Anthropology of Contemporary Issues

A SERIES EDITED BY
ROGER SANJEK

Distant Companions

SERVANTS AND EMPLOYERS
IN ZAMBIA, 1900–1985

Karen Tranberg Hansen

Cornell University Press

Ithaca and London

First published 1989 by Cornell University Press.

International Standard Book Number (cloth) 0-8014-2217-5
International Standard Book Number (paper) 0-8014-9546-6
Library of Congress Catalog Card Number 88-47771

Printed in the United States of America

Librarians: Library of Congress cataloging information
appears on the last page of the book.

The paper in this book is acid-free and meets the guidelines for
permanence and durability of the Committee on Production Guidelines
for Book Longevity of the Council on Library Resources.

For Olga Hansen-Hauge

Contents

Illustrations, Maps, and Tables

Illustrations

Tables

Preface

"When I was taught anthropology," wrote James Murray, who from 1929 on spent over thirty years in the colonial service in Northern Rhodesia, "we learnt how to put bird seeds in skulls, about totemism and exogamy, and a Mr. Malinowski startled us all with a theory about ignorance of paternity. We also read little bits in a long book called 'The Golden Bough.' I do not think anybody taught us about masters and servants. Certainly I cannot remember Dr. R. R. Marett doing so."[1] And Shirley E. Roberts added this perspective when responding to my request for information about her life and times with servants: "I would find it exceedingly difficult to explain to a modern American the kind of life led by a colonial child of 50 years ago without writing a treatise on the subject—and I haven't the time."[2]

Between these two statements lies the troublesome story I have been concerned in this book to retrieve and unravel from about 1900 in Northern Rhodesia through the mid-1980s in Zambia. Masters then assumed that they defined both the identity of servants and the nature of their relationship. The new anthropologists of the post–World War II era ask different questions about the structuring of social relationships from those asked by James Murray's teachers. Relationships long taken for granted are today becoming problematized in research enterprises that are informed in fresh ways by history, the other social sciences, and literary criticism. The study of gender relations, in particular, has not developed from any one single theoretical tradition. This has offered me a challenging range of frameworks

---

1. James Murray, personal communication, October 19, 1986.
2. Shirley E. Roberts, personal communication, November 1, 1986.

from which to choose in constructing an explanation of questions of power, ideology, and economics.

Masters and servants are both the products and the makers of this story, and their relationship persists, in a transformed shape, in postcolonial Zambia. While masters and servants were not studied in Murray's days, the very fabrication of these terms and of men's and women's place in the evolving social order and their contemporary changes is one of the central objects of this book. I use these—and many other words such as primitive, houseboy, and piccanin—without quotation marks or italics not because I accept their normative weight, but because I wish to acknowledge their role in structuring relationships of domination and subordination by race, gender, and class. The practices these terms helped to structure were anchored variously in time and space. To situate my study in those contexts, I have used the contemporary place names and English orthography. My observations close toward the end of 1985, just before a major International Monetary Fund–induced devaluation of the Zambian currency and the introduction of a foreign-currency auctioning system set a severely depressed economy on a further economic downslide. Later economic developments in Zambia may have adversely affected the already strained relationship between servants and their employers which I describe in this book. A hard-earned way of making a living is likely under these circumstances to become even more difficult, and the vexing relationship between this book's two main sets of actors who meet at a distance in the private household may become even more troublesome in its changed reenactment.

The terms employed in the colonial discourse flattened servants out, rarely allowing any sense of servants as individuals, as persons with lives and desires of their own, to enter. Yet although the colonial employer had the upper hand, the relationship between servant and master was a product of their joint interaction, and servants participated crucially in structuring it. I am concerned to restore that sense of life and agency to servants and to depict them as individuals rather than invisible working hands, and so I seek where possible to identify them by their names and to anchor them beyond the locus of work in the context of their own social lives. I identify their employers by name wherever possible as well. The exception to this occurs in my discussion of a large sample survey I conducted in Lusaka from 1983 to 1984, in which anonymous respondents were selected at random.

The Zambian case is but a variation on the story of domestic labor which has no final, or single, conclusion, for it is still unfolding. Domestic service is not an archaic remnant of feudal practices persisting only in remote corners of the late twentieth-century world. It represents a labor process that takes many different forms, and it employs growing, not decreasing, numbers of workers in an advanced capitalist economy such as that of the United States today. The book's relevance must be seen in this context. As a study with comparative implications, its findings pertain not only to southern Africa, Africa as such, or the Third World, but to our discussion in the West about ongoing changes in the gender division of labor in the wake of the transformation of the postwar world economy. To highlight my work's pertinence in this wider context, I take the kinds of calculated leaps at which a trained historian might wince: from past documents to observations from the early 1980s, and from Zambia's capital to the metropolitan United States. I hope the challenge this offers to conventional thinking about domestic service will balance the possible loss of detail in the progression of the sequential narrative of the Zambian story.

This book is a product of my long-term research interest in Zambia, which took me to Lusaka, first between 1971 and 1972 and again in 1981. This particular study draws on two periods of fieldwork carried out in Zambia during 1983–1984 and 1985, made possible by a grant from the United States National Science Foundation, no. BNS.8303507, 1983–1985. During all my stays in Zambia I have been a Research Affiliate of the Institute for African Studies at the University of Zambia in Lusaka. Different stages of the research were supported by a grant-in-aid from the MacMillan Fund of the Graduate School of the University of Minnesota for archival research in England during the summer of 1982, and by two faculty research grants from Northwestern University, facilitating my return to Zambia in 1985 and additional archival work and interviews in England during the summer of 1986.

For advice and help in the launching and completion of this study I am indebted to many individuals in Zambia, the United States, ånd England. Among them are university colleagues at all points of this triangle, the professional staffs of several libraries and archival collections, former Northern Rhodesians now living in England, directors and support staffs of the Institute for African Studies at the University of Zambia, my host households in Lusaka, and my research assistants. Simon Ottenberg and Pierre L. van den Berghe whetted my interests in politics, ethnicity, and race relations in graduate school, and Sue Ellen Jacobs taught me the importance of considering gender as an analytical category. Susan Geiger, Allen Isaacman, and Charles Pike encouraged the first conception of the research. Special acknowledgments are due to Dick Hobson for mediating many contacts with former Northern Rhodesians in England and for cheerfully responding to my many questions; to Arnold Epstein and J. Clyde Mitchell for scrutinizing their memory and research notes for information about domestic servants during the 1950s; to Deborah Gaitskell and Andrew Roberts for historical advice; and to Ilse Mwanza for facilitating my activities as a research affiliate in Lusaka. But the servants and their employers in Lusaka who tolerated my curiosity deserve more than my gratitude, for without their participation this study would not have been undertaken. Among the many special persons to whom I owe so much I do wish to recognize one by name: Norah Rice of Mtendere township in Lusaka, my assistant, confidante, and chaperone in a variety of activities between 1971 and 1985, who during all these years has played the singlemost important role in making me understand what autonomy means from a low-income woman's perspective in urban Zambia.

Because this project has spanned some years, some of my observations have found their way into print. My article "Domestic Service in Zambia," *Journal of Southern African Studies* 13 (1986), summarizes some findings from Part I and Chapters 6 and 7 in Part III. "Household Work as a Man's Job: Sex and Gender in Domestic Service in Zambia," *Anthropology Today* 2 (1986), draws in part from Chapters 3 and 7. The song on pages 163–164 appeared in Peter Fraenkel, *Wayaleshi* (London: Weidenfeld and Nicholson, 1959), pp. 51–52, and is reprinted with the publisher's permission. Plate no. 2 is reproduced from a photograph in the Rhodes House Library at the Bodleian Library, Oxford University, and reproduced here with the permission of S. R. Denny, who owns the copyright. The remaining plates are reproductions of photographs from private collections and appear with the permission of the individuals who own them.

Several persons influenced the shaping of this book at various stages. Judith Butterman, Kusum Datta, Susan Geiger, Maria Grosz-Ngate, Dorothy Helly, Hugh McMillan, Jonathan Ngate, Ibrahim Sundiata, Robert Welsch, and Judith Wittner read individual chapters, and Susan and Henry Antkiewicz, John Comaroff, Carol Stack, Margaret Strobel, and Pierre L. van den Berghe read the entire draft. I wish to thank them all for the interest they took in reading, commenting, criticizing, and advising me in their concern to keep my tendency to ramble within manageable bounds. If I have not listened well enough, they know whom to blame. The book is dedicated to my mother, who gave me the kind of home and preparation for working life I would wish for all servants in Zambia: devoid of hierarchy and with freedom to choose.

K.T.H.

Evanston, Illinois

Abbreviations

The following abbreviations have been used in the notes:

NAZ   National Archives of Zambia
NAZIM   National Archives of Zimbabwe
PRO   Public Records Office, England

Distant Companions

Introduction: The Problem and Its Context

Maids are the thing to have, according to a journalist commenting on the unexpected response to the "Win a Maid" contest launched in January 1986 by *Family Circle*, an American magazine with a huge readership among mainstream women. When the magazine editor in charge of the contest returned after a two-week vacation, her office was filled with boxes and bags of mail entries to the contest.[1] At the end of March 1986, a weekend magazine accompanying one of Chicago's Sunday papers featured a sweepstakes contest sponsored by a company specializing in household cleaning aids; it offered free maid service once a week for a year as the grand prize. Illustrating the contest rules was a photograph of the face of a woman in a maid's uniform, with lace cap and collar and a willing smile, along with cleaning aids, mop, and broom.[2]

It is in such notices, as well as in the growing number of classified newspaper advertisements placed by women willing to hire out their labor for household work as housekeepers, cleaners, cooks, and childminders, or combinations of these, that the late-twentieth-century face of domestic

1. Bob Greene, "A Contest Tailor-Maid for Today's Woman," *Chicago Tribune*, January 27, 1986, sec. 4, p. 1.
2. *Chicago Tribune*, Weekend Magazine, March 21–23, 1986, end page. This was not a unique incident but part of a pattern that indicates how commercial interests are attuning themselves to their customers' needs and desires. Among others of the same kind, Tanqueray, the English gin bottlers, launched a sweepstakes with the prize of an "English butler for a season or $25,000" in *Gourmet*, May 1986, p. 29, and Rubbermaid, a kitchen-gadget firm, featured a "win-a-maid-for-a-year sweepstakes," worth $2,500 in cash in the *New York Times Magazine*, part 2, Good Health, March 29, 1987, p. 45.

service in America comes clearly into focus.[3] These observations command us to question the long-held sociological assumption that paid household work has all but disappeared in contemporary Western society. And in several developing countries such as Zambia, the growth of domestic service as a segment of the wage labor force prompts additional questions concerning its predicted decline in the course of the industrialization process. Taken together, these two sets of observations invite us to reconsider the comparative dynamics of paid household work, its relation to wider economic processes and their shifts both at home and abroad; its changing faces, that is, different labor forms such as live-in and day work; the nature of the work done in private households; gender differences in the labor process; and of the consequences of all of these factors for the private lives of servants and their employers.

A good place to start exploring these questions is Zambia, a developing country in the southern part of the African continent, the geographical locus for this work. If the contests described above strike a nerve among American women, so they would in Zambia, which has only in recent years emerged from its former colonial status. The great majority of servants in the past were men as they are today, although women have entered this occupation, particularly as nannies, in growing numbers since independence. Domestic service is not "naturally" women's work everywhere, and certainly not in Zambia. There, the question of servants is of crucial concern to madams (as female employers of servants invariably are called in southern Africa), for many of the same reasons—and for some different ones—as in the United states.

During the colonial period in what was then known as Northern Rhodesia and also since 1964 in independent Zambia, servants were and are a sine qua non of social and economic position, yet their white employers considered them problematic and their chiefly Zambian employers today still do so. The colonial period's unequal master-servant relationship used race to distance domestics from employers. The lack of postcolonial economic development in Zambia has accentuated the opportunity gap between servants and employers. A changed relationship of distance has emerged in domestic service in which the colonial era's racial distinctions have been replaced by class-based ones. In comparison, during the expansion of the United States' economy in the early decades of this century, white female immigrant live-in domestics found better jobs and left the occupation to minority, especially black, women and, lately, to new female immigrants often of Third World origin who now largely do day work. More recent economic transitions and the growing need for families to have

3. This statement is based on my observation of the classified columns of "household help, wanted" and "situation wanted" in the *Chicago Tribune* from January 1986 through May 1987.

[2]

dual wage earners have increased the need for domestic help, which is proliferating in many forms—live-in, day work, and commercial contracting. These changed economic developments are creating a new class of domestic workers in the United States whose relationship to employers is characterized by inequality. While the evolving story of domestic service in Zambia provides an important study in its own right, it offers a comparative case that casts critical light on our own situation. Rapidly changing economies, the different, and changing, roles of men and women in paid and unpaid household work, and a growing class gap between poverty and wealth come into play in both Zambia and the United States in the mid-1980s. This situation was not anticipated by conventional sociological wisdom and it requires new thinking.

In this book I describe and analyze continuities and changes in domestic service in Zambia from 1900 to 1985 by a retrospective examination of how the world of domestic servitude was created, maintained, sometimes changed, and at times resisted as a result of the interaction between servants and their employers, both men and women. I also seek to capture how that changing world was experienced in the everyday lives of servants and employers; how their relationships with members of their own households and others in the wider society shaped this peculiar world of work; and how the world beyond the household as a work locus at times was affected by servants' activities. Good household management revolved around strictly upheld distinctions between the servant and the employer, and it also turned on sexual criteria. Human-made distinctions, construed as essential difference in culture, race, class, and sex, turned the servant's personhood in otherness, and the changing construction of difference is a central concern throughout this book.

Why write a book about an occupational domain that according to conventional sociological wisdom has been considered to be obsolete in contemporary society?[4] That belief was based on a limited number of studies, conducted mainly in northwestern Europe and North America, which described changes in domestic service as involving a transition from male to female by the end of the 1700s, and its remaining women's main source of urban wage income till the second or third decade of the present century, when wage-labor opportunities opened up in new fields.[5] In the wake of

4. Lewis A. Coser, "Servants: The Obsolescence of an Occupational Role," *Social Forces* 52 (1973): 31–40.

5. For standard description and analysis of this scenario, see, e.g., Vilhelm Aubert, "The Housemaid—An Occupational Role in Crisis," *Acta Sociologica* 1 (1955–1956): 149–158; Pamela Horn, *The Rise and Fall of the Victorian Servant* (New York: St. Martin's Press, 1975); and Theresa McBride, *The Domestic Revolution: The Modernization of Household Service in England and France, 1820–1920* (London: Croom Helm, 1976).

that process the time-honored species of the genus servant, the live-in domestic, supposedly disappeared. Extrapolations from this pattern of near certainty were extended to the developing world with the suggestion that a similar process would occur there.[6]

This thinking has died hard for a number of reasons. One has to do with the lack of serious scholarly attention given to this occupation in the West and elsewhere. An occupational domain that for two centuries or more had been the single largest wage employment avenue for women remained largely forgotten. In the scholarship on the developing countries, the working lives of domestic servants were barely explored, in spite of the fact that paid domestic service often provided one of the earliest means to incorporate subject peoples into a newly created world of wage labor. Miners, railway workers, and traders in the markets were perhaps more conspicuous, and certainly more often targets for study.[7]

Another reason concerns the unilinear assumptions of modernization theory that have influenced our thinking about development. They center around ideas of convergence of the economic development path in the industrial world and newly industrializing countries. Modernization theory has not held up well in the face of the actual development experience in most parts of the Third World. And advanced capitalism at home has not been accompanied by the expected promethean industrial expansion. Rather, the old manufacturing structures are crumbling as the West is undergoing partial deindustrialization and transnational corporations locate manufacturing plants in Third World countries, in an overall process that is shaping a new international division of labor.[8] In the course of this transformation process, the composition of the Western wage labor force is changing, not only by sector, but also by sex. The manufacturing sector is shrinking while employment in service industries and service-oriented work is on the rise. The opportunity gap is widening. Today in the United States women of better and worse means are meeting in contractual employment relationships centered on household and child care which are recasting the live-in domestic service relationship of a previous era into new labor forms.

6. David Chaplin, "Domestic Service and Industrialization," *Comparative Studies in Sociology* 1 (1978): 97–127.

7. For an overview of prominent topics and themes in the study of African labor history, see Bill Freund, "Labor and Labor History in Africa: A Review of the Literature," *African Studies Review* 27 (1984): 1–58.

8. Folker Fröbel, Jürgen Heinrichs, and Otto Kreye, *The New International Division of Labour: Structural Unemployment in Industrialised Countries and Industrialisation in Developing Countries* (Cambridge: Cambridge University Press, 1980), provides a general statement on this emerging process. Special attention to gender in this process is offered in June Nash and Maria Patricia Fernandez Kelly, eds., *Women, Men, and the International Division of Labor* (Albany: State University of New York Press, 1983).

Far from having disappeared, one labor form of domestic service, namely day work, undertaken by workers who live out, appears to be growing.

The processes outlined above are not so far removed from Zambia as they might appear. Economic opportunities among all population segments in that country are linked subordinately to developments in the West. While Zambia is not hosting any global industry for assembly of Western manufactured parts for export to the West, it is intimately linked to world market ups and downs through exports of its chief source of revenue, copper. Aside from mining, there is little local industry or manufacture, and what little there is depends heavily on imported raw materials. When the downturn in the world economy of the early 1970s hit Zambia, the economy stagnated and overall employment shrank. Yet within this decline, the domestic service sector and the government sector have continued to grow. Rapid urbanization with one of the highest rates in Africa, if not the Third World, daily adds new potential workers to a labor force, of whom fewer and fewer find wage work. The opportunity structure has become markedly skewed and the gap between poor and rich is widening.[9] With it, new distinctions are being forged between fellow citizens as more and more black Zambians go to work as servants for black Zambian employers. As a result of the postcolonial indigenization of the economy, more Zambians than ever before work in middle- and upper-level positions in government, parastatal companies, and in the few remaining private firms. Clerking, teaching, and nursing jobs are held increasingly by Zambian women. These households account for the growth since independence in 1964 of the servant-employing class. They, the new expatriates, and the remaining old-timers of white or Asian background all employ servants.

Women in Zambia want household help. Not maids, but male servants, for their preferred servant is a man. They have few positive remarks to make about women servants, who are relatively recent entrants to this particular segment of the labor force. Today, paid domestic service is not gender-typed as woman's work everywhere, nor was it so historically. The Zambian case allows me to question the application of a biological metaphor in accounts of the social relations in domestic service which stress the occupation's function as a "natural" extension of women's reproductive role. Gender roles are not given; they are made. Their construction depends on a complex interweaving of cultural factors and social practices with economic forces and questions of power, and their unraveling is central to this book.

9. For analysis of recent socioeconomic conditions in Zambia, see Cherry Gertzel, ed., *The Dynamics of the One-Party State in Zambia* (Manchester: Manchester University Press, 1984).

I set about the task of describing the empirical processes that affect servants and their employers by approaching domestic service at several different, sometimes overlapping, levels of analysis, linking cultural, demographic, and labor market factors over time. I seek to incorporate a sense of history, and I aim throughout to capture how servants and their employers experienced their unequal companionship in a changing world in a way that brings life to their world. My concerns are with changes in the nature of the servant-employer relationship, with special attention to differences in the labor process depending on whether the servant is a woman or a man; with changes in the type of work that is carried out in private households; with the effects that the work of a domestic has on the servant's own household and-off-the-job activities, and the ways in which such social practices in turn affect the job situation; with the structure of the labor force in domestic service, over time and in relation to overall employment patterns, and by sex. I am also concerned with the changing relationship among domestic servants, and between them and other workers—that is to say, with the questions of whether or not—and, if so, when—they constitute a class in terms of objective indicators as well as of felt identity of interests. The final issue I explore concerns the broader dynamics in paid household work between a developing country like Zambia and a Western country, such as the United States. In that effort, I seek to bring my findings from Zambia to bear on developments closer to home, and ultimately on the task of throwing light on the place of paid household work in the changing economic context of advanced capitalism.

The Problem of Domestic Service

But why domestic service? What's the study for, anyway? as some of the people I interviewed asked when I approached them in Lusaka, Zambia's capital, between 1983 and 1985. There is more to this than culture, demography, and labor market factors in Zambia, although these factors all bear upon it in complex ways. I wish to stress that the at times fascinating, yet mostly depressing, story of domestic service in Zambia speaks to larger issues. As I hinted at before, some of these issues concern inequalities in opportunity and income—in short, class—which prompted the creation of and fuels today's reproduction of a dependent, subordinate labor form— paid domestic service—in various disguises across time and space. Its continued existence is not to be understood as an archaic remnant of the early phases of capitalist development. Vast present-day income gaps coupled with distinctions in consumption styles are central to the production of domestic service, which in turn plays a focal role in reproducing these distinctions. Because of this double centrality, domestic service is a key

[6]

occupational domain to study for purposes of clarifying the mediation of poverty and wealth which takes place in the encounter across the private household's class chasm beyond the factory gates and the office, and is so intimately linked to developments in these institutions.

The comments just made may read as if the larger issues in this study are revealed merely by attributing an economic function to domestic service: it reproduces class privilege. Such an explanation might perhaps work, if made on the basis of aggregate statistical data and national input-output statistics. But it would tell us little about the making of this particular labor form. Nor would it tell us how the relation sometimes was resisted, at times changed if not transformed, yet reproduced over time into one or several simultaneously existing forms of paid domestic labor. And the explanation would leave out completely any understanding of this occupational domain as a created world of labor, a product of the lived and changing experiences of women and men, servants and employers, as well as other members of the society of which they are all part.

The larger issues of this book, then, revolve around inequality, and specifically what it has meant and how it has been experienced in the relationship between men and women servants and their employers from different generations and of various cultural, national, or ethnic backgrounds, from about the turn of the century through the mid-1980s in Zambia. Inequality is at the core of their relationship. It is the basis that structures the labor process and informs the asymmetrical encounters between the chief actors in domestic service—servants and employers—whose created places are construed as belonging to distinctly different worlds. Domestic service, I claim, at least in the live-in version I set out to trace retrospectively in Zambia, and perhaps as well under conditions of day work, can only operate smoothly in situations where servants and employers are considered different from each other. These differences are constructed and informed by essentialist notions of race, culture, sexuality and class. Highlighted differentially, but not incidentally, across time and space, these differences mask, at least temporarily, the co-presence and participation of servant and employer in a shared world.

This paradox of conspicuous presence and social invisibility first struck me when I stayed with Danish relatives in Nairobi before traveling up-country on my first stint of fieldwork as an undergraduate in 1969. I grew up in a society permeated by egalitarian values and in a home free of any gender- and aged-based hierarchy. My father died when I was five years old, and my mother, then forty-eight, went back to work to support her household of three girls and one boy aged between five and seventeen. There was never any question of women not doing things on their own, for we had to. Our participation and initiatives were counted on, and our presence acknowledged. And there were no authoritarian restrictions placed to limit our ambitions. My reaction in Nairobi was one of distinct dislike of what I experienced as the awkward presence of the paid hand who was regarded more as a thing than a person. This experience repeated itself in 1971 when I began my first of several research periods in Zambia, whenever I stayed in a servant-keeping household. Although my research over the years has taken me into Lusaka's low-income areas, where I have tried to clarify the forces that influence women's work in the home, yard, market, and city, I remain puzzled and troubled by the deeply sedimented weight of domestic service, which it seems to me most people in Zambia take for granted.

As an anthropologist socialized in a nonhierarchical setting who has had to study about different societies and social structures around the world, I have been made to understand that some societies are structured by ideologies of inequality which place distinct groups of people in asymmetrical relationships of domination and subordination. India, for one, is often referred to as a society in which people accept inequality, rather than question it.[10] With the anthropologist's conventional stance of cultural relativism, I ought perhaps to have viewed servant-employer relationships in Zambia from that perspective. Given the two sides' interdependence, here was a relationship that, in the language of cultural relativism, could be seen as benefiting all. Yet my problem, and the problematic and troublesome persistence of domestic service, was not an archaic or paternal one. Old habits of domestic service had not been broken, servants had not acquired many marketable skills from life-long work in private households, nor had they been able to create new lives. The problem in nonacademic terms was that the relationship in practice made exploitation almost inevitable. The colonial era's authoritarian tradition of white men's mastery over subject races who lived and worked in fear of coercive rules and regulations had not so much disappeared as been transformed, into a kind of servitude that both servants and their employers find troublesome and would rather not be part of, were the economic situation different. To understand this, cultural relativism is of no use.

The Making of Difference

My choice of terms in the preceding discussion implies certain conceptual and theoretical assumptions. I am influenced by the recent rapprochement between history and some branches of anthropology and the other social sciences.[11] This influence is reflected in my concern to explore and

10. Louis Dumont, "Caste, Racism, and Stratification: Reflections of a Social Scientist," *Contributions to Indian Sociology* 5 (1961): 20–43.

11. This rapprochement is particularly evident in interdisciplinary studies of social history, family history, labor history, and popular culture. It draws inspiration from, among others,

explain the dynamics of change within domestic service as well as to account for the causal relationship between shifts in domestic service and changes of more macrolevel forces. I do so in a processual sense, recognizing that although societal structures and their development in many ways restrain and limit local-level activity, individuals are more than cogs in wheels. They are human social actors who are aware of the constraints on their activity and who through conscious interaction and goal-directed activity are centrally involved both in making the world of which they are part and in changing it.[12] Given this orientation, I seek to attribute to servants a sense of life and agency and to highlight their role in some of the far-ranging changes that have affected and are transforming their society. And, I suggest that the lack of attention historians and anthropologists have paid to this particular social and economic domain in part reflects the limits of explanatory frames that ignore the individual as a human agent. In more ways than one, the previous generation's scholarly community reacted like most employers of servants: they took them for granted.

The attitude of taking servants for granted touches a central nerve in the making of difference. The unequal relationship across the private household's class divide is maintained through practical arrangements that create distance between the chief actors. Unequal distribution of economic means and differential access to power underpin the relationship whose tenuous balance is threatened once personality and affect become implicated in day-to-day interaction. The conceptual and theoretical problem at stake here is the making of difference, conceived in a manner that has implications quite unlike the we/they distinctions often drawn in the books on race relations a generation or so ago.[13] The basis of this distinction was taken for granted and the questions that were asked concerned the functional ramifications of race relations in society.

The construction of difference has been an object of recent literary work, some observations from which I wish to adopt in this study. Edward Said's work of literary criticism, *Orientalism,* describes the creation of the Orient and Orientalism as a European invention.[14] Disregarding local social and cultural complexity, a notion of Orientalism emerged in literature which had less to do with the real Orient and its peoples as free subjects of

---

the historical work of Eric Hobsbawm and E. P. Thompson, the sociological work of Anthony Giddens, and the anthropological work of Pierre Bourdieu. For a discussion of this trend, see the contributions to "Anthropology and History in the 1980s," *Journal of Interdisciplinary History* 12 (1981): 227–275.

12. This, of course, was the important message of E. P. Thompson's *The Making of the English Working Class* (London: Gollancz, 1963).

13. See, for example, Peter I. Rose, *They and We: Racial and Ethnic Relations in the United States* (New York: Random House, 1974).

14. Edward W. Said, *Orientalism* (Harmondsworth: Penguin Books, 1985).

thought and action than with the idea of Europe as superior compared with all non-European peoples and cultures. Said discussed and analyzed Orientalism as "the corporate institution for dealing with the Orient—dealing with it by making statements about it, authorizing views of it, describing it, settling it, ruling over it: in short, Orientalism as a Western style for dominating, restructuring and having authority over the Orient."[15] For its strategy, Orientalism manufactures new differences out of what is a manifestly different, or alternative and novel, world. In this, it makes use of a sense of "positional superiority, which puts the Westerner in a whole series of possible relationships with the Orient without ever losing him the relative upper hand."[16]

In Africa, at least till fairly recently, Europeans saw blacks as fit only for domination.[17] They viewed blacks through a lens of contrasts and were struck by how different Africans were from themselves: in terms of skin color certainly, by not being Christian, and because of social and political arrangements very unlike those in Europe; worse still, they lived on vast, unexplored, wild lands they did little to harness for productive purposes. Many elements of these early views remained embedded in the discourse that, at the level of officialdom as well as in private households, came to structure the relationship between whites in dominant positions and their black subjects throughout the colonial period—although the relative emphasis on each element did shift over time, and might perhaps vary, depending on who did the colonizing.[18]

My excursion into the realm of literary discourse is not a detour; it strikes at the core question of how difference becomes structured, and why it takes its particular shape. For it is not only literary writers or professional anthropologists, who view the other as different and removed from the self in space and time.[19] Ordinary people do so; the colonialists did it, as did the servants in Northern Rhodesia. Servants and their employers in postcolonial Zambia continue to do so, as we ourselves do in the West, construing difference and otherness in such class or classlike terms as *subculture, culture of poverty,* and *underclass,* to mention just a few of recent prominence in the United States. Regardless of progress in society,

15. Ibid., p. 3.
16. Ibid., p. 7.
17. For the literary construction of the African on French terms, see Christopher L. Miller, *Blank Darkness: Africanist Discourse in French* (Chicago: University of Chicago Press, 1985).
18. For the French, see William B. Cohen, *The French Encounter with Africans: White Response to Blacks, 1530–1880* (Bloomington: Indiana University Press, 1980). Early British attitudes are described by H. Alan C. Cairns, *Prelude to Imperialism: British Reactions to Central African Society, 1840–1890* (London: Routledge and Kegan Paul, 1965).
19. Johannes Fabian, *Time and the Other: How Anthropology Makes Its Object* (New York: Columbia University Press, 1983).

unequal gender relations continue too often to be accounted for in terms of difference, that is, essentialist sexual notions. But difference or otherness is a multifaceted phenomenon.[20] When implicated in creating the boundary between the black manservant and his white employer within the colonial household in Zambia, difference stood for the complex interaction of race and culture which then connoted civilization. When servants made trouble and employers complained about their unpredictable behavior, they would refer to their servants' strange customs and tribal mores. Under the thin surface of acquired household mores always lurked the essential African, that is, the primitive. When it came to women servants, trouble was attributed to immorality and promiscuity, that is, essential sexuality. Today's servants continue to make life difficult for their employers. Their Zambian bosses see menservants as members of another class whose needs and problems are quite unlike their own and whom they therefore can treat differently. Regarding their problems with women servants, employers are still less neutral in identifying the difference that matters: sexuality. For women are said to be less tractable than menservants because of their struggle either to get rid of or to find a husband and/or lover. Domestic service in Zambia was, and still is, structured around the making and remaking of differences.

The Power of Difference

In order to relate issues of class and power to the construction of difference I need to draw on additional explanatory insights and situate what looks like an island unto itself—the private household with its purposefully interacting agents—within the wider society of which it is a part, so that activity at each level may be understood to have bearing on the other. Domestic service is not quite a total institution in Erving Goffman's terms.[21] It is an open-door institution from which inmates have several exits, which have varied over time and differed to some degree, depending on the political, economic, and cultural setup of the surrounding society. These open doors all influence what goes on in the household between servant and employer, but differentially so. The difference results from the participants' unequal power, which enables the employer to issue commands more often than the servant can choose not to obey. Said's notion of positional superiority is relevant here, as is the version of power formulated by Anthony Giddens.[22]

20. See contributions to the special issue "'Race,' Writing, and Difference," *Critical Inquiry* 12 (1985).
21. Erving Goffman, *Asylums* (Garden City, N.Y.: Doubleday Anchor, 1961).
22. Anthony Giddens, *Central Problems in Social Theory: Action, Structure, and Contradiction in Social Analysis* (Berkeley: University of California Press, 1979).

Many of Giddens's concerns—the conscious actor, intentional activity and its central role in the reproduction and change of society—are shared by others.[23] Fredrik Barth, for example, has discussed how intentionality leads to institutionalization, and Pierre Bourdieu how practice becomes habitus.[24] These concepts, however, neither analyze the effects of time nor do they explain how power becomes an element of action. Michel Foucault sees modalities of power everywhere, but in an evocative rather than analytical way.[25] But Giddens's framework does more than invoke such notions: it provides a way of analyzing them.

In his attempt to incorporate the relationship between human agency and structure into social theory, Giddens develops the notion of structure as process, which he gives the aptly descriptive name of *structuration*. The informal rules people devise in their day-to-day conduct are in his framework thought of as social practices that constitute the structuring properties implicated in the reproduction of social institutions. These structuring properties are both the media and the outcome of interaction: they enable as well as constrain. This twofold aspect of interaction produces what Giddens speaks of as the duality of structure.[26] Power is an integral part of this process, for it refers to transformative capacity. Instantiated in action as a regular and routine phenomenon, it relates to rules and resources, though in itself power is not a resource in this framework. Rather, "resources are the media through which power is exercised, and structures of domination reproduced."[27] Power, in matter-of-fact words, is a means of getting things done as well as of choosing not to do them. It refers to relations of autonomy and dependence in interaction, to the capability of actors to get others to comply with their wants.

Because power is a two-way relationship, servants in Zambia retain some autonomy even though they are dependent actors in relation to employers in the household situation. This power is exemplified in their choice not to do, or to perform in their own way, the orders an employer issues. Although the employer is the more autonomous actor owing to the more effective means of compliance at his or her command—that is, the capacity to sack, to withold pay, and not to provide references or to provide bad ones—he or she is in some degree dependent on the servant. Using the

23. Sherry B. Ortner, "Theory in Anthropology since the Sixties," *Comparative Studies in Society and History* 26 (1984): 126–165.

24. Fredrik Barth, "Models of Social Organization," *Royal Anthropological Institute*, Occasional Paper, no. 23 (1966); Pierre Bourdieu, *Outline of a Theory of Practice* (Cambridge: Cambridge University Press, 1977).

25. Michel Foucault, *Power/Knowledge: Selected Interviews and Other Writings, 1972–1977*, ed. Colin Gordon (Hassocks: Harvester Press, 1980).

26. Giddens, *Central Problems*, pp. 69–78.

27. Ibid., p. 91.

discourse of servants, the decision not to obey, or to do things his or her way, is a response to "too much work" and to the employer's "talking too much" or "too loud." Servants pursue such practices with the practical knowledge that household work never stops. For once one task is done, others will be issued. The employers say that "orders have to be repeated all the time" and that "sevants are lazy"; they "never learn," and to be sure "they're different!" By repeating orders, the employer adjusts his social practice to the conduct of the servant, who thus retains some power in structuring the household situation and in a way that affects how both servant and employer are getting things done over time as their activity unfolds in space.

This simple example of Giddens's duality of structure at work, chosen from many to be discussed in the body of this work, shows us conscious agents par excellence. The social practices they use in their interaction help to create and reproduce the informal rules that structure their interaction as well as the resources they draw on differentially. In the course of doing so, servants and employers monitor each other's conduct reflexively. Their mutual monotoring is influenced by two levels of consciousness, according to Giddens: "discursive" and "practical."[28] Discursive consciousness refers to peoples' capacity to "give reasons" and "rationalize" their conduct; practical consciousness, to the "stocks of unarticulated knowledge" people use implicitly to orient themselves to situations and when interpreting the acts of others. What servants and employers say about each other involves both these levels.

Servants and employers find their institution hard to understand in discursive terms; but each of them knows, in a practical sense, a great deal about its workings because they participate in it. What they say about each other does not constitute a description or explanation of their relationship. Rather, their statements about each other are part of that relationship, helping them to define each other.[29] Incorporating into my analysis the sometimes contradictory concepts that employers and servants use about each other will, I suggest, throw fresh light on the domestic service institution and present it in a way that reckons with human agency and is not static.

In their mutual monitoring when interacting in the household, servants and employers make use of social practices that become predictable and stable over time. These practices develop into routines, which in turn become patterned in space, that is to say, they become institutionalized. The rules and resources both parties draw on in their routines can be recombined into different forms, changed, and new ones can be created

28. Ibid., pp. 24–25.
29. Ibid., pp. 248–253.

from scratch.[30] These techniques, which are contained in the stocks of servants' and employers' practical consciousness, help to reproduce their interaction through time and affect the way relationships are ordered across space.[31] Notions that servants and employers have of each other as being different underpin this structuration.

The Difference Class Makes

The employers' power over servants results from their control of resources which they can bring to bear on the work situation to effect their servants' compliance. This control is a result of their advantaged position in society in class terms, at least when compared with the servants, who have nothing to sell but manual-labor power. Few servants in Zambia today have even seven years of schooling, whereas most of the persons who employ them have at least high-school education. Far from all being in professional jobs or holding executive positions, the majority of employers are on government payroll. Even the least affluent of employers have regular monthly incomes (sometimes earned by both spouses) which facilitate access to class privilege—the means by which the difference between servant and employer, is made and re-created.

Class in this book is defined in Marx's terms: by relation to the means of production. It has an objective and a subjective face. The problem that besets its discussion is that although we as observers can readily identify class in terms of objective indicators, people themselves do not always share an identity of felt interests in such broad terms.[32] Most of the world's history shows us that in fact they have rarely done so. Race, ethnicity, and gender complicate the question, as does a variety of sectional interests. Racial segregation, minority status in ethnic and gender terms, cultural practices, and religious prescriptions among others, singly or combined, can affect how a person experiences his or her world as a worker. It is with the unfolding of such experiences that I am concerned here: how servants' experiences have been shaped by broader economic forces in the surrounding society if not the wider world, by the labor process within domestic service, and by social practices that take place beyond the work locus. With

30. Ibid., pp. 198–230.
31. These notions are elaborated in Giddens's *The Constitution of Society: Outline of the Theory of Structuration* (Berkeley: University of California Press, 1984), in which he develops the idea of localization, pp. 110–161.
32. Advocates of an orthodox version of Marxism assert that collective action is motivated by class-based interests that arise from the given economic circumstances. This focus on the economic sphere neglects people's own involvement in structuring interests and affecting the economic situation in which they find themselves. Recent attention to the labor process has helped to qualify the overly deterministic explanation of how the relation to the means of production influences class consciousness.

this perspective, I have sought to problematize the question of class action by emphasizing the structures by which work and neighborhood or work and households are connected or set apart.[33] An examination of the changing interrelationship among the three loci of work, neighborhood, and household over the course of economic and political turns will, I suggest, throw light on the question of why servants rarely identified themselves in class terms.

Domestic servants are workers like other workers. They all sell their labor power in return for wages. Yet the domestic servant is more "special" than, say, the miner or factory worker. The labor process in domestic service differs in important respects from that in a larger enterprise where laborer and employer rarely meet in person and compliance with the requirements of the job is achieved through a technical division of tasks carried out in a routine pattern and through scientific management.[34] In the interpersonal labor process in domestic service compliance is created through direct supervision. Although legal rules may exist concerning terms of work, they are rarely applied, certainly not in Zambia. The employers decide how to deal with their servants by judging their personal qualities rather than their skills and/or efficiency.

The labor process in domestic service is hierarchical, asymmetric, and deeply charged with idiosyncratic factors. The privatized nature of the job, its special locus in the employer's household, where most servants labor in isolation from other workers when on duty, do perhaps accentuate a servant's sense of personal dependence on the employer's goodwill. This sense in turn may adversely affect the servant's experience of sharing identity with other workers, particularly if he or she resides on the employer's property in a high-income residential area, further distanced from the mass of ordinary workers. The peculiar personalness of the relationship between worker and employer in domestic service, the special nature of the work, which produces use value rather than exchange value, and the odd living

---

33. For Western examples of this approach, see C. Calhoun, *The Question of Class Struggle: Social Foundations of Popular Radicalism during the Industrial Revolution* (Chicago: University of Chicago Press, 1982), and I. Katznelson, *City Trenches: Urban Politics and the Patterning of Class in the United States* (New York: Pantheon, 1981). For African examples, see the contributions to Frederick Cooper, ed., *Struggle for the City: Migrant Labor, Capital, and the State in Urban Africa* (Beverly Hills, Calif.: Sage, 1983), and for South Africa, Belinda Bozzoli, ed., *Town and Countryside in the Transvaal: Capitalist Penetration and Popular Response* (Johannesburg: Ravan Press, 1983).

34. There are several different types of control over industrial workers on the job and a rich literature on the forms such controls take and why. The works of Harry Braverman, *Labor and Monopoly Capital: The Degradation of Work in the Twentieth Century* (New York: Monthly Review Press, 1974), and Michael Burawoy, *Manufacturing Consent: Changes in the Labor Process under Monopoly Capitalism* (Chicago: University of Chicago Press, 1979), infused this field of research with new vigor. A useful source is R. Edwards, *Contested Terrain: The Transformation of the Workplace in the Twentieth Century* (New York: Basic Books, 1979).

arrangement combine to put servants in an ambiguous situation vis-à-vis other segments of the working class. The interpersonal aspect and domestic nature of this labor process also mark the experience of work as a private one. Since the work experience is rife with ambiguities and troubles, it becomes difficult to talk about it objectively, that is, discursively in Giddens's terms, perhaps because the participants are too close to their material.

Most servants in Zambia today seek from their jobs only the money and the housing that often comes with the job. They have few illusions about acquiring benefits that might improve their prospects for upward mobility. The perks are too few and insignificant in an economy with runaway inflation, and their skills derived from labor-intensive toil are hardly salable in other occupational domains. The question then arises, why do servants consent to carry out a job that reinforces dependency in many situations?

Most servants struggle for tomorrow in two senses: they strive to make a living for themselves and their own household members on a day-to-day basis, and they strain their substandard means in an attempt to ensure that their children never will have to make their living as domestics. On both fronts, servants have to overcome odds that for many are insurmountable. While they all desire to exit from domestic service, few succeed. They all know why, at least at the level of practical consciousness: their job has "no future," they say. Many comply with the demands of the hierarchically structured labor process for fear of losing their meager living, and this they rationalize in practical terms: "Half a loaf is better than none." They also hope that the employers sooner or later will help them. These servants do not, in my view, suffer from a dependency complex as set forth by Octave Mannoni.[35] When, following Giddens, dependency is counterposed to autonomy, a sense of personal agency is retained.[36] For even in consenting to the creation and maintenance of their own dependence, servants show themselves as autonomous actors with some power to affect the outcome of their dependent interaction within the employer's household. They com-

35. Octave Mannoni, *Prospero and Caliban: The Psychology of Colonization* (London: Methuen, 1956). The colonized in Prospero and Caliban perceived the colonizer as a father surrogate to be respected and obeyed, while at the same time he was responsible for his charge. Mannoni's dependence was based on trust that, if the relationship between superior and inferior broke, resulted in feelings of desolation and despair on the part of the colonized (pp. 132–162). For a play, written by a white author in Zambia on this theme, see David Wallace, *Do You Love Me, Master?* (Lusaka: NECZAM, 1977).

36. A. L. Epstein also qualifies the meaning of trust and dependency in the relationship between colonizer and colonized. See his "Autonomy and Identity: Aspects of Political Development on the Gazelle Peninsula," *Anthropological Forum* 2 (1970), esp. pp. 431–432, and "Unconscious Factors in the Response to Social Crisis: A Case Study from Central Africa," in *The Psychoanalytic Study of Society*, vol. 8 (1979), pp. 3–39.

ply, but within limits. If the work situation becomes intolerable and if they find better avenues, they make the ultimate autonomous decision: they quit.

Servants' behavior while at work is thus shaped not only by the demands placed on them there but also by processes beyond the workplace, principally those that relate to their own households and the changing needs of its members. Some of these extrawork forces are influenced by cultural practices, others by associations with neighbors, fellow workers, people in other lines of work, and friends and relatives. Servants thus have conflicting interests that all affect how they perceive their place in Zambia's evolving class structure. The interests that a servant feels an identity with may change over time and they may be different for men and women. They may vary with the servant's familial status and length of domestic employment, so that a long-time servant who is the head of a household may identify the locus of his or her interests in a different way from one who is young, unmarried, and relatively new to domestic service.

The Making of Gender

So far, I have taken my actors as given: servants and their employers. But at the turn of the last century in Zambia there were no givens. When a small white population had settled and gradually began to grow, and in the process felt the need for workers to do the dirty and time-consuming work involved in creating and maintaining households without amenities, there was no ready pool of domestics willing and able to perform household service. There certainly was no script in which roles, gestures, and routines had been laid out in advance, although employers used their experience of servant-keeping at home in their dealings with Africans in the new territory. Persons of African background had to be made into servants in a manner that had much in common with the domestication of wild animals. They were considered "raw," and even today, some employers speak of "breaking in" their servants.

The resulting social practices were structured not only in terms of class and power, but also by gender. Initially, and for a long time, these servants were not women, but men. Employers in Northern Rhodesia, far from taking women servants for granted, avoided them. For reasons I discuss at length later, many continue to do so today.

Most recent studies of domestic service have emphasized the central involvement of females in such work and have, consciously or not, applied a biological metaphor to explain the subordination a servant experiences in the social relations that structure the household and the wider society. In a felicitous argument, Karen Sacks has pointed out that the biological metaphor is part of the anthropological research tradition.[37] Yet the discipline of anthropology does not hold the *droit de seigneur* on this thinking. It is prevalent in the other social sciences and shared among broad segments of society who tend to think of gender as a product of biological differences that set women and men apart. Such a view has prompted many scholars of domestic service to use the nineteenth-century domestic service pattern in the West to universalize the present situation and thereby underestimate its singularity.[38] The result is a contrasting and stressing of presumably given differences between women and men, rather than the raising of questions about how such differences themselves are created. For gender roles are not given. They are made, and created as a result of women's and men's changing social and economic experiences. The gender division of labor is socially constructed. How, when, and why its slots are allocated to the two sexes become issues for investigation rather than questions to which biological "nature" supplies ready-made answers.

Zambia provides an interesting setting in which to explore how gender roles are made and changed. I do so by asking questions about how employment practices were routinized in the opening decades of this century and how they become institutionalized in the longer term, even while at times being remade in different forms and undergoing changes. The employment practice at issue is the preference for the male servant, which persists to the present day, and its reverse, the reluctance to employ women as servants.

Domestic Service: Literature and Scholarship

I noted above that till fairly recently, domestic service remained a relatively unexplored domain in scholarship in the West and in the Third World. The nature of the occupation itself helps to explain its invisibility, and shifts in social science interests suggest reasons for the more recent proliferation of studies on domestic service.[39]

In northwestern Europe and North America, live-in domestic service

37. Karen B. Sacks, *Sisters and Wives: The Past and Future of Sexual Equality* (Urbana: University of Illinois Press, 1982), pp. 24–64.

38. This is a slightly changed paraphrase of M. Z. Rosaldo's description of how non-anthropologists are misusing anthropological data, in "The Use and Abuse of Anthropology: Reflections on Feminism and Cross-Cultural Understanding," *Signs* 5 (1980): 389–417.

39. Some of the most well known of these studies are: Leonore Davidoff, *The Best Circles: Society, Etiquette and the Season* (London: Croom Helm, 1973), Jean J. Hecht, *The Domestic Servant Class in Eighteenth-Century England* (1956; London: Routledge and Kegan Paul, 1980); David M. Katzman, *Seven Days a Week: Women and Domestic Service in Industrializing America* (New York: Oxford University Press, 1978); Horn, *Rise and Fall*; and McBride, *Domestic Revolution*.

has indeed declined as a major occupational domain for women. When women replaced men as servants toward the end of the eighteenth century, they tended to be young, from rural backgrounds, poorly educated, and unmarried. At this time the decline of household production was eliminating the economic role for unmarried women at home and the urban economy offered them little else than low-paid jobs as household servants. Live-in domestic service was something many such young women expected to do for a while but not to engage in as a lifetime occupation. They hoped, as do women in Zambia today, to marry, preferably men of slightly better means than their own fathers and then to establish their own households. The fate of Samuel Richardson's Pamela illustrates the scenario: the dowryless servant girl marries her rich master, thus solving her problem of how to make a living.[40] Domestic service was not considered a particularly nice job, and what official census figures we have on this occupation in Europe and North America in the past are likely to underreport the actual numbers of servants: domestics might have been reluctant to admit the nature of their occupation to census takers. In the United States, where few native-born American women made themselves available as live-in domestic workers, newly immigrant European women were typically drawn into service, and many married "up."[41]

But domestic service has not disappeared as an important occupational domain for women in late twentieth-century America. When white women left domestic service, it remained an occupational venue for minority women. For historical reasons such as slavery, and because of continued discrimination in the labor market by race and sex, poorly educated black American women never left domestic service. Abolition exchanged domestic slavery for contractual servitude, and black American women have persisted in domestic service along with its transformation from live-in to day work.[42] The upward mobility thesis had little relevance to their living and working experience in a class-structured society with deep de facto racial divisions.[43] Neither they nor the later additions of minority women—for

40. Samuel Richardson, *Pamela: Or Virtue Rewarded. In a Series of Familiar Letters from a Beautiful Young Damsel to Her Parents* (London: Harrison and Company, 1785).
41. Janice Reiff Webster, "Domestication and Americanization: Scandinavian Women in Seattle, 1888 to 1900," *Journal of Urban History* 4 (1978): 275–290; Stephen Steinberg, "Why Irish Became Domestics and Italians and Jews Did Not," in his *The Ethnic Myth: Race, Ethnicity, and Class in America* (New York: Atheneum, 1981); and Daniel E. Sutherland, *Americans and Their Servants: Domestic Service in the United States from 1800 to 1920* (Baton Rouge: Louisiana State University Press, 1981).
42. On this point, see Judith Rollins, *Between Women: Domestics and Their Employers* (Philadelphia: Temple University Press, 1985); and Katzman, *Seven Days.*
43. Evelyn Nakano Glenn, *Issei, Nisei, War Bride: Three Generations of Japanese American Women in Domestic Service* (Philadelphia: Temple University Press, 1986); and Rollins, *Between Women.*

example, Chinese, Japanese, Mexican, Central American, and Carib-
bean—to the army of day-working domestics in the United States can
expect much upward mobility in today's shrinking economy. As in the past,
many of today's domestics remain uncounted, and we have little substantive knowledge about the nature of this occupational domain today. [44]

The upward mobility thesis, derived from the experience of one segment
of women domestics during an expanding phase of the West's economic
history, has been exported to the developing world, where, with a few
exceptions, it has been useless. [45] In general, few studies have been undertaken of domestic service in the Third World. Most of the existing work
concerns Latin America, where most servants are young migrant women
from rural backgrounds. They have been described as moving through a
series of gradually better-paying service jobs that serve as a route up. [46] But
while there still are many women domestic servants, their occupation appears to be declining as a major urban employment source in many Latin
American cities. [47] Studies from India show a somewhat different situation,
as does the available information on domestic service from China and
Malaysia. [48] In all these cases, cultural factors complicate the employment
relationship. The Indian situation, for one, is complex because of the division of labor embodied in the caste system. Extraeconomic factors structure work recruitment, determining which caste as well as which sex may
perform which tasks for whom. An exception occurs in the recruitment of
Christian servants, both women and men, in a manner perhaps neutral to
the religious and gender terms of the caste system. In the state of Kerala,
unmarried Christian girls from poor rural backgrounds seem to be preferred as domestic servants in many affluent urban Christian households,
where they work for varying lengths of time before returning to marry in

44. Shellee Colen, "'With Respect and Feelings': Voices of West Indian Child Care and
Domestic Workers in New York City," in *All American Women: Lines That Divide, Ties That
Bind*, ed. Johnetta Cole (New York: Free Press, 1986), pp. 46–70.
    45. The main proponent of this thesis is Chaplin, "Domestic Service."
    46. For example, Emily M. Nett, "The Servant Class in a Developing Country: Equador,"
Journal of Inter-American Studies 8 (1966): 437–452, and work by Margo L. Smith, e.g.,
"Domestic Service as a Channel of Upward Mobility for the Lower-Class Woman: The Lima
Case," in *Female and Male in Latin America*, ed. Ann Pescatello (Pittsburgh: University of
Pittsburgh Press, 1973), pp. 191–207. Ximena Bunster and Elsa M. Chaney qualify this view
in *Sellers and Servants: Working Women in Lima, Peru* (New York: Praeger, 1985).
    47. This is indicated by Harley L. Browning, "Some Problems of the Tertiarization Process
in Latin America," in *Urbanization in the Americas from Its Beginnings to the Present*, ed.
Richard P. Schaedel et al. (The Hague: Mouton, 1978), p. 160.
    48. Papers presented to symposium on domestic workers at the Eighty-fourth Annual
Meeting of the American Anthropological Association Washington, D.C., December 4–8,
1985, bear this out. Among them, M. Jocelyn Armstrong (University of Illinois), "Female
Domestics in Industrializing Malaysia," and Rubie S. Watson (University of Pittsburgh),
"Domestic Workers: Wives, Concubines, and Maids in Chinese Society."

the rural areas.[49] Domestic service is a socializing experience, but this case illustrates the irrelevance of such knowledge outside of the employing household. The women were unable to transfer their work-related experience so as to move beyond their original position in the social structure.

Aside from the Latin American cases just referred to, none of the non-Western studies of domestic service supports the upward mobility thesis. The thesis ignores the critical role that race and ethnicity can play in structuring relations in production. That role is exemplified in black American and other minority women's continued experience in domestic service in the United States. It is also illustrated by the countries of eastern and southern Africa, particularly during the colonial period and in the Republic of South Africa today, where race and sex were primary factors in the state's structuring of roles in production.

The existing studies of domestic service in Africa pertain almost exclusively to the southern region.[50] The remainder consists largely of descriptions done offhandedly in the context of studies with different focuses across the African continent. Recently, several studies, particularly from West Africa, have highlighted the role of young female relatives in performing household work without pay.[51] Commonly referred to as fostering, this practice is a research topic in its own right—and I shall have something to say about the Zambian variety in the main body of this book.

The South African studies offer a kaleidoscopic story of women of all races and men passing through domestic service.[52] After the abolition of slavery in 1834, poor Afrikaaner women and British women brought over from Europe worked as domestics in white households. As members of household staffs consisting mainly of African men, these white women's

49. V. Tellis-Nayak, "Power and Solidarity: Clientage in Domestic Service," *Current Anthropology* 24 (1983): 67–79.
50. Among the chief studies are Michael G. Whisson and William Weil, *Domestic Servants: A Microcosm of "The Race Problem"* (Johannesburg: Institute of Race Relations, 1971); Eleanor Preston-Whyte, "Race Attitudes and Behavior: The Case of Domestic Employment in White South African Homes," *African Studies* 35 (1976): 71–89; special issue on domestic labor of the *South African Labour Bulletin* 6 (1980); Jacklyn Cock, *Maids and Madams: A Study in the Politics of Exploitation* (Johannesburg: Ravan Press, 1980); and Suzanne Gordon, *A Talent For Tomorrow: Life Stories of South African Servants* (Johannesburg: Ravan Press, 1985).
51. Roger Sanjek, "Maid Servants and Market Women's Apprentices in Adabraka," paper presented to symposium on domestic workers at the Eighty-fourth Annual Meeting of the American Anthropological Association, Washington, D.C., December 4–8, 1985; Enid Schildkrout, "The Fostering of Children in Urban Ghana: Problems of Ethnographic Analysis in a Multi-Cultural Context," *Urban Anthropology* 2 (1973): 48–73; and "Age and Gender in Hausa Society: Socio-Economic Roles of Children in Urban Kano," in *Sex and Age as Principles of Social Differentiation*, ed. Jean S. LaFontaine (London: Academic Press, 1978), pp. 109–138.
52. Cock, *Maids and Madams*.

presence proved problematic, and they were replaced by African men soon after the turn of the century. African men persisted in domestic service on the Witwatersrand till the late 1930s, but were replaced by coloured and Affrican women in the Cape much earlier.[53] With growing demands for African labor in the mines, women gradually became more numerous in this occupation also on the Witwatersrand. Today in South Africa domestic service is considered an African woman's job, and it remains a life-long occupation through which married and unmarried women as well as single mothers pursue a series of deadend jobs.[54] In white-dominated Rhodesia, domestic service remained a male preserve longer than in South Africa.[55]

The vexations that reflect the difficulty of maintaining difference between servant and employer within the household have been captured forcefully by the literary imagination. Indeed, novelists and writers have had more to tell us about the nature and nuances of the servant-employer relationship than have social scientists. Servants and their employers have been recurrent figures in European, North American, and African literature.. The literary writer's servant is there in an active variety: as loyal tool, mercenary opportunist, active agent, disturber of the social order, representative of the rising bourgeoisie, forerunner of the revolution. As a metaphor the figure of the servant has been used to highlight intimate psychosexual power relationships, to represent the African oppressed, as a symptom of nationalist awakening, or as a yardstick against which the health or sickness of postcolonial African society is measured.[56] African writers, black and white, have used the figure of the servant for all of these things, yet not exactly in the same manner. In several works by black writers produced in Zambia, servants do figure, though not prominently. Domestic employment is just one detail in the context of the lives of the main characters.[57]

53. Charles van Onselen, "The Witches of Suburbia: Domestic Service on the Witwatersrand, 1890–1914," in van Onselen, ed., *Studies in the Social and Economic History of the Witwatersrand 1886–1914* (London: Longman, 1982), vol. 2, *New Nineveh*, pp. 1–73; Deborah Gaitskell, Judy Kimble, Moira Maconachie, and Elaine Unterhalter, "Race, Class, and Gender: Domestic Workers in South Africa," *Review of African Political Economy* 27/28 (1984): 86–108.

54. Eleanor Preston-Whyte develops this point in "Families without Marriage: A Zulu Case Study," in *Social System and Tradition in Southern Africa: Essays in Honour of Eileen Krige*, ed. John Argyle and Eleanor Preston-Whyte (Cape Town: Oxford University Press, 1978), pp. 55–85.

55. Duncan G. Clarke, *Domestic Workers in Rhodesia: The Economics of Masters and Servants* (Gwelo: Mambo Press, 1974), and chapters on servants and their employers in A. H. K. Weinrich, *Mucheke: Race, Status, and Politics in a Rhodesian Community* (New York: Holmes and Meier, 1976).

56. Stewart Crehan, "Master and Servant: A Comparative Literary Survey," mimeographed paper presented at the University of Zambia, n.d.

57. Andreya Masiye, *Before Dawn* (Lusaka: NECZAM, 1970); Grieve Sibale, *Between Two Worlds* (Lusaka: NECZAM, 1979); and Gideon Phiri, *Victims of Fate* (Lusaka: NECZAM, 1972).

Taking the literature from the southern Africa as my example, there are differences in the way black and white writers construct the servant's viewpoint. Doris Lessing and Nadine Gordimer, writing on Southern Rhodesia and South Africa respectively, have offered acutely sensitive and at times shocking descriptions of the domestic service institution.[58] But few writers have surpassed Ezekiel Mphalele's "Mrs. Plum."[59] This story gives voice to the African woman servant, depicts the economic and interpersonal situation that emerges in the servant-keeping context, and highlights that servants, despite all odds, retain some power in the relationship. Since the writer's imagination often captures popularly shared sentiments that are rarely part of the official discourse, insights gained from literary works on domestic service may be brought to bear creatively on more conventional social science analysis.

Why has this particular occupational domain received so little scholarly attention? Since they rarely formed a class in objective and subjective terms, servants might have been invisible to those labor historians who have viewed labor mobilization and strikes as the chief evidence of class. Defining class in such terms would tend to eliminate servants from the terrain of class analysis proper, for they often appeared uninvolved in the political arena. Servants may have been ignored by mainstream social scientists because they have considered domestic labor to be women's work, and for a long time they saw no need to problematize or raise questions about its agents. But domestic service has had a long history in the West as a typical man's job—and in some parts of the world is still thought to be so. Thus we must look farther than gender for an explanation of why the occupation was for so long neglected by scholars.

I suggest that the additional reason concerns the special nature of the labor process in domestic service. As the subordinate actors in a hierarchically structured work relationship, servants rarely spoke freely. Although they were conspicuously present in wealthier households, servants were rendered virtually "absent" by the social practices that became routinized in household work. Most of what we know about servants is expressed in the discourse of their employers. With some interesting exceptions, servants have left few personal records.[60] In their efforts to make

58. Servants figure frequently in the writings of these two authors and are among the key actors in Lessing's *The Grass Is Singing* (London: M. Joseph, 1953), and "A Home for the Highland Cattle," in her *Five: Short Novels* (London: M. Joseph, 1953); and Gordimer's "Ah, Woe Is Me" and "Happy Event," in her *Selected Stories* (London: Jonathan Cape, 1975), and *July's People* (New York: Viking Press, 1981).

59. Ezekiel Mphalele, "Mrs. Plum," in his *In Corner B* (Nairobi: East African Publishing House, 1967).

60. These exception include Peter Beard, collector, *Longing for Darkness: Kamante's Tales from Out of Africa, with Original Photographs (January 1914–July 1931) and Quotations from Isak Dinesen* (New York: Harcourt Brace Jovanovich, 1975); Liz Stanley, ed., *The Diaries of Hannah Cullwick, Victorian Maidservant* (London: Virago Press, 1984); and Hans

servants visible, scholars have had to tease information out of their employers' letters, diaries, and biographies, to read between the lines of travel descriptions, in addition to sifting through employment data and legal records. These data have already been edited in the recording process and from them we are most likely to glean a flat, stereotyped description of servants which lacks a sense of life.

Studies that make use of oral history data and "life histories" capture a better sense of lives and active interaction. This methodology is central to much recent research in social history.[61] I see the recent proliferation of domestic service studies as a part of this effort and concern to capture the lived experience of ordinary women and men, the ways in which their activities contributed to maintaining as well as to changing the societies in which they lived. A parallel concern has fueled recent scholarship in African history, which has sought to demonstrate the results of African initiative in the face of repressive colonial economic and political structures and of continued postcolonial dependency relationships.[62] To tease out the African voice requires ingenuity and imagination, for if the West is poor in terms of conventional records on ordinary people, Africa is even more so.

Drawing on interdisciplinary insights, I explore in this book how domestic service in Zambia historically and at the present time came to be taken for granted as a perquisite of social and economic position. I suggest that the occupation in that country is developing its own trajectory, which is not a delayed repetition of patterns found elsewhere. To explain the difference I reckon with the critical roles of race and sex in structuring relations of production during the colonial period and of class and sex during the postcolonial period. I have attempted to clarify how and why the African woman's gender role was fabricated in such a way that she was excluded from most urban wage labor, particularly domestic service. Economic, demographic, and political factors shaped the gender division of labor in domestic service, but so did cultural and ideological factors. These factors, in slightly altered configurations, continue to do so in Zambia today. In my comparative discussion of late twentieth-century dynamics in paid household work, I seek to bring my findings from Zambia to bear on developments closer to home. Today, it seems everybody in the United States wants relief from housework. I seek to make sense of this resurgence of

C. and Judith-Maria Buechler, *Carmen: The Autobiography of a Spanish Galician Woman* (Cambridge, Mass.: Schenkman, 1981). To this list might be added Elsa Joubert's recording of Poppie's story, *The Long Journey of Poppie Nongena* (Johannesburg: Jonathan Ball, 1980).

61. Oliver Zunz, ed., *Reliving the Past: The Worlds of Social History* (Chapel Hill: University of North Carolina Press, 1985).

62. William Beinart and Colin Bundy, *Hidden Struggles in Rural South Africa: Politics and Popular Movements in the Transkei and Eastern Cape, 1890–1930* (Berkeley: University of California Press, 1987), and Cooper, ed., *Struggle for the City.*

interest by relating the forces that have recreated the need for paid household workers in our contemporary economies to world economic developments. Household work, whether paid or not, is a critical economic domain, and this study challenges us to do more research on the ways it articulates with other occupational avenues over the course of local and worldwide economic booms and busts.

PART I

A Fixture of Colonial Society

Domestic service has a distinct educational value.
—Northern Rhodesia Annual Report upon Native
Affairs (1930)

[1]

The Creation of a Gender Role:
The Male Domestic Servant

Domestic service was very much a fixture of colonial society in Northern Rhodesia. Servants then were in the foreground and the background of their employers' lives. They were everywhere. In this chapter I piece together from scattered sources a historical narrative about domestic servants—the kind of work they did, their employers, the relationship between the two—and about employers' views of servants from around the turn of the last century through the interwar period. In so far as the sources allow me, I also offer glimpses of servants' reactions to their employers and about their activities outside of the work locus in colonial households. My account ignores the earliest years of colonial rule, partly because of lack of sources and partly because of the rough-and-ready nature of life on this expanding frontier, where concerns with household management and domesticity had little meaning.[1] While the early residents had African menservants, there was no place for African women in the early encounter save as objects to fulfill the most basic sexual needs of the frontiersmen. And there was little place for white women except in missionary households.

My concern in this chapter is to capture how whites, believing in the grandeur of Empire and not far removed ideologically from late Victorian mores and norms—to use the terms of their discourse—reacted to the "wilds" of the "far interior of Darkest Africa" and how they initially sought

1. Northern Rhodesia was administered by the British South Africa Company (BSAC) under a charter from the British Crown, beginning in North Eastern Rhodesia 1893–1894 and in North Western Rhodesia in 1897. Before the BSAC administration, this region was sometimes referred to as Transzambezia. The two separate territories were amalgamated in 1911, and in 1924 the Colonial Office in London took over the administration. I use the term Northern Rhodesia for the entire colonial period, except in situations where a regional reference needs to be specified.

to make Africans, particularly their servants, over in their own image. Colonial whites considered Africans to be members of societies so totally different from their own in social, cultural, and moral outlook that they appeared to be part of the wilds across which they lived scattered, and akin to the local flora and fauna. In the view of a contemporary observer: "in all their actions they are so like animals that I question they have any brains."[2] In domestic service, Africans were to become domesticated. To socialize Africans for subordinate roles in white households in the new political and economic order, colonial employers instituted a hierarchical labor process that accentuated the difference between themselves and their workers. In the discourse that accounted for this difference, race, class, and sex converged in complex ways confounded by notions of the other as primitive, tribal, dirty, and mentally inferior. As I demonstrate in subsequent chapters, these factors converged in varying patterns over time, and in unlike ways for the two sexes, thus constructing gender images of the other that never remained completely static.

During the period covered in this chapter, three generations confronted each other as servants and masters: from the turn of the century through World War I; the 1920s and early 1930s into the Great Depression; and the remainder of the interwar period. I examine how Africans were domesticated, so to speak. *Kaffirs*, like cattle, had to be worked and handled.[3] They had to be taught the domestic arts in the manner of whites, first by men, for few white women lived there during the earliest part of this period. In Northern Rhodesia, domestic service became constructed predominantly in African male gender terms. (The question of women in domestic service is taken up in Chapter 3. It suffices here simply to note that after the arrival of more white women, eyebrows were raised when colonial officials, most of whom were bachelors during their first tour of office, employed African women as domestics.)[4]

There are three points to make before I begin. First, because of the unevenness of my sources, my account probably does not convey the full range of domestic service employment practices. I have found no information on the servant-master relationship during this period in Afrikaans-speaking households, or in Asian or African domestic arrangements. My account focuses predominantly on the urban end of colonial society and

2. D. D. Lyell, *Hunting Trips in Northern Rhodesia, with Accounts of Sport and Travel in Nyasaland and Portuguese East Africa, and also Notes on the Game Animals and Their Distribution* (London: Horace Cox, 1910), p. 98.

3. This statement paraphrases a job advertisement inserted by H. G. Koch of Kalomo in the *Livingstone Mail*, December 18, 1909: "White man to work on farm; must know how to work Kaffirs and cattle."

4. Roy Stokes, personal communication, December 18, 1983.

ignores white farming households and missionary establishments in the rural areas.

Second, the dynamics I seek to reveal throughout this book are the products of a complex intertwining of three systems of stratification: by race, gender, and class. Since race to a great extent masked class relations during the period under review in the book's first part, the effect of my overall concern is to deemphasize variation among the employing classes and to focus on the governing race: the British. The fact that some African, Asian, and Afrikaans-speaking households also employed servants does not mean that the master-servant relationship in British households was atypical or out of the ordinary. After all, this was the time of Rule Britannia, the British considered themselves the dominant race, and they set the norms and standards against which other practices were evaluated.

Third, because I am concerned to unravel the changing effects of race, gender, and class on the domestic service institution, my presentation tends to revolve around instances of whites dominating Africans and one sex lording over the other. This emphasis may be contrary to the observations of some individuals who were participants in the colonial situation and who have praised the creation of bonds of trust and personal friendships between themselves and their servants. To be sure, feelings of affect and compassion developed in some cases, after a fashion, that is, for the distance between the white master and the black servant in the colonial situation remained too wide in class and cultural terms for genuine friendship with equal participation and shared authority to develop. Whether or not one liked a servant, he was a distant companion. He remained a servant and thus an inferior.

Servants and Other Inventory

The published literature on Northern Rhodesia readily leaves the impression that contract migrant labor to farms and mines was the only, or main, form of wage labor which developed during the colonial period in this region. Yet from the earliest days of white entry into what became known as Northern Rhodesia, two other forms of labor placed African men at the disposition of white employers: porterage and personal service.

Till the coming of the South Africa–based railway that bridged the Zambezi River in 1905 and reached Katanga in the Congo in 1910, if not till the advent of motor transportation in the 1920s, porterage is likely to have offered the largest employment avenue for Africans within the territory itself, yet on an intermittent, mostly dry-season, basis. Before the railway reached Katanga, the town of Broken Hill, where zinc and lead had been

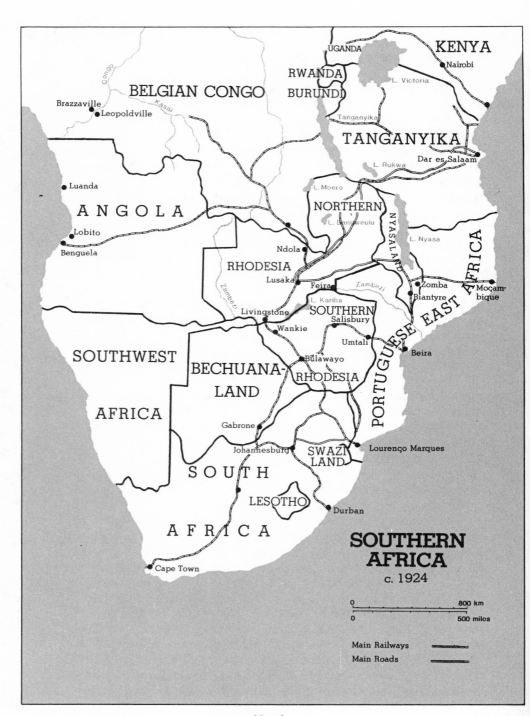

Map 1.

mined since 1902, served as the railhead for the Congo and the small mines in the Ndola and Kasempa districts. This town was the center for a number of private transport companies. In 1908 they employed a total of 27,818 carriers to transport cargo and passengers.[5] As more whites took up farming, especially after the Boer War, the need for African farm workers and domestic servants grew. Up to and including the World War I years, African farmhands outnumbered those employed in domestic service. By 1930, more Africans were employed as servants than as farm workers, and only for a brief period during the postwar years did farm workers again outnumber servants. Large numbers of Northern Rhodesian Africans worked on farms, in mines, and in private households in the south and in Katanga in the north and had done so since before the turn of the century. But domestic service was one of the chief avenues for African employment within the territory itself until mining was begun on a large scale in the north in the late 1920s.

The men who entered domestic service had left their villages to earn money for taxes that had been introduced across the territory, in some regions just before and in others just after the turn of the century.[6] Some of these men must have chosen domestic service in preference to being recruited for contract migrant labor in the south; others proceded on their own to the generally better-paying jobs in the south. Still others shuttled back and forth between jobs within the territory and outside it.[7] Given the grim work conditions on farms and mines, domestic service is likely to have been a choice favored by many.

Some of these African men had been introduced to service in missionary households where they were taught cleaning, washing, ironing, and cooking in the manner of the whites. Among them were some of the first Christian converts. But many left the mission stations, disliking the coercive regimes.[8] Others were socialized into domestic service in the households of the tiny but slowly growing white population—among whom a

5. Michael Gelfand, *Northern Rhodesia in the Days of the Charter: A Medical and Social Study 1878–1924* (Oxford: Basil Blackwell, 1961), p. 115.

6. For general historical background, see Lewis H. Gann, *A History of Northern Rhodesia: Early Days to 1953* (New York: Humanities Press, 1964), and Andrew Roberts, *A History of Zambia* (New York: Africana Publishing Company, 1976).

7. Charles van Onselen has shown how migrants sought to make the most out of their economic misfortune. The most successful worked their way by stages from the lowest-paid jobs on farms and mines in Southern Rhodesia to the less lowly paid jobs on the Rand. *Chibaro: African Mine Labour in Southern Rhodesia, 1900–1933* (London: Pluto Press, 1976). Many Africans, including servants, from Northern Rhodesia also migrated in stepwise fashion.

8. Robert I. Rotberg, *Christian Missionaries and the Creation of Northern Rhodesia, 1880–1924* (Princeton: Princeton University Press, 1965), pp. 42, 52–55.

[33]

disproportionate number were bachelors[9]—in the small administrative headquarters and on farms scattered across the territory. And still others were taken on as personal servants or cooks in caravans that made their way through the territory to enjoy the sport—meaning big game hunting—explore the wilds, or a combination thereof.

The labor process that evolved in caravan service and private households shared little with what variously has been labeled dependent labor, servitude, or slavery as previously practiced in many societies in this region.[10] Such practices did not exclude dependent workers from the groups for whom they labored. They had less status, but there were mutual obligations between them and the persons who enjoyed their services. The colonial labor process depended on commoditization of labor. In it, status was exchanged for contract and obligations toward a worker were stipulated in return for rights: the employer's demand for the worker's labor power.

Information about this employment relationship during the early decades of this century may be gleaned from travel descriptions, local memoirs, and reminiscences and should be used with caution. Cairns, using the literature from 1840–1890, warns readers "to make a deliberate effort to not see Central Africa as an arena where all the important activities were carried out by a growing handful of Europeans in the midst of an environment in which Africans, elephants and natural obstacles are lumped together as background landscape."[11]

Most books of this period, whether travel accounts or memoirs, contain advice to travelers and prospective settlers. Sometimes in the form of an

9. Because of climatic vagaries and the risks of malaria, sleeping sickness, yellow fewer, and other tropical diseases, Northern Rhodesia was known as the "white man's grave," and it was not till after World War I that white women began to arrive in larger numbers. For a discussion of illness and health during the period of early settlement, see Gelfand, *Northern Rhodesia*. See also Table 3 in Chapter 2 below for sex ratios.

10. In African studies, the term *slavery* comprises a variety of relationships. In recent work on the subject, Robertson and Klein note that slavery "has been variously defined in terms of property relationships . . . or in terms of the slave's kinlessness. Whatever definition is used, the slave is involuntarily servile, has a marginal position within [the] social unit, and is subject to the control of others." Claire C. Robertson and Martin A. Klein, eds., *Women and Slavery in Africa* (Madison: University of Wisconsin Press, 1983), pp. 3–4. For a comparative discussion of slavery in Africa, see Suzanne Miers and Igor Kopytoff, eds., *Slavery in Africa: Historical and Anthropological Perspectives* (Madison: University of Wisconsin Press, 1977). Cross-cultural comparisons of African and Asian slavery are available in James L. Watson, ed., *Asian and African Systems of Slavery* (Berkeley: University of California Press, 1980). For other Central African examples, see Mary Douglas, "Matriliny and Pawnship in Central Africa, *Africa* 34 (1964): 301–313; Arthur Tuden, "Slavery and Social Stratification among the Ila of Central Africa," in *Social Stratification in Africa*, ed. A. Tuden and L. Plotnikov (New York: Free Press, 1970), pp. 47–59; and Marcia Wright, *Women in Peril: Life Stories of Four Captives* (Lusaka: NECZAM, 1984).

11. J. Alan Cairns, *Prelude to Imperialism: British Reactions to Central African Society, 1840–1890* (London: Routledge and Kegan Paul, 1965), p. 30.

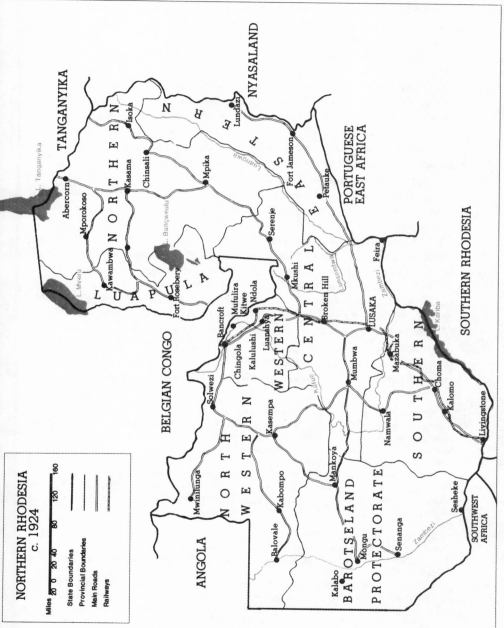

Map 2.

appendix, in other cases merely as prescriptive remarks thrown in, these accounts offer an inventory of items and provisions to bring from overseas and advice about items locally obtainable. Porters and servants were part of the local inventory and readers were told which brands (e.g., different tribes; raw natives versus mission boys) were better or worse, how to deal with them in terms of remuneration and food, and what to expect, or rather not to expect, of them in terms of work discipline.[12] These early travelers moved on foot and/or were carried in *machilas* (hammocks).[13] (Horses and ox wagons were of little use in the territory north of the Zambezi because of the tsetse fly.) Others journeyed on bicycles.[14] During the 1920s automobiles appeared,[15] yet in outlying districts, feet, machilas, and bicycles, or a combination, remained in use much longer.

The travelers' experiences in this remote interior, delivered in books with expansive titles, display a self-confidence bordering on arrogance, rooted in late Victorian mores and habits and in the knowledge that Europe, if not Britain, was the center of the world and the standard against which everything else was measured. Among them Mary Hall, a young British woman of means who had traveled "all the great continents of the world," accounted for how she was the first woman who "quite alone" managed to complete the trek from Cape to Cairo soon after the turn of the century.[16] Mrs. Arthur Colville described what it was like to cross from Chinde in Portuguese East Africa to the interior of Northern Rhodesia in a machila in 1908–1909, while her colonel husband, of fame from the Kabarega campaign in Uganda, described the sport.[17] About the same time, a young British novelist, Charlotte Mansfield, traveled in machila through

12. For a classic of this genre, see Sir Francis Galton, *The Art of Travel, or Shifts and Contrivances Available in Wild Countries* (1854; London: John Murray, 1893), which appeared in at least eight editions. The book contains a special section on "management of Savages" (pp. 308–310). For an example from this region, see the chapter entitled "Some Native Traits" in Lyell, *Hunting Trips*, pp. 98–101, and the chapter entitled "Odds and Ends of Information" in his later book, *Nyasaland for the Hunter and Settler* (London: Horace Cox, 1912), pp. 89–90. His contemporary Owen Letcher in *Big Game Hunting in North-Eastern Rhodesia* (London: John Long, 1911) also included an inventory chapter with information for visitors and sportsmen, entitled "The Natives of the Country, and some Questions Affecting Them."

13. Mrs. Arthur (Olivia) Colville, *One Thousand Miles in a Machila: Travel and Sport in Nyasaland, Angoniland, and Rhodesia, with Some Account of the Resources of These Countries; and Chapters on Sport by Colonel Colville, C. B.* (London: Walter Scott Publishing Company, 1911).

14. Frank H. Melland and Edward H. Cholmeley, *Through the Heart of Africa: Being an Account of a Journey on Bicycles and on Foot from Northern Rhodesia, Past the Great Lakes, to Egypt, Undertaken when Proceding Home on Leave in 1910* (London: Constable, 1912).

15. Selma Whitehouse, *Moonlight, Giraffes, and Frying Pans* (London: John Lane, 1928), describes the first automobile trip from Johannesburg through Northern Rhodesia.

16. Mary Hall, *A Woman's Trek from the Cape to Cairo* (London: Methuen, 1907).

17. Colville, *One Thousand Miles.*

the small towns and administrative stations of Northern Rhodesia.[18] And self-proclaimed suffragette Edith Cecil-Porch, in a book she authored under her later husband's name, described the recruitment of travel companions in England for a trip beyond the Zambezi to see the world and to seek adventure.[19] In these books and others like them Africa and Africans are depicted, much as Cairns suggested, mostly as backdrops against which fairly rich whites went out to play.

A caravan was much like a traveling village. Mary Hall's feeling of being "quite alone" was thus an experience of racial and cultural difference between herself and the retinue of porters and servants. A typical retinue would consist of ten to twelve men to carry the machila. (The hammock covered with a canopy was swung either on one pole or on two parallel poles and carried by two or four men on their shoulders. They would be relieved by others after a short while, the pole being changed from one man's shoulder to his replacement's while running.)[20] Large numbers of porters carried provisions and equipment in headloads of standard weights, varying regionally from thirty to sixty pounds, under the supervision of a head porter, referred to as *capitao*. The number of porters per passenger ranged between twelve and thirty.[21] The suffragette's party of four employed fifty porters.[22] Last but not least came the personal staff, consisting perhaps of cook, tableboy, plate washer, and sometimes a personal boy. Local whites would be equipped in much the same fashion when on *ulendo* (bush travel), though the number of porters and servants might be somewhat smaller.[23]

Porters and servants were engaged often with the help of local officials at the major transportation centers: Fort Jameson in the east, Abercorn in the northeast, Livingstone in the south, and Broken Hill on the railway line. The length of their journey, weight of loads, and remuneration were agreed on in advance. If a personal servant misbehaved or absconded en route, he was often replaced by a porter who received on-the-job training for service.

---

18. Charlotte Mansfield, *Via Rhodesia: A Journey through South Africa* (London: Stanley Paul, n.d., ca. 1909).

19. Mrs. Fred Maturin (Edith Cecil-Porch), *Adventures beyond the Zambezi of the O'Flaherty, The Insular Miss, the Soldier Man, and the Rebel Woman* (London: Eveleigh Nash, 1913).

20. J. M. Moubray, *In Central Africa: Being an Account of Some of the Experiences and Journeys of the Author during a Stay of Six Years in That Country* (London: Constable, 1912), p. 46.

21. Gelfand, *Northern Rhodesia*, p. 115.

22. Maturin, *Adventures*, p. 22.

23. For descriptions of ulendos by early officials, see various articles in the *Northern Rhodesia Journal*, among them E. Knowles Jordan, "Feira in 1919–1920," 4 (1959): 63–71, and "Chinsali in 1920–1922," 5 (1964): 540–548.

Much of the personal staff and the machila men had servants to carry their travel kits and see to their comforts.[24] The "cook [was] a man of dignity and carrie[d] only himself."[25] The matter of the servants' servants caused the travelers some surprise. They seemed to appear out of nowhere, suddenly being part of the caravan.[26] In addition, though not so often commented on by the travelers of the early part of this century, Africans from the various localities traversed by the caravan often attached themselves to it, sloughing off between the villages.[27] Among them also were women who cooked and provided sexual services to the African staff as well as to white men who traveled unaccompanied by women.[28]

Personal servants mediated many contacts among the travelers, the rest of the retinue, and the local Africans. Because travelers rarely spoke any local languages, some found it useful to employ mission boys who had learned some English. When reaching Nyasaland from South Africa, Mary Hall needed a servant who could speak English and Swahili. She hired Robertson, one of the "native pupil teachers" at the Church of Scotland Mission in Blantyre, who accompanied her to Tanganyika as her sole interpreter.[29] Colonel and Mrs. Colville engaged a man named Moffat as cook. He had also gone to school at the Blantyre mission, and Mrs. Colville described him as a first-rate servant and a good cook. But in the prescriptive remarks to other travelers or settlers, her position changed: "his spurious education destroys his simple nature, and in some cases he degenerates offensively in his manners."[30] This remark may reflect the received wisdom on servants which the Colvilles picked up along the way. Many employers were wary of mission boys, whose smattering of education was held to make them less respectful to whites. Because they had been Christianized and/or educated, mission-trained men were perhaps less different from the whites; they may have caused problems of discipline by asking too many questions. "If he can possibly help it," commented J. M. Moubray, a mining engineer who traveled throughout the territory between 1903 and 1908, "the white man will never employ a mission boy . . . many [of whom]

---

24. Moubray, *In Central Africa*, p. 47.
25. Mansfield, *Via Rhodesia*, p. 177.
26. Maturin, *Adventures*, pp. 27–28, 271–272.
27. Dugald Campbell, *In the Heart of Bantuland: A Record of Twenty-nine Years' Pioneering in Central Africa among the Bantu Peoples with a Description of Their Habits, Customs, Secret Societies, and Languages* (1922; New York: Negro Universities Press, 1969), p. 278.
28. Instances of sexual relations between white travelers and African women were frequently reported in the travel/exploration literature from before the turn of the last century but seem to have been filtered out of this era's descriptions. See Chapter 3 for more discussion of sexuality and race.
29. Hall, *Woman's Trek*, p. 53.
30. Colville, *One Thousand Miles*, pp. 19, 20, 303.

are rogues of the first water." "My own natives," he continued, "by which I mean my personal boys and hunters . . . were aliens." He preferred Yao men from Nyasaland.[31]

In hiring servants, many travelers and settlers preferred nonlocal men. And travelers made observations about the "good" boys from foreign territories when they stopped to visit resident whites. When making up their inventory in Nyasaland before setting out on their machila trek, the Colvilles hired Edward, from Chinde in Portuguese East Africa, as a personal servant.[32] Edith Cecil-Porch's party engaged a servant staff of four Tanganyika boys at Livingstone, among them her future husband's headman, interpreter, and body servant in one. Hymn-book, as they called him, was a Christian, "which, if anything, rather set us against him."[33] The BSAC clerk at Kalomo before 1911, E. Knowles Jordan, also hired two Tanganyika boys.[34] When visiting Kalomo in 1903, then the capital of North Western Rhodesia, Lady Sarah Wilson commented on the work of the servants: "I was much impressed in a Kalomo house with the small details of a carefully arranged dinner table, adorned with flowers and snowy linen; the cooking was entirely done by black boys, of these the 'Chinde' boys from the Portuguese settlement are much sought after, so thoroughly do the Portuguese understand the training of natives."[35]

But more so than any others, Nyasa boys were said to be good in Northern Rhodesia.[36] A stereotypic preference has remained to the present day in Zambia for servants, if not from Malawi, then from Zambia's eastern province, which borders on Malawi. In Southern Rhodesia in turn, whites preferred northern natives, Nyasa, and Chinde boys.[37] And in South Af-

---

31. Moubray, *In Central Africa*, p. 34.

32. Colville, *One Thousand Miles*, p. 20.

33. Maturin, *Adventures*, p. 20.

34. E. Knowles Jordan, "Early Days in Kalomo and Livingstone," *Northern Rhodesia Journal* 1 (1950): 21.

35. Sarah Wilson (Lady Spencer-Churchill), *South African Memoirs: Social, Warlike, and Sporting: From Diaries Written at the Time* (London: Edward Arnold, 1909).

36. John B. Thornhill, *Adventures in Africa: Under the British, Belgian, and Portuguese Flag* (London: John Murray, 1915), p. 10.

37. The preference for "northern natives" in domestic service is mentioned in Ethel Tawse Jollie's *The Real Rhodesia* (London: Hutchinson, 1924), a book akin to a household management guide, displaying white settler ideology. The smart Northern Rhodesian servant is idealized in Gertrude Page's novels set in Southern Rhodesia before World War I. Among them are *Jill's Rhodesian Philosophy* (London: Hurst and Blackett, 1910); *The Rhodesian* (London: Hurst and Blackett, 1912); *Where the Strange Roads Go Down* (London: Hurst and Blackett, 1913); *Follow After* (London: Hurst and Blackett, 1921); and *Love in the Wilderness* (London: G. Bell and Sons, 1907). The preference for servants from Portuguese East Africa is noted by Hugh M. Hole, a writer of settler history and once civil commissioner of Bulawayo. According to Hole, the indigenous Mashona were not of any value as cooks, wagon boys, farm or mine laborers. "For domestic purposes, we selected mainly boys imported from the territories on the East coast, where they had long been accustomed to work for the slothful Por-

rica, the northern boys had a very fine reputation. Wherever they were, employers thus seem to have preferred nonlocal servants. The tour reports written by colonial administrators in Northern Rhodesia are replete with statements on the order of "local natives make bad servants." In 1919, for instance, in Chilanga subdistrict, which included the small town of Lusaka, the great majority of African wage laborers were from other parts of the territory or Nyasaland. The subdistrict then had a total white population of 576, of whom 217 were men, 129 women, and 230 children. More than half of them were Afrikaans-speaking South Africans, and about half of the adult male population were farmers. The African labor force consisted of 1,300 men, of whom 300 worked as servants and 650 as farm laborers. The rest worked on the small mines, in quarries, on the railways, or as capitaos. An additional 700 men were employed by the administration and 284 carriers were supplied for war-related work in the north.[38]

The 300 servants in the Chilanga subdistrict in 1919 came from two principal regions: Nyasaland and the north.[39] The tour report lists the latter as Bemba, yet they are likely to have included some Inamwanga, neighbors of the Bemba who lived on both sides of the border between Northern Rhodesia and Tanganyika. They may have been among the Tanganyika boys mentioned earlier. The men who came from afar had left behind wives and dependents. Local Africans did not turn up readily for farm work or for domestic service. If they could make a living in their villages, they seem to have preferred that. When they did take on wage labor jobs, they were likely to have had too many conflicting claims placed on their labor and time by relatives from the home villages. This may have adversely affected their constancy in wage labor and helped to bring about the high turnover rates about which white employers complained as well as the preference for nonlocal workers.

For their work, servants were paid in cash and kind. The latter, known as *posho* or ration, seems to have consisted of cloth, at least during the first decade of this century. Arriving by train at the railhead at Broken Hill in

---

tuguese employers, and had become fairly efficient as house servants." *Old Rhodesian Days* (London: MacMillan, 1928), p. 46. He also mentioned that while many servants were from the east coast, others came from more distant parts: Zulus from Natal, mission boys from Blantyre in Nyasaland, and even some from as far as Uganda. They were all, according to his account, attracted by the high rates of pay, based on "the South African scale" (p. 51).

38. NAZ/KDC 6/1/6. Annual Reports, Chilanga Subdistrict, Luangwa District, 1917–1928. Annual Report for the Year Ending March 31, 1918.

39. Ibid. Annual Report for the Year Ending March 31, 1919, which gives the following ethnic/regional division of labor among Africans employed in the subdistrict: cattle herds: Barotse or Mashukulumbwe; wagon drivers and plough boys: South Africa or Barotseland; houseservants and cooks: Fort Jameson, Wemba Division, and Nyasaland; sawyers, carpenters, bricklayers: Nyasaland; farm laborers: Mumbwa, Namwala, and Kasempa; railway laborers: Mkushi, Ndola, Mwomboshi; Fishermen and canoe boys: Wata from Namwala.

1906 after five years in Southern Rhodesia, John M. Springer, an American Methodist missionary, and his wife provisioned their caravan for a trek to Luanda at the Atlantic coast, noting the "good custom for rationing a caravan. Each man is given a yard of blue or white calico, and he buys his food for a week with it. . . . In addition, we gave our men two ounces of salt each week."[40] When crossing from Nyasaland, where they had paid full cash wages, into North Eastern Rhodesia in 1908, the Colvilles also remarked on the change in remuneration. For in North Eastern Rhodesia posho had to be paid in calico, two yards per man per week. Small amounts of salt were also handed out. From there on, three posho loads were added to their caravan: one of calico and two of salt, the latter to be used as currency in the interior.[41] In addition to the rise in remuneration, there was also regional variation. On the North Eastern plateau, according to Cullen Gouldsbury and Hubert Sheane, posho consisted of four yards of calico per month—this, as in the previous cases, in addition to cash wages.[42]

Travelers' accounts show less concern with the socialization of servants than do those given by white residents. After all, travelers were in transit and not out to carve out small islands of white civilization for themselves. Their comments about servants may perhaps be somewhat exaggerated because they were unprepared for the stark difference between life as they knew it at home and their experience of it in what they considered the wilds beyond the Zambezi. On the other hand, some of their descriptions offer glimpses of servants at very close range.

Women writers, in particular, frequently commented on servants. The carriers' and servants' "domestic affairs afforded constant interest" to Edith Cecil-Porch when she rested in camp while her two white men companions pursued the sport. She commented on the blasé attitude of the smartly attired personal servants toward the half-naked carriers, their separate sleeping arrangements, the division of labor in the caravan kitchen where the cook's "slaves" did the main part of the work, and on the "brudders" and the women who hung around the camp kitchen when the caravan made stops. Her musings are sometimes quite negative, for example, when she called all the servants "perfidious" for giving the same lame excuse—the death of a relative—when one morning they turned up unable to work after a night of drinking in a nearby village.[43]

But on one matter there was no mincing of words: the cook was good. In fact, most travelers were very impressed with the skills of their cooks, who

40. John Mckendree Springer, *The Heart of Central Africa: Mineral Wealth and Missionary Opportunity* (New York: Jennings and Graham, 1909), p. 79.

41. Colville, *One Thousand Miles*, pp. 129, 173–174.

42. Cullen Gouldsbury and Hubert Sheane, *The Great Plateau of Northern Rhodesia: Being Some Impressions of the Tanganyika Plateau* (London: Edward Arnold, 1911), p. 323.

43. Maturin, *Adventures*, pp. 21–22, 27, 100, 328–329.

managed to prepare courses of several dishes, using mainly tinned food-stuffs carried along in the loads, and chickens, eggs, vegetables, and fish bought from local Africans. If there were white men in the party, game shot en route was cooked as well. Fresh bread was baked daily on many cara-vans. The Springer's cook, a mission boy brought from Umtali in Southern Rhodesia to Luanda "was the best fitted of all the boys to fill the role of helper, interpreter, and general man. . . . He was also a splendid cook and had the art of a superior chef—the ability to make tasty dishes out of almost nothing."[44] While on trek, although in the wilds, life was not necessarily simple. Some, like Colonel and Mrs. Colville, traveled in style. They shared an imperial pint of champagne twice a week, and on other nights they drank whiskey and sparklet, with a glass of Madeira after dinner.[45]

Because personal servants ministered to the daily needs and comforts of their traveling employers, they came into contact with them more fre-quently than did other Africans in the caravans. Nevertheless in the eyes of their employers, servants remained just that: part of an inventory, distant companions. Whatever else the servants did as individuals was of little consequence to their employers so long as it did not interfere with the execution of their work. At most, drunken brawls annoyed the employers, and the pecking order among servants and carriers amused them. These two aspects of the personal affairs of the African staff seem to have been the main ones noted by the travelers. Not the private life, background, or idiosyncracies of servants as individuals but their habits, spoken of collec-tively, of drinking, gambling, and consorting with women.

It simultaneously amused and annoyed the whites to notice how much their personal servants liked to dress up European-style. They were amused by the ill-matched garments and annoyed because the well-dressed African appeared less like a piece of inventory and more like a white. Almost without exception, travelers' accounts contain comments to that effect. In the words of Mrs. Collville: "The black man is essentially vain. There can be no doubt that the wearing of European clothes in his own hot climate has an extraordinary and deteriorating effect on his mind. Dressed up in the cast-off clothes of his master, or the shoddy garments of the native store, he really think he impersonates and is on a level with a white man. . . . It is a great pity stringent rules are not made to prevent natives from apeing the white man's dress, especially in a young colony.[46]

Such contempt for African attempts to dress in style also reflected the attitude of white residents. Consider the sarcastic evaluation of such efforts

44. Springer, *Heart of Central Africa*, p. 59.
45. Colville, *One Thousand Miles*, p. 40.
46. Ibid., p. 133.

in the following note, from which we can glimpse an occupational culture in the making among servants in Livingstone in 1909:

> Last week a gentleman requiring his evening clothes found the coat missing. On questioning his boy the latter fetched the garment from his k[a]ya [hut]. Investigation revealed he had worn it the previous evening at a dinner party given by some of his friends to their acquaintances of both sexes. Subsequent inquiries [revealed] . . . that other peoples' clothes were missing. . . . A native dinner party, with the gentlemen attired in evening dress, stand-up collars, white vests, and possibly patent leather shoes, the ladies being doubtless "en decollette" must have been an inspiring sight, and the fact that such a function has been successfully held is . . . evidence of the rapid advance of civilization.[47]

The comments by this Livingstone resident ignore almost completely any serious reckoning with the functions that European dress may have played in the social lives of servants when away from work. The story, whether true or false, had a sorry ending, for the chief actors received several strokes of the cane.

The travelers also commented on the lifestyle of the resident whites they visited in the tiny settlements. Against the background of what the travelers considered as the wilds, The Society appeared as small islands of civilization. Since there were few visitors, local whites were very welcoming and opened their homes to entertain up-country shooting parties, ladies of fame, and people of means bent on enterprise. Lady Sarah Wilson (Spencer Churchill) was impressed by the emptiness and youth of the territory when she visited Livingstone and Kalomo in 1903.[48] The white population was estimated to number only 850 in 1904, and 1,497 at the time of the first census in 1911 when the African population stood at some 820,985.[49] In this vast territory in which the visitors saw so many economic potentials, they noted "one draw-back . . . there are not enough [white] women." Dinner parties consisted of eight men to two women in North Western Rhodesia, wrote novelist Catherine Mansfield after her visit around 1908/9.[50] In 1911, white men outnumbered white women by three to one.[51] Miss Mansfield commented: "the [white] inhabitants are ambitious and surprisingly up to date in their ideas. . . . The officials are

---

47. "Notes and Memos," *Livingstone Mail*, February 9, 1909, p. 6.
48. Wilson, *South African Memoirs*, p. 303.
49. George Kay, *A Social Geography of Zambia* (London: University of London Press, 1967), p. 26. The African population figures are taken from NAZ/BS 2/134. BSAC Administration. Annual Reports, North Western Rhodesia, 1911, and North Eastern Rhodesia, 1911.
50. Mansfield, *Via Rhodesia*, p. 142.
51. Kay, *Social Geography*, p. 26.

cultured men and their wives *charming women"* (italics added). She was entertained in style: a garden party hosted in her honor by the wife of Administrator Wallace at Livingstone with more than seventy guests for tea on the verandah while "a native band of drums and fifes discoursed music on the lawns below." The mine officials at Broken Hill declared half a day's holiday at which she entertained them; there was piano playing and singing, and the local magistrate was the best banjo player she had heard off the professional platform.[52] In the life of resident whites "sport is naturally at present the chief pastime. . . . Everyone reads, many are musical, and conversation has as much and often more interest in than 'the bored talk in European towns.'"[53] Such enthusiasm was not shared by all travelers, and not all towns were equally cultured. Lusaka was merely a railway siding that had arisen in 1905 alongside the building of the railroad to the north. It was still a small village when Edith Cecil-Porch's party made a one-week stop in 1913, and its population was predominantly of Afrikaans-speaking background. In addition to being unpleasant, the place was boring. Comments Miss Cecil-Porch: "I can't think of how they faced life, for it had none of the compensations of ours . . . practically no society, no pleasures, nothing!"[54]

Few texts from the days of frontier life describe how unmarried white men went about the practical tasks of tropical housekeeping. Many, as I discuss in the next chapter, took African wives who may have carried out part of the housework. Yet Heaton Nicholls, a BSAC official, reports that when he and a white colleague trekked from Southern Rhodesia to the Kafue Flats in Northern Rhodesia to take up a new assignment, they "tried [their] hands at cooking with the aid of Mrs. Beeton's cookery book and by substituting for her ingredients anything available."[55] I doubt that they did the regular cooking. Their caravan is likely to have included a cook and perhaps a personal servant in its inventory.

As most other texts, Nicholls's autobiography offers no glimpses of how

52. Mansfield, *Via Rhodesia*, pp. 142–144, 164–165.
53. Ibid., p. 142. Miss Mansfield's book was commented on extensively in the local press by two writers who took her to task, not for her descriptions of The Society, but for exaggerating the wildness of her exploits. They pointed out, among several other things, that she hardly traveled unaccompanied; in addition to African servants, she had European male escort at several points of the journey; she did not trek through unexplored parts but followed well-trodden routes that other white women had traveled before her; and she traveled most of the route from the Cape to Cairo not overland but whenever possible by railways, gunboats, and steamers. Miss Mansfield's Africa is thus a constructed product, her descriptions of the extensive wilderness and the small islands of white civilization in the colony meant for consumption by readers in Great Britain. "'John Bull' and Miss Mansfield," *Livingstone Mail*, October 2, 1909, p. 4, and "Cape to Cairo," *Livingstone Mail*, November 13, 1909, p. 2.
54. Maturin, *Adventures*, p. 385.
55. G. Heaton Nicholls, *South Africa in My Time* (London: Allen and Unwin, 1961), p. 52.

servants were domesticated into their work roles by white men living without permanent female company, black or white. The men I spoke to or corresponded with, who came to Northern Rhodesia in the late 1920s, typically had a servant referred to them by an old-hand on their arrival to Livingstone or Lusaka. Some of these servants accompanied them to up-country posts, but others vanished, not willing to relocate to a different language area. At bush stations, wives of missionaries or officials subsequently recommended servants. James Murray had employed a cook, Chongo, recommended by missionaries near Mkushi in 1929. When he became district commissioner at Mkushi in 1934, he "decided to import a wife. She soon discovered that my monthly consumption of sugar, flour, . . . soap and tea were enough for a boarding house and Chongo's hours of work were drastically increased. There was no time off between 8 and 12, there was much dusting, floor polishing to be done and more or less endless washing of . . . table cloths and even dish cloths. Puddings had to be made for lunch and supper and there was interference in the kitchen. Chongo naturally left."[56] By contrast, when Gervas Clay in 1936 brought his wife, Betty, to Barotseland where he had been stationed since 1930, the cook stayed put. Clay engaged him upon the recommendation of the wife of the local district commissioner. Betty left things to the cook without much interfering. As the youngest daughter of Lord Baden Powell, she had little practical experience in housework and the cook in all likelihood introduced her to tropical housekeeping. When leaving Britain she had no idea of what life in the bush would be like, she told me, but retrospectively and with good-scouting attitude, she spoke of it as adventure and excitement. The cook stayed with them till he died, after which the houseboy was promoted to cook.[57]

If travelers were impressed by the skills of their personal servants, especially their cooks, the few white women settled in the territory at this time had already begun to complain about their domestic trials with servants. Most of them had a fair number, because servants' wages were low and because it was assumed, rightly or wrongly, that Africans were incapable of doing more than a simple job. So there were separate cook, house-, laundry, scullery, wood-, water-, garden boys, and so forth.[58] Their numbers seem to have ranged from six to twelve. White women faced the task of turning what they called raw natives into domestic workers, skilled at keeping house like in London, under circumstances where many basic amenities were lacking.

56. James Murray, personal communication, October 19, 1986.
57. Betty and Gervas Clay, personal communication, July 5–6, 1986.
58. Robert C. Tredgold, *The Rhodesia That Was My Life* (London: Allen and Unwin, 1968), p. 16.

Edith Cecil-Porch, two men companions with trophies, and servants during caravan trek. Reprinted from Mrs. Fred Maturin (Edith Cecil-Porch), *Adventures beyond the Zambezi* (London: Eveleigh Nash, 1913), p. 384.

The household staff of S. R. Denny, Kasempa, c. 1930. From left to right, probably: piccanin, washboy, cook, houseboy, and tableboy. Reproduced with permission of S. R. Denny, from photograph deposited in the Bodleian Library at Rhodes House, Oxford University, MSS Afr. s. 791(3).

Where both husband and wife were present in a colonial household, the man seems to have been more lenient than the woman in evaluation of servants. This at least is the tenor of comments in a 1909 newspaper write-up by one Harold Reynolds:

> Why does the native so strongly object to a missus? . . . The Bwana is content to take things as they come. Sometimes he gets angry and his wrath is very terrible, but it is only for a few minutes. . . . But the missus is often angry. . . . [A] woman tries to teach the native to do things her way. One native in a hundred can learn, but the other ninety-nine must do things in their own way or not at all. . . . Remember, *in the degree that you charm so shall be your powers.* . . . Do not attempt to teach the native overmuch; realize his limitations, and do not attempt to drill into that wooly head that which its mental capacity cannot possibly grasp. You will only ruin your constitution and your temper. . . . Be your own delightful self and you will perform *the whole duty of woman in tropical climes* [italics added].[59]

Cullen Gouldsbury, BSAC official on the northeastern plateau in the 1910s, expressed similar sentiments in his semifictional account of domestic life in these parts. While his description of household affairs highlights the indispensability of servants to the effort of creating The Society of the time, he and his wife reacted in very different ways to the household staff. Whereas wife Beryl classified servants by "a standard of smelliness or unsmelliness, or of those who are suitable for housework and those who are not" and when she was in a bad mood viewed the African "instinctively, as a beast," Gouldsbury himself thought that they were an asset who, with education, eventually would advance.[60]

In Gouldsbury's and BSAC colleague Hubert Sheane's 1911 impressionistic account of life on the plateau, servants were an important part of the inventory. Following the conventions of this era, their book includes prescriptive sections. Servants are featured under "ways and means" and readers informed that good servants can be engaged at Zomba and Blantyre in Nyasaland. Boys fill a section of their own and are described as being a matter of taste. The book offers recommendations about how many to employ, in which functions, and at what wages. For the smooth running of the household, one boy should be appointed head servant and have some degree of authority over the rest so as to relieve the master from overseeing everyone.[61]

Some of these servants advanced through the ranks and worked for the same employers for many years. Some masters grew fond of their servants,

59. "At Random," *Livingstone Mail*, December 25, 1909, p. 6.

60. Cullen Gouldsbury, *An African Year* (London: Edward Arnold, 1912), pp. 25, 106, 169.

61. Gouldsbury and Sheane, *Great Plateau*, p. 309, 323–324.

after a fashion, and took them along to see the world. Codrington, an early administrator of North Eastern Rhodesia, once took his favorite boy to England on leave.[62] Stewart Gore-Browne, later of political fame in Northern Rhodesia, took along two servants, Bulaya and Kakumbi, when he went to England at the beginning of World War I. He wanted them "to see and learn . . . the very best of our things . . . and how we really live. Something to set against the mining towns which [in Northern Rhodesia] is what passes for the height of English habit and living. [He] wanted to educate them and not to spoil them."[63] When Gore-Browne left for the front, he made arrangements for Bulaya and Kakumbi's return to Northern Rhodesia. On the morning of their departure, Bulaya had disappeared; only Kakumbi went back and joined Gore-Browne's African staff on his return from the war. Bulaya meanwhile had some menial jobs, then enlisted in the army and spent time in France and Palestine. In 1922 arrangements were made once again for his return to Northern Rhodesia, but he absconded. He later became an actor and married an Englishwoman.[64]

Some employers took servants along on vacation trips to South Africa.[65] These servants and those of famous men certainly did "see the world," although it is uncertain how they interpreted it and what sort of educational lesson they got from it. Codrington's servant was scared to tears when taken to the hippodrome for entertainment.[66] And Northern Rhodesian officials viewed Bulaya's self-selected education with suspicion, considering it unwise to encourage his return: "he could hardly be expected to readjust himself to the ordinary conditions of life in a native village, nor could he continue to live like a European in this territory."[67]

Other servants used Bulaya's strategy, though on a lesser scale, seeking to make the best out of their restricted opportunities. Many moved from household to household, diversifying their careers with shorter or longer periods of rest in their villages and with other types of jobs inside and especially outside the territory. Those who joined caravans are likely to have moved around in a similar manner. Some might have traveled widely, like Amoni, a Swahili boy "from somewhere below the [Northern] Rhodesian border," who at Kigoma on the eastern shore of Lake Tanganyika

62. Mansfield, *Via Rhodesia*, p. 147. The administrator was the highest position of local authority during the period of BSAC rule.

63. Robert I. Rotberg, *Black Heart: Gore-Brown and the Politics of Multiracial Zambia* (Berkeley: University of California Press, 1977), p. 69.

64. Ibid., p. 70 n. 19.

65. This practice is noted in some of ther annual reports, among them NAZ/KDC 6/1/6. 1918 and 1919.

66. Mansfield, *Via Rhodesia*, p. 163.

67. Statement by Governor H. J. S. Stanley to Secretary of State for the Colonies in 1925, cited in Rotberg, *Black Heart*, p. 70.

attached himself to the caravan of Colonel Alexander Powell, an inveterate American traveler with a self-proclaimed insatiable curiosity and fascination for savage countries, who in 1924 crossed the continent from coast to coast, accompanied by his wife and a male friend.[68] Amoni had acquired a sketchy knowledge of English at a mission school and been trained by a British colonial officer in southern Tanganyika in the arts of valeting, laundering, cooking, and waiting on table. When his employers went on leave, he had accompanied them to Dar es Salaam and was returning to his wife and village in Northern Rhodesia, where he would wait until he had to meet them on their return. He had been six weeks en route, walking intermittently with stops of two to three days in villages along the way, when he met the caravan. The Powells engaged him as a servant and he accompanied them all the way to the Atlantic Ocean. The "faithful, willing and efficient" Amoni was left in the charge of a local American missionary who was to find someone with whom he could travel back to Northern Rhodesia. Amoni also received presents: blankets, lanterns, and the remaining supplies plus "enough money to make him a rich man among his own people." He waited at Matadi on the Atlantic coast for about a month and then accompanied a European as far as Lake Tanganyika. On this trip he was less successful for, as he later wrote to Colonel Powell, "my new Bwana forget to pay me."[69]

If they did not pick up a new job when the caravan trek was over, servants might seek other avenues, perhaps in the same way as Saidi, gunbearer and capitao of the Colville caravan. Wishing to travel by train from Broken Hill to Livingstone, the Colvilles needed a cook as no food was available during the long train journey. Moffat, their caravan cook, wanted to walk back to Nyasaland together with the rest of the staff, thus leaving the Colvilles in a bind. Then Saidi volunteered, and he proved to be a very good cook. He had "suddenly discovered that he wanted to see the Victoria Falls and that afterwards he would like to earn six months' wages at Bulawayo before returning to Nyasaland."[70] At Bulawayo he might have become one of the much praised Nyasa boys. If not returning to Nyasaland, he might have decided he wanted to see Goli (the city of gold), as Johannesburg was known to Africans, for wages increased as workers moved south.

Servants' wishes to see other places and receive higher wages prompted them to leave positions they disliked. Employers constantly complained about the turnover rates, lack of efficiency, and the servants' poor work

68. E. Alexander Powell, *The Map That Is Half Unrolled: Equatorial Africa from the Indian Ocean to the Atlantic* (New York: Century Company, 1925), p. 7.
69. Ibid., pp. 102–106, 217, 343.
70. Colville, *One Thousand Miles*, pp. 132, 242.

habits.[71] To make Africans work on terms defined by whites, some employers believed in using harsh discipline and instilling work compliance through fear. In his account of life at Livingstone from the end of the last century to about 1919, Percy M. Clark, the town's photographer and its first commercial curio dealer, gives the following advice after describing how he had beaten several houseboys with the *sjambok* (Afrikaans for whip), which he always kept handy, for giving cheek to their "missus": "I say that a dog and a native are on a par. One should give them a good hiding when they really have earned it, but one should never thrash either until one's temper has cooled."[72]

With the arrival of more settlers after the opening decades of colonial rule in Northern Rhodesia, hints, informally observed conventions, and personal idiosyncrasies became unsatisfactory as regulative mechanisms. In the new legal framework, inventoried servants became wards of their employers. The laws that guided employment were informed by paternalistic attitudes. The Masters and Servants Ordinance, first implemented in North Western Rhodesia in 1908 and extended over the amalgamated territory in 1912, amended 1913 and 1925, was modeled on legislation in southern Rhodesia and ultimately influenced by South African laws.[73] It was rationalized by current notions of sanitation and civilization which when taken together saw cultural achievements and capacities as products of distinct racial backgrounds.[74] Africans were considered to be primitive, raw natives who did not know what was good for them, whereas whites were civilized and responsible for their protection and uplift. As in seventeenth-century England, the term *servant* meant anyone who worked for an employer for wages, except skilled workmen.[75] The labor regulations

71. Cairns, *Prelude to Imperialism*, pp. 31–32, describes these problems as they were experienced by whites who came out between 1840 and 1890, giving examples from their encounter with the Matabele and the Baganda. He suggests that tribal pride in both cases was a barrier to undertaking work for whites. The Matabele could not understand the practice of hiring servants: "they must own them." Unable to recruit Baganda workers, missionaries employed Muslims from the coast, who in turn began spreading Islam among the Baganda and eventually were dismissed.

72. Percy M. Clark, *The Autobiography of an Old-Drifter: The Life-Story of Percy M. Clark of Victoria Falls* (London: George G. Harrap, 1936), pp. 249–250.

73. Statutory Law of North Eastern Rhodesia, 1908–1911; of North Western Rhodesia, 1910–1911; and of Northern Rhodesia, 1911–1916, and NAZ/NR 3/73. Employment of Natives Ordinance, Amendments.

74. On this, see Philip D. Curtin, "Medical Knowledge and Urban Planning in Tropical Africa," *American Historical Review* 90 (1985): 594–613.

75. I am aware that this is a controversial statement. See the debate between MacPherson and Lasslett: C. B. MacPherson, "Servants and Labourers in Seventeenth-Century England," in his *Democratic Theory: Essays in Retrieval* (Oxford: Clarendon Press, 1973), pp. 207–233, and Peter Lasslett, "Market Society and Political Theory," *Historical Journal* 7 (1964): 150–154.

stipulated among other things that employers house their servants (but not wives and dependents), feed them, and take care of their medical problems.

The stereotype of the good and faithful servant that had developed during caravan travels did not necessarily apply to the relationship between a domestic servant and a resident employer. Misdemeanors had to be dealt with legally, and not in the ad hoc fashion that was characteristic of the traveling caravan. Under the Masters and Servants Ordinance, breaches of contract were considered criminal offenses for which servants were punished with fines or imprisonment with or without hard labor. Breech of contract was an inclusive legal term, encompassing absenteeism, drinking, careless or improper work performance, use of property without permission, damaging of property, refusal to obey commands, insulting language or behavior, and disruptive behavior when in or on the employer's premises. This legislation defined fairly innocuous events as crimes, such as the following 1912 incident concerning public nuisance brought before the magistrate court at Livingstone, involving: "three full-grown natives, two attired in parodies of European clothes, and the third in the white smock and cap of a household servant . . . dancing to the music of . . . a Kaffir piano." In the magistrate's opinion: "they must not create a disturbance in Sackville Street on a Sunday afternoon, the white man's day of rest. These Kaffir pianos are an unmitigated nuisance, and if they want music and dancing they must go into the *veld* [Afrikaans for bush] and enjoy themselves where they will not cause annoyance."[76] They were fined five shillings each or three days' imprisonment with hard labor.

The need for coercive legislation to control the activities of African workers, including servants, bears evidence of an ongoing battle between colonial employers and African migrant workers barely a generation removed from the work rhythms of small-scale cultivation, cattle husbandry, and fishing. In private household service this battle positioned servants and employers in a labor process that involved a new work discipline and new forms of authority, aimed at breaking-in raw natives as workers. It entailed, as noted above, a process of domestication. The employers' constant complaints of inefficiency and laziness may have captured one aspect of this process: their servants' difficulties in adopting, or attempts to resist, new labor regimes that required continuous work rather than seasonally changing or task-determined routines.[77]

76. "Monday Morning at the Police Court," *Livingstone Mail*, September 21, 1921.
77. E. P. Thompson, "Time, Work Discipline, and Industrial Capitalism," *Past and Present* 38 (1967): 56–97.

The Institutionalization of Domestic Service

The knowledge that African menservants acquired from caravan work remained useful even after motor transportation made caravan travel almost superfluous. Some of the porters and men who had specialized as travelers' companions turned to resident domestic service for a living. Former caravan servants and mission boys played important roles in shaping the domestic service patterns their novice resident employers developed. Their employment opportunities increased, for new towns grew up almost overnight in the north, where copper mining was begun on a commercial scale in the late 1920s. The capital was moved from Livingstone to Lusaka in 1935, and all the towns grew tremendously, especially during the World War II years. Many whites were employed in the mining industry, some took up commercial farming, and the Asian population, negligible in size during the first decades of the century, grew and scattered across the country's small towns, where the majority made a living from family-based trade with Africans.[78] Health conditions had improved, and the malaria danger had lessened, owing to the draining of swamps and the use of better prophylactics. Between 1921 and 1946 the adult white sex ratio became more balanced, so that by 1946 there were 91 white women for every 100 men.[79] Many more white women joined their civil servant husbands than did previously, although the Colonial Office as late as the post–World War II years discouraged junior officers from bringing out wives during their first tour of office.

The number of African men who did wage labor away from their villages had increased as well. According to Andrew Roberts, by 1936 more than half of the able-bodied male population was working away from home, as many outside the territory as within it.[80] Linked to the imposition of taxes, the creation of a labor force of this magnitude was part of a rural transformation that by the mid-1930s had undercut the possibilities for peasant agriculture to such an extent that most Africans had become dependent for their livelihood on wage labor.[81] Between 1928 and 1930 a series of com-

78. The Asian population had grown from 39 in 1911 to 176 in 1939. At the close of the war in 1946, it had shot up to 1,117 according to *Report on the Census of Population of Northern Rhodesia Held on the 15th October, 1946* (Lusaka: Government Printer, 1946), p. 9. The Asian population has not been extensively studied. The main work was undertaken in the late 1950s by Floyd and Lillian O. Dotson, *The Indian Minority of Zambia, Rhodesia, and Malawi* (New Haven: Yale University Press, 1968).

79. Kay, *Social Geography*, p. 27.

80. Roberts, *History of Zambia*, p. 191.

81. This is among the chief points made in *The Roots of Rural Poverty in Central and Southern Africa*, ed. Robin Palmer and Neil Parsons (Berkeley: University of California Press, 1977), pp. 173–174, 291. It has to be qualified by a recognition of the fact that the effects of incipient capitalism and the legal measures used to advance it neither filtered through all rural

missions had reclassified African lands into reserves located away from areas of white settlement.[82] Some of these reserves were on unproductive soils and/or were too small to sustain their growing populations. Agricultural quotas discriminated against African cultivators, giving white settler farmers along the line-of-rail preferential access to market their crops.[83] Using legal measures to condition white privilege, the colonial government at the same time deprived rural Africans from using new productive means other than selling their labor.

African wages were not shaped by the supply and demand of labor but by the colonial government's ideas of the amount needed for subsistence of a single worker rather than of his family. These workers were predominantly men, for working conditions were set up to prevent workers from bringing wives and dependents to town. The lives of African men in the towns were shaped by political, economic, and residential segregation by race and circumscribed by rules and regulations concerning where and with whom they could live and work and how they could move between and within urban and rural areas.[84] Housing was tied to the job, and once a worker lost his job or finished a work contract, he was supposed to return to his village to join his wife, who in his absence had tended fields and cared for children and the old. Such, at least, was an African worker's career in the administration's view. As I discuss later, not all men workers returned, and not all African women remained in the rural areas. The direction of their movement was temporarily reversed during the Great Depression, when mines and businesses laid off both African and white workers and many Africans did return to their villages. After the depression years, rural to urban migration continued, involving men, women, and children.

Among the local white population, opinions on the desirable course of native administration began to differ, especially after the Colonial Office's publication of the 1930 Passfield Memorandum, which stated the paramountcy of native interets in matters of local policy. Some interpreted the

---

regions with the same speed nor affected the different population segments in the same fashion.

82. Gann, *History of Northern Rhodesia*, pp. 136–138, 215–224, 372–373.

83. See, for example, Maud Muntemba, "Thwarted Development: A Case Study of Economic Change in the Kabwe Rural District of Zambia, 1902–1970," in Palmer and Parsons, eds., *Roots*, pp. 365–395, and Brian Siegel, "The Response of Resentment: The Lamba Vegetable Trade of the Rural Zambian Copperbelt," paper presented at the "Culture, Economy, and Policy in the Colonial Situation" conference held at the University of Minnesota, Minneapolis, 1981.

84. Among these ordinances were the Employment of Natives Ordinance (1929); the Native Registration Ordinance (1929); the Vagrancy Ordinance (1929); the Natives on Private Estates Ordinance (1929); the Township Ordinance (1929); the Municipal Corporations Ordinance (1927); the Public Health Ordinance (1930); and the Native Beer Ordinance (amended 1930).

memorandum as a blueprint for guided paternalism, whereas others viewed it with horror and held up the Union of South Africa or Southern Rhodesia as models, wishing to see Northern Rhodesia become a "white man's country," perhaps even amalgamated with the south.[85] Yet in spite of such divergencies in public outlook, and regardless of occupational differences and those of rural or urban location, the colonial residents shared one thing: the employment of African male domestic servants. And of all Africans, only servants were allowed to live in the white parts of town so as to minister to the needs and comforts of their employers.

In structuring their household regimes, white employers drew on two models: the British, where domestic service till the interwar years was the chief urban income source for wage-laboring women, and the South African, where, with the exception of the Cape, African men had dominated in service after the abolition of slavery but were beginning to be replaced by women. Class condescension and racism thus informed servant-keeping practices in Northern Rhodesia and helped to shape the labor relation between black menservants and their white employers.

Employers' Lifestyle

In bush stations and towns, the presence of more white women helped to develop household arrangements and patterns of lifestyle in familiar ways. A previous generation of white men's approximation of an "African way of life," meaning cohabitation or concubinage with African women, came gradually to be viewed with contempt—though it certainly continued, albeit perhaps more in remote areas and in the manner of casual encounters. Such encounters were best left unmentioned, and against the background of what they held to be strange and uncivilized mores, white householders sought to recreate a world of their own design. Winifred Tapson, a typist for the North Charterland Company and a farmer's wife, noted this quality of the familiar in her description of life at Fort Jameson in the late 1920s: "Here was this relatively large community of white people, men and women and children, *pitched into a wilderness of black people and surrounded by a negation of civilized life*" (italics added).[86]

---

85. Legislators had discussed the idea of amalgamation during the 1920s, and some expressed extreme opposition to the "attrocious suggestions" of the "obnoxious white paper," i.e., the 1930 Passfield Memorandum on native paramountcy as the goal of local colonial activity. Their concerns are highlighted in the Legislative Council Debates and several newspaper articles, from among which the above terms are taken, e.g., *Livingstone Mail*, January 29, 1931, p. 6.

86. Winifred Tapson, *Old Timer* (Cape Town: Howard Timmins, 1957), p. 29. For a historical study of settler behavior with focus on the creation of cultural boundaries between colonizer and colonized, see Dane Kennedy, *Islands of White: Settler Society and Culture in Kenya and Southern Rhodesia, 1890–1939* (Durham, N.C.: Duke University Press, 1987).

This quality of the familiar also struck travelers. When on a motor tour from Johannesburg headed for Nairobi in the late 1920s, Selma Whitehouse and her four companions stopped among other places at Broken Hill, where Mrs. Whitehouse was impressed by the cosmopolitan nature of life. There they met mining engineers from Canada, France, and South Africa: "we have travelled 1500 miles to get here through Darkest Africa, [and] here we came into a colony of people who might live anywhere. . . . [We] have come upon this little community with its country club, and its golf course, and its at-home days!" When the party reached Kasama, her praise continued: "they are all cultured and charming people, and with charming wives they live here in the wilds, keeping house as if in London."[87]

The Society certainly had its divisions, for the "boma [administrative headquarters] people and the mine managers [were] the social heads of the place."[88] Below them ranked, according to other writers, missionaries and settler farmers, the latter particularly of Afrikaans-speaking background. European businessmen, often Greeks and Jews, ranked in between them, whereas Asian traders were placed at the bottom. They are hardly ever mentioned in this era's literature, and as non-Europeans, they were probably not viewed as part of The Society. The Afrikaans-speaking farmers tended to be looked down upon. Many of them were poor by white standards, their Calvinist ideology was offensive to some, their harsh treatment of African farm workers left much to be desired, and the lifestyle of many was rough. During her travels in Northern Rhodesia, Eileen Bigland met many "Dutchmen in different walks of life." The year was 1939 and she was not impressed: "Most of them belonged to the genus bully and . . . [held] that judicious ill-treatment was the best way to make an African work hard. They were full of horrific tales of the native customs and habits."[89]

In spite of these differences, members of the various segments of the white population shared the same concern with regard to their own households: to recreate a familiar style of living in this remote interior of Darkest Africa. The chief burden of this task fell on white women, who in turn relied on numerous African menservants to carry out most of the actual work. The women who have written about their lives in Northern Rhodesia were clearly supplementary actors in the colonial scheme. Though they were unpaid, the importance of their work should not be overlooked. In the words of Sir Charles Jeffries, the deputy undersecretary of state for the colonies, such women made their contribution by their wifely support, "looking after their [husbands'] health and comfort, keeping house, dis-

87. Whitehouse, *Moonlight*, pp. 42–43, 57–58.
88. Ibid., p. 46.
89. Eileen Bigland, *Pattern in Black and White* (London: Lindsay Drummond, 1940), p. 107.

pensing hospitality, enduring when need be separation in order that children may be brought up the way their fathers would wish."[90]

But such "incorporated wives," whose ascribed social character was a function of their husbands' occupation and culture, had a role beyond wifehood.[91] They helped to define the local standards of white civilization. These standards were assumed to set educational examples for African menservants who labored under white women's supervision within colonial households,[92] and to be of great help to African women.[93] White women's work, in other words, revolved around day-to-day reproduction of labor, and of social reproduction of a racially divided and class-structured colonial society.[94]

Glimpses of this life may be found in, among others, Emily Bradley's *Dearest Priscilla*, a book written to advise a fictitious young woman friend on her way to a tropical colony as the wife of a junior official. For it, Mrs. Bradley drew on her own experience as the wife of a colonial civil servant in Northern Rhodesia between 1929 and 1942. Her main role in the colony, Mrs. Bradley told young Priscilla, was to see to it that her husband's creature comforts were supplied at home. With servants to condition their gracious living, married white women in Northern Rhodesia, according to Mrs. Bradley, lived in a man's world where their chief role was that of silent partner. In this scheme of things, the master (Bradley's term) came

90. Sir Charles Jeffries, *Partners in Progress: The Men and Women of the Colonial Service* (London: George G. Harrap, 1949), pp. 155–156.

91. Hilary Callan and Shirley Ardener, eds., *The Incorporated Wife* (London: Croom Helm, 1984), p. 1. For colonial African examples of analyses using the concept of the incorporated wife, see Deborah Kirkwood's two chapters on Rhodesia and Beverly Gartrell on Uganda in the Callan and Ardener anthology. For a discussion with special focus on Nigeria, see Helen Callaway, *Gender, Culture, and Empire: European Women in Colonial Nigeria* (Urbana: University of Illinois Press, 1987). For a general discussion of white women's problematic place in the colonies, see Margaret Strobel, "Gender and Race in the Nineteenth- and Twentieth-Century British Empire," in *Becoming Visible: Women in European History*, ed. Renate Bridenthal, Claudia Koonz, and Susan Stuard, 2d ed. (Boston: Houghton Mifflin, 1987), pp. 375–396. For additional glimpses of the development of white colonial lifestyles in other parts of Africa, see chap. 8, "The DO's Wife and the Governor's Lady," in Charles Allen, *Tales from the Dark Continent: Images of British Colonial Africa in the Twentieth Century* (London: Futura, 1980), pp. 128–147, which contains a colorful narrative, based on interviews with retired colonial civil servants, only very few of whom lived and worked in Northern Rhodesia. For the British Empire in general and a glorious sentimentalizing recollection about it, see Valerie Packenham, *Out in the Noonday Sun: Edwardians in the Tropics* (New York: Randon House, 1985).

92. This point was often stressed when officials and legislators discussed domestic service.

93. Jeffries, *Partners in Progress*, p. 156.

94. Olivia Harris and Kate Young distinguish three aspects of reproduction which affect gender relations in different ways: biological reproduction, reproduction of labor itself, and social reproduction. See their "Engendered Structures: Some Problems in the Analysis of Reproduction," in *The Anthropology of Pre-Capitalist Societies*, ed. Joel S. Kahn and Joseph R. Llobera (Atlantic Highlands, N.J.: Humanities Press, 1981), pp. 109–147.

first, as "it was the rule rather than the exception out there . . . that the men can get along without us."[95]

A life with many servants offered white women the possibility of leisured living. Once she had given the "morning order" to her servants and decided the meals of the day, a wife could spend the rest of her time on handiwork and reading, painting, and drawing. Some, like Mrs. Bradley, wrote. Many developed fondness for gardening and took pride in growing English flowers in the tropics. The routine was broken by teas and gossip with neighbors and games such as bridge, golf, and tennis in the club.[96] Some men played soccer and cricket. Rifle clubs existed in many towns and some had ladies' auxiliaries.[97] Outside of bush stations there was the whirl of white colonial society, consisting of sundowners, cocktail parties, dinner engagements, and dances.[98]

From reading the society columns of colonial newspapers, the external observer might assume that this lifestyle was busy and engaging for an urban colonial wife. Month after month the columns are filled with notices about marriages and *braaivleis* (Afrikaans for barbeque); holiday dances, club dances, and charity balls; swim galas, cricket, soccer, and fishing competitions; rifle club parties; yearly agricultural shows; Women's Institutes exhibits; and flower shows. These notices show how spaces of the wilds had become domesticated into small islands on which whites sought to recreate the sense of "keeping house like in London."

The white colonists, observed Dorothea Irwin, a newly arrived American woman on the copperbelt in the late 1920s, "were very long on ritual

95. Emily Bradley, *Dearest Priscilla: Letters to the Wife of a Colonial Civil Servant* (London: Max Parrish, 1950), pp.112, 168–169. After their stay in Northern Rhodesia, the Bradleys worked in the colonial service in the Falkland Islands and the Gold Coast. Kenneth Bradley was a prolific writer and published, among others, *The Diary of a District Officer* (London: MacMillan, 1943), describing a district officer's life during 1938 at Fort Jameson, and *Once a District Officer* (New York: St. Martin's Press, 1966), a lively description of his wide experience in the colonial service. Emily Bradley likely modeled her work on the already existing narrative genres of women travelers and new settlers who published their experiences in the form of letters, diaries, and guidebooks. For two early works of this genre, written before the end of the last century by white women whose travels in Nyasaland took them across the extreme boundary regions of North Eastern Rhodesia, see Jane F. Moir, *A Lady's Letters from Central Africa* (Glasgow: James Maclehose and Sons, 1881), and Helen Caddick, *A White Woman in Central Africa* (London: T. Fisher Unwin, 1900). For analyses of white women's travel writing during the closing years of Queen Victoria's reign, see Catherine Barnes Stevenson, *Victorian Women Travel Writers in Africa* (Boston: Twayne Publishers, 1982), and Katherine Frank, who comments among others on Helen Caddick, "Voyages Out: Nineteenth-Century Women Travellers in Africa," in *Gender, Ideology, and Action: Historical Perspectives on Women's Public Lives*, ed. Janet Sharistanian (New York: Greenwood Press, 1986), pp. 67–94.

96. Bradley, *Dearest Priscilla*, pp. 84–110.

97. Tapson, *Old Timer*, pp. 43–46.

98. Bradley, *Dearest Priscilla*, pp. 84–110.

and precedence, calling, entertainment, etc., in strict order of rank." Their life did have its satisfactions, as noted in her letters home. As wife of the general manager of Roan Antelope at Luanshya from 1928 to 1933, the chief mine then in Northern Rhodesia, she experienced the pleasures as well as the hard work of an incorporated wife. In January 1933 the Irwins hosted Governor and Mrs. Ronald Storrs, who were well known for their fastidiousness on proper observances. She and her servants had spent several days preparing for a dinner party for sixteen guests in a new house built and furnished to the Irwins' specifications. The party appears to have been a success save for "my boys [who] went entirely mad with excitement and ceased functioning completely! . . . Towards the end of [the] many courses the boys cracked under the strain, and weird things happened thick and fast. Glasses that should have been put on were snatched away, one course was forgotten completely." Yet Mrs. Irwin's satisfaction and pride is evident: "It was really a job of work, that dinner. I figured that to serve the wines in proper order took 112 glasses. . . . The table did look lovely, . . . long and narrow, with lace, low bowls of roses, and dull blue candles. The whole home came in for much admiration—they said they had heard in Livingstone that it was the most charming house in the Rhodesias, and they thoroughly agreed."[99]

White colonial life developed its own conventions of dress; social hierarchies of who could be invited with whom and seated next to whom; and codes for calling and leaving cards. The custom of calling survived in the colonies after it had faded away in England. It meant that newcomers called on seniors while equals and juniors called on the newcomer. Callers left cards or signed a visitors' book, perferably without being seen. Invitations would rarely be issued until after such calls had been made. Remembering this custom in Livingstone in 1930, Vernon Brelsford, then a newly arrived junior official, commented: "it was said that a bachelor in Livingstone who 'played his cards with skill' could drink or dine out almost every night."[100]

The observation of such practices not only reinforced relative rank in the colonial hierarchy but also established a "them and us" difference between whites and blacks. Conventions and order helped minimize outward contacts, made whites appear even more civilized, and lessened the chance for standards to drop. Some people functioned happily in this setting, whereas others felt it dulled their personal initiatives. Gore-Brown for one, himself a member of lower British nobility, preferred his remote estate in the

99. Dorothea Irwin, *Far Away and Long Ago* (privately published, n.d.), p. 68, pp. 106–107.

100. "Northern Rhodesia in the 1930s," bibliographical notes by Vernon Brelsford, ed. and intro. Dick Hobson (London: unpublished manuscript, 1985).

Bemba bush to the artificial standards of white settled life in the towns. His remarks, especially on white women, after a visit to the small town of Kasama in the late 1920s starkly contrast with those of Selma Whitehouse, referred to previously. "How glad," he wrote, "one is not to live here. Eight households, not necessarily very congenial to each other, having to do everything, everyday, together—the men do a little mild office work . . . the women I suppose order dinner. They don't garden because there is no water . . . and they don't read (there was a library once, but white ants are eating the books). They play golf, and they plan tennis, and they sit in each other's houses & talk about 1) each other, 2) the badness of a) native servants, b) the government, 3) the roads. They aren't vicious, and they are extraordinarily kind, but oh my word they are dull and they are aimless."[101]

If white women disliked domestic arts and found parties and conversations boring, they had a hard time. The lot of the wife of a colonial official was not every woman's cup of tea. This according to Charles Jeffries, who noted that "the Appointments Departments of the Colonial Office have sometimes been heard to express the wish that they could select officers' wives as well as the officers."[102] A dislike of the scene, coupled with the many of difficulties they encountered when enjoying what compared to African lifestyles must have been high society, prompted some white women to leave. Some marriages went on the rocks,[103] and some women developed "nerves." Those who accommodated faced isolation from relatives and friends and, often, separation from their children if they made the hard choice of sending them to boarding schools. The compulsive attention paid to housekeeping and servant management and to the problems experienced in the process was perhaps one important way of passing time.

The Importance of Good Housekeeping

For the running of a proper colonial home, wrote Emily Bradley to her fictitious young friend Priscilla, a white woman needed to be surrounded by a retinue of specialized boys in the house and on the grounds. When the Bradleys established their first household at Fort Jameson in the late

---

101. Quoted in Rotberg, *Black Heart*, pp. 159–160.
102. Jeffries, *Partners in Progress*, p. 156.
103. A member of the adult female postwar generation, Barbara Carr, who divorced her husband and left for South Africa, discusses several of these problems in two books that display an intense dislike of the local African scene. She grew up as the daughter of a colonial official in Nyasaland, went to school in England, and returned to supervise her widowed father's household before marrying and moving to Northern Rhodesia. Her few positive comments concern Mateyo, a Ngoni servant from Nyasaland her parents had had for fifteen years, who went with her to Northern Rhodesia. He was "the only real buffer between me and my savage surroundings!" *Not for Me the Wilds* (Cape Town: Howard Timmis, 1963), p. 59, and *Cherries on My Plate* (Cape Town: Howard Timmis, 1965).

1920s, they employed nine servants: a cook and a houseboy each with a piccanin helper. Around the house, to tidy the grounds, fetch water and wood, five other men were employed.[104] From the point of view of the employer, the servants formed a hierarchy of domains: kitchen, house, and grounds. Winifred Tapson also had nine servants in Fort Jameson in the late 1920s. They formed a strict division of labor with the kitchen at the top where the cook reigned, absolutely. Next to him in location, though not in status, was his factotum, a diminutive piccanin. He was the cook's right hand, his ten fingers, his legs and his arms. Called the *sukumpika* or *sukumbula* in the literature, he was the washer of pots and pans and the link between the cook's domain and the house and the grounds. Within the house, the head houseboy guarded the *dona's* keys and possessions. Next came the tableboy who waited on table, the bedroom boy who brought the morning tea and folded back the mosquito net, and the bath boy who carried the tin bath in from the outside, filled it with heated water and tempered the temperature before announcing in front of the bedroom door that the bath was ready. On the fringes of this hierarchy floated the dregs of the household, the washboy, the wood boy, and the water boy, whose task it was to provide a never ending supply of those basic necessities.[105]

With so many hired hands, colonial households might seem to have functioned smoothly and white women householders enjoyed unbounded leisure. This is not how many women viewed it. When establishing her new home in Northern Rhodesia, Dorothea Irwin was dismayed by her servants' inefficiency. As she wrote in her first letter to relatives in the United States, she was struck by their numbers but also frustrated. The mining town, which was then opening up, was "growing very fast in population—about 500 to 600 whites, and Lord knows how many blacks. 400 black domestic servants, imagine! But every [white] carpenter's assistant keeps two or three servants. You never saw anything like it. And what ridiculous objects they are! If I could sweep all of mine out and have one good woman worker, I could do in a day what I have not been able to do in a week."[106]

Quite specific household management advice is provided in Emily Bradley's 1939 *Household Book for Africa*, again based on her experience in Northern Rhodesia. This book was written especially for the bachelor "faced with the bewildering problem of housekeeping" before the days when British wives commonly accompanied their civil servant husbands out to Africa.[107] The writing of this book had been suggested to Mrs.

---

104. Bradley, *Dearest Priscilla*, p. 58.
105. Tapson, *Old Timer*, pp. 47–54.
106. Irwin, *Far Away*, p. 68.
107. Emily Bradley, *A Household Book for Africa* (London: Oxford University Press, 1939).

Bradley by Ralph Furse, long-time recruiting officer for the Colonial Service, who on a 1935/36 tour of Africa made a stop at the Bradleys in Mumbwa. So impressed was Furse by "the heart of a lettuce in the midst of a desert" that he there and then talked her into the project.[108] Mrs. Bradley must have been well-known locally for her skills in household management. In 1938 she was detailed to assist a junior officer just arrived at Lusaka in buying supplies to bring to the rural outpost at Isoka. It included everything from a full case of whiskey and 150 pounds of flour to a bottle of capers.[109]

The second edition of Mrs. Bradley's book, titled *A Household Book for Tropical Colonies*, was published in 1948. She aimed it "also to the wives, especially beginners who are equally worried by housekeeping and the bachelor girls who have both homes and jobs to look after."[110] In it, she described the work routine in a colonial household, beginning with the morning order given to cook and houseboy as they appeared with their trays when their mistress opened the storeroom. The cook's tray would have on it tins with lids for coffee, tea, porridge, and salt and cups and basins for the dishing out of food for the day. The houseboy's tray had a sugar basin, a cruet, and a marmalade jar. The containers on each tray were then filled daily according to the menu decided on. This practice, according to Bradley, "saves endless anxiety over the unwonted disappearance of food."[111]

She also described the duties of a good cook. He might need quite a bit of coaching till the mistress could trust him to do things as she liked them done, without constant reminding and correction:

1. He must: (a) keep the kitchen scrubbed and the towels and oven cloths washed daily.
(b) Boil the drinking water thoroughly in a clean kettle and pour it into sacks to cool, one each night. Sacks should be washed out frequently with coarse salt, cold water, and a few crystals of potassium permanganate.
(c) Boil the milk, keeping saucepan, cooling basins and straining muslin spotless.
(d) Keep his tins for tea, coffee, crumbs, fat, salt, etc., clean and covered. He must not store his own treasures among the food.
(e) Keep his apron clean. Don't employ a boy who is not clean. Good boys are

---

108. Ralph Furse, *Aucuparius: Recollections of a Recruiting Officer* (London: Oxford University Press, 1962), p. 253, in which Furse also told that Emily Bradley was an American. Furse misidentifies the book in question, referring to *Dearest Priscilla* and not *A Household Book*.
109. Rhodes House. MSS Afr. s. 664. J. C. Walter papers.
110. Emily Bradley, *A Household Book for Tropical Colonies* (London: Oxford University Press, 1948), p. vii.
111. Ibid., pp. 16–18.

African cook. Photograph from the reprint of the *Northern Rhodesian Handbook* (Lusaka: Government Printer,
1953), p. 94. Original photograph probably from the 1940s.

Michek and Kosam at Kawamba, 1947. From the collection of Mary and Reginald
Thompson. Reproduced with permission.

most fastidious about their hands. A persistently oderous boy must be dismissed if he does not respond to frequent baths with carbolic soap.

2. A good cook should be able to make bread, soup stock and good white sauce at least; to cook vegetables carefully (not soggy over-cooked potatoes and cabbage!); to roast meat so that it is brown on the outside, soft and juicy on the inside, and not greasy; to understand the method of making:

(a) Cake: i.e., cream butter and sugar.

(b) Scones and pastry: i.e., rub fat into flour.

(c) Batter: i.e., make a hole in the flour.

(d) Brown soups and sauces: i.e., fry onion in fat.

(e) White soups and sauces: i.e., melt butter, add flour, etc.; boil onion in milk.

He should also be able to devise a variety of breakfasts, and make good coffee and tea.

Concluding her description, Emily Bradley suggests that a boy who understands two-thirds of the above should be taken on gratefully and the mistress then set about bringing the other third up to standard.[112]

The number of servants employed depended on locality, that is, rural versus urban, and on the amenities present. Toward the end of the Bradleys' stay in Northern Rhodesia, the number of servants in their household had declined to five. They then lived in Lusaka, their two sons were away at boarding school, and they had at that point the benefit of such technological improvements as piped hot and cold water, flush toilet, and fuel delivery.[113] They probably also had electricity and refrigeration.

In addition to locality and the sort of amenities present, the employment of specialized servants also depended on the composition of the employing household. With the birth of children, new needs arose. The real need at this stage of the family's development cycle, according to Mrs. Bradley, was "that of an attendant." Since she herself had no daughters, it was never necessary to employ another woman, white or black, to help with childcare. All she had was a "nurse-boy to push the pram and wash the nappies." But from friends who had white nannies she understood there were many snags: "All the problems of leisure and pleasure applied to them as well as the mistress. There was no opportunity for them to have any sort of social life on their own apart from their employers. They were part of the family, belonged to the club, and Mother and Nanny took turns about playing games, or attending club dances. African [male] servants made difficulties of discipline over another white woman in the house whose position they didn't quite understand." Properly trained children's nurses were almost nonexistent in Africa, she told Priscilla. "Anthropologically or sociologically

112. Ibid., pp. 19–20.
113. Bradley, *Dearest Priscilla*, p. 59; following quotes, pp. 230, 58, 230–231, and 231–233.

speaking," she continued, "a young African woman of good family does not take up children's nursing. . . . Her life is governed by her family from cradle to altar, within rigid tribal codes, and a few years of independence between her parents' home and her husband's is as unthinkable to them as it was in our own society not so long ago." That it was almost unthinkable for whites in Northern Rhodesia to employ African women in domestic service is corroborated by the numerical record on servant employment.[114] Emily Bradley's remarks on how to manage a colonial household help us to understand why, but perhaps, as I suggest later, there were reasons other than those she gave.

The men who worked as domestics were often recruited upon the recommendation of neighbors or colleagues or of a trusted African worker on the staff of the household or of the husband's place of employment. They were sometimes the "brothers" or friends of already known African workers. Others "came with the house" and worked for its new residents. As mentioned earlier, some white women did prefer raw natives fresh from the bush whom they could domesticate themselves. But in general, workers with traceable work records were preferred. When presenting themselves, servants looking for work carried reference books. These were checked for length of employment, with what sort of people, and the hopeful servant was asked if he drank.[115] In her advice on hiring, Emily Bradley never mentioned the need to ask questions about the servant's personal background, his marital status, or ethnicity.

The available statistics tell little about the servants' ethnic backgrounds. Employers continued to consider Nyasa boys, meaning men from the border regions of Northern Rhodesia and Nyasaland, among the best, as well as very congenial workers. If indeed domestic service was characterized by an ethnic division of labor in which men from that region dominated, it is likely to reflect the poor conditions in peasant agriculture and the lack of rural employment alternatives.[116] Large numbers of migrants did come from the Eastern Province, where there were land shortages after the allotment of reserves and where wage labor on tobacco farms had shrunk after the 1938 slump in the tobacco market. Some of these men may have made their way into service, but just how many is uncertain.

Employment was usually first on a trial basis to ensure that the two parties could get along. After a while the woman householder would, according to Bradley, "doubtless discover whether Cook is amenable to instructions and likes learning new things, and whether or not the houseboy

---

114. See Tables 5 and 6 for numbers employed in domestic service categorized by sex.
115. Bradley, *Dearest Priscilla*, p. 53.
116. H. Leroi Vail, "Ecology and History: The Example of Eastern Zambia," *Journal of Southern African Studies* 2 (1977): 129–155.

has been working on the theory that what the master doesn't see won't worry him."[117] If the servant's behavior was tolerable, a monthly contract would be made, with wages paid weekly, fortnightly, or, more commonly, once a month. Food or ration money, sometimes referred to as *posho*, was also provided, as were occasional castoffs such as clothing from the employing household. Emily Bradley recommended giving servants a day off each week and one Sunday in three, or even occasional weekends, especially if the servant's wife and children did not live with him on the premises. A two-week holiday with pay once a year or every two years, particularly if the servant's village was far away, might be part of the contract.[118] Rates of pay, time required at work, and holidays all depended on arrangements between employer and servant since no formal regulations were established.

Space and Place in the Colonial Household

The almost compulsive attention to the do's and don'ts of housekeeping conveyed in Emily Bradley's recommendations may reflect an unconscious attempt to control a situation ripe with contradictions. The racial stratification of colonial society was supported in part by mechanisms for maintaining distance.[119] These mechanisms were both social, prescribing etiquette and comportment, and spatial, requiring segregation. Servants were in these white households, but never *of* them. The physical proximity of servants and employers belied the chasm between them which the racial and economic premises of colonial society created.

The Masters and Servants Ordinance and its later amendments stipulated among other things that employers should house their servants. Cooks and houseboys were often accommodated in servants' quarters, known by the Portuguese term *kaya*, in their employers' backyards. The hierarchical relationship between master and servant was manifested in the layout of the grounds with the servants' quarters built alongside the sanitary lanes from which nightsoil, in the days before flush toilets, and garbage were collected. Where such housing was unavailable, or when employers did not want them to reside on the premises, servants received an allowance and had to find shelter in the African parts of town, commonly referred to as compounds, or if at an outstation, in a nearby village. To facilitate their coming and going, especially their late-night return after

---

117. Bradley, *Dearest Priscilla*, p. 47.
118. Ibid., pp. 59, 65.
119. See Pierre L. van den Berghe, "Distance Mechanisms of Stratification," in *Readings in Race and Ethnic Relations*, ed. Anthony H. Richmond (Oxford: Pergamon Press, 1972), pp. 210–219.

evening chores since a 9 P.M. curfew prohibited Africans' moving about in the white parts of town, employers wrote "night passes" for their non-domiciled domestics.

A properly managed colonial household was part of civilized society and as such it was on permanent display.[120] The labor behind the display was done by numerous African servants who from the perspective of their employers were members of an otherwise formless African mass and somehow had to be socialized into work on white terms. To differentiate them from other Africans, servants not only were housed on the periphery of their employers' premises and given special passes to enter white areas; they were also set off from other Africans by their manner of dress. House-servants were supplied with at least two complete uniforms, usually a khaki tunic and trousers for day wear, the equivalent in white for the evening, small hats or fezzes, "plus aprons for cook, and soap all round."

The display and upkeep of white civilized standards required work efficiency. To promote it, madams observed the hierarchical division of labor among house, kitchen, and grounds and the elaborate rules of etiquette which governed conduct. These rules and conventions served both to set servants off from other workers and to mark the social distance between them and their employers within the household. White women were advised to "talk slowly, simply, and distinctly" when speaking to servants in English and to treat them with "tolerance and understanding, but not with familiarity. Discipline should be firm, but fair."[121] The paternalistic tone is clear: servants were considered children.

Generically, and regardless of age, all servants were referred to as boys, as were, for that matter, all other African men save perhaps chiefs and headmen. Servants were rarely addressed by their own names. Many white employers would garble a cook's or houseboy's African name into something more manageable for the Anglo-Saxon tongue. Some became known under biblical names such as Amos, Elijah, Isaac, and Moses. Others were called Sixpence, and Pumpkin, Wireless, Bicycle, Cigarette, or

120. The distinction between domestic or private versus public sphere becomes relative in this situation and is perhaps related more to an ideology of power and control than to differential involvement across space. This distinction was elaborated especially by Michelle Z. Rosaldo, who suggested that women's status in various societies was influenced by the degree of differentiation between the two domains: "Women, Culture, and Society: A Theoretical Overview," in *Woman, Culture, and Society*, eds. Michelle Z. Rosaldo and Louise Lamphere (Stanford: Stanford University Press, 1974), pp. 17–42. This distinction has since been viewed as simplistic and of doubtful historical and cross-cultural value. For more on the relativity of space and its social and ideological partitioning, see Shirley Ardener, ed., *Women and Space: Ground Rules and Social Maps* (New York: St. Martin's Press, 1981); and Callan and Ardener, *Incorporated Wife*.

121. Northern Rhodesia Information Department, *Northern Rhodesia Handbook* (n.d. Lusaka: Government Printer, 1950; reprint of an earlier version, n.d.), p. 78.

Cabbage. The servants on their part did not always know the exact names of their employers, who were referred to and addressed as bwana or master, or missus, dona, or madam.

Servants rarely wore shoes when in the house. They were not to rest in chairs or sofas, read newspapers, listen to the radio or play the radiogram in either the employer's presence or absence. Servants were not to use the facilities of the main house. Some areas were off-limits to prevent pilfering: kitchen stores and liquor cabinets. Africans in general were by law forbidden till the late 1940s to buy and use "European liquor."[122] In many households it was locked up and guests might help themselves "as the boys do not even handle it."[123] But bedrooms seem not to have considered private space. Most white colonists had morning tea brought to the bedside and boys made their beds and washed their sheets.

When on duty, servants were not supposed to talk unless they were spoken to. Communication around domestic work was itself a hierarchical situation, especially in households where "Kitchen Kaffir" was the main communicative mode.[124] This hybrid language, which had arisen through contact between whites and blacks in South Africa, was used to some extent in Northern Rhodesia, especially by settlers who came up from the south, but it never developed into a lingua franca. Consisting mainly of command and obey expressions, Kitchen Kaffir provided a language of subordination. Unlike in India, where white women were encouraged to learn the local languages and English-speaking servants were distrusted, their sisters in Northern Rhodesia went to no great lengths to learn any of the local languages.[125] While employees of the provincial administration, the police,

122. When European wines and beers had been made available to Africans, a group of white women wrote an indignant letter to the editor. They referred to weekend domestic disruptions due to their servants' indulgence in "Kaffir beer," i.e., commercially brewed beer meant for African consumption. Yet Kaffir beer was checked for its alcohol content, they noted, so why introduce Africans to more? "Kaffir beer brewed and sold under observation may be good for the African, and it is natural for him to drink it. . . . Why introduce him to another of our vices?" Letters to the Editor, "Housewives Concern," by "The Group," *Central African Post*, October 13, 1948, p. 3. But an African man responded that "legislators knew that there was no harm in allowing wines and beers to Africans, because it won't make him worse. I would agree, if gin and other things were allowed to him. . . . European liquor which has been allowed to be purchased by the Africans is 20% weaker than the present beer brewed by Africans" (i.e., illegal, home-brewed beer and distilled alcohol, and not the Kaffir beer sold in the municipal beerhalls). He concluded: "I think time is coming when a housewife shall have to face the houseduties when the men African servants will demand more pay. What will happen then?" Letters to the Editor, "Housewives and Africans," by "One of Those Africans," *Central African Post*, October 28, 1948, p. 3.
123. Bradley, *Dearest Priscilla*, p. 60.
124. Kitchen Kaffir, Chilapalapa, or Fanagolo is a hybrid language consisting of elements from Zulu, English, and Afrikaans.
125. Charles Allen, ed., *Plain Tales from The Raj: Images of British India in the Twentieth Century* (London: Futura, 1976), p. 90.

and the army were required before advancement to pass examinations in one or more of the major African languages spoken in the territory, other officials, including professional magistrates and the judiciary, were not and used African interpreters.[126] Some of their wives picked up an elementary vocabulary of a local language, especially if they lived for several years within the same language area. Since most colonial officials were transferred across regions frequently, the opportunity to absorb a local language was limited. Many servants learned household English on the job, while others had acquired a rudimentary knowledge of that language in schools. Servants who did not master English well were likely to be caught in all kinds of problems: mixing the wrong ingredients into recipes, not doing what they were told to do, or doing it very differently.

The linguistic problems arose because Bantu languages express pronouns and negations in different ways from English. Imagine the domestic strife that may have been caused by the servant's wrong use of gender when describing his madam's unexpected visitor to his returning master. Such mistakes, as well as their inconsistent use of English pronouns and the negative affirmative were the stuff that servant stories were made of. Exchanged at women's teas, such stories helped consolidate the image of the servant as inferior to his madam and accentuated the distance between the two in the otherwise shared space of the household. Not necessarily malevolent, such stories construe servants as inherently irresponsible, having no sense of time, lazy, lacking understanding, and therefore in need of constant supervision and coaching. Mary Thompson provided, among others, "a true story of a bachelor, a farmer who liked to read over his solitary meal and his servant would put a book by his plate. One evening he did a rare bit of entertaining and each guest found a book placed neatly before him at the dinner table."[127]

The etiquette of dress was also of great concern. Revealing clothing should not be worn in the presence of servants. Some colonials dressed in evening garb for dinner at home. At formal events, hats, gloves, and pumps were de rigueur for women. While such dressing habits might reflect those current in European bourgeois circles at the time, they did not necessarily express what was practical in the tropics. Even cinema visits required dinner jackets and robes if a high-standing colonial official was present. Stories were told, humorously, of officials traveling on up-country tours and dressing formally for their camp dinner in the bush. But "keeping up appearances" and "dressing for dinner" in the heart of the bush were not fiction. According to W. V. Brelsford, "many of these lonely bachelors

126. Roy Stokes, personal communication, December 18, 1983.
127. Mary Thompson, personal communication, August 24, 1982.

believed such habits were essential for the maintenance of morale."[128] The humor that accompanied such stories does not convey what the concern for proper appearance achieved: a reassuring of the familiar, the maintenance of civilized standards, and an ideological legitimation of difference between white and black and of white domination over black.

If they dressed "like Europeans," Africans challenged the function of dress to mark social difference, and whites reacted with predictable hostility. White travelers during the early decades of this century treated with condescension servants' attempts to dress up "like them," and the antagonism did not abate with time. In a 1949 newspaper article advocating racial segregation, the writer of "Some Illusions of the Bantu" noted that although the African could live comfortably on much less than whites, "he wants to wear boots and hats and European clothing—which are unhealthy and unsuitable—, and his wife wants to wear dresses, silk stockings and high-heeled shoes and hats—also unsuitable and unbecoming." Even when they step out of place and into whites' clothing, this writer concluded, "they will never be anything but poor imitations of the higher race."[129]

The colonial household was built on contradictions of space and place which involved both servants and their employers. It was the employer's territory, but because it was on permanent display, the household was hardly a private domain. It was open to other whites for inspection. And to the servants, it was a very public place: it was their work locus and they knew every nook and cranny as well as what went on inside. In some instances, it also enclosed their home, and then not only space but also time was public. Servants domiciled on the premises were on constant call; even if their work chores were done, they were still considered available. Ironically, the result was the same for both servant and employer: the private domain was one of time, and it existed primarily when servants were off duty and not called on.

All aspects of life were regulated for the domiciled servants: whether or not to live in, when and which visitors could call, what sort of activity might be undertaken in leisure time. In fact, this unequal incorporation into the household was something they shared with their madams. White women in the colony did not hold a particularly strong position. They were prisoners of the ideology that associated women's place in the home with the upkeep of civilized standards and supported inequality between women and men.

---

128. W. V. Brelsford, *Generations of Men: The European Pioneers of Northern Rhodesia* (Lusaka: Government Printer, 1964), p. 120.

129. "Some Illusions of the Bantu," *Central African Post*, October 27, 1949, p. 5. The writer suggested racial segregation as the solution to the problems. He recommended that readers consult a notably racist and segregationist book written by a white South African, H. R. Abercrombie, *Africa's Peril* (London: Simpkin Marschall, 1938).

Being wives of men in power, their status derived from their husbands' occupations and their personal lives merged into officialdom just as servants' personal lives to a large degree were subsumed by their employers. White women's willingness to play charming and delightful wives for their husbands was conditioned by an acceptance of the colonial hierarchy in its racial and patriarchal dimensions.[130]

Most white women had but one domain in which to exercise personal power: in their own homes over their menservants. Housekeeping may have had its satisfactions, for it allowed women to run their homes and boss servants. Their charge to hire and fire servants gave them at least a taste of power. Perhaps the difference between white men's relaxed attitude and white women's tough attitude to servants must be seen in this light. White women's disciplinary stand was both a shield to protect themselves as employers against workers and a means to exercise some authority without overtly challenging the inequality in their relationship to their husbands.

In this situation, race and sex impinged in complex ways on what was fundamentally a class relationship between employer and servant. This relationship became charged because of the spatial proximity of the white madam and her black manservant. The convergence of race, class, and sex within the tight space of the colonial household made it difficult for the two chief actors to remain unaffected by the opposite sex.

The rules and regulations, etiquette and decorum that developed in colonial household employment accentuated the social difference between servant and boss but did not disguise that one was a man and the other a woman. How did white women and African men react to this? African men's work in colonial households gave them intimate knowledge of white habits, for servants washed and ironed every item of their employers clothing and made the beds. They also, of course, saw their employers' misconduct and possible indiscretions.

White women in Northern Rhodesia are likely to have viewed their African men domestics first as members of the inferior race, different from whites, less capable, more like children, and only secondarily as male and thus sexually threatening. Undoubtedly, sexual phobias were bandied around at white women's teas as were stories told in beerhalls of African servants seducing their white madams, whether true or false. But the collective sexual hysteria that swept South Africa between 1890 and 1914 did not occur in Northern Rhodesia. Very few "black peril" cases were recorded there. Mrs. Bradley reasoned that "it is a hard fact of sociological

---

130. For an insightful discussion of a variation of this situation, see Jane Hunter's work on American women missionaries in China in the early 1900s, *The Gospel of Gentility* (New Haven: Yale University Press, 1984), esp. pp. 128–173.

statistics that 'black peril' is only rife in more civilized places where white people have lost or thrown away the respect of the colonized races."[131] Of how menservants viewed their white madams little is known. They are as likely to have told stories of their madams as the latter did of them. They probably saw them as whites first, members of a privileged class who wielded power over them. White women were, after all, the bosses who could hire and fire and report any misdemeanors such as drinking, pilfering, and misuse of property. Menservants' inferior status may have muted the sense of troublesome sexuality which lay beneath the surface of the social practices that structured their relationship with white women employers.

Whatever ties of affection developed between servant and employer—for of course there were kind and generous employers and obliging and faithful servants—their relationship was inherently hierarchical and characterized by domination and subservience. The inequality was accentuated in clothing, speech and demeanor. The use of a classificatory label rather than a name rendered the African's personal circumstances irrelevant to the work situation. The wearing of uniforms and the nonuse of shoes when inside set the servant off from both employer and fellow Africans. The Kitchen Kaffir spoken in some households crudely exemplified a language of subordination. The demeanor of not talking unless spoken to, of being present without being seen, reduced the person to an object. These were the official points of contact between the servant world and that of their employers. Taken together, such social practices construed the servant as different from, other than, his employers.

By the interwar period when the sex ratio of whites had balanced, domestic service had developed from a set of common practices originating in the days of caravan travel and mission stations into a taken-for-granted world of unequal relations and routines. This occupational domain had, in Giddens's terms, become institutionalized.[132] One result of this process was the construction of gender in domestic service as male. Further, it meant the establishment of practices and rules that helped to lessen two inherent contradictions in domestic service: the shared space of the dominant and the subordinate within the white colonial household; and the sexual confrontation between the African male servant and his white female boss.

The construction of the male servant's role as an object or commodity, almost a nonperson, may—in the terms of Mary Douglas and Victor Turner—locate him in a social and cultural limbo at a structural margin, marked

---

131. Bradley, *Dearest Priscilla*, p. 56.
132. Anthony Giddens, *Central Problems in Social Theory* (Berkeley: University of California Press, 1979), p. 80.

off from the mainstream of society.[133] The servant's ambiguous role seems also to fall within the analytical domain of the drama of face-to-face interaction, captured so sensitively in Erving Goffman's work. Thus at one level of analysis, the colonial household may be viewed as a total institution[134] in which recurrent features of social interaction can be observed at close range. In such a situation the reciprocal stereotyping and the presentation of selves[135] in tactics of subservience and domination[136] can be studied in a regime where, as Goffman puts it: "two different social and cultural worlds develop, jogging alongside each other with points of official contact but with little mutual penetration."[137]

Yet, the colonial household was *not* marked off from the rest of society and it was only in a limited analytical sense a total institution. That limited sense is confined by the terms used by the dominating group to differentiate servants from themselves and other Africans. Their discourse applies to an atemporal, repetitive everyday routine within the closed space of the colonial household and, as I demonstrate at length in Chapter 3, ignores the effects that servants' activities beyond the work locus had on the organization of household work.

Servant Problems: Questions of Control and Regulation

African menservants were part of white colonial households in the manner of pots and pans. As household commodities, they were the subject of much discussion: ways of handling them, their price and work capacity. If servant stories were frequent conversation topics at women's teas, so were discussions of servant problems, chief among which were complaints about their lack of hygiene, poor work efficiency, insubordination, pilfering, and high turnover rates. These perceived problems were overwhelmingly attributed to servants themselves. Women's second gripe was their husbands' lack of attention to domestic affairs which exacerbated the problems with the servants. Finally, "the government" was criticized for not doing anything to straighten up recalcitrant servants.

Some madams complained that their husbands were oblivious to their

133. Mary Douglas, *Purity and Danger: An Analysis of the Concepts of Pollution and Taboo* (London: Routledge and Kegan Paul, 1976), pp.115, 145, and Victor W. Turner, *The Ritual Process: Structure and Anti-Structure* (Ithaca, N.Y.: Cornell University Press, 1969), pp. 102–107.

134. Erving Goffman, *Asylums* (Garden City, N.Y.: Doubleday Anchor, 1961).

135. Erving Goffman, *The Presentation of Self in Everyday Life* (Garden City, N.Y.: Doubleday Anchor, 1959).

136. Erving Goffman, "The Nature of Deference and Demeanor," *American Anthropologist* 58 (1956): 473–502.

137. Goffman, *Asylums*, p. 9.

problems with servants. Because he was relatively divorced from the daily execution of household work, a husband might make a request of a servant that contradicted madam's instructions. The confused servant who chose to follow master's orders was likely to be blamed by his missus, especially if he argued. A husband's whims could thus upset established routines, so that noninvolvement might have been the safest approach to domestic matters. Yet husbands were not always allowed to remain neutral; they were called on when things got out of hand and if authoritarian decisions needed to be made. In the domestic power struggle, however, they were not always immediate allies. A wife, when she complained of getting "yards of cheek" from a servant might, as one of them satirized on a newspaper woman's page, get the following unsympathetic answer from her husband: "I've always got on well with the boys. It's all a question of knowing how to handle them." This same writer resorted to staging a near nervous break-down, making her husband's life a misery, before he agreed to sack an offending cook. When taking on her next cook, she realized that he proba-bly had been laid off from his previous job for the very same reasons that she had wanted her former kitchen worker dismissed. And so her story continues, life interrupted by continual servant problems and inaction on her husband's part, until she finds the solution she recommends to her servant-employing sisters: keep out of the kitchen.[138]

There were of course good- and bad-natured servants, well-intentioned and harsh employers; some servants had better skills or were quicker to learn than others; and some madams and masters had long experience as servant employers in colonial settings whereas others were greenhorns. Some women made bad bosses and some servants, themselves heads in their own households, had a tough time taking orders from a woman, white or black. The worst combinations of any of these factors were likely to produce bad results. "Between the two extremes," commented the native commissioner in Livingstone in 1926, "of the man who spoils his servants, allows himself to be robbed by them and keeps so large a staff that little is required in the way of work for any individual member of it and he who regards his single servant merely as a 'nigger' who is to do everything he is told from chopping wood to boiling eggs and making beds, there lies a large range of moderate people who try to treat their servants fairly but require some return in the shape of efficient performance of duties. This class neither prosecutes defaulters nor is it prosecuted as a general rule; it pre-fers to suffer and avoid court. That it does suffer . . . is too well known."[139]

138. From the Woman's Angle, "Too Many Cooks," by E. G. R., *Central African Post*, May 25, 1950, p. 7.

139. NAZ/ZA 1/9. Department of Native Affairs. Licensing and Registration of Domestic Servants, 1929. Native Commissioner, Livingstone, to Secretary for Native Affairs, Living-stone, May 13, 1926.

In an attempt to lessen problems, authorities suggested in 1926 the passage of a legal ordinance requiring the registering and licensing of servants. The need for some regulation had been expressed particularly by white residents of Livingstone, then the territory's capital and hub of its Society, and Broken Hill, then its main industrial center. "The trouble is," argued the native commissioner, that we are "permitting the growth of a class, numerous members of which live by preying on the European to an extent unbelievable by anyone who has not had intimate personal experience of the difficulties of employers and employees in relation to each other."[140] The district commissioner from Broken Hill was in accord, and further explained that white employers suffered "at the hands of native domestic servants who invariably give false names when engaged, desert when the inclination takes them, demand wages for uncompleted terms of service . . . , and continuously pilfer and consequently many European women detest the sight of a native and believe them to be quite beyond the control of government."[141]

Time was ripe for some sort of regulation to keep servants in line, to eliminate the "bad hats," and to open the way "for the native who genuinely intends to adopt domestic service as a living and to do his best in his chosen walk of life."[142] When considering what to include under a licensing ordinance, officials consulted domestic service regulations from other colonial territories: a Northern Nigerian proclamation of 1905; licensing rules from Uganda passed in 1924, from the gold Coast of 1924, and from Nyasaland.[143] Among the most frequent suggestions made by officials for areas to be covered by a licensing ordinance were medical examinations to exclude servants with venereal and infectious diseases; compulsory testing of references in the *situpas* (servants' passbooks); prohibitions of misuse, copying, and forging of passbooks; and revoking of licenses of servants who were irregular or who deserted.[144] The police sergeant at Livingstone suggested a clause to deny licenses to servants who had committed or attempted to commit rape of white women and girls or who had indecently assaulted or shown curiosity toward them.[145]

140. Ibid.

141. Ibid., District Commissioner, Broken Hill, to Secretary for Native Affairs, Livingstone, July 28, 1928.

142. Ibid.

143. Ibid. Gazette copies from various colonial territories are included in this file.

144. Some whites made money from copying and forging certificates in character books. The district commissioners' offices were authorized to write out clean copies of dirty and worn character books. They were to destroy the originals but did not always do so, and some old character books would be passed on or sold to other Africans. "It enables rogues and scoundrels of all descriptions to obtain employment which they would not get without a certificate of character book." Ibid., Sergeant-Major, Police Warrant Officer of Mazabuka to officer in command of town and district police in Livingstone, February 2, 1927.

145. Ibid., Acting Assistant Magistrate, Livingstone, to Secretary for Native Affairs, Livingstone, May 10, 1929.

As on almost all subsequent occasions when officials considered "doing something about" domestic service, they failed in this instance, for there were many stumbling blocks. Not all the laws of other colonies were relevant or applicable to Northern Rhodesia. A licensing ordinance might in the future have to be extended to areas not administered by current township regulations and thus changes in rules might be required.[146] The medical establishment was not sufficiently extensive to examine all servants.[147] The compulsory giving of character references could be used to the disadvantage of servants as "there exists . . . the class of Europeans who out of sheer spite owing to some small grievance gives a native an undeservedly bad character."[148] And if an ordinance were to be inclusive, it would apply also to "Europeans in domestic employment and it seems . . . hardly necessary to license European women who are forced to earn their living as house keepers, lady helps, nurses, etc."[149] Servants in Northern Rhodesia thus were never licensed, and in later years, when the need for legal regulations was brought up, the dismal failure of a licensing scheme in Kenya was generally referred to as setting a bad precedent. Most problems between servants and employers continued to be dealt with interpersonally.

Employers typically attributed their problems to the simplicity or badness of their domestic servants rather than to the work regime in the white household and its emphasis on order and regulation. Because the domestic space was both a site on permanent display of proper civilized standards and at the same time the locus of work for the servant, a white woman's freedom to pursue whims and idiosyncracies was to some extent limited by the servant's presence, by when and where he pursued his household tasks. From this fact might arise the idea of servants controlling their madams' lives which has been so creatively elaborated by such writers as Doris Lessing.[150] It is true that decorum was felt necessary in the interaction with servants, and in this sense servants' presence influenced their employers' habits. But this is a different matter from servants controlling

146. Ibid., Native Commissioner, Livingstone, to Secretary for Native Affairs, Livingstone, August 23, 1926.

147. Ibid., Native Commissioner, Livingstone, to Secretary for Native Affairs, Livingstone, May 13, 1926.

148. Ibid., May 18, 1926.

149. Ibid., District Commissioner, Broken Hill, to Secretary for Native Affairs, Livingstone, July 28, 1926.

150. This theme is developed, for example, in Doris Lessing's short story "A Home for the Highland Cattle," in *Five: Short Novels* (London: Michael Joseph, 1953), and in her novel *The Grass Is Singing* (London: Michael Joseph, 1953). Lessing's setting is Southern Rhodesia. Nadine Gordiner has given this theme political relevance in *July's People* (New York: Viking Press, 1981), where she suggests a postrevolutionary stage in South Africa in which a white family flees with their servant to his remote village; there the authoritarian, hierarchical relationship that once structured his work in their household is reversed, and he literally assumes control over their lives.

their employers' lives. A servant's desertion or drunkenness certainly inconvenienced the pursuit of an employer's lifestyle, and a mistress obviously felt done for when having lost, say, five servants in one month. But there were many to replace them and she still had de facto control. She could sack the servants whose work habits interfered most with her own likes and dislikes.

That servants occasionally asserted their independence and employers sometimes suffered may imply that some servants attempted to turn the institution of domestic service to their own advantage. The terms that governed servants' work were set by whites, but they could nonetheless be used to challenge the institution (which was not at all as hermetic as the previous discussion might imply). Although their situation was perhaps special, servants were members of their own households and workers among other workers, and these other relationships also affected their work as servants.

Servants and Their Other Lives

In the late 1920s, when copper mining began on a commercial basis in the north, a large African labor force was hired for the mines, for the ongoing construction work, and as domestic servants for the rapidly growing white population (see Table 1). This massing of Africans required tighter administration. From the end of the 1920s through the early 1930s a series of new rules and ordinances restricted the movements of Africans between rural and urban areas as well as within the towns.[151]

This era's labor legislation consolidated the Masters and Servants Ordinance and its various amendments into the Employment of Natives Ordinance of 1929. The word *servant* was omitted from its title and the legislation extended to cover every category of African employee, including skilled workmen. It tightened the contract system, making workers liable to criminal punishment if they deserted before completing contracts. Criminal remedies continued to be meted out for misconduct, "because the civil remedy would be ineffective in regard to natives who have little sense of responsibility, usually possess no property, often have no fixed place of abode, and generally are quite indifferent to dismissal."[152] The ordinance also gave the servant "a criminal remedy against his employer for nonpayment of wages. . . . Although some natives have achieved a veneer of education and skill and have by contact with Europeans became in some ways amenable to the ordinary standards of civilized life, even the most

151. See note 84.
152. Northern Rhodesia. *Legislative Council Debates* 10 (1929), col. 56.

advanced of them are still very irresponsible, credulous and gullible and require the protection of the criminal law against many European employers."[153]

Paternalism continued to inform labor relations and perhaps supremely within servant-employing households, where some masters thought they eventually would "make over" and civilize their servants. Because servants worked in their employers' space and their behavior was governed by their employers, masters commonly believed that they "knew" their servants—and thus, by extension, all Africans. A stereotype had arisen of servants as "ridiculous objects . . . [yet] rather appealing, too; very gentle and anxious to please, in all their blunders and weird ways."[154] Because of their "simplicity," servants were also considered impressionable, and up till World War II it was generally thought that they would pick up civilized mores under white supervision and apply this knowledge in their own lives. Many whites thought that there was "hope" for the domestic worker. When the new capital of Lusaka was planned in the early 1930s, a personal servants' compound was laid out, separate from the general African compound, with the belief that "the boy through [his] association with European family life, has reached a higher standard of domestic culture and civic behavior than the more unsophisticated labourer, and is therefore likely to prefer to associate with his fellows."[155]

Did servants accept their masters' estimation of their own worth? With the class- and race-conscious white household in front of them, servants certainly learned that manners and dress symbolized white colonists' claim to civilized status. The condescending remarks that whites made about their smartly attired servants were based on the assumption that Africans accepted whites' system of evaluation. But European clothing, and I return to this in Chapter 3, also took on new meanings informed by African cultural practices and helped shape the urban African world of leisure in distinctive ways. Employers and administrators saw only one side of their servants' lives: that part which emerged in the domestic encounter, the part governed by whites' rules. And although these rules circumscribed the behavior of Africans, they did not determine it. The notions that led to

153. NAZ/ZA 1/9/18 no. 25, vol. 1. Department of Native Affairs. Labor: Masters and Servants Ordinances, 1927–1929.

154. Irwin, *Far Away*, p. 67.

155. Kenneth Bradley, *Lusaka* 1935 (privately published, 1935; reprinted in *In Situ*, October 1981, p. 13). Always conscious of differences of status and rank among themselves and between themselves and others, the British also distinguished among Africans. "Special servants," such as those employed in Government House, had their separate residential area at a distance from their place of work but still within walking distance of it. For the convenience of employers, the personal servants' and the government servants' compounds were closer to the white residential areas than was the general African compound located at Lusaka's extreme southwestern corner.

Table 1. Number of African men employed in Northern Rhodesia, by occupation, 1927–1948

Occupational category	1927	1928	1929	1930	1931	1932	1933	1934	1935	193⬛
Government	3,708	2,979	4,777	5,101	8,146	7,580	4,582	4,111	8,023	5,4
Agriculture	16,063	15,600	10,655	10,885	10,508	6,530	5,624	8,981	10,033	9,⬛
Other indus- trial										
Manufacture	1,224	2,073	3,270	2,886	2,791	2,391	1,648	1,675	4,830	3,9
Building	2,502	2,236	2,277	4,420	10,133	2,464	1,640	3,769	2,005	1,7
Mines	9,493	11,036	17,608	28,004	21,888	27,851	9,920	14,245	17,298	18,3
Railways	3,223	3,500	4,399	6,808	3,204	9,666	1,582	1,592	1,500	1,6
Domestic ser- vice	7,482	8,431	8,832	12,470	16,315	11,966	9,335	10,388	10,296	10,⬛
Other		5,412	6,485	6,069	6,177	7,631	5,029	3,791	3,986	5,2
Total	43,695	51,267	58,303	76,743	79,162	76,079	39,360	48,552	57,971	55,7

Source: *Northern Rhodesia, Blue Books*, 1927–1948 Lusaka, Government Printer.

the formulation of these rules and to the stereotyping of the domestic servant never reckoned with the servants' real characters as individuals or as members of African households with personal affairs, projects, and plans of their own.

The observance of strict interactional rules and the compulsive attention to housekeeping implied that everyone and everything had its place and order reigned over all. But it was a deceptive impression. Not everything was under control, for the terms that structured domestic work did not extend much beyond the locus of work in the colonial household. This inherent limit to the regulative framework impeded the civilizing, educational function that whites ascribed to domestic service in the early years and produced unexpected responses. There was always the lingering suspicion that servants would "revert to type," forgetting everything they had learned, for Africans were considered to be, after all, tribal and by definition different. Then there were servants who took matters in their own hands and, by asserting their independence, sought to transcend the restrictive work regime within domestic service. These responses to domestic service are illustrated by the cases of three menservants recorded in the official colonial registry of correspondence from 1924 to 1951.

The first alternative, "the native who genuinely intends to adopt domestic service as a living and to do his best in his chosen walk of life,"[156] was a product of the terms set by the masters. One such servant was Jameson, the head servant at Government House in Lusaka. In 1936 the acting

156. To paraphrase a statement made during the discussion of a registration scheme for servants, taken from the same source as note 142.

1937	1938	1939	1940	1941	1942	1943	1944	1945	1946	1947	1948
6,703	5,329	5,541	5,541	5,541	1,500	12,500	12,500	14,000	24,000	26,000	26,000
8,595	12,826	13,500	13,500	13,500	13,500	12,000	14,000	15,000	26,000	26,000	25,000
5,353	5,520	6,288	6,288	4,500	4,000	4,400	4,400	5,000	9,000	10,000	12,000
4,332	5,560	6,856	6,856	5,160	4,000	1,200	2,750	2,500	12,000	12,000	14,500
23,689	23,754	29,524	33,396	32,400	41,330	41,987	35,000	33,000	31,000	34,000	36,500
1,700	5,395	5,500	2,600	1,938	2,587	2,573	2,860	2,800	3,100	3,400	3,350
10,021	11,511	13,000	13,000	13,000	18,000	18,000	20,000	20,000	17,500	17,500	19,000
5,747		8,348	8,348	8,348	8,000	6,300	7,000	8,000	20,000	20,000	20,000
66,140	69,895	88,557	89,529	84,387	92,917	98,960	98,510	100,300	142,600	148,900	156,350

governor of Northern Rhodesia wrote a letter to Ormsby Gore in the Colonial Office in London requesting a pension for Jameson's retirement. (No arrangements for African pensions existed at this time, so a special request was necessary.) In his letter, he noted that "this native . . . entered the service of the Administration of North Eastern Rhodesia as a tennis boy in 1906, and has given continuous and faithful service as a member of the household staffs of all Administrators and Governors from Sir Robert Codrington down to Sir Hubert Young."[157] Jameson may have been the favorite boy Codrington took with him on a visit to Britain in the first decade of this century. In any case, a yearly pension of three pounds was granted to him. Little else is known about him. The official record is silent on how he spent his retirement and used the skills he had acquired in colonial domestic service (as an old retainer, an independent economic man, or a returned migrant, for example). But his conduct as a servant is likely to have been obliging and accepting.

The second response to domestic service, reverting to "type," was to some extent the case with Kakumbi, one of the two servants Gore-Browne had taken to England.[158] Although Kakumbi was "one of the nicest fellows

157. PRO/CO 705/93. Grant of a Pension to Jameson, Head Native Servant of Government House, Lusaka. Letter from Acting Governor, Northern Rhodesia, to W. G. A. Ormsby Gore, M.P., Colonial Office, December 12, 1936.

158. The possibility of reverting to type puzzled and troubled well-meaning white employers. Kenneth Bradley has aptly captured this tension in his short story "Tomo," in *Africa Notwithstanding* (London: Lovat Dickson, 1932), pp. 119–182, which revolves around the retirement of an old colonial commissioner's long-time personal servant and his wife to their village.

you could have," domestic serrvice did not successfully civilize him. As Gore-Browne continued in a 1922 letter home, "Not a single scrap he has picked up from all he saw in England & during the war, though his eyes were wide open & took a jolly keen interest in everything. . . . yet he still lives in a rubbishy hut full of bugs, still stuffs a few seeds into a patch of ashes on the ground which he doesn't even trouble to hoe, still brews beer, from such grains as he does grow, in the summer and grows hungry in the winter.[159]

Bulaya, Gore-Browne's servant who chose to not return to the life of a servant in colonial Northern Rhodesia, exemplifies the third response: asserting independence. His case shows that servants did not always accept their social inferiority to whites or assimilate white norms without question. Some did seek to transcend their situation—although usually on a less grand scale than Bulaya, who became an actor in England and married a white woman. They must have done so in ways defined by their own experience and what they saw as alternatives. These three responses to domestic service are likely to have overlapped at times during an individual servant's life.

Peter Fraenkel, broadcasting officer in Lusaka in the 1950s, in his book *Wayaleshi,* offers us a rare case from the war and postwar period which illustrates this process. His account details many of the aspects I have been sketching and is especially illuminating because it presents the servant as a person with an ethnic background, family ties, a social life, and, last but not least, a purpose and conscience of his own.[160] Fraenkel writes of the life and work of Amon, a Lenje man, born Amon Chapusha, who with two years' primary schooling had learned to read but barely to write. At ten he began to work for a poor Afrikaans-speaking farmer, some thirty miles from his village, as a nurse-boy for the baby. He left that household after being severely beaten. Next he was taken on by a nearby British farmer, a retired civil servant known for his contempt of the poor white Afrikaaners. Amon worked as a kitchen boy, peeling potatoes and chopping firewood. He stayed for several years, advancing to houseboy, cleaning rooms and serving at table. Then he decided to seek his fortune in town: "Money was very little on these farms. I got 15 shillings and food per month. Also, I was bored." It was around the late 1930s that he came to Lusaka and was employed by Fraenkel's parents, Jews from Breslau, first as a houseboy, then as cook.

Amon was a variable worker, writes Fraenkel. If there was anything new and interesting to do, such as preparing a dish he had never tried or

159. Rotberg, *Black Heart*, p. 121.
160. Peter Fraenkel, *Wayaleshi* (London: Weidenfeld and Nicolson, 1959). All quotations are from pp. 124–130.

Amon Chapusha and his wife. Lusaka, 1950s. From the collection of Peter Fraenkel. Reproduced with permission.

repairing the plumbing, he was enthusiastic and enterprising. Routine work he found boring and did indifferently.

Amon married, but his wife soon gave him grounds for suspicion. He tried to divorce her, but there was difficulty because she was the daughter of a minor chief. ("I suspect," comments Fraenkel, "that his own marital record was not as clean as he claimed.") Amon's life made him listless. He did not know what to do with his spare time as there were few channels for his talents. He had no ambition to excel at tribal dancing or beer drinking because they were "uncivilized." He once bought an English primer and tried to learn English. During Fraenkel's vacations from boarding school he helped the African, but when school was on Amon lost interest. Yet he had a restless, inquiring mind, and he started to ask awkward questions.

"If we all were created in God's image, why are some of us black and white? What colour is God? If God really loved the world why did he create some to enjoy life and some to suffer?" One day he surprised Fraenkel: "This story about Adam and Eve and the snake and the apple, I think the Bible is speaking in riddles like our own people. What it really means is that Adam had discovered how sweet women were. What do you think?" These questions were the fruit of lengthy theological speculation and controversy he heard in his compound from lay preachers of the Watchtower Bible and Tract Society, or Jehovah's Witnesses, on their house-to-house

[81]

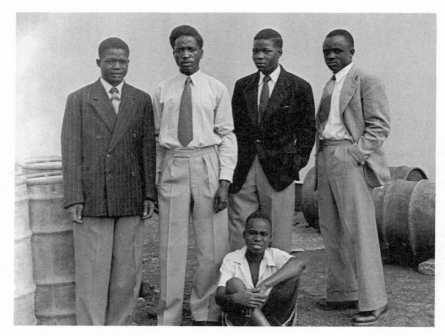

Amon Chapusha (extreme left) and co-workers at Express Dry Cleaners, Lusaka, 1950s. From the collection of Peter Fraenkel. Reproduced with permission.

visits. The society had grown to become the biggest single denomination in Northern Rhodesia during the 1930s and 1940s. In Lusaka in the 1930s, 75 percent of the African population were among its adherents.[161] It alone of all the Christian denomination was not tainted by identification with the white establishment, for while "the society" called for salvation, it was also political. In the 1940s its teachings increasingly criticized the economic and political order on which white privilege was based.[162] Its message appealed to Amon. He brought a Nyanja Bible and began to read in his spare time, in the kitchen, under the bananas in the garden, and in his little round mud-house in the compound. There was no priestly hierarchy to hinder the progress of a humble, uneducated man. Soon he began to accompany lay preachers on their rounds and he joined the choir. His former gossiping

161. Norman Rothman, "African Urban Development in the Colonial Period: A Study of Lusaka, 1905–1964" (Ph.D. diss.: Northwestern University, 1972), p. 340.
162. Rothman, pp. 340–344. For a historical study of the Watchtower movement, see Sholto Cross, "The Watchtower Movement in South Central Africa, 1908–1954" (Ph.D. diss.: Oxford University, 1973).

was transformed into preaching with an urgent purpose. His ability came to be recognized and he was happier than Fraenkel had ever known him.

Amon found that the irregular hours of domestic service interfered with his preaching, and he had ambitions. He asked to be transfered to the Fraenkel dry-cleaning business. There he immediately made himself help-ful by repairing the electrical equipment and delivery bicycles. He was soon a sort of foreman.

After Amon had worked for the family for twelve years, Fraenkel senior disposed of the business. Amon turned down another servant job to start a dry-cleaning business of his own. Working from his house in the com-pound, he developed a flourishing trade among Africans and some whites. He expanded and employed several younger relatives. His enterprise eventually folded, when a nephew employee ran off with the clothes taken in for cleaning and Amon had to pay for them. He did not have enough money and disappeared to his village.

The unhappy ending does not diminish the importance of Amon's story. His experience is probably not unique among the many unrecorded stories of African servants who, conscious to their disadvantageous position in colonial society, found alternative means (many through the Watchtower) to transcend their situation.

During the period covered in this chapter, an educated African man's employment horizon was limited to a job as interpreter in the courts, a lowly clerical post, or teaching. Beyond that, there was manual labor, including domestic service, and African menservants remained fixtures of household employment throughout the colonial period. The construct of the good and faithful manservant, at times inefficient and lazy because of men-tal incapacity but obligingly taking orders with a simple mind and no questions asked, had changed by then and servants were increasingly con-sidered "subversive." Before the how and why can be discussed in Chapter 3, African women must be brought into the story. The written record has given them little room other than as tangents to men, as mothers and daughters, sisters and wives, lovers and prostitutes. Despite their subsidi-ary role, however, women were by their absence in fact central to the shaping of colonial domestic service as a male institution.

[2]

Women for Hire?
Sex and Gender in Domestic Service

How and why did the development of a colonial labor force in Northern Rhodesia exclude African women from domestic service? The trajectory of *what* took place, namely men's prior entry into wage labor as a result of the administration's attempt to create a rural-urban division of labor by sex, is well known. To explain *why* and *how* it occurred, I go beyond functionalist explanations, according to which the division of labor is held to benefit capital by enabling it to pay substandard wages to male workers whose reproduction costs were borne by the unpaid work of women either on rural farmsteads or in urban households.[1] I wish to demonstrate the implication of cultural factors in this process.

To be sure, any explanation of the gender division of labor in domestic service needs to be placed in the broader context of the new economic and political processes that were set into motion by the penetration of first settler, then mining, capital. It was also shaped by demographic factors and settlement patterns among the scattered white and African populations. Last, but not least, there were cultural and ideological factors, which on both the white and the African side of the colonial encounter affected the way each group constructed societal norms, the place of the two sexes in the system of social relations, and their images of each other.

In this chapter I attempt to unravel the various and changing roles that economic, demographic, political, cultural, and ideological factors played in

---

1. Lionel Cliffe, "Labour Migration and Peasant Differentiation: Zambian Experiences," *Journal of Peasant Studies* 5 (1978): 326–346, and George Chauncey, Jr., "The Locus of Reproduction: Women's Labour in the Zambian Copperbelt, 1927–1953," *Journal of Southern African Studies* 7 (1981): 135–164.

structuring domestic service by gender. Cultural and ideological notions about sex and gender reinforced the convention, developed during the opening decades of colonial rule, of not employing African women as servants. As the economy changed, this convention was rationalized as commonsensical knowledge that white women did not want African women in their homes because their sexuality was threatening. Because this argument, in the words of an observer of race relations in the 1950s, "reveals an assortment of lust and fears that were usually kept out of sight and about which it [was] not polite to talk,"[2] I have marshaled evidence and made deductions from sources other than conventional historical documents. My concerns are with a battery of gender images shaped in the early days of contact between a primarily male white population and local African women and men. I trace how they were produced—as opposed to whether they are true or false—through an examination of contemporary texts concerning the nature and effects of interactions between and among whites and Africans of both sexes from the turn of the last century onward. Many disparate elements comprise the discourse, and their relative weight in the overall characterization changed over time, accommodating to a small degree the shifts in colonial society and the world beyond it. Yet the outcome remained fixed, for Africans remained different, other,[3] and African women in Northern Rhodesia even more so, inferior to their men and most certainly to white women.

The Rural/Urban Division

Before the Great Depression, the potential supply of African women for urban wage labor was limited. The system that supplied migrant workers to farmers, businesses, small mines, and private householders within and outside Northern Rhodesia was geared exclusively toward men. They worked on temporary contracts, housed and fed by employers for the duration, after which they were expected to return to their villages. The administration was concerned to prevent the growth of an urban African proletariat and considered the village and the tribe to be the permanent reference point for migrants.

The viability of village life depended overwhelmingly on the work of women, for in his region's agricultural system they played the major pro-

2. Quoted in Patrick Keatley, *The Politics of Partnership: The Federation of Rhodesia and Nyasaland* (Harmondsworth: Penguin, 1963), p. 269.

3. Mary Louise Pratt, "Scratches on the Face of the Country; or What Mr. Barrow Saw in the Land of the Bushmen," *Critical Inquiry* 12 (1985), pp. 119–122.

ductive role. Men could more easily be dissociated from their villages, especially if they returned at critical points during the cultivation season when their labor was most needed.[4] In the colonial scheme, it was very important to keep women back on the farm. Their work subsidized migrant workers' substandard wages and ensured the reproduction of a new generation of workers without cost to the administration. Despite the reserves policy, which reduced the available land for many African groups, and marketing decisions that adversely affected the price of their produce, Africans' farm output did not disappear from the market. As long as it remained profitable to participate in the food market, many African women continued to depend on their fields for income, supplemented by remittances from absentee husbands, brothers, and sons. Before the 1930s special policies would have been necessary to extract that rural female labor supply for work in the cities had the economy needed their labor power. Thus the question of using African women for urban domestic service did not arise: they were hardly available.

These circumstances changed once the slump had ended and many more men went on labor migration. In some societies, such as the Bemba, where hunger had been a recurring seasonal phenomenon, malnutrition became more prevalent.[5] Women, children, and old people on the reserves were unable to meet their own demands for food without permanent support from men. Various studies from the 1930s onward indicate a growing gap in food consumption between African rural and urban populations.[6] More women and children migrated to the towns, sometimes alone, at other times accompanied by husbands, fathers, or guardians. During World War II, when Northern Rhodesia experienced extreme food scarcities, the colonial government tried to stem this urban influx, devising a variety of measures to get women and children back to where they belonged: the villages, as food producers. These attempts were largely ineffectual. This observation suffices here to demonstrate that by the time of the post–World War II campaign for African womanpower, there was a large supply of urban African women from whom white householders could have recruited servants.

---

4. Audrey I. Richards, "Bemba Marriage and Present Economic Conditions," *Rhodes-Livingstone Papers*, no. 4 (1940); William Watson, *Tribal Cohesion in a Money Economy* (Manchester: Manchester University Press, 1958); and Jaap van Velsen, *The Politics of Kinship* (Manchester: Manchester University Press, 1964).

5. Richards, "Bemba Marriage."

6. Betty Preston Thomsen, "Two Studies in African Nutrition," *Rhodes-Livingstone Papers*, no. 24 (1954); Bruce Fetter, "Relocating Central Africa's Biological Reproduction, 1923–1963," *International Journal of African Historical Studies* 19 (1986): 463–478.

The Sexuality Argument

In Northern Rhodesia the demand of white colonists for servants was shaped by factors that construed a good servant as a man. White attitudes to African women revolved around sexual anxiety. This anxiety meant different things to different people, depending on their sex, race, and class. It first and foremost meant white men's sexual need for African women, and white women's uneasiness, concern, and fear caused by the knowledge of such sexual encounters. This sexual anxiety runs as a single common thread through the entire colonial period, providing an important key to understanding the gender division of labor in white servant-keeping households.

The Cook's Woman

The question of sexual relations with African women was "of obvious interest," states Alan Cairns in his study of British reactions to Central African society before the imposition of BSAC administration in the 1890s.[7] This interest did not abate with the coming of British colonial rule but persisted in conflict with or accommodation to the cultural norms and social pressures that gradually emerged within the slowly growing white population among whom the sex ratio remained skewed till about World War II.

The "simple life" of the earlier period, as described by a pioneer from North Eastern Rhodesia, included the change from the "palmy days of transition, when there were no game laws, reserves, or licenses necessary, and when men could and did shoot scores of elephants,"[8] to the stepwise introduction of a civil administration, taxation, the building of roads and bridges, the establishment of a postal system, and the building of railways. Slave-trading Arabs had been eliminated, gunrunning reduced in scale, and white missionaries, hunters and prospectors, traders, farmers, and administrators began to settle down more peacefully to the task of adopting the "exigencies of an African environment to their own standards of comfort and well-being."[9] Regardless of occupational background they all needed

---

7. H. Alan C. Cairns, *Prelude to Imperialism: British Reactions to Central African Society, 1840–1890* (London: Routledge and Kegan Paul, 1965), p. 53. For a general discussion, see Ronald Hyam, "Empire and Sexual Opportunity," *Journal of Imperial and Commonwealth History* 14 (1986): 34–90.

8. Dugald Campbell, *In the Heart of Bantuland: A Record of Twenty-nine Years' Pioneering in Central Africa among the Bantu Peoples, with a Description of Their Habits, Customs, Secret Societies, and Languages* (1922; New York: Negro Universities Press, 1969), pp. 298, 304.

9. Robert I. Rotberg, *Christian Missionaries and the Creation of Northern Rhodesia, 1880–1924* (Princeton: Princeton University Press, 1965), p. 49.

menservants to minister to their household needs. Their cooks often procured "the cook's woman," as she came to be known, who provided sexual
services to the master on a temporary or longer-term basis.

Among some whites there was a partial equation of frontier life, up to
and including the early years of the BSAC administration, with sexual
freedom and indulgence. Their response to sex across the racial divide
depended to some extent on their occupation and relative standing in the
evolving hierarchy of white colonial society. The ethical and moral norms of
missionaries prohibited them from sexual intercourse with African women,
but traders and hunters felt no such obligations.[10] Although exact figures
are difficult to obtain, "what information there is available indicates that the
practice was widespread, despite many attempts to stamp it out."[11]

Little is preserved in the written record of what later contemporaries
said and thought about the sexuality issue. Outside of all-male mess parties, it might not have been discussed. What remains is scattered between
the lines of travel descriptions, memoirs, and colonial dispatches, and can
be gleaned from the retrospective, almost all male writings in publications
from the 1950s and on, when the days of grand patriarchs and women who
knew their place were reckoned soon to be a bygone era. The images such
texts convey are twice refracted, as it were. They celebrate the good old
days, which were hardly romantic but tough, and they speak in a libidinous
voice about sexual relations, which in the tense racial atmosphere of the
1950s were considered an impolite topic for public discourse. While some
of the evidence is necessarily anecdotal, it nevertheless portrays practices
that were the rule rather than the exception during the first decades of
white settlement.

The tropical habit of keeping a cook's woman developed during the
pioneer era under frontier conditions where a small, nearly all male population required physical cooperation across race at a time when a class
barrier had not yet been established (See Tables 2 and 3). R. Murray-
Hughes recalls life at Kafue-Namwala about 1912: "Among all those stal-
wart, healthy, young—and old—pioneers, whatever their calling—administrators, police, traders, farmers or miners—there were no psychopathic
cases . . . : our community was essentially sane; and this was due to an
institution known as 'the cook's woman,' which she was not. An arrangement openly acknowledged in the neighbouring Belgian and Portuguese
territories had to be camouflaged in an English colony where Mother
Grundy still ruled; and much less being allowed the run of the house and

10. Cairns, *Prelude*, pp. 54–55.
11. Lewis H. Gann, *A History of Northern Rhodesia: Early Days to 1953* (New York:
Humanities Press, 1964), p. 151.

Table 2. European population of Zambia, by year, 1904–1965

Year	Population
1904	850
1907	1,050
1911	1,407
1921	3,634
1925	4,620
1927	7,540
1930	14,000
1931	13,846
1932	10,550
1934	11,460
1935	12,000
1940	15,190
1946	21,907
1951	37,079
1954	53,000
1956	65,277
1957	72,000
1958	71,000
1960	73,000
1961	74,640
1962	77,000
1963	76,000
1964	74,000
1965	70,000

Source: George Kay, *A Social Geography of Zambia* (London: London University Press, 1967), p. 26.

given a status equivalent to the Chinese concubine, our 'mistress' was given her clothes and monthly allowance in the usual English manner."[12]

Most of the hunters, transport riders, and traders of this era adopted an "African way of life" and had either one of more African wives, writes Richard Sampson in his biography of George Westbeech, trader and hunter, one of the first whites to enter into and settle in this region. The strain between him and his South African–born white wife grew because of his drinking and sexual habits and culminated in her return to the Transvaal in 1877. She had heard too many stories of his consorting with African women up and down the Zambezi Valley. With her Boer condemnation of mis-

12. R. Murray Hughes, "Kafue-Namwala in 1912, Part 2," *Northern Rhodesia Journal* 5 (1962): 106.

Table 3. Age and sex structure of the European population of Zambia, 1911–1956

Year	Males as % of total population	Women (over 20 years) per 100 men	Men aged 25–44 years as % of total population	Children under 15 years as % of total population
1911	74.5	17.5	49.0	15.5
1921	62.5	48.0	30.0	25.0
1931	63.0	48.5	29.0	21.0
1946	51.5	91.0	20.0	29.0
1956	53.0	83.0	22.0	33.0

Source: George Kay, A Social Geography of Zambia (London: London University Press, 1967), p. 27.

cegenation, she was still saying forty years later how ashamed she was to have been married to Westbeech because of his sexual activities.[13]

Although BSAC administration was imposed over these northern territories in the 1890s, it was fragmented and scattered, leaving room for enterprise in business and administration as well as in matters of sex. Some white men set themselves up as, or were made, chiefs and settled down almost as feudal lords, according to W. V. Brelsford's recollections of pioneer days. Such was the case of Harrison Clark, known as "Changa Changa," who made a treaty with a chief in the Portuguese East Africa border region. Because he was not placed in a BSAC post, he complained to the company office in Salisbury, arguing that he carried out the tasks of most of the company's administrators: he collected hut tax in kind (grain, chickens, and cattle) and seized one tusk of every elephant killed in the country. Whenever he saw "a girl he [fancied] he [took] her as his mistress for a few days, and when tired of her, he [sent] her home"; he had even taken one of the chief's wives.[14] In the same region near Feira lived another trader, "Kachachola" Bloomfield, who is said to have had at least eight or nine African wives and to have left at least thirty-six children among them.[15]

Sexual relationships between white men and African women were most common in those areas with good potential for trade and hunting—for example, in the Caprivi Strip and in Barotseland—or for other employment, such as the construction of the Bulawayo-Katanga railroad.[16] When

13. Richard Sampson, The Man with a Toothbrush in His Hat: The Story and Times of George Capp Westbeech in Central Africa (Lusaka: Multimedia Publications, 1972), pp. 13, 69.

14. W. V. Brelsford, Generations of Men: The European Pioneers of Northern Rhodesia (Lusaka: Government Printer, 1965), p. 24.

15. Ibid., pp. 70–71.

16. For more discussion, see Cairns, Prelude, pp. 55–57, and ibid., pp. 96–109.

railway building halted for about two years at Broken Hill in 1906, most of the white workers settled down with African women.[17] Labor recruiters met at Sesheke on the Zambezi River to recruit a quota of workers from Barotseland and to return them on completion of their contracts in the south. There was also a market for the sale of cattle from Barotseland and from North Eastern Rhodesia. It was here at Sesheke that traders congregated, doing most of their business once the African workers came upriver returning from migrant work. For most of the time these white men hunted, fished, and had "affairs with the Lozi women."[18] One of this band of traders who lived and died on the Zambezi in Barotseland was Arthur Harrington, about whose household many stories were told. He was said to have six African wives, whom he would visit, each in her own hut, according to a carefully checked schedule.[19]

The most famous of these men set up their menages in quasi-feudal style. Among them were Arthur Davidson, one of the biggest landowners in Northern Rhodesia, who was so fond of African women that he entertained two at the same time in his castle in Ndola.[20] Best known of all was "Chirupula," alias J. E. Stephenson, who helped open up the Kafue Hook and what became the copperbelt to the BSAC administration. In soap opera fashion, his biographer relates how he "went native," first with a woman procured by the cook, and next with an African princess.[21] In his own biography, Stephenson said very little about his African wives or about the nature of their household. He does note that "in those parts and in those days there were no European women. . . . But there were lots of women—ladies, too, if you like—of a different complexion: there was no scarcity at all."[22] He resigned in 1906, allegedly after he was refused promotion because of flaunting civilized norms. He then took up farming in the Mkushi district and built a strange-looking castle, which he called Stonehenge. Stephenson's biographer notes that most of his acquaintances "kept native concubines . . . only as long as European society remained strictly masculine, but as soon as white women appeared in the outposts, they sent the African girls back to their villages, and their golden-skinned babies were either farmed out to some sympathetic missionary or left to wander in the wilderness."[23] Stephenson himself had not done so; he

17. Dick Hobson, "Recollections of Captain John Brown," *Northern Rhodesia Journal* 3 (1958), p. 516.

18. Brelsford, *Generations*, p. 96.

19. Ibid., p. 114.

20. Ibid., p. 142.

21. Kathaleen Stevens Rukavina, *Jungle Pathfinder: Central Africa's Most Fabulous Adventurer* (New York: Exposition Press, 1950), pp. 57–67.

22. J. E. Stephenson, *Chirupula's Tale: A Bye-Way in African History* (London: Geoffrey Bles, 1937), p. 29.

23. Rukavina, *Jungle Pathfinder*, pp. 143–147.

publicly recognized his children and supported them. And he complained of the coming of the "ubiquitous Nosey Parkers" who declared that men "who lived naturally—legally . . . according to the ways of the country and the period—were 'living in sin'."[24]

The private menages of Davidson and Stephenson were the frills on an increasingly race-conscious colonial society, tolerated because of these men's pioneering roles but certainly no longer *comme il faut.* In a voice that puts women in their place, Brelsford comments that "some white ladies probably felt quite daring and advanced by receiving such renegades as Davidson and Stephenson in their homes."[25] If he had let them speak for themselves, he may have learned that such ladies might not have wanted to do so, judging from comments about men who had "gone native" made by Barbara Carr from fort Jameson in the 1940s: "I noticed with disgust in the club at Christmas . . . that one or two of the older bachelor game rangers . . . whom I knew lived with native women, were dancing clumsily with the sweet, innocent teenage daughters of some of the townspeople and my blood boiled. These men had an uncomfortable look in their eyes when we wives spoke to them and I now watched them with disgust."[26]

White men's days of carefree sex belonged to the pioneer era. While prejudice increased in the small but slowly growing white settlements along the line-of-rail, these practices persisted where there was less social pressure to conform, especially in bush stations. In her account of life at Fort Jameson in the 1920s, Winifred Tapson noted the commonality of interracial sexual cohabitation and the "hiding everywhere . . . of little scatterings of half-caste children." In her view, the loneliness of pioneers absolved them: "those men are hardly to be blamed for rejecting in their self-chosen exile, a life of monastic exactitude."[27] By that time, however, colonial authorities took a hostile view on concubinage and cohabitation, deeming such relations as unfitting for men in positions of authority. The official stance, however, did not necessarily reflect actual practice. One case, discussed at length in the colonial correspondence just before 1910, illustrates this ambivalence.

This case arose in the wake of complaints made by Charles Venables, a farmer near Chirundu, who alleged that Native Commissioner MacNamara of Guimbi (now Gwembe) subdistrict, had inflicted brutal assaults on Africans for not paying taxes. In the ensuing correspondence, Venables threw in the additional allegation that MacNamara cohabited with African wom-

24. Stephenson, *Chirupula's Tale*, p. 29.
25. Brelsford, *Generations*, p. 143.
26. Barbara Carr, *Not for Me the Wilds* (Cape Town: Howard Timmins, 1963), p. 175.
27. Winifred Tapson, *Old Timer* (Cape Town: Howard Timmins, 1957), p. 19.

en.[28] These charges were proven true and MacNamara dismissed in 1910 for "having habitually practiced concubinage with a native woman. This practice is most degrading to a white officer . . . and incompatible with the maintenance of the prestige of a British Government."[29] That same year, one Mr. Graham brought similar charges against R. L. Harrison, native commissioner of Mkushi, who after a severe reprimand was allowed to remain in his post, because he had recently married a European woman.[30]

Matters involving Venables did not end at that point. A letter from the high commissioner's office in South Africa noted that Venables had "been in the practice of cohabiting with native women." He was reprimanded and told he was not entitled to criticize since his own conduct was "calculated to degrade the white man in the eyes of the black and to impair the prestige of the governing race."[31] Provoked, Venables dispatched an accusatory fusillage to the imperial secretary in London, excusing himself by his youth and loneliness and by reference to the commonality of concubinage. His charges included officials within the Northern Rhodesian administration and read in part:

> I beg to remind you that His Majesty's Government have within recent years permitted the territories of North Eastern and North Western Rhodesia to be administered by an official who kept a plurality of native concubines . . . [and] are now permitting and have permitted for years the district administration of these territories to be conducted by a staff of officials a large proportion of whom keep or have kept native concubines . . . [or even] made a practice of cohabiting indiscriminately with native women throughout their districts. . . . There are scattered throughout these territories half-caste children and families of half-caste children, the offspring of . . . officials. . . . One of these territories in fact, has been administered by an official who kept a veritable harem of native women.[32]

Venables's accusations caused an uproar, prompting confidential and official dispatches among these northern territories, Cape Town, and London.

---

28. The brutality charges, but not the sexuality issue, are discussed in Fergus Macpherson, *Anatomy of Conquest: The British Occupation of Zambia, 1884–1924* (London: Longman, 1981), pp. 123–128.
29. PRO/CO 417/482. Telegram from High Commissioner, Johannesburg, to Acting Administrator of North Western Rhodesia, Livingstone, about MacNamara. April 11, 1910.
30. PRO/CO 417/485. Letter from Imperial Secretary C. H. Rodwell to Harrison. September 13, 1910. Gann and Duignan refer to a 1909 case of an early official, R. A. Osborne, who had flogged and fined and then sacked his African cook, whom he found sleeping with his "African wife." L. H. Gann and Peter Duignan, *The Rulers of British Africa, 1870–1914* (Stanford: Stanford University Press, 1978), pp. 241, 387 n. 56.
31. PRO/CO 417/482. Letter from Imperial Secretary C. H. Rodwell to C. N. B. Venables. April 21, 1910.
32. PRO/CO 417/493. Letter from Venables to the Imperial Secretary. May 11, 1910.

High Commissioner Lord Gladstone read Venables's letter as a straightforward explanation and accepted his statement that although he had had relations with an African woman of superior background, that is, royal descent, he had not practiced concubinage with native women. But he took exception to the implication of the last part of Venables's letter, that the high commissioner was condoning concubinage.[33]

The acting administrator of North Western Rhodesia in Livingstone, L. A. Wallace, could not let Venables's remarks pass unchallenged either. For when Venables charged that North Eastern and North Western Rhodesia had been administered by officials who kept a harem of native concubines, the persons referred to could only be Codrington, the former resident administrator, and Wallace himself. Codrington died in 1902 and Wallace had never seen or heard any sign of his "plurality of concubines." If the statement referred to himself, "it could so easily be proved to be an absolute lie without the most far fetched, most flimsy foundation on fact." Wallace was perturbed because of the publication of a recent novel that featured Codrington under a scarcely disguised name as administrator of North Western Rhodesia and told the same story of an administrator of North Eastern Rhodesia "with the same morbid presumption of official vice."[34]

These dispatches highlight the sensitivity of the sexuality issue. While in the official view concubinage had been condoned in the pioneer days and perhaps accepted as a liability of hunting and trading life, it could not continue. Metropolitan prudery had to be reckoned with. To that effect a confidential letter was circulated throughout the BSAC territories.[35] The amount of disagreement it engendered reveals that the practice was more widespread than the administration figured.

Local dissent, and the ambivalence surrounding the sexuality issue, is brought out squarely in a letter sent by the acting administrator of North Eastern Rhodesia at Fort Jameson to the high commissioner in South Africa in response to the circular on concubinage. In L. P. Beaufort's opinion:

---

33. Ibid. Letter from the Imperial Secretary to Venables. June 6, 1910.

34. Ibid. Letter from L. A. Wallace to Lord Gladstone, September 30, 1910.

35. The confidential letter on concubinage mentioned in the colonial correspondence has not been retained in the official files. It is *not* the confidential circular on concubinage issued by the Colonial Office in London in 1909 and distributed in two different versions to a selection of colonial dependencies. That 1909 circular was not distributed in the areas over which the high commissioner in South Africa was in charge, i.e., Basutoland, Bechuanaland, Southern Rhodesia, and North Western Rhodesia, nor was it sent to North Eastern Rhodesia, then under the Crown Colonies Department. PRO/CO 854/196. Colonies General. Circular Despatches. Confidential and Secret Circulars, 1907–1915. Longhand list of distribution of circulars. January 11, 1909. See also Ronald Hyam, "Concubinage and the Colonial Service: The Crewe Circular (1909)," *Journal of Imperial and Commonwealth History* 14 (1986): 170–186.

Concubinage of a European with a single native woman, maintained with constancy and decently veiled, stands on a footing so different (from promiscuity, libertinage, and general incontinence) that it would be of very doubtful justice or expediency to condemn it before it had given rise to scandal or trouble. . . . Were I to be told that any proved case of concubinage, apart from its ill consequences, should be severely dealt with, I should doubt the wisdom of the order.

Such a concubinage is often defended on many grounds, e.g., a. health, b. the acquirement of native language, c. ideas and mode of thought, d. and the warning of projected crimes and risings. It has been e. of material comfort and advantage to many a lonely European, f. it is not the least degrading to the women of this country, nor the least likely in itself to give rise to native trouble, g. if it does not enhance the official's status in the native eye, it at least saves him from the contempt of many among them and from the suspicion of the worst moral state they are apt to impute to a man living by himself.

Concluding, Beaufort remarked: "if [the circular] is intended to threaten displeasure at every case of concubinage, I would respectfully dissent from its expedience or justice."[36] To this, the high commissioner duly but tersely replied that it was both undesirable and impossible that the practice of concubinage with native women, which "repeatedly had been the cause of great scandal in the past," should receive either countenance or condonation.[37]

Concubinage, as described in these dispatches, implied enjoyment first and sin as an afterthought. White men wanted to have their cake and eat it too, decently veiled, and the colonial administration, at least at this point in time, was unable to regulate local sexual mores. Of MacNamara, a later source reports that he was reinstated after a temporary suspension and became employed at Livingstone as a labor agent.[38] And the story continued of Venables, who had helped stir the uproar. Enjoying a very comfortable remittance from Britain, on his farm about 1912, "he didn't live alone by any means. His companions were half a dozen little maids, who he insisted were all daughters of chieftains and princesses in their own right."[39]

Concubinage persisted in Northern Rhodesia, not only in outlying districts but in the towns along the line-of-rail, among prospectors, traders of

36. PRO/CO 417/484. Confidential Letter from Acting Administrator of North Eastern Rhodesia L. P. Beaufort to the South African High Commissioner. October 4, 1910. In all the records consulted for this region, this is the only one containing a reference to homosexuality, albeit obliquely.
37. PRO/CO 417/484. Letter from Lord Gladstone to Beaufort. November 14, 1910.
38. Tom Chicken, "Memoirs of Abandoned Bomas No. 3: Ibwe Munyama, Part 2," *Northern Rhodesia Journal* 3 (1958), 419. But see MacPherson, *Anatomy*, p. 125, who disputes this.
39. Hughes, "Kafue-Namwala," p. 106.

various nationalities, and officials, and everyone knew of it. As white society became increasingly race conscious, British people in positions of influence, like Beaufort, made a great fuss, emphasizing the need at least to cloak the practice. "Not even the lowest [white man] on the social and moral scale would ever dream of offending the susceptibilities of white women by parading his black paramour in a place where white women lived," commented a newspaper contributor after a visit to Elizabethville in the Congo in 1912. "Not so the Belgians in Katanga." This incensed writer described how he had seen a fully uniformed Belgian officer walk down Elizabethville's main avenue arm in arm with his native woman and in passing greet a white woman accompanied by her husband. He had on another occasion refused to be seated at a Belgian officer's table laid out for three until the "unofficial black wife" had been relegated to the kitchen.[40] In Northern Rhodesia, although the practice normally was never discussed openly, concubinage was considered acceptable so long as white men did not display their black mistresses in public. That opinion persisted among some segments of white society up to the eve of independence when one of them, who disapproved of the way developments were turning, said to a friend: "I don't 'old with it. I don't 'old with it—. They will be dancing with 'em next."[41]

"Miscegenation certainly occurred," states Gann, though "its full extent is difficult to gauge. . . . Documentary and verbal evidence . . . makes it seem likely that intermingling occurred more often than the census figures indicate; it is likely that the enumerations failed to keep count of a number of coloured children living with their mothers in the villages.[42] These children lived "in the manner of the Africans," as members of the legislative council termed it in later years when they with embarrassment recognized the "unfortunate practices leading to the production of half-castes . . . in earlier days." Such children were distinguished from those who lived "after the manner of Europeans . . . many of whose fathers were men of good standing and education, university men, civil servants, expert engineers, etc."[43] Those special few, that is, the African women kept on a long-term basis by men such as Davidson and Stephenson, became the founding ancestresses of descent groups that are readily recognizable in Zambia today.

But such men were exceptions. Most white men took African women in the way they had taken everything else, land and labor, and when it was not forthcoming, then by force. Regardless of the purported motive of

40. "Conditions in Katanga," *Livingstone Mail*, December 14, 1912, p. 7.
41. Gervas Clay, personal communication, January 15, 1986.
42. Gann, *History*, p. 184.
43. Northern Rhodesia. *Legislative Council Debates* 33 (1939); May 20–June 6, cols. 196–197.

replacing slavery with civilized trade, huntes, traders and prospectors, missionaries, and administrators were all in search of game—trophies and ivory, mineral wealth, customers, souls, land, or subjects to administer. The use of extraeconomic means in this process has been well documented but its sexual dimension has barely been explored.[44] As African men were coerced into wage labor through the tax nexus, so many African women were taken from their local groups at white men's behest and against their own wishes. Chirupula's infatuation with his "ebony Venus" seems an exception and is perhaps overdramatized by his romanticizing biographer.[45]

Glimpses of how white men got their "game" exist among the evidence in the MacNamara and Harrison cases in 1910. Men servants would be dispatched to a village to find a woman. Sometimes a chief or headman would be asked if he had a young woman to spare; at other times servants would procure women, using their powers of persuasion or coercion. Presents, such as a shawl or money, might pass hands as well. To please their masters, servants would at times bring them women without having been asked. These women would then stay at the white man's place for the night, or a few days. While on tour as well, white men would seek out women for sex. Once MacNamara "had come all through the district and had not been able to get a girl; at each village [he] only saw the old hags who brought out the grain."[46] When taking a woman, the white man or his African servant might inquire about her marital status. Unmarried girls seem to have been preferred, perhaps to avoid troubles with husbands, fathers, or guardians. Yet a Lala woman implicated in the *Graham* v. *Harrison* case was divorced by her husband on her return from Harrison's.[47] Thus not all African men may have approved the practice.

The relationship of the pioneering generation of white men to Africa and her peoples was thus largely one of an expropriation. Such relations helped create, among others, the twin characters of the male domestic servant and the cook's woman, who, however, became differentially incorporated into the racially divided and class-structured society that was taking shape around them: African men providing labor power and African women providing sexual services. In this new division of labor, African men performed a role that had no parallel in the societies from which they came, whereas women's role was constructed in terms of their sex and by functions assumed to be primordial. Whites saw African women, as I discuss shortly, as

44. On coercion, see Macpherson, *Anatomy*, pp. 57–201; on imperial history and sex, see Hyam, "Empire and Sexual Opportunity."

45. Rukavina, *Jungle Pathfinder*, p. 62.

46. PRO/CO 417/482. Guimbi Subdistrict Inquiry, North Western Rhodesia. Extracts from the evidence, *Venables* v. *MacNamara*, pp. 343–344. April 25, 1910.

47. PRO/CO 417/483. Mkushi District Inquiry, North Western Rhodesia. Extracts from the evidence, *Graham* v. *Harrison*, p. 127. January 1910.

available Madgalens. The administrators' discussion about concubines and cohabitation is therefore more than a tempest in a teacup: it reaches to the core of the nature and definition of the relation of white to black and is of course centrally concerned with the construction of sexuality.

Black and White Perils

White reactions to sex between men of the dominant race and women of a conquered race have varied widely. In his comparative historical analysis, George Fredrickson has shown that white South Africans condoned such relations much longer than the white colonists in North America. Such reactions do change, however, and by the period covered in this chapter—that is, from the beginning of this century up to World War II—white South Africa had closed in upon itself and had made such relations illegal under the law. Fredrickson attributes this development to differences in the social and political conditions in the two societies. In his view, such conditions serve better to explain white reactions to race mixing than do cultural ideas of, for example, attractivenes or compatibility,[48] or at least they are more readily supportable from the historical record.

Sexual relations between white men and African women and a convention of employing men servants persisted longer in Northern Rhodesia than in the countries to the south. This persistence was due in part to demography and economic and political developments that helped texture the sexual aspect of the system of race relations in different ways in the north and the south.

In the early 1900s, the white-to-black population ratio and the proportion of white women to white men were much higher in the south than in Northern Rhodesia. The white South African population had by then established a sense of civilized life in which white women's presence was a powerful incentive to end concubinage. White Southern Rhodesians, although they lagged behind their South African neighbors in these respects, were already intent on creating a white man's country in the territory and on getting rid of BASC rule, and they were far ahead of Northern Rhodesia in terms of population and sex ratios.[49] The economies of South Africa and

48. George M. Fredrickson, *White Supremacy: A Comparative Study in American and South African History* (New York: Oxford University Press, 1981), p. 125.

49. In South Africa in 1904 there were 111,700 whites and 349,100 Africans, and in 1911 the whites formed 21.4 percent of the total population, according to Pierre L. van den Berghe, *South Africa: A Study in Conflict* (Berkeley: University of California Press, 1970), p. 288, table 2. There were 431 white women to 569 white men per 1,000 in 1904, a ratio that had evened out by 1926 to 490 women to 510 men, according to *Southern Rhodesia. Report of the Director of Census, Regarding the Census Taken on the 4th May, 1926,* Part I (Salisbury: Government Printer, 1927), p. 14. In 1904 in Southern Rhodesia there were 12,623 whites (*South Africa: Census Returns of British South Africa* [London: HMSO, 1904], p. 20), and

Southern Rhodesia were more developed than in the north, where the white population was small and dispersed across the country in tiny settlements that grew slowly till the postdepression if not the post–World War II years (see Tables 2 and 3). In the context of this fairly unsettled and scattered white population whose self-consciousness and community were still in the process of being formed, white women householders' efforts to create and uphold a civilized way of life turned into anxiety. "Civilization" was threatened by crossracial sex between white men and African women. "European women," according to Gann, "were incensed at the idea of liaisons between white men and black women which they considered to be degrading to both, while men, especially those living on lonely farms, sometimes worried what might happen to their womenfolk if they were left alone amidst backward tribesmen."[50] This statement is only partially correct. White women disliked the thought or the knowledge of sexual involvements between white men and African women. But numerous observers, who lived in or passed through Northern Rhodesia, commented on the unproblematic relationship between white women and African men, and I return to this issue shortly.

The sexual anxiety in Northern Rhodesia centered on African women, not men. This fact helps explain why whites in the north did not share the "black peril" hysteria that swept South Africa and Southern Rhodesia before World War I, when white women on an unprecedented scale accused their African menservants of rape. In my view, this difference between north and south was shaped by the nature and extent of white men's sexual encounters with African women in the early decades of settlement in Northern Rhodesia, by the persistence and condoning of such practices during later years, and, as I discuss below, by the image whites constructed of African women's sexuality. "Nothing so embittered 'race relations' in urban South Africa before the First World War," comments Charles van Onselen in his dramatic study of the Rand, "as these 'black peril' scares, and nothing has been so little studied."[51] Since the Southern Rhodesian scare has to my knowledge received scant scholarly attention, and since news of it filtered across the Zambezi, I have chosen to discuss it to highlight the contrasting sexual anxieties of the two territories.

---

289 white women to 711 white men per 1,000. The unbalanced white sex ratios had evened out by 1926 to 443 women to 557 men per 1,000 (*Southern Rhodesia: Report . . . of Census*, p. 14). In Northern Rhodesia (see Table 2) the white population numbered only 850 in 1904. I have found no white sex ratios for that year. Only by 1946 had the white sex ratio in Northern Rhodesia evened out to 91.0 women to 100 men (see Table 3), yet by 1956 it had dropped to 83.0 women to 100 men. The early censuses in Southern and Northern Rhodesia give no estimates for the white proportion of the total population.

50. Gann, *History*, p. 200.

51. Charles van Onselen, *Studies in the Social and Economic History of the Witwatersrand, 1886–1914*, vol. 2, *New Nineveh* (London: Longman, 1982), pp. 45–46.

Southern Rhodesian and South African whites were outraged when the high commissioner in South Africa, Lord Gladstone, in 1910 commuted the death sentence of houseboy Alukuleta, who was alleged to have attempted to rape a white woman in Umtali, a town on the border between Southern Rhodesia and Portuguese East Africa. Letters to the press called for stringent laws to protect white women. There were mass meetings in Bulawayo and on the Rand in March 1911.[52] "The Women of Rhodesia," that is, Southern Rhodesia, sent a petition to the secretary of state for the colonies, calling for protection by the law, explaining, "Our homes lie in scattered townships and on isolated farms, and we are alone for the greater part of the day with male natives, who are practically the sole domestic servants obtainable. These natives are only savages, often thus brought in contact for the first time with civilization. . . . [White] men could not bring their wives here, nor rear their daughters in this country without making stringent laws to protect them."[53] There is evidence of scattered "black peril" cases in Southern Rhodesia during subsequent years.[54] Yet "black peril" was not objectively a real epidemic of rapes by black men of white women in that country. It was rather a subjective construct of the white mind, a product of social interaction informed by a master-servant relationship, the logistics of which intimately threatened the hierarchical structure of the white colonial household. The class barrier, masked by race, had to be maintained, and in both South Africa and Southern Rhodesia laws against intermarriage and miscegenation between white men and African women were passed.[55] The underlying sentiment is expressed in one of many

52. NAZIM/S 144/4,5. BSAC Administration. Black Peril, 1910–1912. See also Philip Mason, *The Birth of a Dilemma: The Conquest and Settlement of Rhodesia* (London: Oxford University Press, 1958), pp. 246–253, and Dane Kennedy, *Islands of White: Settler Society and Culture in Kenya and Southern Rhodesia, 1890–1939* (Durham, N.C.: Duke University Press, 1987), pp. 138–147.

53. PRO/CO 417/496 no. 141. The Black Peril, Southern Rhodesia. Petition from the Women of Rhodesia, 1911.

54. Rape statistics were collected in Southern Rhodesia at least through 1918. About 30 cases were reported in 1911 in which African men were charged with crimes of rape or attempted rape of white women but in none was the death penalty imposed (PRO/CO 417/511 no. 311. Rape Statistics, Southern Rhodesia. 1911 returns). Of the 32 cases dealt with in court during the first half of 1912, 2 concerned alleged rape of white women, 6 of white children under twelve years, and the rest concerned rape of African women; no death sentences were passed (PRO/CO 417/512 no. 465. Rape Statistics, Southern Rhodesia. 1912 returns). There were 59 incidents reported for all races in 1916, 54 in 1917, and 52 in 1918. No death sentences were passed in any of these cases, the majority of which involved Africans rather than whites. Most of the African men who were convicted and given varying sentences were found guilty of assaults with the attempt to commit rape (PRO/CO 417/617. Rape Statistics, Southern Rhodesia. 1918 returns). Rape statistics may have been collected beyond the years for which I have been able to find statistics.

55. In South Africa, the Immorality Act of 1927 outlawed sexual intercourse between whites and Africans. Marriage between whites and all nonwhites was outlawed in 1949 under the Prohibition of Mixed Marriages Act. In 1950 and 1957 the Immorality Act of 1927 was

letters to newspaper editors in the wake of "the social scare" signed by Mrs. Robert Crawford Hawkin (Marie Botha Hawkin), sister of General Botha: "I have often heard strangers to South Africa express wonderment at the rigour of our authority over the blacks. They do not realize that if white men with their women are to live in a black country they can do so only as masters."[56] Some of these letters called for the recruitment of African women into domestic service to avoid problems between African menservants and their white madams. In 1905 a report was compiled on the issue by the South African Native Affairs Commission, which recommended promoting the employment of African women domestics.[57] Yet, till the 1930s, most domestic servants on the Rand were men, whereas at the Cape more women, especially coloureds, were working in this occupation.[58] And in 1930 in Southern Rhodesia, the premier suggested and the legislative assembly requested a commission to inquire into the question of employing African women as servants. Its report did not support the suggestion.[59] The Federation of Women's Institutes of Southern Rhodesia had in the late 1920s conducted a survey of white attitudes to African women domestics, submitting a memorandum about their findings to the premier and suggesting that he appoint the above-mentioned committee. Among those who supplied information was the widow of a BSAC administrator, Mrs. E. Tawsee Jollie, a well-known author and the first woman elected to the legislative assembly. She objected to employing men in service because of the "black peril" threat. But aside from herself, she told the FWI, only missionaries employed servant girls in Southern Rhodesia.[60]

In 1910, in the charged atmosphere characterized by angry outcries about the Umtali case, High Commissioner Lord Gladstone commented on the suggestion to recruit African women as servants: "female domestic

---

amended to prohibit intercourse between whites and all nonwhite groups. These laws persisted till 1985. Legislation about immorality and intermarriage was instituted in Southern Rhodesia in 1903 in the Immorality Suppression Ordinance, by which a white woman convicted of illicit intercourse with an African might be sentenced to two years of hard labor, and the African to five years. An act of 1916 made it an offense for a white woman to make indecent suggestions to an African man and for an African man to make such overtures to a white woman; but such behavior was not criminal between a white man and an African woman. For discussion, see Mason, *Birth of a Dilemma,* pp. 238–253.

56. NAZIM/S 144/4. BSAC Administration. "The Umtali Case." Newspaper clippings, letters to the editor, 1911.

57. Cited in Deborah Gaitskell, "'Christian Compounds for Girls': Church Hostels for African Women in Johannesburg, 1907–1970," *Journal of Southern African Studies* 6 (1979): 45.

58. Deborah Gaitskell et al., "Race, Class, and Gender: Domestic Workers in South Africa," *Review of African Political Economy* 27/28 (1984): 86–108.

59. NAZIM/S 1561/48. Female Domestic Labour. Labour Memoranda and Minutes, 1941–1947. Report on Native Female Domestic Service. November 17, 1932.

60. Ibid. Report of the Standing Committee on Domestic Service by the Federation of Women's Institutes of Southern Rhodesia, pp. 63–64.

servants are not a practical possibility till the Matabele and Mashonas advance sufficiently to see that their women are better employed thus than in doing most of the hard labour . . . on the land."[61] To these comments he annexed a short memorandum, "[The] Native Servant Problem," in which he referred to practical difficulties and argued that the suggestion was "utterly opposed to native sentiment: a native, asked to allow his daughter to be trained in the service of a European Lady, would view the matter in much the same way as an Essex farmer would a proposal that his daughter should proceed to London to enter service as a coachman or chauffeur." He concluded that women in Rhodesia, for a long time to come, would have to be served by males, meaning "very small boys, seldom over the age of 12 and often much younger."[62]

Among the practical difficulties the high commissioner alluded to was the "white peril": the reversal of the sex and race relationship which exposed African women to sexual advances and/or attacks by white men. A few of the letters mentioned the "white peril" and that African women had no way of saying no when approached by their masters. "We may not forget," noted a writer in a Southern Rhodesian newspaper in 1911, "that from the side of the native there is a White Peril. It is common knowledge that in these parts native women are not immune to the attentions of men, whose skins may be white, but who are white men in no other senses."[63] The same year one reader wrote to one of the South African papers: "Thousands of young natives and coloured women are seduced by white men. . . . I believe the crime of a white man in seducing a native girl to be quite as great as rape committed by a black man upon a white woman."[64]

If, *pace* van Onselen, "black peril" scares are central to understanding the white attitudes and ideology that structured race relations in South Africa, and, we may add, Southern Rhodesia, then their absence from Northern Rhodesia was a result of a very different climate of opinion. Richard Gray made this suggestion and included Nyasaland, from where at the time of his writing in 1960 not one case of rape of a white woman by a black man was recorded. Comparing and contrasting the racial policies of the south and the north, he noted that the situation in Nyasaland was less conducive to sexual hysteria since most whites there thought of themselves as paternal trustees. But in Northern Rhodesia policy ideas clashed, for the settler segment of the white population wanted to create another white

61. PRO/CO 417/496 no. 142. Case of Alukuleta. Memorandum by High Commissioner Lord Gladstone. March 29, 1911, p. 99.
62. Ibid., p. 100.
63. NAZIM/S 144/5. BSAC Administration. "Black Peril." Newspaper clippings.
64. Ibid.

man's country as in the south, while white colonial officials called for a liberal interpretation of paternal trusteeship.[65]

Gray's reading of Northern Rhodesian historical records is somewhat misleading. For there had indeed been cases of rape of white women by black men during the period he refers to. They were, however, very few in number and, unlike in the south, they did not give rise to collective hysteria. While Gray is correct in stating, not that none, but that very few "black peril cases" have been brought to light from Northern Rhodesia, he is so for the wrong reasons. His explanation telescopes political ideologies that belong to the era of the 1930s and after. But during the period in question, that is, from the turn of the century through World War I, Northern Rhodesia was very much influenced by the south, economically as well as politically. The absence of the "black peril" scare in Northern Rhodesia had less to do with politics and economics than with sexual assumptions and demography in this much later and unevenly settled, and fitfully administered, part of the subcontinent. There were as yet few white women in Northern Rhodesia. When the Colonial Office took over its administration in 1924, it was still very much man's country. The sexual anxiety here continued to center on African women.

The different texturing of the sexual aspect of the system of race relations in the north and the south was acknowledged in the regional discourse in several ways. Cullen Gouldsbury, a BSAC official in Northern Rhodesia from 1908, had been employed in Southern Rhodesia from 1902. A prolific writer of prose and poetry, his 1907 novel *God's Outpost*, set in Southern Rhodesia, caused a stir among the local whites and was withdrawn from circulation, apparently by the BSAC.[66] In it, Gouldsbury allowed local gossip to construe as sexual the relationship between a white male missionary and a young Shona woman. This affair might have been too much for the class- and race-conscious Southern Rhodesians, and the suggestion has been made that the publication of the book was the reason for Gouldsbury's transfer to the remote north.[67] Best-selling Southern Rhodesian author Gertrude Page wrote several novels but only one deals with interracial sex—and in it, significantly, she situates her plot in Northern, not Southern, Rhodesia. Her *Silent Rancher* is in all likelihood the novel that Acting Administrator L. A. Wallace referred to in his correspondence with the high commissioner in South Africa on concubinage. Page's brother was a

65. Richard Gray, *The Two Nations: Aspects of the Development of Race Relations in the Rhodesias and Nyasaland* (London: Oxford University Press, 1960), pp. 181–194.

66. Publisher's introduction to Cullen Gouldsbury, *Rhodesian Rhymes* (Bulawayo: Books of Rhodesia, 1969), p. 6

67. Anthony John Chennels, "Settler Myths and the Southern Rhodesian Novel" (Ph.D. diss., University of Zimbabwe, 1982), mentions this, p. 418 n. 23.

farmer at Fort Jameson from whom she was likely to have had firsthand accounts of the local scene.[68] The "black harem" of the administrator in her book was common knowledge, and it was brought to his prospective white bride's attention during her ship passage. The woman passenger who breaks the news feels that "the mere idea [of miscegenation] outrages the white woman," and that it is "a grave evil menacing [the country's] future." When she informs the prospective bride about the matter, she explains to her that many white women overlook their husband's sexual habits. "They have very little choice. Some do not mind. It hits you harder . . . because . . . you are naturally so ideal . . . and unsophisticated."[69]

Although the northern whites heard about the southern "black peril" hysteria, they did not share it. They read the newspapers from the south, and from 1906 the *Livingstone Mail* provided extensive commentaries on the situation. According to my own reading, a total of seven "black peril" cases were commented on in the press between 1906 and 1931,[70] and the newspaper's editor took particular pains to stress their rarity. In his response to a letter to the editor, for example, he noted that the writer's "reference to 'Black Peril' cases suggests that they are common, whereas we know they are not."[71]

The editorial commentaries explain the difference between Northern Rhodesia and the countries to the south by referring to the presence in South Africa of "riff-raff," that is, working-class whites who did not know what proper standards were and allowed themselves to be taken advantage of, and to half-educated African servants who did not keep their place. Northerners did not always agree with the outcome of the legal cases in the south. For example, Sam Lewis from Bulawayo was brought to trial for shooting his African servant Titus, who was alleged to have made indecent

68. Ibid.

69. Gertrude Page, *The Silent Rancher* (London: Hurst and Blackett, 1909), pp. 272, 282.

70. The first case, heard in court in March 1911, involved an African servant charged with burglary and the intent to commit rape of a white woman in Livingstone. He received six months' hard labor and 20 strokes with the cane: *Livingstone Mail*, March 4 (1911), p. 10, and September 16 (1911), p. 4. A case in Livingstone in 1914 concerned an African servant charged with intent to commit rape of a railway ganger's sixteen-and-a-half-year-old daughter. He was sentenced to five years' hard labor during which he was to be "treated like a savage beast," and given 24 lashes of the cane: *Livingstone Mail*, March 20 (1914), p. 3, and March 27 (1914), p. 7. A kitchen boy at the North Western Hotel in Livingstone was taken to court for having entered the bedrom of a white woman guest with the intent to commit rape in 1924. He got five years' hard labor and 24 lashes of the cane: *Livingstone Mail*, April 19 (1923), p. 4. In Broken Hill in 1924 a houseboy was taken to court for having hidden himself in the closet of a fourteen-year-old white girl: *Livingstone Mail*, November 13 (1924), p. 4. Another case was reported in 1925: *Livingstone Mail*, February 26 (1925), p. 7, and two were brought to court during 1931, one involving an alleged attack by an African servant of a white woman in bed: *Livingstone Mail*, August 26 (1931), p.10, and one an indecent assault, involving an African servant charged with molesting a white child: *Livingstone Mail* September 23 (1931), p. 3.

71. *Livingstone Mail*, February 26, 1925, p. 7.

overtures to Lewis's daughter. Although the shooting took place long after the incident, Lewis was acquitted by the white jury. In the north, according to the editor of the *Livingstone Mail*, while making "allowance for the abnormal conditions in [Southern] Rhodesia, the general opinion seems to be that the acquittal was a miscarriage of justice."[72]

The difference between the north and the south is delineated by other writers as well. G. Heaton Nicholls, later a famous political figure in South Africa, was employed by the BSAC in Northern Rhodesia from 1902 to 1907, first as a member of the police force to train the Barotse native constabulary and later as a district officer headquartered at Mumbwa.[73] His novel *Bayete! "Hail to the King"!*, written in South Africa in 1915, draws on some of his experiences in the north and involves (in a sensationalist plot) a case of "black peril" in South Africa. In the course of the narrative, one of his protagonists comments: "no case has occurred in native areas where white women are leading lonely lives in perfect safety amidst a teeming native population. The crimes are the product of our cities . . . and are the result of our indiscretions, not to put it more mildly." His visitor, stationed north of the Zambezi, agrees with him: "The White women in Zambezia are treated with the utmost respect by natives. . . . in their wild state they respect the whites."[74] Cullen Gouldsbury is one of several writers who echo this sentiment. He described how he would leave his wife by herself at night, with some *askaris* around the boma to be sure, when he was away on *ulendo*. To do so would be impossible, he contended, in civilized South Africa. But in the north, "a native would as soon purloin the offerings of flour from his village god's hut or the trinkets of beads from his brother's grave as attempt a criminal assault upon a white woman."[75]

According to these texts white women householders in Northern Rhodesia commonly employed African menservants without much ado about sex. They used the language of culture and difference rather than of sexual fear to speak of their concerns and problems with African menservants. Although some incidents of "black peril" took place during later years, they were shaped by different forces from those in the south.[76] But during the period preceding Colonial Office administration very few such cases oc-

72. "Sam Lewis Case," *Livingstone Mail*, August 19, 1911, p. 6, and "The Sam Lewis Case," *Livingstone Mail*, August 26, 1911, p. 7.

73. G. Heaton Nicholls, *South Africa in My Time* (London: Allen and Unwin, 1961), pp. 43–67.

74. G. Heaton Nicholls, *Bayete! "Hail to the King"!* (London: Allen and Unwin, 1923).

75. Cullen Gouldsbury, *An African Year* (London: Edward Arnold, 1912), pp. 70–71. See also, Owen Letcher, *Big Game Hunting in North-Eastern Rhodesia* (London: John Long, 1911), p. 231.

76. The incidents referred to by Gray, *Two Nations*, were described in the unpublished evidence given to the Royal Commission on Rhodesia and Nyasaland, 1938, the so-called Bledisloe Commission.

curred. That the sexual anxiety in Northern Rhodesia at this time revolved around African women can to some extent be explained by such demographic factors as the white population's disparate sex ratio and some white men's using African women to fulfill their sexual desires. Further, the system of contract migrant male labor may explain why white women chose African men for their domestic servants, since according to that system, African women were supposed to remain in the villages. Yet there were loopholes in the system, and African women did migrate to the towns from early on. If African women were available for sporadic sexual contact or prolonged cohabitation with white and African men in towns, they certainly formed part of the potential labor supply from which white women could have recruited their servants. What demography and the migrant labor system do not explain, then, is the sexual image of the African woman which was constructed in the white mind and provoked anxiety in white women's mind.

Images of African Women

African women's sexuality is a well-worked theme in the literature.[77] To be sure, the image of African women which I derive from reading texts from the period of early white settlement in Northern Rhodesia is fairly similar to that painted by sources from other parts of Africa: the black woman as a creature of exaggerated sensuality, almost animallike, hot blooded, precocious, of "easy virtue." But although the theme is widespread throughout the continent, its constituent elements were combined in a variety of ways in different regions, and the resulting permutations are far from incidental. In Northern Rhodesia, the piecing together of disparate impressions about African women produced a discourse that accentuated their sexuality much more dramatically than was the case in the countries to the south. The Southern Rhodesian literature also depicts African women as immoral, but their immorality is far less essential and pervasive than it is seen to be in the north.[78] As I suggested earlier, it was this image

77. See Philip Curtin, *The Image of Africa: British Ideas and Action, 1780–1850* (Madison: University of Wisconsin Press, 1964), p. 216; Dorothy Hammond and Alta Jablow, *The Africa That Never Was: Four Centuries of British Writing about Africa* (New York: Twayne Publishers, 1970), pp. 148–156; and Winthrop D. Jordan, *White over Black: American Attitudes toward the Negro, 1550–1812* (Baltimore: Penquin Books, 1971), pp. 32–40.

78. For early studies from Southern Rhodesia, see D. Carnegie, *Among the Matabele* (London: Religious Tract Society, 1894; reprint, Westport, Conn.: Negro Universities Press, 1970), and F. W. T. Posselt, *Fact and Fiction: A Short Account of the Natives of Southern Rhodesia* (1935; facsimile reprint, Bulawayo: Books of Rhodesia, 1978). Among later studies, see W. Bazeley, "Manyika Headwomen," *NADA* 17 (1940): 3–5; H. C. Childs, "Family and Tribal Structure and the Status of Women," *NADA* 35 (1958): 65–70; Michael Gelfand, *African Crucible: An Ethno-Religious Study with Special Reference to the Shona-Speaking*

of the "oversexed" African woman which fostered anxiety among the northern whites about the "white peril" while their southern neighbors feared the black.

This image arose from whites' reactions to the African societies they encountered in Northern Rhodesia, and in particular from whites' perception of these Africans' social organization, kinship and marriage practices—their flexible marriage arrangements, polygyny, polyandry and matriliny—as manifestations of immorality. The commonality of the two latter practices distinguished Northern Rhodesia from its southern neighbors.[79]

What sources were available up through the 1920s to inform local whites about the societies in the middle of which they lived? There were "ethnographies" consisting of the observations made by missionaries and administrators; there was a prolific travel literature; and there were more detailed memoirs and autobiography. This literature has been used by scholars for a variety of purposes.[80] Here I offer but a few glimpses of the white discourse about local African sexual mores, an issue not distilled out and dealt with in the works most usually referred to.

The Ila, for example, a cattle holding, fishing, and horticultural society on the Kafue flats, received "bad press" from the early days. William Chapman, a missionary of the Primitive Methodist society who had worked in their region since 1905, wrote in 1911: "[they] are a people whose national business is polygyny, their national pastime beer drinking, and their national sport fornication."[81] J. H. Venning spent time at Kalomo during World War I. In his memoirs of life in Northern Rhodesia from 1893 to 1962, he described the Ila as the "most immoral tribe in the country, but

---

People (Cape Town, 1960), and also his "The Shona Attitude to Sex Behavior," *NADA* 9 (1967): 61–64.

79. Matriliny and polyandry were also widespread in the neighboring country to the north, the Congo, and some of the points I make about African women and sexuality may perhaps apply there as well. Because the countries to the south provided the reference point for contrasts and comparisons when white Northern Rhodesians discussed labor policy and native administration, I have not explored the discourse on sex in texts from the Congo in any detail. In the Congo, African men dominated in domestic service. White women, commented an observer of household relations in the capital in the mid-1940s: "generally prefer . . . to be served by men or boy servants. [They] have one hundred good reasons to prove that it is not preference but sheer necessity, the most obvious being that men are already trained to do that kind of work. . . . At the bottom of their dislike for women servants . . . is the underlying fear of the attraction of the black woman for the European man." Suzanne Comhaire-Sylvain, "Food and Leisure among African Youth of Leopoldville (Belgian Congo)," University of Cape Town, *Communications from the School of African Studies,* new series no. 25 (1950), p. 54.

80. Cairns, *Prelude,* delineates British reactions to Central African society in the half decade preceding the imposition of BSAC rule from 1840 to 1890. Rotberg, *Christian Missionaries,* details the role of missionaries in "opening up" Northern Rhodesia over the period leading to direct colonial rule in 1924. Macpherson, *Anatomy,* has added Zambian sources to demonstrate the coercive nature of the conquest.

81. Cited in Rotberg, *Christian Missionaries,* p. 40.

one should rather call them amoral . . . [for they] seemed devoid of any moral code in matters of sex."[82] In Edwin Smith and Andrew Dale's two-volume ethnography from 1920, the discourse is much the same. The authors, a missionary and a BSAC magistrate begin their chapter about relations between the sexes with this effusion of offense at their subject:

> there is much that is unpleasant in this part of our subject. [But] to write of the Ba-Ila and omit all reference to sex would be like writing of the sky and leaving out the sun; for sex is the most pervasive element of their life. It is the atmosphere into which children are brought. Their early years are largely a preparation for the sexual function; during the years of maturity it is their most ardent pursuit, and old age is spent in vain and disappointing endeavours to continue it. Sex overtones all else. . . . To them, the union of the sexes is on the same plane as eating and drinking, to be indulged in without stint on every possible occasion.[83]

Dale and Smith also noted that while men and women might indulge their sexual instincts, they must respect proprietary rights. A woman's sexuality was her husband's property; he might give a friend this right just like he might offer a meal; but if the friend took without permission he might be fined. "It is," they stated, "a matter of property, not moral reprobation."[84]

According to Dale and Smith, all Ila men wished to marry early and to have as many wives as possible, some of whom were slaves who lived as concubines. The Ila also practiced a type of polyandry in which husbands allowed their wives to live with lovers for a shorter or longer period. Adultery was rampant, and, moreover, Ila wives often would "go and prostitute themselves" after making agreement with their husbands, who in turn claimed damages for adultery.[85] The reviewer of Dale and Smith's book was at a loss for words: "this is not for family reading; . . . some portions have been done into Latin, the better to conceal them. . . . Of their sex relations it is impossible to speak here; they are, to a European thinking man, one mass of obscenity."[86]

Dale and Smith were not alone in commenting on polyandry; it was assumed to be widespread. Stephenson discussed its practice among the Lala.[87] Brelsford, who was stationed at Mumbwa in Ila country in the early 1930s, published a paper on *Lubambo*, a type of polyandry, in an anthropo-

82. J. H. Venning, "Memories of My Life in Southern Africa, from 1893 to 1962," unpublished papers deposited at Rhodes House, MSS Afr. S. 1490, p. 121.

83. Edwin W. Smith and Andrew Dale, *The Ila-Speaking Peoples of Northern Rhodesia* (London: MacMillan, 1920), p. 35.

84. Ibid., pp. 35–36.

85. Ibid., pp. 64, 67–69, 72–73.

86. "Review of *The Ila-Speaking Peoples of Northern Rhodesia*," *Livingstone Mail*, December 2 (1920), p. 6.

87. Stephenson, *Chirupula's Tale*, pp. 46, 231.

logical journal.[88] Dugal Campbell, who lived in various parts of this territory for twenty-nine years around the turn of the century as a missionary
and later a labor recruiter for the Katanga mines, noted in his "ethnography" that polyandry was common in Central Africa among the Bemba, the
Lunda, the Luba, and among the Luena of Angola.[89] In later years, during
the 1950s, the "loose morals" of Congolese Kasai women on the copperbelt
were attributed to their polyandrous background.[90]

Matriliny, the organizing principle of the majority of the African societies
within this region, was also seen as predisposing African women toward
immorality. J. M. Moubray, a mining engineer who traveled throughout
the territory between 1903 and 1908 commented in this regard: "In Central
Africa the morals of many tribes are somewhat lax. It is a mistake to
suppose that uncivilised people are generally very moral, this being often
the exception than otherwise. This laxity as regards the moral code is
recognised to such an extent among many of the tribes that, instead of
inheritance passing from father to son, as in European countries, it passes
from father to sister's son."[91]

The image of the sexually free, morally lax African affronted the late
Victorian/early Edwardian British ideals and the assumption that sex was to
be contained within the conjugal bond.[92] The contrast between turn-of-
the-century British social norms and what was considered to be a wild,
primitive, and sexually permissive environment can be seen to have
prompted extreme but different reactions in white men and white women.
White men may have regarded African women as an outlet for sexual
experiences outside those available in the conventional conjugal relationship and may thus have been sexually attracted, whereas white women's
reaction may have combined disgust and envy. Among most African societies in this region, young girls were taught quite explicitly during initia-

88. Vernon Brelsford, "Lubambo: A Description of the Baila Custom," *Journal of the
Royal Anthropological Society of Great Britain and Ireland* 63 (1933): 433–439.

89. Campbell, *In the Heart*, pp. 163–164.

90. John Taylor and Dorothea Lehmann, *Christians of the Copperbelt: The Growth of the
Church in Northern Rhodesia* (London: SMC Press, 1961), p. 73, and Dorothea Lehmann,
"Marriage, Divorce, and Prostitution of African Women in a Changing Society," in *Report of
the Annual Conference of the Northern Rhodesia Council of Social Service on Marriage and
the Family* (Lusaka: Government Printer, 1961), p. 34. For an ethnographic account, see
Mary [Douglas] Tew, "A Form of Polyandry among the Lele of the Kasai," *Africa* 21 (1951):
1–12.

91. J. M. Moubray, *In Central Africa* (London: Constable 1912), p. 69.

92. This ideal and its changes are described by Lawrence Stone, *The Family, Sex, and
Marriage in England, 1500–1800* (New York: Harper and Row, 1979). On sexual attitudes, see
Eric Trudgill, *Madonnas and Magdalens: The Origins and Development of Victorian Sexual
Attitudes* (New York: Holmes and Meier, 1976), and Peter Gay, who qualifies these observations in many respects in *The Bourgeois Experience: Victoria to Freud*, vol. I, *Education of
the Senses*, and vol. 2, *The Tender Passion* (New York: Oxford University Press, 1984 and
1986).

tion rites how to perform sex and how to please partners.[93] White women's perceptions of African women's sexuality exacerbated their sense of being different and strengthened the need to keep African women out of the colonial household. To lessen sexual anxiety, social distance from African women had to be maintained—by both men and women, as Hammond and Jablow have noted: "an Englishman neither marries, employs, nor befriends an African woman. The only possibility is a *sub rosa* offer, making sexuality the only basis for any relationship at all."[94]

The question of whether the condition of moral laxity existed before contact with whites or was its result was rarely addressed in the literature. One exception is worth noting. It concerns the Lamba, who lived in the area that later developed into the copperbelt. Lamba women were depicted as "champions" among prostitutes during the period of the copperbelt's rapid growth and, much like the Ila, inherently immoral.[95] But Clement M. Doke, a missionary in the Lamba region from 1914 to 1921, in a 1931 monograph tempered the prevailing view with an analysis that vested responsibility with the Europeans: "exaggerated statements have often been made concerning the looseness of the natives of Central Africa. . . . It must be remembered that in these days the introduction of European customs and mode of life, with all the contacts which that means, has undermined tribal control, throwing the social fabric into the melting pot. There are not now those restraints which were potent a few years ago, with the result that today there is certainly a tendency to moral looseness. But we cannot put this down to Lamba social organization, which is definitely opposed to moral laxity."[96] Most whites, however, continued to view African women's "loose morals" as the result of tribal practices. Immorality was a primordial attribute, and African women were therefore dangerous.

Bachelor Towns and the Immorality Issue

The authorities' attempts—no matter how ineffective—to restrict and control African women's movements between villages and towns bear evidence that the image of moral laxity and promiscuity formed during the

93. Audrey I. Richards, *Chisungu: A Girl's Initiation Ceremony among the Bemba of Zambia* (London: Faber and Faber, 1951), C. M. N. White, "Elements in Luvale Beliefs and Rituals," *Rhodes-Livingstone Papers*, no. 32 (1961); and V. W. Turner, *The Drums of Affliction: A Study of Religious Processes among the Ndembu of Zambia* (Oxford: Clarendon Press, 1968).

94. Hammond and Jablow, *Africa That Never Was*, p. 153.

95. Brian Siegel, "The 'Wild' and 'Lazy' Lamba: Ethnic Stigmatization and Resentment on the Central African Copperbelt," paper presented to the International Conference on History of Ethnic Awareness in South Africa, Charlotteville, N.C. April 7–10, 1983.

96. Clement M. Doke, *The Lambas of Northern Rhodesia: A Study of Their Customs and Beliefs* (London: Harrap, 1931), p. 158.

early decades of contact continued to be the operative one in later years. A slight shift in nuance occurred, however, as immorality and promiscuity came increasingly to mean prostitution.

The Ila of Mumbwa subdistrict had already been the subject of much invective concerning sexual matters. Referring to Ila women who had gone off to the line-of-rail towns, Native Commissioner J. W. Sharrat-Home cried out in 1923: "We want the women sent back. In what way will the law assist us?"[97] Because of their laxity in sexual matters, "those who know them best regard the Baila, mainly through this course, as a dying race. . . . the people themselves are largely responsible. . . . free love may be said to be paramount throughout the district."[98] This particular concern about the Ila had arisen because of the poor health, venereal disease, lack of children, and absence of married women and girls noted by officers on tour in the subdistrict. Bringing these observations to the district commissioner's attention, the native commissioner reminded him:

> the Baila (so we learn from the official handbook of the territory) are "chiefly noted for their low state of morality" . . . [and these] remarks [are] not much out of place if applied to the Balenje or Balovale. . . . Morally the sub-district has probably never reached a very high standard, [and] it might now be called the brothel of Northern Rhodesia. . . . Since the advent of civilization and its new standards of wealth for the natives—money, calico, blankets, butcher's meat, and the excitement of compound life—the outward and visible rewards of immorality have become much greater, and women of the sub-district have not been slow to take advantage of the inducements offered.[99]

According to this native commissioner, local Africans first were introduced to these articles of wealth some ten to fifteen years earlier when small mines operated in the region. Nonlocal Africans were brought in to work them; when the mines were closed down, these workers took Ila women with them to the towns. Since then, many unmarried women had begun to "gravitate towards the life of comparative luxury and ease to be secured by selling their bodies to any native wealthy enough. . . . During the past ten years the number of women leaving the district has increased enormously and to-day they are to be counted in hundreds."[100]

97. NAZ/BS 3/303. Prostitution and Temporary Unions of Women of Mumbwa Sub-District in Settled Areas, 1923–1924. Native Commissioner, Mumbwa, to District Commissioner and Magistrate, Mumbwa. February 18, 1923.

98. Ibid. District Commissioner and Magistrate, Mumbwa, to Secretary for Native Affairs, Livingstone. March 4, 1923.

99. Ibid. Native Commissioner at Mumbwa to District Commissioner and Magistrate, Mumbwa, February 18, 1923.

100. Ibid.

This official once again ascribed the problems with the Ila to "the loose-ness of the marriage tie among the natives, and the looseness of their ideas as to what constitutes marriage." According to his observations, there were three ways of forming unions: a nonlocal African man might buy a girl from her Ila family; a woman might make an agreement with a man to live with him as a concubine "and receive clothing and other presents" for her ser-vices; and, there was prostitution, "pure and simple . . . in the narrow sense of the word." Among the prostitutes were unmarried women elders brought out of the district for the purpose of procuration. The official knew three such cases, plus many stories about real trafficking: "I have heard of one case where a woman who had been living with an alien in Livingstone came home and stayed a month or two, and then returned to Livingstone with six unmarried girls . . . [and] of a certain man in the north of the district who makes periodic pilgrimages to the Lubumbashi mine [in the Congo], never with less than 4 or 5 girls." He held that such trafficking took place because aliens wanted and were willing to pay for concubines; wom-en wanted clothes and had no moral compunction about how to get them; and their fathers, usually not approving, were not strong enough to resist the sight of money. And, finally, because an African worker, separated from his rural wife, "being a sensual animal, demands some temporary accommodation. . . . This demand local women do their best to supply."[101]

Colonial male officials ascribed African men's desire for female company solely to their sexual needs; because African women supposedly lacked moral scruples, they readily supplied their services. While they might not be "common prostitutes or streetwalkers," once they came to town, there was little "to prevent them from whoring." Such were the opinions of Magistrate Melland, who raised the issue of controlling women's move-ments "in view of the unsettling effect in the district of a life of prostitution being lived by hundreds of native women; the spread of veneral disease, and especially of the infection of young girls."[102] In a circular letter to the officers in his area he related how he had attempted to reduce the traffic in women in the Kasempa district, by allowing Kasempa headmen to prohibit women and girls from going to towns if they were suspected of prostitution. Women who disobeyed were arrested and fined; some were imprisoned without the option of a fine. Melland suggested that this approach might be successful elsewhere and was advised by the secretary for native affairs that the following orders were likely to be considered reasonable: "a) no unmar-ried woman or married woman unaccompanied by her husband shall leave the district without permission from the Native Commissioner; b) natives

101. Ibid.
102. Ibid. District circular letter from District Commissioner and Magistrate, Mumbwa. July 7, 1923.

of other districts wishing to marry local women must come before the Native Commissioner and satisfy him that Native Custom has been satisfied. No alien must take a woman out of the district without proving to the satisfaction of the Native Commissioner that she is his lawful wife."[103]

High Court Judge P. J. Macdonnell, however, criticized the circular letter as well as the order. He doubted that it could "be considered a general lawful order that women are not to go to the [towns] for *any purpose*." Furthermore, the judge noted, the circular letter did not distinguish between prostitution and concubinage; its remarks implied that a person would be found guilty unless she proved her innocence. Such an order would give the "headmen too autocratic powers and curtail people's liberties." Under colonial law, headmen had local not personal power. The legal advisor suggested that Magistrate Melland had been misled about the powers of headmen and pointed out that Melland, qua judge, had no legislative but purely judicial powers: a judge "administers; he doesn't make the law."[104]

Melland disagreed. In reasoning why headmen ought to be allowed to prevent women from going to towns for any purpose, he had cited his own judgment of a court case concerning a woman who had cohabited with a man at Bwana Mkubwa mine without permission of her parents or the headman. She had been ordered off the compound premises, yet she had returned, and the mine authorities sent the case to the boma. Although the man promised to marry her and the parents approved their union, Melland could not see that these circumstances "acquitted her of having lived an immoral life at Bwana Mkubwa mine in defiance of lawful order." The native commissioner at Ndola set her free, but Melland would have convicted her.[105]

Commenting on the legal advisor's opinion, Magistrate Melland explained his position: "I appreciated the difference between concubinage and prostitution, [yet] I considered the line too fine. . . . Natives have only one word 'marry' for marrying a woman, or taking her as a mistress or concubine; the women who come to Broken Hill and other [towns] for the purpose referred to do not use this word, they do not say they come here 'to marry,' but use the word—*kusebenza*—'to work' . . . which I have

---

103. Ibid. Secretary for Native Affairs to District Commissioner and Magistrate, Mumbwa. July 17, 1923.

104. Ibid. Judge Macdonnel to Registrar, Livingstone. October 25, 1923. Legal Advisor to Secretary for Native Affairs, Livingstone. December 1, 1923.

105. Ibid. Annex to circular letter (see note 117). Native Commissioner, Ndola, Criminal Case No. 71 of 1923. May 12, 1923. This may be the case referred to by Helmuth Heisler, *Urbanisation and the Government of Migration* (New York: St. Martin's Press, 1974), p. 69, about the1924 quashing of a conviction of a woman found guilty of disobeying an order issued under Proclamation 8 of 1916 from Mumbwa subdistrict. My sources date the event to 1923.

taken to mean to follow the profession of prostitutes."[106] Melland did withdraw his circular letter, noting that the ruling was "from an administrative aspect, a severe blow to me. . . . I am always telling [the Africans] that we stand behind them in maintaining their customs (with certain exceptions) and I have tried to live up to this."[107]

During the last year of the BSAC administration, the secretary for native affairs at Livingstone commented to the district commissioner at Fort Jameson, who was concerned about the exodus of women, that "the problem of restricting immorality by legislation is a thorny one but some action seems desirable in the interests of the native population."[108] His view was shared by many, but the problem of implementing legislation stemmed in part from colonial officials' interpretation of what was customary in terms of sexual relationships. The official legal stance was that custom should be maintained, within the limits of what whites considered to be morally acceptable. If prostitution were to be a matter for colonial law, it had to be part of the fabric of customary law and to be punishable within that framework. Officials cited section 15(11) of Proclamation 8 of 1916, which imposed on headmen the duty to "suppress . . . prostitution, procuration and all matrimonial or sexual relations contrary to custom of the tribe and harmful to the wellbeing of the village." Yet this formulation did not enable legal advisors to state definitively that the departure of women from tribal areas for purposes of prostitution constituted a criminal offense in the "natural customary law" of any given tribe—that is, a crime punishable by death or mutilation. If it was punishable merely by a fine, women's departure could not be regarded as a criminal offense under customary law.[109]

Despite the debate, no overall legal action was taken to restrict women's movements to towns in the 1920s. Rural native authorities were left to deal with the problem within the limits of their local powers, in other words, by proposing rules that, if accepted by the secretary for native affairs, became orders within their territories. If part of the problem was due to white officials' attempts to reinvent custom,[110] another part was due to the in-

---

106. Ibid. District Commissioner and Magistrate, Broken Hill, to Registrar, High Court in Livingstone. November 5, 1923.

107. Ibid.

108. Ibid. Secretary for Native Affairs, Livingstone to District Commissioner, Fort Jameson. September 27, 1923.

109. Ibid. Legal Advisor and Public Prosecutor's Office to Secretary for Native Affairs. December 20, 1923.

110. Martin Chanock and Marcia Wright have argued that white legal officials changed the law considerably when, during the early decades of colonial rule, they sought to identify and codify customary law, thus in fact making it. See Martin Chanock, "Making Customary Law: Men, Women, and Courts in Colonial Northern Rhodesia," and Marcia Wright, "Justice, Women, and the Legal Order in Abercorn, North-Eastern Rhodesia, 1897–1903," in Jean Hay and Marcia Wright, eds., *African Women and the Law: Historical Perspectives* (Boston:

ability of the native authorities to stem the tide of migration to towns, not only of women but also of children and adult men. The problem all parties faced reflected their inability to cope with ongoing social and economic changes in the colony. These processes did not stop and the debates concerning women's migration to towns and prostitution and immorality continued, with a hiatus during the depression, till the post–World War II years. To set the stage for the subsequent reemergence of the immorality issue, we may do well to take note of the women's words: they had gone to town to work. If Melland was correct in interpreting work as prostitution, he did not adequately explain the economic circumstances that prompted it.

It was not inherent immorality, lack of moral compunction, or loose marriage ties that made women dispense their sexual services. The literature from the 1930s, 1940s, and 1950s shows that actually the extent to which they did so on a purely commercial basis was limited.[111] Women made cohabitational and housekeeping arrangements with men, often without being legally married, because it was one of the very few ways in which they could ensure economic support in towns. The changing socioeconomic urban scene that left few wage labor options open to African women thus provided the context for the shifting focus in the official discourse from "immorality" to prostitution. The deteriorating rural socioeconomic conditions that had prompted women's migration to towns were obscured during the lean years of the 1920s and the poor years of the depression, when many African town dwellers were forced to return to the rural areas because of the lack of employment. But they were revealed once men returned to work in towns and mines and officials sought to reinstitute the old geographical division of labor by sex, separating men workers in towns and mines and women cultivators in the rural areas. When economic activity picked up momentum after the depression, authorities once again became concerned with the movement of women and children to the towns.

The mining companies did not share their concern. During the 1930s they had begun to encourage men to bring their families to live with them in the compounds in Luanshya and Broken Hill. The presence of wives who cooked and tended to their men's needs improved labor productivity without the companies' having to pay higher wages. George Chauncey has

---

African Studies Center, 1982), pp. 53–67, 33–50; also Martin Chanock, *Law, Custom and Social Order: The Colonial Experience in Malawi and Zambia* (Cambridge: Cambridge University Press, 1985).

111. See, for example, Godfrey Wilson, "An Essay on the Economics of Detribalisation in Northern Rhodesia, Part 2," *Rhodes-Livingstone Papers*, no. 6 (1942), pp. 66–69; Chauncey, "Locus of Reproduction"; and A. L. Epstein, *Urbanization and Kinship: The Domestic Domain on the Copperbelt of Zambia, 1950–1956* (New York: Academic Press, 1981).

delineated the way in which mining capital in this instance benefited by the compound, not the village, being the locus of reproduction.[112] The presence of children, especially boys, served a similar purpose. They did cleanup work in mines and compounds, worked in white households, and cooked, cleaned, and did laundry for single male migrant workers; they also did household chores for African miners' wives and garden work for those who had plots.[113]

Colonial and native authorities were alarmed at these developments, but not for the same reasons. Colonial authorities were concerned with the problems that were beginning to arise from the rapid growth of substantial African populations in the towns, which were not designed to house and service them. The officials also dreaded the consequences of detribalization in the rural areas, that is, the undermining of traditional authority. Responding to the chief secretary's call in 1936 for an inquiry into the causes and effects of labor migration from the tribal areas, the native commissioner from the Central Province noted: "The source of the greatest harm is the wives who have accompanied [the men]. They have learned loose habits and are apt to refuse to carry out the normal household duties. . . . Another disadvantage is the gradual deterioration of the children who grow up under compound conditions."[114]

Alarming comments came in from other regions. The district commissioner from Lusaka district noted that "the women in the compounds have virtually nothing to do. . . . With hours of idleness on their hands it is not surprising that they often fall from grace when strange men appear. . . . It is certain that in the town many married women are tempted to become common prostitutes."[115] The report from Broken Hill stressed a situation of chaos and wholesale immorality, the latter attributed as usual to loose marriage ties of intertribal unions. Many men who had left wives and families behind contracted temporary marriages after arrangements with parents or guardians, who "simply hired the girl out for profit." And from Mkushi district "one evil . . . is the desire of an appreciable number of women to share in the pleasures of town life, which upsets the [rural]

112. Chauncey,"Locus of Reproduction," p. 137.
113. Numerous examples of children's work in towns are given in the official correspondence. See, for example, NAZ/SEC 1/1316. Labour: Employment of Children, 1938–1945; NAZ/SEC 1/1350. Repatriation of Unmarried Women; and my own "Labor Migration and Urban Child Labor during the Colonial Period in Zambia," paper presented to the Conference on the Analysis of Census Data from Colonial Central Africa, University of Wisconsin at Milwaukee, August 18–22, 1986.
114. NAZ/SEC 1/1312. Administration of Native Labour. Investigation of Labour Conditions in Northern Rhodesia. Senior Provincial Commissioner, Central Province, Lusaka, to Chief Secretary. October 18, 1937.
115. Ibid. Report on the Causes and Effects of Native Labour Migration in the Broken Hill District. June 7, 1937, p. 15.

menfolk a good deal. These women when arrived at the labour centres adopt whoring as a livelihood, or at least concubinage."[116] Officials also worried about the large numbers of young boys above ten years of age who had gone to towns: "A youngster . . . almost invariably grows up to be a thoroughly bad character, but even when his sojourn is only for a few years or less, he naturally absorbs much that is evil."[117]

From the point of view of the rural native authorities, there were two important concerns: the *machona*—the "lost ones," the men who had left, never to return—and the loose sexual habits of women in towns. But as more marriageable men disappeared to town, so did women. Perhaps understanding women's dilemma, the Mkushi local courts adopted the practice of granting divorces to women who had been deserted by their husbands and not received support for two years. And wives who received money or other support from absent husbands who did not return when called back after three years were also granted a divorce.[118] Young rural women of marriageable age, divorcees, and widows unable to find husbands of their own choice were likely to become one of several wives of elderly men or remain single poor dependents of their aged parents or guardians.[119]

The reports stress collectively that prostitution and contempt for customary law and authority were the two most striking and dangerous results of town life. When women married or cohabited with men from other ethnic groups, rural native authorities lost their ability to control marriages. They were less likely to receive remittances from men who had married intertribally in town. And migrant workers who returned from town had seen a different world. Wanting perhaps to do things in new ways, they began to question the decisions of tribal authorities. As more young people went to towns and more children grew up urban areas, it became less likely that traditional mores would be imparted to the young generation, who then might lose respect for the old.

Acting out of these concerns, when the migration process quickened after the depression, rural native authorities began to call for official restrictions on women's and children's movements. And this time, unlike in the 1920s, their pleas received a sympathetic hearing from colonial authorities. Over the following years, most native authorities passed orders prohibiting unmarried women, children, and wives unaccompanied by husbands from leaving their villages without permission of guardians, headmen, or chiefs. But the native authorities had few means of enforcing these orders, and so

---

116. Ibid. Report on Emigrant Labour, Mkushi District. 1937.
117. Ibid. Broken Hill District, p. 15.
118. Ibid. Mkushi District, p. 2.
119. Cliffe, "Labour Migration."

the exodus continued. Great trouble was taken to little avail. Patrols were placed along some of the major migration routes to check for women's permission papers. Transport companies that operated along these routes were requested to do the same. The African drivers easily circumvented these arrangements; they hid women in the lorries and gave them "a lift in exchange for their pleasant company on the journey; no money passes."[120]

A bill was drafted in 1936 for the repatriation of natives from the urban areas,[121] and the native authorities continued to try, with the colonial authorities' approval, to prevent women from leaving the villages and to collect them from towns once they had done so. Rural native authorities would sometimes send *kapasus* to town to round up women and children. Chiefs and headmen also paid occasional visits to towns for the same purpose and were sometimes assisted by the compound police. But many women and children did not remain in the villages for long, and the native authorities continued to be perturbed by the matter. Colonial authorities did little about the situation during World War II, but in 1944 they began to allow the Urban Native Courts, established in 1939, to issue marriage certificates to couples after receiving approval from the rural native authorities. Since this consent was often slow in coming, urban African couples frequently took matters in their own hands. By the close of the war, the question of women's right to live in towns had become more complicated.

There was lack of consensus among African men about whether women's proper place was rural or urban. The issue was often the topic of heated discussion in the newly created regional councils (or provisional councils, as they came to be called), which had been established in 1943, and comprised representatives of African rural and urban authorities. At a meeting in Ndola in 1945 of the African Provincial Council for the Western Province, for example, Adam Frog, a representative from Ndola, commented that when "the chiefs were asked why they had not looked after the women better they replied that they had no place to keep them, and that there were few men in the villages and the women just disappeared, they did not know how. They asked the Government to find a way of keeping women in the villages." Mwachande, from the Swahili native authority, argued that the "trouble was that the girls did leave the villages and the town dwellers gave them sugar and meat and all sorts of things. In the villages they get only bad food . . . and they did not like living there. When they were arrested and kept in the villages the town dwellers came and fetched them back again." But Dauti Yamba from Luanshya wondered "why the women

120. NAZ/SEC 1/1350. Repatriation of Unmarried Women from Industrial Areas, 1940–1949. Provincial Commissioner, Fort Jameson, to District Commissioner. June 25, 1940.
121. Heisler, *Urbanisation*, p. 99.

were singled out. He thought the men were to blame too. . . . It could never be a happy village where there were no men and the women had to do everything with no man to help them. If the loafers were sent home they could settle down with the women in the villages."[122] At another council meeting for the Western Province held in Kitwe in 1945, the remarks of Esau Tembo were similar: "in my area . . . the people said that if boys are allowed to go to towns to work for Europeans, why cannot the girls also be allowed to go to towns. . . . Sometimes these girls go to visit their relatives or friends and sometimes the people who look after them in towns are their own guardians. It was also said that if the girls are stopped from going to towns, it means that they are being put to prison, because today there are not many boys living in the villages who can help the girls."[123]

At a 1946 meeting of the African Representative Council, formed that year, Nelson Nalumango from the Southern Province characterized "types" of women: "There is a married class and there is a class of working women and the third class is the class of undesirable women. . . . You find them in Lusaka today and next day you find them on the copperbelt and by January you hear they are in Wankie [a coal mining town in Southern Rhodesia] and the week after they are in Livingstone and wherever they go they cause a lot of trouble. People fight over them . . . they are the people whom the government should compel to go back to the villages."[124]

Rural native authorities had only local power; they depended on the colonial authorities to effect changes in the movement of women and children. Such an effort was made in 1946 when the colonial government empowered Urban Native Courts to enforce rural native authority rules and to return women and children who had come to towns without permission.[125] In this decision we can see how the official discourse was focused on the notion of prostitution; we can also see how the resulting negative image of African women shaped legal practices. But the protracted discussion that preceded the decision belied actual social practices in the changing colonial situation. At the time the decision was made, there were thousands of women and children in the towns, and repatriation orders

122. NAZ/SEC 1/1350. Repatriation, which includes a variety of minutes and extracts from meetings with African representation on which notes 123 through 125 below are based. Minutes of the African Provincial Council, Western Province, Meeting at Ndola. October 1945.

123. Extracts from Minutes of Meeting of the African Provincial Council, Western Province, at Kitwe. 1946.

124. Extracts from Minutes of First Session of the African Representative Council. November 1946.

125. Extracts from Minutes of Fifth Meeting of the African Provincial Council, Northern Province. April 1948. Comments by Secretary for Native Affairs. But see Heisler, *Urbanisation*, p. 99, who states that this policy was introduced in 1952.

were difficult to enforce. Perhaps it was this reality that led the government in 1953 to authorize the Urban Native Courts to issue marriage certificates to African couples in towns without prior approval of rural native authorities.

The Campaign for African Womanpower

African women and children continued to be repatriated from towns to rural areas after World War II. Yet the outcry against their presence in towns seems to have abated,[126] perhaps because wartime issues claimed the authorities' attention. Labor was scarce within the colony, and many African men served in the armed forces. The economy gained new momentum during the world war and the Korean War, when the copper industry boomed, secondary industries developed in munitions and autoparts, and the construction sector grew. Continued labor shortages throughout industry, government, and agriculture after the war invited new thinking on work and how to house workers.

In this situation of labor shortages, the colonial government formally adopted the mining companies' practice of providing some workers with family housing in order to reduce the rate of turnover and increase productivity. But their policy of "stabilization without urbanization" was half-hearted for it aimed at providing better housing for a small ratio of the African urban population rather than improving the standards of living for all. Africans were still not considered urbanized, their rural ties were not to be severed, and the great mass of the African urban working class continued to make their own work and housing arrangements.

The towns grew rapidly. Lusaka's African employed population increased almost six-fold from 1931 to 1946 and almost tripled, from 7,544 to 22,444 between 1946 and 1956 (see Table 4).[127] Some of this growing population was accommodated in new housing, built after the 1948 passage of the African Housing Ordinance which enabled local authorities to build African suburbs with married quarters in addition to the usual hostels for bachelors. An African Housing Board was set up and in Lusaka two new municipal townships were begun, one of them the model African suburb, Chilenje. Several more townships were planned here as elsewhere, but not built. The territory's entry into the Central African Federation in 1953

126. This observation may be erroneous and a result of the lapse in publication of some of the colonial reports during the war.

127. Part of Lusaka's six-fold growth between 1931 and 1946 was probably due to the move of the capital from Livingstone to Lusaka in 1931. The 1931 and 1946 figures are taken from *Report on the Census of the Population of Northern Rhodesia Held on 15th October, 1946* (Lusaka: Government Printer, 1949), table 2, p. 69, and the 1956 figures from *Census of the Population, 1956, Federation of Rhodesia and Nyasaland* (Salisbury: Central Statistical Office, 1960), table 80, p. 165.

Table 4. Number of Africans employed in urban areas of Zambia, by area, 1931, and by sex, 1946

	1931	1946		
Urban area	Total	Males	Females	Total
Broken Hill Township	2,441	2,890	69	2,959
Broken Hill Mine Township	2,318	3,286	36	3,862
Lusaka Township	1,280	7,485	59	7,544
Livingstone Municipality	4,786	6,306	63	6,369
Nchanga Mine Township	2,988	4,181	34	4,215
Kitwe Township	[na]	2,544	37	2,581
Nkana Mine Township	7,889	11,235	63	11,298
Luanshya Township		1,887	24	1,911
Roan Antelope Mine Township	7,796	10,540	86	10,626
Roan Antelope North (Suburb)		321	9	330
Mufulira Township	3,548	1,707	37	1,744
Mufulira Mine Township		8,013	73	8,086
Ndola Municipality	4,481	5,933	85	6,018
Manners Township (Suburb)		662	9	671

Source: *Report on the Census of the Population of Northern Rhodesia Held on 15th October, 1946* (Lusaka: Government Printer, 1949), Table 2, p. 69.

meant a new division of powers among the colonial, federal, and territorial governments. This, coupled with an economic decline in the last half of the 1950s, meant that revenues for housing were scarce. In fact, there was a housing shortage for all races.

In the late 1940s' atmosphere of rapid economic growth and severe labor shortages, colonial authorities singled out domestic service as a sector in which too much African male labor was "wasted." African men could be put to more profitable use elsewhere, their argument ran, so why not employ African women as servants? They were considered lazy and idle anyway, so service would be good for them. The ambiguous and at times contradictory attitudes of whites and Africans, males and females, to the woman question in domestic service were laid open in the debate that followed. This debate provides a unique historical moment that gives dramatic evidence about the workings of colonial gender ideology and of the social impacts of its sexual assumptions.

The question of employing African women in service-oriented work had been raised before the 1940s. The legislative council had already in 1929 suggested the employment of African women servants in girls' schools and as ward-maids in European hospitals. The proposal floundered because of the lack of separate living quarters for such African women in the hospital in Livingstone and the boarding school in Choma.[128]

128. NAZ/ZA 1/9 no. 49. Department of Native Affairs. Licensing and Registration of Domestic Servants. Secretary for Native Affairs to Chief Secretary. September 4, 1929.

Later, at the height of the repatriation attempts, native authorities were asked their opinion about the entry of young African women into service. Most of them were against it. This rejection was expressed, among others, by native authorities from the copperbelt region, from Mpika, and by Lungu and Mambwe native authorities at meetings in 1938 concerning the education of boys and girls. Yet representatives of the Abercorn Local Native Welfare Association, which had a more modern outlook than the chiefs, considered such employment suitable for unmarried women after, but not before, they had received some education.[129]

When during World War II the call for African women workers was made more urgently, it was first seen as a partial solution to wartime labor shortages in the farm sector. A circular from the chief secretary's office to all labor officers, provincial commissioners, and district commissioners encouraged them to undertake "the most effective propaganda . . . to overcome prejudices . . . to persuade women to do more [agricultural work] in order that a higher proportion of men may be released for essential war work."[130] The call was extended to domestic service at the beginning of the war: "we could raise another battalion of men who could do better than sweep floors."[131] The chief secretary and the labor commissioner doubted from the outset that they would succeed, for, "as you are aware", the latter reminded the former, "the difficulties are great in this territory."[132] Although the chief secretary did draft a propaganda article for inclusion in the vernacular newspaper, *Mutende*, encouraging African women to seek work as servants, no concerted campaign was set into motion at this time.[133] As in 1929, the lack of suitable accommodation was viewed as the main obstacle. The colonial administration did not act on a resolution on social welfare, adopted by the 1943 synod of the Methodist Church in Northern Rhodesia, which recommended that the government establish hostels either independently or through the management boards in towns, where employed African women could be trained under "suitable European control."[134]

129. NAZ/SEC 1/1316. Labour: Employment of Children 1938–1945. Native Education on the Mines. Notes of meeting with Senior Provincial Commissioner, Provincial Commissioner, and Director of Native Education, May 14, 1938. Dispatches on Education from District Commissioner, Abercorn, to Provincial Commissioner, Kasama. August 27, 1938; and from District Commissioner, Mpika, to Provincial Commissioner, Kasama. December 14, 1938.

130. NAZ/NR 3/143 md/14. Labour Department. Lative Labour Conditions. Labour Supplies. Womanpower. Circular no. 8 of 1943: African Womanpower, to All Labour Officers, Provincial Commissioners, and District Commissioners. March 17, 1943.

131. Comments by Harry Franklin, Director of Information. Northern Rhodesia. *Legislative Council Debates* 82 (1954), July 26–29, col. 284.

132. NAZ/NR 3/143. Labour Commissioner to Chief Secretary. June 1943.

133. NAZ/NR 3/143. Chief Secretary to Labour Commissioner. June 1, 1943.

134. NAZ/SEC 1/1350. Repatriation, Methodist Church Synod. November 1943.

The call to hire African women workers was voiced again in the late 1940s, when the economy had picked up and white immigration was growing, especially in the mining towns and the tobacco-growing areas. There were labor shortages in all sectors of the economy, particularly farming. White farmers clamored for government support to ease their labor shortage.[135] The demand for servants also increased, for most whites, including the new arrivals, commonly employed several. Many of the new immigrants came from South Africa, where at this time African women had almost displaced African men in domestic service. Yet in Northern Rhodesia the immigrating whites adjusted with alacrity to the prevailing practice of employing African menservants, assimilating local conventions in household employment. They, and other private householders, complained about the supply of good servants, meaning men.

When white male officials staged the postwar African womanpower campaign it was, as in the previous instances, first aimed at lessening the farm labor shortage by encouraging African women to work as farmhands. White farmers along the line-of-rail, the area where the majority of the commercial farms were located, suggested that native authorities be charged with making propaganda to encourage African women and young persons to turn out for farm work.[136] Several farmers had experimented with the employment of women and some had even fetched women from the nearby reserves. Others managed to talk the wives of male farmhands into helping with hoeing and harvesting. But many wives "refuse[d] blankly to do any work whatsoever."[137] In the farmer's view, the administration was biased toward the mines and the towns and did not do enough for them. The labor reports from the late 1940s and early 1950s show that farmers frequently criticized the authorities for inactivity on "the loafer issue." Loafers in towns, assumed to be hangers-on, persons without work and shelter living by their wit, could presumably be engaged in agricultural work. On that score farmers had little success, and, in fact, it is doubtful that the towns were full of loafers during the labor shortages of the early fifties. When township authorities made an effort to relieve the farmers' troubles by arranging for a supply of women and youth from the city compounds, the farmers chose not to accept them.[138] In the farmers' view, there were too

135. In an effort to support white farmers, the government established the African Labour Corps, which between 1942 and 1952 made conscripted African male workers available for farm work at wages that were subsidized by the government. See Kusum Datta, "Farm Labour, Agrarian Capital, and the State in Colonial Zambia: The African Labour Corps, 1942–1952," *Journal of Southern African Studies*, 14 (1988): 370–392.

136. NAZ/NR 3/143. Chief Labour Officer to Secretary for Native Affairs, Lusaka. September 28, 1950.

137. NAZ/NR 3/199. Annual Reports. Senior Labour Officer, Lusaka, 1950–1960. Philpot reporting from the Southern Area, 1950.

138. Ibid.

many problems involved in employing African women. Only in tobacco grading was some success achieved, which was attributed to women's manual dexterity and "natural suitability" for the task. A touring labor officer summarized the farmers' attitudes to African women's work as: women can't work; they are too lazy; or women won't work even if offered high wages and full rations because their husbands won't allow them.[139]

These complaints were elaborated by a labor officer after an inspection tour of white farms in the territory's southern part. His remarks highlight the authorities' limited understanding of African women's work and reveal the emphasis on education as a solution to "the woman problem." His assumptions were shared by much of white colonial society and were central in the subsequent debate.

> It is generally felt by farmers that as the only work [an African woman] has to do is to cook her husband's food she might show some gratitude for services rendered by helping to keep the compound clean and doing some occasional work on the farm. . . . There is no regular attendance [in farm work] and there is little doubt that on the whole the African woman is very much more trouble than she is worth on a farm, but she is unfortunately a necessary evil, she is the cause of a large amount of the discontent among the labour, she is filthy in her person and in her habits and is more often than not riddled with disease, she is pig headed and uneducated and till such time as she is brought into line, educated, and taught at least, some of the decencies of life, she will not be able to become a helpful member of the community.[140]

Farmers would have been unlikely to receive much support from the administration, who understood that rural African women's productive work in cultivation was crucial in efforts to maintain subsistence. From the viewpoint of colonial administrators, it was not at all advisable to recruit women from the reserves: "the main point is that we don't want to take women away from villages growing food. . . . We are encouraging the African to grow more food and women and children are concerned in this. . . . There is a *need to harness womanpower where not otherwise usefully employed.* There are more males in domestic service than any other industry save mining. *I wish we could get women in the town compounds to work* (italics added).[141]

The continuing debate revolved around the question of how to get urban African women into domestic service. Reducing the number of men employed as servants would be part of a solution to the shortage of labor on

139. Ibid. Tour Reports of Farms West of Lusaka. July 1951.
140. Ibid. Tour Reports of Farms in the Mazabuka, Monze, and Pemba Areas. 1948.
141. NAZ/NR 3/198. Tour Reports of Labour Officers, Lusaka, 1950–1955. May 1951; and NAZ/SEC 5/331. Native Labour. General Policy 1949–1951. Comments on dispatches by Commissioner of Labour and Mines. September 28, 1950.

farms, according to the Northern Rhodesia Farmers' Unions,[142] and in towns, in the view of male colonial administrators and such philanthropic groups as churches and welfare organizations. The issues of primary concern in the discussion of how to bring about a gender transformation in domestic service had been anticipated in the previous debate. One was the question of how to house women servants, another, the matter of training, and a third was the question of whether women servants should be single or married.

The suggestions offered on these issues in Northern Rhodesia are likely to have been influenced by the experience with African women domestics in the south. In Southern Rhodesia in the early 1930s, the legislative assembly had established a committee to prepare a report on the subject. It took extensive evidence from employers in the main towns, from location officials and educational staff, church representatives, African welfare associations, and white women's voluntary organizations. The committee also gathered information about women's hostels in South Africa, where they had operated since before the turn of the century,[143] and about the Native Girls' Hostel in Umtali in Southern Rhodesia, run in 1933 by the Women's Foreign Missionary Society and the American Methodist Episcopal Church. Commenting on the report in 1932, the chief native commissioner of Southern Rhodesia recommended that the government should not, at that time, take any specific steps to encourage African women to come to towns to work. But since that movement had already begun, steps should be taken to direct it into "safe channels" by providing hostels and domestic training, especially for detribalized urban women.[144]

Providing hostels seemed to be an idea then in vogue, its precedent dating back to Britain in the 1860s and 1870s, when large numbers of leisured Victorian women had entered the workhouses to train poor girls for domestic service.[145] The Federation of African Welfare Societies in Southern Rhodesia involved themselves in the training of women domestics in Umtali in the early 1950s. Some thirty young women were accommodated at the center for three to four months and taught "household English," the use of kitchen utensils, washing, cleaning, mending, waiting on table, and simple cooking.[146]

142. Comments made by B. Goodwin of the Northern Rhodesia Farmers' Union at a conference called by the government on African labor problems. "Too Many Natives in Domestic Service Say Farmers," *Central African Post*, October 19, 1950, p. 12.

143. Gaitskell, "Christian Compounds."

144. NAZIM/S 1561/48. Female Domestic Service. Labour Memoranda and Minutes, 1931–1947. Comments by H. U. Moffat.

145. F. K. Prochaska, "Female Philantropy and Domestic Service in Victorian England," *Bulletin of the Institute of Historical Research*, 54 (1981): 79–85.

146. NAZ/NR 2/27. African Welfare. General Correspondence. African Welfare Bulletin, by the Federation of African Welfare Societies in Southern Rhodesia, Bulawayo, no. 97. May 1953.

The Northern Rhodesian government, however, did not approach the question as systematically as their southern neighbors had. No general investigation was undertaken, although labor officials met and various private bodies, representing white employers and philanthropic groups, made their opinion known. While there was general agreement that African women had to be trained for domestic service, diverse suggestions were made for their housing. The chairman of a location superintendents' conference at Ndola in 1947 anticipated that white employers would be so glad to get properly trained African women servants that they would be willing to extend their homes to house them. Such accommodation would be, he suggested, "in [the employers'] own interests, for these girls would at the same time be protected from unwise attention of the local bloods and would be available on the premises to look after European children left in the evening by their parents."[147]

This official had reacted negatively to the suggestion of building women's hostels in the middle of the white residential areas or in the African townships. But most of the other suggestions involved such hostels. The idea was elaborated by the Anglican bishop of Northern Rhodesia, Robert Selby Taylor, who in 1949 invited government officials to a meeting at which he intended to set up a committee to work out a proposal for the establishment of a domestic training center in Lusaka. It was to accommodate about thirty African women and to be supervised by white women who would instruct them in "housewifery under European conditions." As he envisioned it, the costs were to be shared between the church and the government.[148] Dealing somewhat summarily with the bishop's idea and sending a subordinate official to the meeting, the secretary for native affairs rejected the notion of strong government involvement: "let him do the training with whatever financial assistance he can get out of Government" and place the responsibility for housing women when employed with the local authorities.[149] On the other hand, the Federation of Women's Institutes in Northern Rhodesia passed a resolution calling for the government to "include within its new African Housing Scheme the building of hostels for African women in employment . . . [to] be supervised by [white] African welfare officers."[150]

Hostels for African women might have seemed an attractive idea for several reasons. By restricting the movements of African women in towns, authorities could reduce the chances of sexual involvements when women were away from work. This advantage was likely to appeal to rural native

147. Comments on conference of location superintendents at Ndola concerning African labor. *Livingstone Mail*, May 2, 1947, p. 3.

148. Northern Rhodesia. *Legislative Council Debates* 82 (1954), July 26–29, col. 268, and 65 (1949), September 7–16, col. 231.

149. NAZ/NR 3/143. Comments on the Bishop's scheme. August 29, 1950.

150. Ibid. The file includes the resolution quoted in the text.

authorities, who continued to object to the allegedly freewheeling town lifestyle of the African women under their jurisdiction. Furthermore, supervision and domestic-service training by white women might serve as a form of ideological control by instilling in African women white middle-class values of home and housekeeping. In this way, presumably, they might eventually become incorporated into the colonial order as house-proud wives rather than partners in sexual play.[151] The managers of industry, however, anxious to recruit male labor, had little to gain by segregating women domestics into residential areas separate from men and away from the white suburbs. And the government itself was not forthcoming with funds to support the building of hostels. When the bishop died in 1951, so did the training and hostel scheme, "largely due to lack of funds and other difficulties.[152] Churches and missions in Northern Rhodesia never involved themselves in housing and training African women domestics to the same extent that they did in the south. They may have seen their primary purpose as training African women not for domestic service, but for self-improvement and home management so as to make them into better mothers. With this task, in fact, they had their hands full already.[153]

While labor officials at several meetings agreed that African men ought to be released from domestic service to work in other areas, their opinions varied as to which women should work as servants and how they should be trained. The participants at a 1950 labor conference recommended training courses of short duration. They regarded African women as "absolutely raw material, . . . if it lasted longer . . . it [is] probable that women would not stick it. . . . An African woman does not normally remain unmarried after the age of 17 and it is possible that floating unmarried women in the big towns would not be very desirable characters to bring into European homes." As an alternative, one official suggested that the wives of men domestics be trained. Such a course might lessen the housing problem; on

---

151. The education of African women was informed by the explicit ideology of making them houseproud. For an early formulation of housepride which influenced colonial policy of African women's education, see PRO/CO 795/158 no. 45469. Miss Gwilliam and Margaret Read, Report on the Education of Women and Girls in Northern Rhodesia, 1949.

152. Northern Rhodesia. *Legislative Council Debates* 86 (1955), November 29–December 16, col. 144.

153. The United Missions to the Copperbelt had begun educational efforts directed toward girls in the mid–1930s, described in Taylor and Lehmann, *Christians of the Copperbelt*. For the ideology that guided women's education, see also Hay Hope, "An African Women's Institute," *Overseas Education* 10 (93): 104–107, and Sean Morrow, "Some Social Consequences of Mission Education: The Case of Mbereshi, 1915–1940," *History in Zambia* 11 (1981): 10–23. Mabel Shaw, headmistress of the London Missionary Society's girls' school at Mbereshi saw the role of education above all as the molding of Christian mothers and wives. She did not agree with the policies of the administration: "It is high time they were reminded that our ideals are not theirs, and that the only kind of education we are interested in is religious" (Morrow, p. 14).

the other hand, they "might have to consider creches where children of female domestics could be left during normal working hours." The secretary for native affairs questioned the suggestion, arguing that "African women (and European women for that matter) who have children at home should stay at home to look after them. In any event native opinion would take years to come round to the idea that women with families should work for wages."[154]

As the 1940s turned into the 1950s, very few African women indeed were employed as domestic servants. The years 1951 to 1957 and 1961 to 1968 are the only time spans for which I have located employment figures categorized by sex (see Table 5 and Table 6). Although the official figures are likely to underestimate the actual extent of service employment, the gender gap is notable. Among the very few women who did work as servants during those years, some are likely to have been introduced to the occupation through a couple of specially organized efforts.

A kind of labor exchange, called the Women's Labour Bureau, was set up in Lusaka in 1950 in a cooperative effort between the Labour Officer and the white female welfare officer in the African Welfare Department of the town's management board.[155] During her daily house visits in the compounds, the welfare officer notified the young girls with Standard IV education who sat at home "doing nothing" of the possibility of working in domestic service. They could "not only train as nurse girls given suitable conditions but some of them could in time become efficient domestic servants." It would be a difficult task, though, for it was "obvious that a great deal of time must be devoted to these girls if they are to learn anything at all."[156] In a 1950 letter to the editor of the *Central African Post*, which ran under the heading "Training for African Women," four white women who described themselves as "enthusiastic supporters of any scheme for training Native girls for domestic service," expressed the same attitude. In their view, such training should be undertaken by "honest-to-goodness women with a sound knowledge of Rhodesian homes and how they are run [because] only women who have lived among Africans have a glimmering idea of the primitive condition of the African female."[157]

154. NAZ/NR 3/143. Commissioner of Labour and Mines. September 28, 1950; and Chief Secretary. September 29, 1950.

155. Welfare departments had been established in all the towns by 1950. The passing of the Colonial Development and Welfare Act of 1940 made financial assistance available for many activities in the realm of social welfare, and a social welfare advisor was added to the Colonial Office staff in London in 1947. When local welfare departments were established in the postwar years, they sought in particular to deal with youth and to counteract the effects of detribalization and drift away from villages. Sir Charles Jeffries, *The Colonial Office* (London: Allen and Unwin, 1956), pp. 151–153, 160–166.

156. NAZ/NR 2/27. African Welfare. General Correspondence, 1944–1954. News Sheet of the African Welfare Department, no. 10. November 1950.

157. "Training for African Women," Letter to the Editor, *Central African Post*, December 14, 1950, p. 3.

The failure of the Lusaka Women's Labour Bureau was anticipated a year later in the welfare department's newsletter: "It would assist the successful running of the bureau if interested Europeans would get in touch with the welfare section giving information as to the type of girl they wish to employ, what accommodation is available and in what type of work."[158] The bureau, according to an official, had placed only two or three women. "The ones I have seen," he commented, "could hardly be described as 'good' girls in every case, and I myself have not taken one so far. Other employers have done so but the girl has got tired within a week and left saying either: a) that the Dona made too much noise, or b) that the journey to the place of work was too great, or c) that the houseboys already on the job drove her away." He doubted that girls would "go in for" domestic service, even if they were trained: "I . . . think that our experience will follow Salisbury's and Southern Rhodesia's generally. There women are going into secondary industry in some numbers, having skipped the stage when they still work in private homes. . . . we shall not be as lucky as our grandparents who lived through the butler/footman era to that of the female servant before they reached the present one of 'do it yourself.'"[159]

When, in 1943 the chief secretary's office suggested the idea of a propaganda campaign, as mentioned earlier, the director of information argued that the time was not ripe for a full-blown effort. He contended that African opinion had proved adamantly negative. And few white employers would be willing to hire women and train them. He nevertheless agreed to help prepare the ground. Among the remaining documentation are copies of letters he wrote to the editor of *Mutende,* to the broadcasting officer, and to the producer of the Central African Film Unit, suggesting "indirect propaganda" to persuade African women, especially in towns, to work for wages. In his letter to the producer of the film unit, he proposed a film that "in a simple and humdrum way" would persuade African women to work, particularly as servants: "a film with a story that would paint this moral . . . that an African woman is happier or better off if she is working than if she is idle."[160]

Propaganda of sorts was transmitted across the territory when the Central African Broadcasting Corporation chose the issue of African women for domestic service for its first program in a new series of roundtable discussions called *African Forum* in October 1952. The topic, "Should African Women Take On Paid Jobs in European Households?," had been announced in advance and an indirect campaign set into motion in a series of talks concerning African women's education. A background write-up in

158. NAZ/NR 2/27. News Sheet, no. 21. September 1951.

159. NAZ/NR 3/143. P. J. Law for Commissioner of Labour and Mines to Secretary for Native Afffirs. November 23, 1951.

160. NAZ/SEC 5/331. Native Labour. General Policy, 1949–1951. Copies of letters included.

Table 5. Estimated number of Africans employed in industry and services in Zambia, by occupational field and by sex, 1951–1957

Occupational field	1951		1952		1953	
	Males	Females	Males	Females	Males	Fema
Agriculture	34,000	3,882	39,500	1,290	40,000	4,1
Butcheries	250		600		900	
Bakeries	650		600		700	
Brickfields	5,000		3,000		4,000	
Building	17,000		17,000		21,000	
Civil engineering						
Cordwood cutting	7,000	105	12,000		8,500	
Factories	10,200	50	4,500	50	3,900	
Domestic service	30,000	250	31,000	600	35,000	7
Flour mills	750		800		800	
Garages	2,000		2,000		2,250	
Government (exc. roads)	7,700		11,080		32,000	
Hotel and catering	1,000		2,148	5	2,200	
Municipalities and local authorities	4,500	62	4,300	40	5,400	
Mines (all)	42,000	150	42,000	190	46,000	1
Quarries and lime works	2,400		3,000		3,300	
Roadwork	5,000		5,000		4,500	
Railways	4,400	5	4,600		4,650	
Saw mills	4,000		3,200		3,500	
Transport companies	3,000		3,000		3,500	
Wholesale and retail distributive trade	10,000	10	65,000	5	6,800	
Native authorities, African employed, self-employed, etc.	11,000	200	24,000		35,000	
Unified African teaching service						
Miscellaneous						
Total	201,850	4,714	229,828	2,180	263,900	5,1

aincludes 500 part-time teachers.
bincludes 500 part-time teachers.
cincludes 500 part-time teachers.
dincludes 500 part-time teachers.

Source: Annual Reports of the Department of Labour, 1951–1957, Table 1(b).

the monthly radio magazine, the *African Listener*, sought to campaign. It highlighted the importance of education for urban African women's household management and their need to learn new ways of cooking to enable them to cater to their husbands' wishes, especially those who worked in white households: "It would also be a very good thing if African women were educated enough to do much of the work in the towns which is now done by men. Does it not seem strange that African men should be seen looking after European children in the towns, scrubbing floors in the houses, cooking food and washing clothes? Europeans think this is women's

1954		1955		1956		1957	
Males	Females	Males	Females	Males	Females	Males	Females
36,000	4,250	31,700	4,000	28,215	3,400	28,820	6,520
1,000		1,085	5	1,295		1,330	
800		750		850		720	
5,000	5	5,170	5	5,050		4,350	5
22,500		29,700		26,610		22,600	
3,500		1,930		2,500			
8,000	120	3,100	50	1,515		1,170	
5,250		5,700	50	5,900	65	6,800	30
30,000	800	32,800	850	33,600	855	33,000	800
800		900		950		1,085	
2,500		2,500		2,500		1,950	
31,725		33,700	250	38,850	260	34,100	300
2,500	10	2,560	10	2,500	10	2,310	30
5,500	60	6,650	5	7,035	5	6,975	85
45,000	100	44,700	100	45,540	450	44,250	500
3,000		2,750		2,250		2,330	
1,200		2,250		2,895		3,050	
4,815		5,250	5	6,410	5	6,300	5
3,500		2,530	25	950		2,480	
3,750		3,850		4,675		4,775	
7,500	15	7,950	15	8,800		9,400	75
30,000	15	21,000	15	21,000	50	20,000	50
3,500	1,000a	3,850	1,050b	4,125	1,455c	4,500	1,350d
1,000		3,000	30	3,600	40	5,000	40
258,340	6685	255,375	6,510	257,615	6,670	247,475	9,790

work; Africans, in their own villages, think so too. If the women did this work it would release many men to do other work which women cannot do—mining, making railways, driving lorries, building houses and offices and so on."[161]

The participants in the *African Forum* roundtable included the labor commissioner and three African men: a clerk in the colonial secretariat and two inspectors of cooperative societies. No African women were invited. These three African men of elite status did not emulate white attitudes.

161. *African Listener* 1 (1952), January, p. 17.

Table 6. Estimated number of Africans employed in industry and services* in Zambia, by occupational field and by sex, 1961–1968

Occupational field	1961		1962		1963	
	Males	Females	Males	Females	Males	Females
Agriculture, forestry, and fisheries	21,852	579	24,384	649	23,899	753
Mining and quarrying	2,635	4	39,636†	482	2,034	
Manufacturing						
Food processing	3,753	28	4,016	7	6,144	102
Clothing and apparel	787	30	902	27	882	8
Furniture, leather, paper and chemicals	1,415	1	1,400	2	1,457	1
Bricks and cement	2,576		2,489		2,337	1
Metals and machinery	3,945		3,990		3,968	1
Building and construction	15,457		13,175		12,717	1
Electricity, water and sanitation	1,933	5	1,087		1,069	
Wholesale and retail trade	7,681	52	7,502	68	8,027	86
Finance and real estate	401		369	1	378	1
Transportation	3,236	1	3,593		3,594	
Local government, education, health, community service	6,611	256	8,517	353	8,386	356
Recreation and entertainment	1,155	10	1,078	56	996	50
Domestic service					27,240	708
Restaurants and hotels	2,683	82	2,632	127	2,503	177
Personal services	402	5	382	12	498	4
Total	76,522	1,053	115,152	1,784	106,129	2,249

*This table covers a less extensive regional scope than Table 5. Thus the 1961–1962 figures are confined to the line of rail in the Southern, Central and Western provinces; the 1963–1964 figures exclude North-Western Province and the Barotseland Protectorate; the 1965–1966 figures exclude North-Western Province and Barotseland Province; and the 1967–1968 figures exclude North-Western Province.

†The enumeration of males and females under the mining and quarrying category in 1962 is conspicuously larger than in previous and later years. I suggest that some employees in larger mines are included in the 1962 figures.

Source. Annual Reports of the Department of Labour, 1961–1963 and 1964–1968, Table I(b). Some eighty occupational groups have been merged for use in this table.

They argued that educated African wives had enough to do in their own homes. A Eurafrican woman (that is, a person of mixed racial background), Agnes Morton, who was a well-known and very popular radio producer of women's programs, took issue with them in the *African Listener*. She suggested work as part-time servants, especially by newly married wives without children. Such employment would help financially and they would learn a great deal from white women. "I am very surprised," she wrote, "that these . . . well-educated gentlemen should cut down the oppor-

1964		1965		1966		1967		1968	
Males	Females	Males	Females	Males	Females	Males	Females	Males	Females
23,307	709	26,071	827	26,561	817	27,100	608	22,782	332
2,650		2,639	7	2,162	7	3,585	2	3,076	2
6,139	171	6,860	122	5,683	169	7,085	191	7,291	188
1,224	42	2,428	177	2,961	115	4,415	201	3,715	170
1,814	9	2,664	17	2,477	22	3,844	18	3,637	33
2,238	4	3,383	7	1,607	1	2,705		2,705	11
5,167	5	4,934	4	4,683	5	6,264	12	7,854	11
15,189	106	22,460	597	21,617	5	22,558	9	26,132	21
1,154		1,349		1,072		1,223		795	
8,753	275	8,573	266	8,875	344	8,466	299	10,922	490
483	2	777	7	754	9	955	15	1,042	36
3,304		3,342	7	3,346	14	5,016	13	5,352	46
11,603	457	12,342	604	9,347	480	13,698	435	7,515	389
1,117	42	1,018	1	1,037	54	829	21	929	48
26,800	700	31,500	800	31,231	1,498	31,508	1,549	36,491	1,758
2,429	208	2,610	258	2,696	252	2,564	336	2,316	359
473	9	605	7	552	9	523	25	867	17
13,844	2,739	133,654	3,706	126,661	3,801	142,348	3,734	143,421	3,911

tunities of African wives of helping financially. This kind of opposition is just to show Europeans that African husbands do not yet trust their wives."[162]

The debate about hiring women for domestic service dragged on through the first half of the 1950s. In "Too Many Cooks," a letter to the editor of the *Central African Post* in 1954, the writer complained that "this country cannot go on forever employing able-bodied adult men in work which is traditionally women's work." In another letter, "Domestic Service Plea," it

162. *African Listener* 12 (1952), December, p. 16. Miss Morton, born between 1910 and 1920, was a daughter of a white district commissioner at Mansa and a granddaughter of the first Chief Kazembe. She had been schooled at the London Missionary Society's school at Mbereshi till standard 4, took standard 5 through 6 in Southern Rhodesia, and subsequently trained as a teacher at Hope Fountain Girls' Institute in Bulawayo, Southern Rhodesia. Before becoming a broadcaster in 1949, she taught domestic science in girls' schools in Northern Rhodesia. She never married. *Zambia Daily Mail*, July 23, 1981, p. 7.

was argued that employment of African women in service would help in the "advancement of the African."[163] And a leading newspaper in 1955 ran an article in which the home environment was pointed to as the greatest handicap for Africans, particularly for women "still content to squat outside their front door and watch life pass them by." In order to advance, women, it was suggested, should replace men in domestic service.[164]

Toward that end a scheme had been launched at Ndola in 1954. Organized by the Federation of Women's Institutes in cooperation with the labor department, the African Charwoman Scheme made part-time domestics available to residents of flats and to white women in retirement homes. It was different from earlier efforts in that it involved not young girls but so-called "suitable" women, that is, women who had worked as servants in Southern Rhodesia or South Africa. The scheme was advertised in the *Northern News*, by the Ndola Chamber of Commerce, and by voluntary organizations.[165] News about it was sent to labor officers in all the line-of-rail towns, who were encouraged to copy the plan. But by 1956 the Ndola scheme had failed and efforts to start similar schemes elsewhere had been unsuccessful. A labor officer explained: "While African women are not yet prepared to become proper full-time domestic servants, when they go to flats or part-time duties they tend to get involved with male servants and the usual difficult complications arise. No doubt under such circumstances husbands would not be prepared to let their wives go and work as charwomen if it might have a bad effect on marital relations.[166]

At that point, the labor commissioner was clearly fed up. All attempts had failed. His remarks added in longhand at the end of the official correspondence indicate his frustrations: "It is a pity but I do not think we can force the issue any more."[167] And it was not forced again. When in subsequent years the question occasionally arose in the legislative council, voluntary organizations were called on to train women for domestic service.[168] None, to my knowledge, ever did.

The economy had entered a period of recession which lasted through the first years of independence. The tide had begun to turn in 1954, when for the first time in many years labor was plentiful. It continued to be in ample supply. There was unemployment among workers of all colors, and several

---

163. "Too Many Cooks," Letter to the Editor," *Northern News*, July 9, 1954.

164. Lead article, *Central African Post*, September 23, 1955, p. 4.

165. NAZ/NR 3/143. Labour Officer, Ndola, to Assistant Labour Commissioner, Kitwe.

166. Ibid. Acting Senior Labour Officer to Secretary, Northern Rhodesia Council of Social Services. January 7, 1956.

167. Ibid. Handwritten comments by Labour Commissioner. 1956.

168. Northern Rhodesia. *Legislative Council Debates* 94 (1958), March 18–May 16, col. 145.

white miners left the copperbelt and the country when copper prices dropped sharply in 1957. In 1958 even farmers had little difficulty obtaining labor. By 1960 there were thousands of unemployed African men in Lusaka and Livingstone.[169] The argument that women should replace men in domestic service so as to release them for more productive work elsewhere was no longer heard.

Economic Logic and Ideological Contradictions

African women did not skip the stage of working in private homes because wage labor opportunities opened up for them in secondary industry. As the womanpower debate shows, they hardly began entering that stage. And secondary industry never developed to any significant degree except in activities that supplied the mining companies.[170] When the mid-1950s' recession hit, African men kept their stronghold on domestic service, and the occupation remained for the entire colonial period predominantly a male preserve. Although men's persistence in domestic service may be attributed to supply and demand, such labor market factors do not explain why women were not recruited into domestic service at the height of the labor shortage at the turn of the 1940s and through the mid-1950s, when both the African and the white urban populations were growing rapidly and labor was scarce across the economy.

Assuming that units of labor were mutually interchangeable, male colonial officals argued that African women should replace men in domestic service to release the latter for work elsewhere. But sex was not an irrelevant factor in the market, and one occupation, domestic service, was construed in gender terms as male. The debate that ensued in the campaign for African womanpower was shot through with contradictions that embody complex ideological assumptions about sex and the gender division of labor in the late colonial situation. The same assumptions were not shared among male colonial authorities, white women employers and their men, and African women and men.

The lackluster performance of all participants in the campaign to hire African women workers may reflect that most of them doubted it would work. The "other difficulties" alluded to during the debate concerned the sexual ramifications of the scheme. Their sex became African women's liability and not an asset that "naturally" predisposed them for domestic

169. NAZ/NR 3/199. Annual Reports. Labour Officer, Lusaka. 1960.
170. Robert E. Baldwin, *Economic Development and Export Growth: A Study of Northern Rhodesia, 1920–1960* (Berkeley: University of California Press, 1966), pp. 37–40.

work. Sex, with that word's many connotations in the colonial mind—immorality, promiscuity, prostitution, in short, sexuality—remained a charged issue. Young African girls were considered dangerous in colonial households for they were assumed to be sexually precocious, and married African women were suspected of adulterous sexual assignations. Then there was the unspoken question of how an African woman servant and the white madam's husband would confront one another.

In the view of white women householders, African women were less controllable than men; they were less submissive and caused more problems in the running of the household. During the African womanpower campaign, white women held that African women were nowhere near capable of taking over from men in domestic service and made little or no effort to aid the situation. Their discourse comes close to depicting African women as a different species—certainly from themselves—and more primitive even than African men. The image was charged with sexuality, the African woman as "easy" temptress and—although it was not made explicit—a dangerous element in the white house.

The discussion about the need for training masked the sexuality issue. It was argued over and over again that African women needed education before they could go into service. White women were unwilling to socialize them into domestic labor on the job as they had done with previous generations of African men. In the past, men's work as servants had not been deemed problematic because they had little education. By contrast, and in the early days, many employers avoided mission boys who had a bit of education. Several had preferred "raw" natives whom they domesticated themselves. But when it came to considering the possible entry of African women into domestic service, their lack of education was held against them. When making this argument, white women presumably chose to disregard that the curriculum in girls' schools emphasized domestic science subjects with the aim of making African women good mothers and proud housewives. Yet these mutually contradictory attitudes about education did not cancel each other out. African women's presence in the white colonial household was too close for comfort.

Given the class structure and the color bar that delimited the vastly different livelihoods of Africans and whites in the colonial division of labor, African women's gains from education, homecraft centers and women's programs, and domestic work in white households were negligable. Housewifery and homepride were defined in terms of what was proper and useful in white households. But scotch eggs, muffins, and rice puddings, the recipes for which were offered to the new readers of the *African Listener*, were difficult to prepare in homes without wood stoves or electric cookers and seem jarringly out of tune with the culinary arts of the African low-income household. Many of the skills African women might supposedly

[136]

acquire from working in white households were similarly irrelevant. They certainly had been so for generations of menservants. Because of the sub-standard wages, African cooks and houseboys could make little practical use of their knowledge of roasts, mince pies, and custards. And the table-boy's manual dexterity in handling various types of flatware, cutlery, and glasses had little application in his own household. Moreover, in their own domestic settings, women were in charge of such matters. If African wom-en were unenthusiastic about homecraft/housewifery classes, it may reflect the inapplicability to their everyday life of much of what patronizing whites taught them. Knitting, sewing, and embroidery seem to have been excep-tions, perhaps because these skills could be used to turn out articles for personal wear or sale and thus supplement the household budget.

Colonial officials had described African men as "loath, not without rea-sons, to allow their wives to work away from home."[171] The reason implied was their wives' likely sexual encounters with other men. Allowing "other men" to include whites, I suggest that several additional factors were influ-encing African men's attitudes toward women's work away from home. Their reluctance to send wives, sisters, and daughters into service in white households may reflect their unwillingness to expose them to a demeaning work relationship for which very low wages were paid. The matter of wages was never addressed in the debate. The few African women who did par-ticipate in the Ndola African Charwoman scheme in 1954 preferred to change from an hourly basis to "whole time employment as being more secure."[172] Their statement implied that part-time domestic service was hardly worthwhile economically.

But perhaps most important was the fact that paid household service conflicted with the demands placed on African women for their own do-mestic labor as broadly defined in cultural terms among the region's vari-ous ethnic groups. Across much of Africa, women and men regard the home as women's place and childcare and household tasks as their most important endeavors. Women's ability to prioritize this work was influ-enced by cultural practices that shaped gender relations within households and by the viability of their household economy. Speaking generally, such viability was affected by the region's productive potential, the economic needs and political capacity of the state to incorporate women as wage laborers, and by women's personal initiatives. Because of the sudden and haphazard nature of the recruitment campaign, African women in North-

171. NAZ/NR 3/199. Annual Reports. Senior Labour Officer, Lusaka, 1950–1960. Citation from 1955 report.

172. NAZ/NR 3/143. Labour Department. Native Labour. Conditions of Service. Labour Supplies. Womanpower, 1943–1956. Labour Officer, Ndola, to Acting Assistant Labour Com-missioner, Kitwe. February 8, 1955.

ern Rhodesia were better able to resist the colonial government's attempt to incorporate them into domestic service than their sisters in South Africa.[173]

At the time of the womanpower campaign in Northern Rhodesia, the demands on African women's domestic labor from within their own households were much the same across class lines. This fact is borne out by the reactions of the male African participants in the *African Forum* radio debate, who objected to the idea of women going into service because they already had enough to attend to in their own homes. Colonial authorities failed to recognize the time-consuming nature of food processing and preparation and the constant demands that children and their care placed on women's attention and time. The demands of child care were particularly incompatible with paid domestic service, as most African women begin bearing children early and continue to give birth every two or three years throughout their childbearing years. Although authorities mentioned the need for creches, it was never attended to. African women of the early 1950s are likely to have shared the view on domestic service held by the women I spoke to between 1983 and 1985: a woman with small children simply does not leave her own household to attend to someone else's. And if she does, it is as a last resort, for who wants to be ordered around by another woman all the time on a slave wage? Whereas men, when all else has failed, and because they are normatively defined as heads of households, took and continue to take domestic service jobs because the economy has offered them few other wage labor opportunities.

Nowhere in the debate were African women called on to express their views. Their voice was silenced and they were assumed to want to work as servants. From the perspective of African women in the towns in the early 1950s, the division of labor which had existed in rural economies had been transformed. The contract migrant labor system that had forced men into wage labor on farms, in mines, and in private households over the preceding decades had gradually undermined rural women's autonomous roles in agricultural production. Their subsequent migration to towns, in spite of opposition by both colonial and rural native authorities, was in part their reaction to the deteriorating rural production opportunities. In this process of transformation, African women and men in towns were grappling with how to organize their urban households, relations among themselves, between themselves and their children and dependents, as well as with others in the towns, including white women and men. African women's un-

173. Belinda Bozolli, "Marxism, Feminism, and South African Studies," *Journal of Southern African Studies* 9 (1983), pp.149–155, reckons both with the capacity of indigenous societies and of the state to subordinate women's labor when explaining the differential proletarianization of women in South Africa, as do Gaitskell et al., "Race, Class, and Gender," pp. 98–100.

willingness to do wage labor as domestics may be seen as their attempt to resist any further loss of the limited independence they were establishing for themselves in their management of urban household activities.

By not "going in for" domestic service African urban women sought to define their own terms of work in ways that left them more freedom than they could hope for by working in low-paying jobs in white households. They are likely to have done so within a familiar frame. Rural women's desire for security within a household where they managed and worked in production, cared for children and grandchildren, contributed food and cooked for the household head[174] did not change drastically in the urban setting. Urban African women wanted to be in charge themselves. Some traded from homes and yards, and the brewers and sellers of beer were sure to do a good business. Other women entered market trade. Because housing was tied to the job and few were employed, some women's terms of work included the exchange of sexual services and food preparation in cohabitational arrangements with men who provided them shelter.

The issue of prostitution and cohabitation with whites was not directly confronted in the African womanpower debate. The matter had been brought up in the legislative council in 1939, but nothing was done about it.[175] In 1942 one issue on the agenda at a public meeting in Mufulira was whether or not to introduce the South African Immorality Act, and a motion was carried unanimously to draw government attention to the matter.[176] The question arose again in the legislative council in 1946.[177] Among the waves of postwar white immigrants who worked in mines and construction were many single men who, like previous generations, sought sexual gratification from African women. At a conference in 1949 the district commissioner from Chingola complained that "few things . . . caused more anger amongst Africans than European men living with African women."[178] A majority of those present voted that the government should introduce legislation to prohibit cohabitation between whites and Africans. Yet the matter was sensitive, for the authorities all knew of pioneers who had lived with African women in the bush for years, and they felt that it would be difficult to discriminate between old timers and others.

A variation on this theme was discussed in the legislative council as late as 1957, when a motion was introduced to make miscegenation a criminal

174. Marcia Wright, *Women in Peril: Life Stories of Four Captives* (Lusaka: NECZAM, 1984), p. 59.

175. Northern Rhodesia. *Legislative Council Debates* 33 (1939), May 20–June 6, cols. 196–197.

176. NAZ/SEC 1/1771. Public Opinion. Western Province, 1942–1945. Notes of a public meeting held at Mufulira on December 7, 1942.

177. Northern Rhodesia. *Legislative Council Debates* 54 (1946), May 6–June 7, cols. 17–18.

178. NAZ/SEC 5/114. Cohabitation, 1949–1957. Minutes of Conference of District Commissioners from the Western Province. 1949.

offense. A well-known racist, John Gaunt, who made the motion, was upset by seeing a good deal of miscegenation in Lusaka, which he attributed to the "getting into this territory certain people who do not have the same standards as the rest." His reference was to "foreign European labour . . . , birds of passage, . . . here to-day and gone to-morrow," who were unlikely to bring their children up "in the manner of the European."[179] His motion failed. Other members felt that miscegenation was inevitable in a multira-cial society and that making it a criminal offense would not reduce it.[180]

Thus everybody knew of, and many objected to, sexual relationships between white men and African women, but legislators chose to do nothing about the situation. Delicate and embarrassing, the issue was rarely dis-cussed in public, while at the same time everyone knew that it could happen and did. The private actions of African and white women were taken in the context of that knowledge. African and white women chose to not encounter one another in a servant/mistress relationship and thereby lessened the possibilities for compromising sexual involvements.

The sexuality argument conveys a rather denigrating view of white colo-nial women in Northern Rhodesia. To quality this view, we must reckon with their status as incorporated wives and with white colonial society's principles of male domination and female dependency. Other than their power to charm in the household context, as a newspaper commentator put it in 1909, white colonial women had little scope for autonomous activity and power acquisition in their own right in this class- and race-conscious society. The harbinger of unspeakable news in Page's novel explained to her friend that many white women overlooked their husbands' sexual hab-its; they had no choice, she said. A colonial white woman's main option was to see her husband as sexual protector, no matter what his extramarital involvements were.

But there were other choices. One was to leave. Barbara Carr recalled this when she "thought of the game rangers and planters and men of the administration, too, who had gone to England and brought back pretty young English brides who, when they discovered that their husbands owned large families of coloured piccanins had fled as fast as their . . . legs could carry them, back to their homes across the sea."[181] Another was to engage in extramarital affairs with white men, although the extent of this practice may have been limited; the evidence does not give impression of bedhopping as practiced by white Kenya settlers in the Happy Valley.[182]

179. Northern Rhodesia. *Legislative Council Debates* 91 (1957) March 12–April 3, cols. 681, 796.
180. Ibid., cols. 683, 793.
181. Carr, *Not for Me*, pp. 174–175.
182. For the lifestyle of these white colonists in Kenya, see James Fox's carefuly researched real-life mystery, *White Mischief* (Harmondsworth: Penguin Books, 1982).

Liaisons between white women and African men were another choice, but it was one considered even more despicable than relations between white men and African women. While they did occur, they were not widespread. Judging from contemporary writers such as Emily Bradley, white women are likely to have been very conscious of themselves as the embodiment of white womanhood and of the propriety expected of them in their roles as wives to powerful men. In the end, to play to the hilt the role of incorporated wife was these women's best choice.

The campaign for African womanpower had been the product of male officials who, vaguely doubting it would work anyway, could easily argue in the abstract the pros and cons of male versus female labor for domestic service, for they left to their wives the practical matters involving servants and their management. It is not surprising that colonial white women defended their place as mistresses of their own households when encouraged by male officials to hire African women. For white women, being aware of white men's sexual involvement with African women, may have seen any potential for such liaisons as jeopardizing their only position of strength. Given the structure of this situation, their decision not to employ African women servants in their homes may thus be interpreted as a singular feat by dependents of exercising personal power over their masters.

The dismal failure of the post–World War II campaign to recruit African women into domestic service was not due, as claimed, to lack of suitable housing, lack of education, or men's opposition. Although these factors influenced the outcome, they masked the key issue of sexuality. The debate about African womanpower may be viewed, I suggest, as a hegemonic moment in the Gramscian sense. Gramsci did not view ideology as unified or homogeneous, but always as made up of diverse and sometimes conflicting elements.[183] Hegemony here means the way these elements are made to "hang together" in a relative, though never complete, unity. The debate about African womanpower at first seems to have been fraught with conflicting assumptions about sex and the division of labor by gender held by society's diverse segments. Male officials continued to view African women in terms of their sexual functions, and white women preferred not to have them in their homes. African men were reluctant to allow women to work away from home, and African women themselves were not overly keen on

---

183. The concept of *egemonia* recurs frequently in Gramsci's writings. Of the texts available in English, a selection on hegemony is included in Quintin Hoare and Geoffrey Smith, eds., *Selections from the Prison Notebooks of Antonio Gramsci* (New York: International Publishers, 1971). The first major clarification of the concept in English is Gwyn A. Williams, "The Concept of 'Egemonia' in the Thought of Antonio Gramsci: Some Notes on Interpretation," *Journal of the History of Ideas* 21 (1960): 586–599. See also Raymond Williams, "Base and Superstructure in Marxist Cultural Theory," in his *Problems in Materialism and Culture: Selected Essays* (London: Verso, 1980), pp. 31–49.

taking paid domestic work. Although their reasons differed, most people agreed: keep African women out of domestic service. As a hegemonic moment, the African womanpower campaign thus temporarily produced consent to the prevailing colonial social order in both its patriarchal and class dimensions.

Non-African Women in Domestic Service

When interviewing former employers of servants in Northern Rhodesia now living in England, I was told of individual cases of African women who worked in households as nannies. One was Julie Mulenga, also called Chikamoneka, a Bemba woman of royal descent born about 1900, who was known in Zambia as Mama UNIP (United National Independence Party) because of her role in anticolonial demonstrations before independence. One of her thirteen jobs over a span of twenty-five years was as nanny to the household of none other than "white-is-right" member of the legislative council, John Gaunt.[184] Julia Mulenga and Betty Kaunda, the president's wife,[185] were among the very few black African women to work in white households during the colonial period.

Although African men dominated in service, the occupation also saw a diverse contingent of non-African (meaning nonblack) women pass through it. Their presence lies hidden between the lines of obscure records that tell us little about them as persons or about their place in the evolving class system of the racially structured colonial situation. I discovered them when interviewing former employers and by examining job advertisements in the colonial newspapers. Such advertisements reveal a series of categories first of white, then of various shades of coloured, women passing through private household employment. Advertisements requesting African women for servants hardly ever appeared, and when they did, it was in the late 1950s or early 1960s.

Northern Rhodesia's first newspaper, published in Livingstone from 1906, featured (by my reading) its first two situation-wanted ads in 1912, when a lady skilled at dressmaking sought a post as a useful companion and an experienced nurse wished to take entire charge of one or two children.[186] There were no further ads till 1918, when three English ladies

184. Bob Hitchcock, *Bwana—Go Home* (Cape Town: Howard Timmins, 1973), pp. 92–93; Ilsa Schuster, "Constraints and Opportunities in Political Participation: The Case of Zambian Women," *Geneve-Afrique* 21 (1983), pp. 16–17. Mama UNIP died in June 1986. Some of her accomplishments are described in a news story, "Chikamoneka: Shining Example to Women," *Zambia Daily Mail*, June 24, 1986, p. 4.

185. Stephen A. Mpashi, *Betty Kaunda* (Lusaka: Longmans of Zambia, 1969), pp. 15–16.

186. *Livingstone Mail*, May 4, 1912.

sought positions as governesses.[187] In 1919 a nursery governess wanted a post in Livingstone, a boarding-house keeper in Livingstone requested a native or coloured cook, and Lusaka's chief quarry operator, G. Marrapodi, requested a "Coolie" or "Chinaman" as gardener.[188] The last two listings are among the few ads for nonwhite household workers before World War II, and include the only request I found for a Chinese worker. From the early 1920s to 1938 white women regularly advertised themselves as governesses or children's nurses, using such terms as "English," "refined," and "domesticated" to indicate their suitability for work in colonial white households.

Who were these women, and where did they come from? The number of white women who came out on their own from England to work in private household service must have been small, for overseas passages were expensive. Unlike in South Africa, there was no recruitment scheme to bring Englishwomen to Northern Rhodesia for such work. I have found no indication of such women being recruited to Northern Rhodesia, although it is conceivable that persons with contacts in South Africa engaged women from this pool.[189] During World War I, some of the white women who went into household service may have been wives of men who went to the front leaving them with few economic means. As I noted in Chapter 1, their presence in service made authorities hedge on launching a registration scheme in the 1920s; it was felt to be beneath the dignity of a white woman, even if poor, to have to register.

These white women did not do the dirty and heavy domestic work; that always remained the job of African men. Through the 1920s and 1930s, white women worked as governesses in colonial households who could pay as, for example, the English gentlewoman, "lately from home," who in 1924 advertised her "wide teaching experience, languages, advanced pianoforte, singing, kindergarten, and dancing."[190] The need for governesses arose from the lack of schools. Before the depression, the educational system for white children was poorly developed, and it hardly affected outlying districts. Only in 1941 did schooling become compulsory for white children between the ages of seven and seventeen who lived within reach of government schools.[191]

Other white women worked as housekeepers, companions, mothers'

---

187. *Livingstone Mail*, May 10, 1918, and December 6, 1918.

188. *Livingstone Mail*, February 21, 1919, and November 21, 1919.

189. Charles van Onselen discusses the problematic role of white women servants on the Rand in his *Studies*, vol. 1, *New Babylon*, "Prostitutes and Proletarians, 1886–1914," pp. 103–162. See also "'The Crying Need of South Africa': The Emigration of Single British Women to the Transvaal, 1901–1910," *Journal of Southern African Studies* 10 (1983): 17–38.

190. *Livingstone Mail*, May 22, 1924, p. 1.

191. Gann, *History*, p. 344.

helpers, and children's nurses. Betty Clay's parents and in-laws sent a British-trained professional nurse out to Northern Rhodesia when she was expecting her first child in the late 1930s. The nurse returned to England after a year. After the birth of her second child, Betty Clay employed as nanny a middle-aged English widow who had previously come out to the colony with colleagues of the Clays' in the administration. Before marrying her late husband, a seaman, she had been a nanny in Egypt. Nanny Woods left the Clay household to marry an Afrikaans-speaking railway worker in Broken Hill. The marriage broke up, and after another period with the Clays, Mrs. Woods became a housekeeper at a hotel and eventually retired to England, surviving into her nineties.[192]

Having a white woman on the staff challenged the rigid hierarchy of color, sex, and class. White women servants are likely to have been aware of their problematic status and may have used marriage as a strategy to leave service. They became scarcer, especially as the economy improved and more unmarried white men arrived. Because of increasing immigration, the demand for them grew, as indicated by the frequency of newspaper requests. Then, too, they may have priced themselves out of the market. When Eileen Bigland traveled in Northern Rhodesia in the late 1930s, she commented that "European nannies were about as scarce as ice in the Sahara—and about as expensive."[193]

What happened to these women, and how many were they? Among those who were single, some married and left domestic service. Others may have set themselves up in the boarding-house and hotel trade, which was growing as a result of immigration. Some may have been young Afrikaans-speaking women from poor family backgrounds, such as the nurse girl whom colonial official S. R. Denny hired in 1937 in Lusaka when his first son was born. He described her as "a kindly soul but not very clean. We used to find piles of dust in her bed, she never seemed to wash her feet. But at least she took the hardest work off M. . . . She finally went off to get married herself and was last seen . . . serving in a shop during the war."[194]

The 1946 census listed a total of 193 white women in personal service, including 75 children's nurses, 41 domestic servants, 8 hotel keepers, 29 hairdressers and beauty specialists, and the rest employed in hotels and clubs. Personal service comprised the fourth-largest sector of white women's wage employment then, with 295 in government work, 260 in retail

192. Gervas amd Betty Clay, personal communiciation, July 5–6, 1986.
193. Eileen Bigland, *The Lake of the Royal Crocodiles* (Norwich: Hodder and Stoughton, 1939), p. 191.
194. S. R. Denny, "Up and down the Great North Road, with Some Sidesteps to East and West," unpublished papers deposited at Rhodes House, MSS. Afr. s. 113. S. R. Denny papers, quoted with author's permission.

trade probably as shop assistants, and 250 in public service.[195] These figures likely underestimate the number of white women who did household-related work, which may have included several young Afrikaans-speaking women who did a short stint as a mother's helper before marriage. The term "governess" disappears in the 1940s, when most requests concerned child care, and employers needed nannies and nurses. The shift in demand probably reflected improvements in the white school system, the consolidation of white family life, and the growth in immigration.

As the white sex ratio evened out and immigration increased, more white families with below-school-age children needed nannies. Through the 1940s the advertisements almost exclusively requested non-African women for work. The Polish refugee scheme in Northern Rhodesia between 1942 and the late postwar years temporarily made available a white female labor force willing to do servile work in white households. In personal reminiscences the women who employed these Polish women describe them in glowing terms. Frances Greenall took on a Polish nanny from the camp outside Lusaka when her daughter was two-and-a-half years old. Having someone to look after her child, she felt free to take a job on the vernacular newspaper *Mutende*.[196] When Ronald and Mrs. Bush had two children aged five and seven and were stationed at Fort Jameson, they employed a Polish woman as nanny. The Poles were very good at handicrafts and mending, recalled Mrs. Bush. Mrs. Bush valued Sophia's services and was sorry to see her leave in 1948 to join her husband in England, from where the couple later went to America.[197] There were communication problems, as between Maria Wawa, who knew no English, and Barbara Carr, for whom Maria worked as a nurse but who knew no Polish. But Barbara was satisfied with Maria's work: "After being used for so long to dealing with native servants, who were lazy, dirty, inefficient, incompetent, careless and rough, it was wonderful to see Mary plunge into the housework, although it was not part of her job. She put every one of my seven native servants to shame, except that to feel shame for not doing work well was quite foreign to them."[198]

These accolades are somewhat clouded, however, by evidence of problems. Reports from Lusaka in 1943 indicate that white women lodged complaints about their new household workers. Their Polish nannies would take a job but leave it at a moment's notice, unconcerned with the difficulties this caused their employers. But aside from "servant problems" that

195. *Report on the Census . . . 1946*, p. 39. The number of 193 white women employed in personal service differs from the number enumerated in Employment Table 8, p. 36, which lists 25 women under 20 and 175 between 20 and 60 years of age in personal service.

196. Frances Greenall, personal communication, October 4, 1986.

197. Mrs. Ronald Bush, personal communication, November 24, 1986.

198. Carr, *Not for Me*, p. 106; and Barbara Carr to Henry Antkiewicz, November 8, 1978.

were not very different from those white women experienced with their African menservants, there were worse matters to contend with. Rumors had been circulating concerning the sexual conduct of Polish women. The Lusaka Women's Institute under the leadership of the wife of a Methodist minister suspected the Polish women in the local camp of providing sexual services for the white officers and enlisted men of two nearby military battalions.[199] Further, Polish women were alleged not only to have relations with African men, but to go so far as to openly solicit them.

Such affairs aroused great indignation and were seen as "undermining the respect due by Africans to all European women." The reputation of the Polish women never recovered. Even after the worst of the opprobrium had begun to die down, there were still "those who affirm[ed] that all the [Polish] women [were] prostitutes." But it was not only the notion of prostitution that caused the offense, white women doing manual labor was threatening in itself: "the sight of a European woman doing hard manual work such as hoeing gardens, carrying sacks of potatoes on their backs, etc. will be detrimental to the position of all European women."[200] As a result, there were some, but not many, ads for Polish nannies in the newspapers. It may be that the presence of these white women, who did manual work in colonial households and perhaps had loose sexual mores, contradicted too dramatically colonial white women's tightly upheld standards of propriety.

In the late 1940s and early 1950s, white madams were fortunate to gain access to a new female labor supply with several desirable features: the ability to speak proper English and knowledge of white housekeeping practices combined with racial characteristics that set them off from both white women householders and male African servants. These women came from the tiny island of St. Helena, in the South Atlantic Ocean, which had a reputation in Britain and South Africa for providing good servants. Its population is a late mixture of East India Company employees, officials, merchants, soldiers, slaves from Africa and Asia, especially Madagascar, some Chinese and, later, liberated African slaves.[201] Despite this heterogeneity, it was a thoroughly English island according to the *Annual Reports:* "The language is English and the English environment has become firmly established. . . . All St. Helenians receive a primary education and their homes, social life and outlook follows entirely the English tradition."[202]

199. Robert I. Rotberg, *Black Heart: Gore-Browne and the Politics of Multiracial Zambia* (Berkeley: University of California Press, 1977), p. 237; and NAZ/SEC 9/1770. Reports on Public Opinion. 1942–1945. April, November, and December 1943.

200. NAZ/SEC 9/1770. Confidential. Central Province. Provincial Commissioner to Chief Secretary, Lusaka, April, November, and December 1943. Western Province, July 1943.

201. *Colonial Annual Report on the Social and Economic Progress of the People of St. Helena* (London: HMSO, 1933), p. 5.

202. Ibid. (1934), p. 5, and (1935), p. 6.

But St. Helena had few economic resources and labor migration provided some relief. There was regular emigration to South Africa and to Britain, especially by St. Helena women, described as "by nature and habit . . . deft and polite, and admirably suited to . . . employment in domestic service."[203] From 1945 a contract system existed for such prospective servants, giving them a permit to work in Britain and South Africa for two years. The scheme persisted in Britain till the late 1960s, when the provisions of the Commonwealth Immigration Act of 1962 became more strongly enforced,[204] and may have ceased in South Africa in 1961 when that country became a republic and left the Commonwealth.

Whites in Northern Rhodesia during the postwar years were able to hire St. Helena women at recruiting agencies in South Africa.[205] Some of these women must have entered the servant pool in Northern Rhodesia. The frequency of advertisements for St. Helena women between 1949 and 1955 indicate that they were much sought after. They must have been almost perfect workers in the eyes of householders concerned with propriety and the upkeep of civilized standards. "The main reason for employing them," recalled a contemporary, "was that they all talked perfect or nearly perfect English whereas coloureds from South Africa would have a very strong South African accent which children were likely to acquire."[206] Although they had mixed racial backgrounds, St. Helena women were seen as different from coloured South African women. They were familiar with the household requirements of English life, yet, although fair, they were sufficiently distinct in racial terms for the two roles of white woman and manual worker not to coincide. They were different in racial terms from African servants and perhaps because of their socialization in the manner of the English on their small island, they may have been more conscious of their expected place in the race and sex hierarchy in the colonial situation. The former Northern Rhodesians with whom I spoke or corresponded all remembered friends who had employed St. Helena women, yet none was able to provide information based on close-range observation of these women's life and work.

The employment advertisements ceased in 1955. If most St. Helena women worked on contract permits, they may have returned to their island or left Northern Rhodesia for the Cape in South Africa.

The disappearance of St. Helena women from the servant ranks in the mid-1950s left Northern Rhodesian white women householders with four child-care options. They could employ a coloured nanny; take on an African nurse boy; hire an African woman; or decide to take charge of their children

---

203. Ibid. (1935), p. 6.
204. *St. Helena Annual Reports* (1956 and 1957), p. 9, and (1966–1967), p. 11.
205. A. St. J. Sugg, personal communication, November 11, 1986.
206. Gervas Clay, personal communication, January 15, 1986.

themselves. Judging from the newspaper advertisements, many white women wanted to hire coloured nannies. Persons of mixed-race background from within Northern Rhodesia were considered to be different and even less civilized than those from South Africa. In early colonial discourse they were not called coloured but half-castes and were held to have the vices of both races, and the virtues of neither.[207] The term *Eurafrican* began to be used for them only in the 1950s. The paper advertisements only rarely requested Eurafrican women for service. When white women needed actual childcare as opposed to someone just to watch the baby—for example, if they were wage employed—they preferred to hire these coloured women of South African background, who were considered more responsible. More white women than ever before worked away from home during the post–World War II years, and they advertised continually for coloured nannies. The abundance of ads may also imply that the employment relationship had its problems.

When black African women were hired as nannies, they were not expected to be in charge or to relieve white women of the chief tasks of child care. These African nannies watched the children, amused them, and played with them. Some may have worked as Betty Kaunda did in the early 1940s, looking after the district officer's baby for a couple of hours after school. She worked in this capacity for a couple of years for a succession of district officers' wives until she left home to go to boarding school.[208] In the early fifties, Mary Thompson had African nannies for both of her sons during their first eighteen to twenty months. She described their function as "a sort of watchdog while I was at the tennis court or in the pool."[209] Ishbel Stokes, herself a trained nurse, saw several such nannies pass through her household on the copperbelt in the 1950s when her two girls were small. She never allowed them to touch the children and described them all as useless, though none of them ever let her down, for example, by leaving the children alone. The most reliable and efficient nanny the Stokeses had was Maria, a beautiful Congolese woman known locally as the dance queen of the Congo. She was fabulous with the children, would entertain them with stories and games. "What our children learned," commented Roy Stokes, " we never knew, or deemed wise to ask, but we are sure that [she] contributed more to their general education than many tedious hours in school."[210]

White women did not always find it necessary to employ someone to help with childcare. Some sent the children to creches and nursery schools

207. Dick Hobson, personal communication, December 2, 1986.
208. Mpashi, *Betty Kaunda*, pp. 15–17.
209. Mary Thompson, personal communication, November 24, 1985.
210. Roy Stokes, personal communication, December 18, 1983.

during part of the day. Many, such as Emily Bradley, who had only sons, were content to have a young African boy to push the pram and wash the nappies. A. St. J. Sugg, a colonial official, and his wife never employed an African man or woman to help with their son's and daughter's care. They would occasionally lay on one or other from the staff of menservants to amuse the children if they themselves went out.[211]

Black African nannies finally became a more frequent sight in white households in towns from the late 1950s and on. Like the Stokes' Maria, some of them were nonlocal Africans. When Eric Dunlop, then labor commissioner, and his wife had twins in 1962, they employed the cook's wife as nanny. She was a well educated, mature woman from Southern Rhodesia.[212] Women like her had come to Northern Rhodesia together with husbands from that territory whom they had married as labor migrants in the south. These nonlocal women were by far the preferred African nannies. Few advertisements for them ran in the newspapers, which may reflect their scarcity, desirability, and the fact that they were likely to be engaged on the strength of personal recommendations. With the growing demand for child care during the late colonial period and the disappearance of white women willing to do such work, these foreign, coloured Africans and their local African sisters became the exceptions to the time-honored practice of employing mainly African men as domestic servants in colonial households. Even so, the few African women then employed did not as a rule work qua domestic servants as house, table, or kitchen workers, and they never displaced African men from these domains. The exception thus confirms the rule: colonial domestic service remained almost exclusively an African man's job.

Sex and Gender in Domestic Service: Structure and Ideology

My observations in this chapter are likely to differ from those made, for instance, by scholars and former residents of East Africa where the *ayah*, the female African servant, was a common sight in white colonial households. They may also be at variance with the situation in parts of Francophone Africa, for example, Mali and Senegal, where *la bonne* was a household fixture. And I have specifically argued that they contrasted with South African conditions from approximately 1930 onward, when women began replacing menservants.

The answer to the gender question in domestic service is complicated and no single explanation will suffice for any of these or other cases. An-

211. Sugg, personal communication, November 11, 1986.
212. Eric Dunlop, personal communication, September 27, 1986.

Theresa Thompson, her nanny, and a friend of the nanny, 1949. From the collection of Mary and Reginald Thompson. Reproduced with permission.

swers will everywhere depend on unraveling the changing interaction of economic, political, and demographic factors with cultural and ideological ones. These factors combine in different ways across space and time with the result that similar employment conventions, the East African ayah and the Senegalese bonne, in fact may involve explanations in which these factors carry varying weight.

In my explanation of the gender question in domestic service in Northern Rhodesia I acknowledged, first, the limits that economic, political, and demographic processes set around this occupational domain. Compared with South Africa (and Southern Rhodesia), the lower level of overall economic development, the lack of coerciveness by the local colonial government, and the smaller white population of Northern Rhodesia resulted in the much longer duration of the convention of employing man as servants. When the economy grew and both the white and the African urban populations increased rapidly during the post–World War II era, and African men's labor power was critically needed outside of domestic service, cultural and ideological factors did not change easily to reflect this shift. On the contrary, their legacy persisted and helped as the years went on to construe the gender division of labor in domestic service in terms that

Carole Stokes and nanny, Kitwe 1955/56. From the collection of Ishbel and Roy Stokes. Reproduced with permission.

The children of the Ronald Bush household and their nanny in the garden in Lusaka. From the collection of Mrs. Ronald Bush. Reproduced with permission.

Erlbert taking Geofffrey Bush, aged 3, to nursery school. From the collection of
Mrs. Ronald Bush. Reproduced with permission.

Michek, his small daughter, and Ian Thompson. Reproduced with permission.

made African men better suited for it than women. This division of labor was so taken for granted in the outlook of white madams that they never seriously considered employing African women servants. Given the legacy of pioneer days, suspicion lingered that African women would be sexually available to the master of the house.

The second part of my argument brought these cultural and ideological factors to bear on my explanation. Recognizing the limits that broader structural factors had set around the occupation, I granted cultural and ideological factors some influence in shaping the gender division of labor in domestic service. I identified sexual anxiety as the core of this ideology and delineated the processes and interactions across race and sex that had helped bring such a belief to the fore. The issue of domestic service in white households, as Belinda Bozolli has observed, "can better be understood as the outcome of a complex series of domestic struggles, rather than as an institution designed to serve the interests of capital in an uncomplicated fashion."[213] I am thus proposing neither that structural and ideological factors operate independently of one another, nor that either set of factors alone determines action, but that they both, in complex and at times contradictory interaction, shape social action and practice.

213. Bozolli, "Marxism, Feminism," p. 159.

[3]

Troubled Lives: Servants and Their Employers in the Preindepedence Era

Private household service remained predominantly an African male preserve during the remainder of the colonial period. The postdepression years had been a period of transition during which urban African men and women, and white officials and employers of servants, grappled with conflicting views of what it meant to be an African worker in the rapidly growing towns. The Passfield Memorandum of 1930, which stipulated the priority of African development with the colonial administration in the role of trustee, had provoked protest from white settlers and their representatives in the legislative council.[1] Yet preciously little African development had taken place by 1938, when Sir Allan Pim prepared a report on the state of affairs in the colony.[2] World War II and the postwar years were another critical period during which the relationship of black to white gradually was redefined in economic and political terms and colonial policy shifted somewhat, in part prompted by the Colonial Development and Welfare acts of 1940 and 1945, which made funds available to individual colonial governments for economic development purposes.

The discussion about the characteristics of the local African population had by then passed out of the hands of missionaries, amateur ethnographers, and civil servants. Professionally trained anthropologists did not speak of revolting customs. Instead, in their concern to present their findings in the idiom of science and objectivity, they spoke of how variously

1. Richard Gray, *The Two Nations: Aspects of the Development of Race Relations in the Rhodesias and Nyasaland* (London: Oxford University Press, 1960), pp. 181–182.
2. *Report of the Commission Appointed to Enquire into the Financial and Economic Position of Northern Rhodesia* (London: His Majesty's Stationery Office, 1938). Colonial no. 145.

structured institutions in the domains of kinship, religion, politics, and economics functioned together to bring about a state of equilibrium.[3] Although anthropology became part of the curriculum in colonial administration in England, the discipline had little impact on local colonial officials' general view of their African subjects. The meaning of the previous era's discourse about the primitive nature and simplicity of the local Africans remained fairly unchanged, even though the idioms in which it was now expressed were tempered by a pronounced paternalism that held that Africans were unable to manage their own affairs.

Because they studied Africans, anthropologists were looked upon with suspicion by the white settlers,[4] particularly in the 1950s when the concern to uphold racial privilege was uppermost in the minds of many. "Frankly, we think that much of this anthropological or sociological study is 'hooey'," remarked the writer of an opinion article in the *Central African Post* in 1953. "In the name of science certain Englishmen enter this country to make . . . studies of the customs and habits of African tribes and in the process they conduct themselves in such a way that they lose the deference traditionally accorded to white men by Africans."[5] In general, the 1950s were highly charged racially and politically, a tension first prompted by widespread African opposition to the Federation of the Rhodesias and Nyasaland, which the Colonial Office nevertheless imposed from 1953 to 1963.[6] This opposition contained the seeds of rapid political mobilization and a nationalist struggle, resulting in political independence in 1964.

In this chapter I explore how African servants lived through these years of rapid change. First I examine servant involvement in labor and leisure activity and discuss whether or not—and if so, what—such activities may tell us about the place of domestic servants in the evolving class structure of late colonial society. Many employers attributed the so-called "problem of domestic service" to the disappearance of the old-time subservient servant.

3. Lewis H. Gann, *A History of Northern Rhodesia: Early Days to 1953* (New York: Humanities Press, 1964), pp. 319–324.

4. For the dilemma facing anthropologists in this situation, see two essays by Richard Brown, "Anthropology and Colonial Rule: Godfrey Wilson and the Rhodes-Livingstone Institute, Northern Rhodesia," in *Anthropology and the Colonial Encounter*, ed. Talal Asad (London: Ithaca Press, 1973), pp. 173–198, and "Passages in the Life of a White Anthropologist: Max Gluckman in Northern Rhodesia," *Journal of African History* 20 (1979): 525–541.

5. "Sociology," *Central African Post*, April 10 (1953), p. 4. This article was followed by a series of exchanges, including a statement by the newspaper's editor and anthropologists V. W. Turner and M. McCulloch in the *Central African Post*, April 17 (1953), and comments in later issues, from England by Lucy Mair, who was associated with the teaching of colonial administrators, and from South Africa by Max Marwick, who had conducted fieldwork in Nyasaland.

6. Arnold L. Epstein has captured some of the tensions of the late colonial situation in his "Unconscious Factors in Response to Social Crisis: A Case Study from Central Africa," in *The Psychoanalytic Study of Society* 8 (1979): 3–39.

As I explain, this problem had less to do with servants as individuals than with changes within the servant-keeping population and the overall change of colonial society. If lives were troublesome for many employers, so they were for servants, especially those who had expected their welfare to be provided for by white employers who in the end were unwilling to live under a future black government. I also elaborate on some of the experiences of old-time servants from whom I collected life-history data.

Servants and Other Workers

Under the law, most urban African wage earners shared inequality: they were all servants in generic, legal terms. Personal or domestic servants differed from the rest mainly in regard to their intimate contact with those in power. Some of them lived on the premises, at a distance to be sure. Contemporary descriptions indicate that many lived in the African parts of town in Broken Hill, Livingstone, and Lusaka, and in some of the copperbelt towns employers insisted on them not living on the premises. According to Clyde Mitchell's 10-percent-sample survey conducted between 1950 and 1955 of all dwellings in which Africans lived in the line-of-rail towns and the copperbelt, approximately 66 percent of the servants lived on the premises, 20 percent were housed in mining and industrial compounds, 12 percent lived in local authority townships and the rest in squatter compounds.[7] In the postdepression years, servants' wages were much the same as those of other workers. Until the mid-1940s, wages were pegged at the level of farmhands' and remained at this level for unskilled workers on the mines as late as 1953.[8] Yet servants are likely to have been better fed and clothed because of castoffs from the employers' households.

If day-to-day living experiences when off work in private households and mines were shared to some extent by servants, miners, and the self-employed, so were the impacts of economic booms and busts during the 1930s. Servants were second to miners in the number of people employed in the rapidly growing mining towns. In towns away from the mining areas such as Lusaka and Livingstone, they comprised the single largest category of wage workers. The territorywide figures of domestic service employ-

7. J. C. Mitchell, table, "Occupation by housing area: Adult males, population estimates" Computer print-out from the unpublished Rhodes-Livingstone Institute Social Survey, 1950–1955, made available by J. C. Mitchell. The survey is discussed in Mitchell, *Cities, Society, and Social Perception: A Central African Perspective* (Oxford: Clarendon Press, 1987).

8. Peter Harries-Jones, "'A House Should Have a Ceiling': Unintended Consequences of Development Planning in Zambia," in *Perceptions of Development*, ed. Sandra Wallman (Cambridge: Cambridge University Press, 1977), p. 141.

ment almost doubled between 1929 and 1930, from 8,832 to 12,470. Over the same period employment in mining grew from 17,608 to 28,004, an increase of the same magnitude. As the two occupations gained momentum from the same process of overall economic growth, so they declined when the depression hit Northern Rhodesia, and both servants and miners were laid off. In 1933 employment in mines stood at 9,920 and in domestic service at 9,335. When the mines resumed their operation in the mid-1930s, both occupational sectors grew rapidly. From 1938 to 1943 employment in mines increased from 23,754 to 41,987 and in domestic service from 11,511 to 18,000. At the end of the war 20,000 Africans were employed as domestic servants in Northern Rhodesia.[9]

Servants and Class Formation

Classes are not defined exclusively by their distinct relation to the means of production in Marx's *an sich*, or objective, sense. Objectively speaking, servants were workers among other workers. Yet a full-fledged working class is not formed until workers develop a subjective identification, class *für sich*, of their shared position. Such an identification is not only affected by the characteristics of the labor process and the locus of work. It is also influenced by such nonwork-related phenomena as the setting in which workers live, their household arrangements and leisure-time activities. Depending on time, place, and the nature of economic constraints, interaction in these social and cultural domains of life may contribute to shape groups of people into categories as classes, or conversely, may hamper such identification.[10] Viewing the process of class formation in this way may help to place domestic servants on the terrain of labor and class struggle in Zambia. The annals of that history consist largely of studies of African miners—their strikes, their struggles for a union, and their political role before to and after independence.[11] These studies have overwhelmingly

9. See Table 1 in Chapter 1.
10. This recognition has been brought to bear, for example, in recent labor-oriented studies in South Africa as well as in a collection of essays focusing on the city. See Belinda Bozzoli, ed., *Town and Countryside in the Transvaal: Capitalist Penetration and Popular Responses* (Johannesburg: Ravan Press, 1983), and Fred Cooper, ed., *The Struggle for the City* (Beverly Hills, Calif.: Sage, 1983).
11. Among the main works are the following: A. L. Epstein, *Politics in an Urban African Community* (Manchester: Manchester University Press, 1958); J. R. Hooker, "The Role of the Labour Department in the Birth of African Trade Unionism in Northern Rhodesia," *International Review of Social History* 10 (1965): 1–22; Robert Bates, *Unions, Parties, and Political Development* (New Haven: Yale University Press, 1971); Michael Burawoy, "The Colour of Class on the Copper Mines: From African Advancement to Zambianization," *Zambian Papers* 7 (Manchester: Manchester University Press, 1972): Ian Henderson, "Wage-Earners and Political Protest in Colonial Africa: The Case of the Copperbelt," *African Affairs* 72, no. 289 (1973): 288–299; J. F. Holleman and S. Biesheuvel, *White Mine Workers in Northern Rho-*

interpreted class through a Western lens. To balance this view, I seek to bring social and cultural practices to bear on my discussion of urban economic relationships.

Servants and other urban workers had a lot in common. Most of them had spent less than a generation as wage laborers away from their villages of origin. They shared the impacts of economywide booms and busts as well as many day-to-day living experiences. In the copperbelt towns, many servants lived in the mining compounds, and some were housed in the municipal townships.[12] Like other workers, their visitation practices and female company were watched by compound managers, to whom they were supposed to bring their complaints. When after a sudden announcement of tax increases in 1935 miners struck in Mufulira, Luanshya, and Nkana, domestic servants were also involved. The commission report compiled after the strike leaves the impression that servants were pressed into participating. The district commissioner's personal servant, who lived in Mufulira mining compound, told District Commissioner Moffat what he had heard about the strike in the compound. It was none of his concern, he said, for "I do different work which has nothing to do with mine work."[13] A chemist at Nkana was told by a servant he had had for eight years that miners were going to force all houseboys to strike. His entire domestic staff of twelve lived in the mining compound and reported to work earlier than usual on the day appointed for the strike. During the day, stones were thrown in white residential areas where servants were at work. The chemist's servants joined in and he suggested they did so to make the strikers believe "they belonged to them." A magistrate's clerk related how natives were running all over the place near Nkana's commercial center, and how houseboys were being chased out of their employers' homes. And in Luanshya, the assistant to the chief secretary reported that "50–60 per cent of the houseboys joined in the strike. The remaining 40 per cent were intimidated into doing the same."[14]

desia, 1959–1960 (Leiden: Afrika-Studiencentrum, 1973): Elena L. Berger, *Labour, Race, and Colonial Rule: The Copperbelt from 1924 to Independence* (Oxford: Clarendon Press, 1974): Peter Harries-Jones, *Freedom and Labour: Mobilization and Political Control on the Zambian Copperbelt* (Oxford: Basil Blackwell, 1975): Charles Perrings, *Black Mineworkers in Central Africa: Industrial Strategies and the Evolution of an African Proletariat in the Copperbelt, 1911–1941* (New York: Africana, 1979); and Jane L. Parpart, *Labor and Capital on the African Copperbelt* (Philadelphia: Temple University Press, 1983).

12. NAZ/SEC 1/1552. Local Government: Housing of Personal Servants of Government Employees, 1943–1947. Labour Commissioner to Chief Secretary, November 18, 1943. Statistics on personal servants' accommodation in the towns.

13. Northern Rhodesia, *Evidence Taken by Commission Appointed to Inquire into the Disturbance in the Copperbelt, Northern Rhodesia, July–September 1935* (Lusaka: Government Printer, 1935), p. 358.

14. Ibid., pp. 31, 379, 539.

The nature of worker response to the 1935 strike is a matter of contention in Zambian labor history. Administrators labeled it "riots"; some scholars have seen it as a spontaneous work stoppage by migrant workers still bound by rural loyalties and dissatisfied with their deteriorating living standard.[15] Another study views the mineworkers of 1935 as proletarianized and interprets the strike as an early example of class action in Zambia.[16] Yet none of these answers need be final, for there is more to class consciousness than simply inferring it from evidence about collective action. The existing studies have ignored, or chosen not to consider, the participation of nonminers in the strike. An account of the strike's broader support invites us to reconsider its possible class basis.

Involving workers across several occupations, this first strike shows a common concern with problems of urban survival. The proposed taxes could only exacerbate those problems and would affect all African urban workers, including servants. An analysis of servants' response to the 1935 strike is difficult to make, since most of the available evidence is from administrators and officials. Evidence taken from African workers by the investigative commission, often using interpreters, was given in an hierarchical, racially structured setting likely to produce stereotyped answers. Although the whites who were questioned by the commission implied that servants were forced into participating in the strike, other clues suggest that the servants' involvement might have been more voluntary. To be sure, because servants labored in white households under the direct supervision of their employer, their activity was constrained. Perhaps this is the reason why Moffat's servant emphasized the difference between mining and domestic service. Yet servants like miners were wage workers. Sociability and friendship patterns arising outside their work places could promote a common solidarity and a sense of shared urban experience. Of the twenty-two who were convicted and sentenced for participating in the strike, only five were miners; two were store capitaos, three were unemployed, and a total of twelve were personal servants.[17]

In objective terms, the grievances precipitated by the tax increase, bad living conditions, and substandard wages were shared across a broad spectrum of occupational categories. Miners, servants, and other African workers in and around the mining compounds, whose everyday lives were adversely affected by colonial governance, took the system to task in ways

15. See Henderson, "Wage-Earners"; Berger, *Labour*; and Charles Perrings, "Consciousness, Conflict, and Proletarianisation: An Assessment of the 1935 Mineworkers' Strike on the Northern Rhodesian Copperbelt," *Journal of Southern African Studies* 4, no. 1 (1977): 31–51.
16. Parpart, *Labor and Capital*.
17. M. R. Mwendapole, "A History of the Trade Union Movement in Zambia up to 1968," ed. and intro. by Robin Palmer and Ian Phimister, *Communications*, no. 13 (University of Zambia: Institute for African Studies, 1977), p. 3.

that on the one hand were influenced by their distinct work locuses, but which on the other showed an understanding of the problems they all faced as workers. This strike, although it did not manifest full-fledged class action, shows how a shared understanding of common problems of living and working in the copperbelt towns was being forged.

In the strike's aftermath, neotraditionalism was put to work in the mining compounds in the form of a system of tribal elders who were to serve as liaisons between compound and mine. The *Mutende* journal was launched to serve as a mouthpiece of administrative viewpoints in the vernacular.[18] More schools were built. The Africans' understanding of their position in the colonial order was growing. But neither servants nor miners had gained any improvements in their economic situation after the 1935 strike. As the mining industry picked up momentum during the close of the 1930s, white immigration grew, especially from South Africa. There were labor shortages in mines and kitchens. The colonial reports from this time are filled with complaints about both servants and employers. A public hearing in Nkana in 1937 was held to consider these complaints. Precipitated by the flogging of a poor white youth in the presence of Africans, participants at the meeting discussed how whites were being debased by Africans, especially servants who were "absolutely disrespectful."[19]

Prices, meanwhile, doubled between 1939 and 1941 and continued to accelerate through the 1940s.[20] When miners struck in Mufulira and Nkana in 1940, wages were again an issue, as were matters of advancement. One of the three mining compounds at or near Nkana mine, called Kitwe compound, housed principally the African servants of white mine employees plus an overflow of African miners from the compounds at Nkana and Mindolo mines. There, according to the evidence of the commission of inquiry, "domestic servants and other non-mine workers [were] being forcibly prevented from going to work."[21] At Mufulira, the district commissioner and secretary for native affairs overheard a personal servant from a white township telling African miners on the picket line information he probably had overheard at his place of work, namely that "Europeans were threatening to 'shoot up' the compound at night but that their cartridges would be blanks only."[22] The crowds behaved quietly, and Gore-Browne,

18. Rosalyn Smyth, "Propaganda and Politics: The History of Mutende during the Second World War," *Zambia Journal of History* 1 (1981): 43–62.

19. Northern Rhodesia, *Report of an Enquiry into the Causes of Disturbances at Nkana on 4th and 5th November 1935* (Lusaka: Government Printer, 1937), pp. 37, 39.

20. NAZ/NR 3/242. Rise in Native Cost of Living and War Bonus, 1941–1947; and NAZ/NR 3/243. War Cost of Living, 1942–1947.

21. Northern Rhodesia, *Report of the Commission Appointed to Enquire into the Disturbances on the Copperbelt, Northern Rhodesia, July 1940* (Lusaka: Government Printer, 1941), p. 6.

22. Ibid., p. 20.

the representative for African interests in the legislative council "marvelled at the 'masterly manner' in which Africans ran their work stoppage."[23] No African reported to work on the mine or in town, and even the night-soil workers and houseboys were absent.

These early examples of labor mobilization show servants, miners, and other workers gradually becoming aware of their position and by strike action also seeking to transcend it. It is tempting to interpret these two early strikes as evidence of the formation of a broad, undifferentiated working class. But these men did not constitute any ready-made class category, and one must be wary not to read "too much class" into the limited evidence. No less than other workers, servants had grievances that they sought to overcome, yet their place in the process of class formation remained ambiguous. Their sense of shared concerns with other workers could easily become fractured because of the peculiarity of their work relationship. On the other hand, their interests could also coalesce, owing to the residence of nondomiciled servants in the African parts of the towns. Each category of worker was likely to have relatives among the other categories, and leisure-time interaction threw many together regardless of occupation. Many workers among all the categories continued to maintain some rural connection, if only because the village continued to provide a place for retirement. Finally, domestic service was, perhaps more so than any other occupation, replenished by the continuing arrival of people from the countryside. The place of servants in relation to other workers was thus more fluid and their alliance wavered, depending on time, place, and the nature of controls that set limits to their pursuit of better lives.

A Servants' Culture?

Did servants develop a distinct occupational subculture that set them off from other workers? What sort of involvement did they have with other Africans in the towns? All the towns had a heterogenous population that catered to the needs of a low waged, mostly male, work force in such areas as food, personal upkeep, services, and recreation. Servants established diverse links to these groups in their comings and goings between place of work, residence, and recreation. As mentioned in Chapter 1, chief among the activities reported by whites were drinking, gambling, and sex. Subscription parties were held once in a while. Known also as "sundowners," they would be held at somebody's house, and participants paid an entry fee. The parties featured beer, music, and women, and were attended by

23. Robert Rotberg, *Black Heart: Gore-Browne and the Politics of Multiracial Zambia* (Berkeley: University of California Press, 1977), p. 220.

Africans from various work backgrounds, including servants.[24] Like other workers, some servants married or took town wives. Others, like Amon, found in the preaching of the Watchtower Society ideas about a society in which men were equal and race did not matter. Some watched or participated in African dancing in the compounds, and still others got together for ballroom dancing.

Ballroom dancing clubs had sprung up in most of the towns in the 1930s and 1940s. They were associations out of whose fees members could expect support at funerals, when going on home leave, or when moving to another town. But they were first and foremost dance clubs, holding practices several times a week and competition dances almost monthly. Dances might also be staged to collect money for special purposes. To support the war effort, the Livingstone Dance Club, together with the African Welfare Association and other clubs, staged a grand competition dance in aid of the National War Fund of Northern Rhodesia in February 1942.[25] In the mid-1950s, the Ndola African Ballroom Association collected money for the Society of the Blind, the Northern Rhodesia Police, and was approached by the Football Association to hold a dance for its benefit. The board members of this association were employed by the Ndola municipality and worked in various capacities at the Ndola welfare center, where the dances were staged. The regular members were predominantly domestic servants.[26]

Servants became known as good dancers. Lifetime servants told me in 1984 how they would stand at the employer's veranda watching the whites dance and then go practice in their quarters. Ballroom competitions were held between the towns to which whites sometimes were invited to "come and see how well the Africans dance"[27] and to judge. At one such event in 1949, held at the African welfare hall in Maramba compound in Livingstone, a then twenty-three-year-old unmarried colonial civil servant was invited by Friday (whose surname he does not know), the headwaiter at the Fairmount Hotel in Livingstone where he messed, to serve as judge. A total of six white judges were present: two married couples, a woman postal office clerk, and the young civil servant. They awarded prizes donated from local businessmen, judging the performers on their dancing of waltz, quick step, and fox trot and selecting a best-dressed man and woman. The standard of dancing was exceedingly high, and the effect of the range of dress startling. The men for the most part wore full evening dress,

24. Anonymous, "An African Sundowner Party," *Northern Rhodesia Journal* 4, no. 3 (1957): 298–302.

25. *The Livingstone Mail*, February 6, 1942, p. 6.

26. Arnold L. Epstein, private papers: file on the Ndola African Ballroom Association (n.d.).

27. Godfrey Wilson, "An Essay on the Economics of Detribalization in Northern Rhodesia, Part 2," *Rhodes-Livingstone Papers*, no. 6 (1942), p. 18.

a lot of it many years out of date but very well taken care of. The women dressed in a variety of styles " almost to a woman in hand-me-downs from the husband's or partner's bwana's dona." Friday, who wore his "Soup and Fish," won the best-dressed male category and, recalled the observer, "service at my table improved accordingly."[28] The source of music, in this case, was a grammophone. But at a competition in the Kitwe African Dance Club in October 1950, a six-piece African band played and tango was included among the styles of dancing.[29]

In his study in Broken Hill, Godfrey Wilson reported that men dancers around 1939 to 1941 chiefly were "drawn from the clerks, the personal servants and the commercial workers, whose knowledge of European ways [was] greater than their fellows."[30] Long-time professional servants who had been dance champions in Lusaka in the 1940s and early 1950s told me that dance club participants included workers from various walks of life. Their performances in Lusaka's old welfare hall drew crowds who enjoyed the fancy display. But according to Arnold Epstein, at Ndola on the copperbelt in the mid-1950s, ballroom dancing was regarded by African white-collar workers as *fya bukaboi*, the quintessence of the "boy" way of life.[31]

The stereotype of the bukaboi drew on a number of fictions at whose core was the notion of the servants' privileged knowledge of the European way of life. This privilege led, supposedly, to their being good womanizers. Alick Nkatha, a musician who worked at the Central African Broadcasting station in Lusaka in the 1950s, struck this particular cord of the bukaboi fiction in his snappy song in Nyanja and town English:

Some young men of today have no sense.
When they see a girl with painted lips
they lose their heads.
Then they speak in English:
Yeah, good,
alas my beauty,
come live with me in the yards.
You're gonna get bread an' butter
I have everything.
New look in *plenty.*
You'll have so many dresses
you'll be changing clothes all day.
And every morning you'll be taking
Morning coffee, toshta an' butter
if you live with me.

28. Brian O'Shea, personal communication, February 1987.
29. *Central African Post*, October 19, 1950, p. 10.
30. Wilson, "Essay," p. 18.
31. Arnold L. Epstein, *Urbanization and Kinship: The Domestic Domain on the Copperbelt of Zambia, 1950–1956* (New York: Academic Press, 1981), p. 105 n.

You'll grow very fat.
If we two appear in public,
young men will be shaking
because of your beautiful clothes.

One of the radio listeners commented: "It is a very educative song. . . . it teaches us to look after our wives properly and to beware of domestic servants. They are morally weak."[32] So, too, thought white welfare officials in Lusaka who were involved in social work and recreational activities in the African townships in the early 1950s, seeking "to harness the enthusiasm of these men and women who more often than not are misfits in their own society."[33] The senior welfare officer commented in 1952: "Dances and concerts are popular, though [there has been] little improvement in either. . . . Partner dances were tried to encourage married couples to dance but they were not successful. European dancing continues to be patronized by men from broken homes, unmarried men and prostitutes, decent married folks are seldom seen dancing. . . . Every effort is made in clubs to keep African dancing in force but jiving is a keen competitor."[34]

The servants' easy way with African women was part of the bukaboi fiction that made them different from other African workers. So, too, did their position on the "inside" of the European way of life. Servants had been a source of information for other workers on white customs of dress, interior design, and manners. Although their wages were low, servants had better access than other workers to clothing in the form of hand-me-downs. Yet all Africans wanted clothing. Africans in Broken Hill in the late 1930s, wrote Wilson "are not a cattle people, nor a goat people, nor a fishing people, nor a tree cultivating people, they are a dressed people."[35] This preoccupation with clothes was not solely an urban phenomenon. Audrey Richards observed in the early 1930s in rural Bembaland that people constantly talked about clothes and took an intense interest in them.[36] Wilson echoed this at the urban end, noting that clothes were discussed "unceasingly, in much the same way . . . villagers discuss their cattle; they are

---

32. Fraenkel, *Wayaleshi*, pp. 51–52. Nkatha's song is reprinted by permission of Weidenfeld & Nicholson, Ltd.

33. NAZ/NR 2/27. African Welfare. General Correspondence, 1944–1954. Lusaka Management Board. African Welfare Department. News sheet no. 12, December 1950.

34. Ibid. Annual Report 1952. African Affairs Department, Welfare Section, Municipality of Lusaka. Comments by A. J. Harris.

35. Wilson, "Essay," p. 18. Africans bought clothes from an expanding nexus of white and Indian stores and self-employed tailors, through mail order firms in Southern Rhodesia, South Africa, and Britain, and from bales of secondhand clothing exported to the Congo from overseas and imported in bundles to Northern Rhodesia by African hawkers.

36. Audrey I. Richards, *Land, Labour, and Diet in Northern Rhodesia* (London: Oxford University Press, 1939), p. 217.

tended lovingly and carefully housed in boxes at night." As noted in Chapter 2, one of rural women's aims when migrating to towns was to get clothes. According to Nkatha's song and to Wilson, women "judge husbands and lovers largely according to the amounts of money they are given by them to spend on clothes."[37]

Clothes were much more than a means of emulating white lifestyle. Clothing had become a new idiom for establishing relationships not only between the sexes but also between the generations, for it was "the chief medium in which obligations to country relatives [were] fulfilled."[38] Finally, the use of distinct types of European clothes in such leisure-time activity as the Kalela dance was informed by African perceptions of class, status, and ethnicity in the urban situation.[39] While in one sense dress in this context may have imitated white civilization, in another sense it also had a subversive function. It caricatured the ambiguous roles some Africans had in the occupational structure, thus implying a critique of the structures's racial underpinnings.

"European-style" dress was by the 1950s far from a servants' monopoly. Servants' association with white employers, representatives of the colonial rulers, no longer carried prestige but was, in fact, resented by other workers. At this time, domestic service was ranked low by employers as well as by fellow Africans,[40] and dances were beginning to lose out in popularity to meetings and rallies of a more political nature. But even for political mobilization, dance clubs had a use. The recently released diaries of the late Simon Kapwepwe, one of the chief participants in pre-independence politics, show four visits to dance clubs in Kitwe in 1951 and registration of club members in the newly formed African National Congress party, just before Kapwepwe went on a study trip to India. After his return, the diaries make no further reference to the clubs.[41] The African opposition to the federation triggered a rapid political transition, in which existing forums for association, among them ballroom dancing clubs, proved insufficient.

Although the majority of the regular members of the ballroom dance associations may have been servants, these clubs are not by themselves sufficient evidence of a specialized occupational culture of servants. Several other factors counteracted such a development, among them residence arrangements, social interactions, and the shared preoccupation with cloth-

37. Wilson, "Essay," p. 18.

38. Ibid.

39. J. C. Mitchell, "The Kalela Dance: Aspects of Social Relationships among Urban Africans in Northern Rhodesia," *Rhodes-Livingstone Papers*, no. 27 (1956).

40. J. Clyde Mitchell and Arnold L. Epstein, "Occupational Prestige and Social Status among Urban Africans in Northern Rhodesia," *Africa* 29 (1959): 29–40.

41. Goodwin Mwangila, *The Kapwepwe Diaries* (Lusaka: Multimedia Publications, 1986), pp. 10–13.

ing. Servants were not as socially isolated as their work regime might imply. In several studies of domestic service in Western Europe and North America it has been argued that servants there lacked a class identity because household employment did not remain their permanent occupation. Since many of them were women, they would marry anyway and leave service. Because of the prospects for upward mobility, servants assimilated aspects of their employers' lifestyle.[42] But in Northern Rhodesia, the color bar blocked mobility in the system and domestic service remained a life-long specialization for many. Certainly there was some imitation of what was displayed as white civilized married life before the cook and the houseboy, but this is a matter entirely different from assimilation of lifestyle. The uses to which clothing was put were influenced by Africans' perceptions of their world and their way of organizing work and leisure. Those who moved in and out of service must have carried into domestic work experiences gained in other settings, and brought these experiences to bear when assessing their place in relation to the employers and to other African workers. As their occupation became devalued, servants did not simply acquiesce to their subordination in the labor process. Many sought to transcend it, in different ways to be sure, depending on their own experience and what they saw as alternatives. Their attempt to form labor unions was one such effort.

The Struggle for Unions

Whatever fitful alliance had linked servants and miners in the 1935 and 1940 strikes faded away subsequently. After the 1940 strike, some improvements were granted to miners, and other categories of workers such as teachers and clerks began to put claims on the system. *Askaris*, or soldiers, returned from the war and, having seen a different world, wanted jobs in towns. Among the returnees were servants who had accompanied their employers and on reaching their destinations were presented with the choice of returning to Northern Rhodesia or enlisting. Ewen Thomson's servant did the latter, fighting in Somalia and Burma, where he was in charge of gas operations. Back in Northern Rhodesia, he drank up his war bonus money in a short time and continued to work as Thomson's servant.[43] Around him, the school system was expanding and, with its emphasis on vocational skills, producing artisans and semiskilled workmen. As a

42. The upward-mobility thesis is advanced in particular by Pamela Horn, *The Rise and Fall of the Victorian Domestic Servant* (New York: St. Martin's Press, 1975), and Theresa McBride, *The Domestic Revolution: The Modernization of Household Service in England and France, 1820–1920* (London: Croom Helm, 1976); both view domestic service as a bridging occupation for young women, facilitating first horizontal, and then, vertical, mobility.
43. Ewen Thomson, personal communication, July 15, 1986.

result, there was a confrontation between the administration's two conflicting concepts of the proper roles of the African worker in town: the migrant worker as a special type of proletarian, and the more stabilized worker entitled to better wages and family housing. The mines had already fought this battle in the 1930s, settling in favor of stablizing the more skilled workers, and in the postwar years the administration grudgingly followed suit. While this meant better working and living conditions for some workers, including limited advancement for skilled miners, it changed little for the broad mass of the urban population.

During the 1940s, the workers who had participated in the 1935 and 1940 strikes began to pursue activities that furthered their own occupational interests. By virtue of their specific positions in the labor force, different categories of workers viewed their concerns as distinct. (This attitude is reflected in the remarks of Simon Katilungu, the leader of the Northern Rhodesia African Mine Workers' Union, at a trade union meeting after a strike in 1954 in Luanshya: "You are miners. . . . You are much better than those other people, the cooks, the clerks, and the delivery boys, and the others who work in towns.")[44] The struggle for unions highlights this difference.

Once mine workers were allowed to unionize in the late 1940s, other workers followed. This action coincided with the postwar economic boom in the mining economy and with shortages in all segments of the labor force across town and country. A wave of white immigrants, mostly of South African background, flocked to the copperbelt, all needing servants. Complaints about high turnover rates and lack of work discipline again filled the pages of labor reports. Servants asked the same questions as other workers, and wanted to establish unions to enforce better work conditions and improve wages. In March 1947 servants met with an African member of the urban advisory council in the welfare center at Mufulira to complain about their low pay. One of the elected members of that council was himself a domestic servant, and in 1946 Africans in Fort Jameson also elected a servant to be member of their urban advisory council.[45] The Mufulira meeting was well attended, and the labor commissioner wondered loudly whether the servants of Mufulira would form an association of their own. "If they do," he wrote, "it will probably be the first of its kind in the world as far as I know."[46] In March 1948 in Kitwe, "certain domestic servants held

---

44. Hortense Powdermaker, *Coppertown. Changing Africa: The Human Situation on the Rhodesian Copperbelt* (New York: Harper and Row, 1962), pp. 136–137.

45. Gann, *History*, p. 385.

46. NAZ/SEC 1/1338 vol. 1, part 2, 1947. Labour Department, Monthly Reports: Mufulira, Personal Servants, March. Comments by P. Law, Acting Labour Commissioner, May. Domestic servants did form unions in other countries. John Illiffe reports from Tanzania that the earliest African trade union (as opposed to a staff association) was the *Chama cha*

meetings among themselves during the month and various rumours of possible wage demands were floating about. . . . A deputation of four men met with the Trade Union Labour Officer and asked for government assistance in getting higher wages, shorter working hours and long service pensions." The labor officer pointed out the "enormous difficulties in the way of government intervention" and suggested that they themselves could help by making careful inquiry about the terms of service before taking on employment.[47] The Kitwe domestic servants did form an association in 1949.

By 1950 servants expressed their dissatisfaction in Lusaka. They staged a strike in May, demanding wage increases, and they held two public meetings. On July 24 they met two labor officers and the government's labor union officer, Comrie. They were told that a union for servants was "impracticable." Such a union, said Comrie, "must be able to meet employers, but not . . . in matters concerning domestic service because in industry the employers are making profit from work done by the employees and this is not so [in domestic service where] a person's household is his private property."[48] The example of the domestic servants' association in Kitwe was then mentioned and the suggestion made that Lusaka's servants might use it as a model, calling on the labor officers for advice.

When Luanshya's hotel, club, and domestic servants met with Comrie in November 1950, they wanted to form a Luanshya waiters' trade union. On this occasion domestic servants were advised by Comrie not to join, "as there was no opposing asssociation for them to meet."[49] By 1952 the momentum had reached Broken Hill, where a branch of the domestic servants' association was formed. Their leaders were "eager but with little grounding in trade unionism." The labor officer saw complex problems in

---

Wapishi na Maboi formed in 1939 by servants in Dodoma. In 1941, a union was formed in Dar es Salaam, where domestic servants were the largest category of workers. A union with territorial scope was created in 1945. It had, at one time or another, at least 12 branches. Apparently, the union was deregistered in 1949. Such a large organization in so unstructured an occupation, Illiffe suggests, encountered difficulty in organizing so scattered and individualistic a labor force that it caused its own undoing. See his "Wage Labour and Urbanization," in *Tanzania under Colonial Rule,* ed. Martin H. Y. Kaniki (London: Longman, 1979), pp. 276–306. In Kenya during World War II, several domestic servants' associations were formed. According to Sharon Stichter, a Kikuyu Houseboys Association was started in 1945 and there was another group known as the Jaluo Houseboys' Association, as well as associations of Indian and Goan houseboys. See her *Migrant Labour in Kenya: Capitalism and African Responses, 1895–1975* (London: Longman, 1982), p. 171.

47. NAZ/SEC 1/1338 vol. 1, part 2, 1948. Kitwe, March. Comments by P. J. Law.
48. NAZ/NR 3/183 1950. Department of Labour and Mines: Monthly Reports, Lusaka, May, July.
49. Ibid. Luanshya, November.

the servants' attempt to organize, and he doubted the outcome: "By what means they hope to conduct any negotiations is not known."[50]

Despite this flurry of activity, no servants' union was formed and the domestic servants' associations also withered away. The interpersonal relationship within the private household made employers unwilling to concede to servants the union rights granted many other segments of the working class. The same unwillingness caused legislators to deny the extension of minimum-wage legislation to servants in the 1950s. Such an inclusion, it was suggested, would involve domiciliary inspection: "It would mean that somebody would have to come into our houses, question our servants to see if they were being paid the right amount, and it is always an objectionable thing if we are to have inspectors coming round to our houses." Since the work of servants varied from house to house, it was considered "wrong" for each household to have to use the same standard of payment. A factor complicating the issue of minimum wages was that many Africans also employed servants. This practice had been noticed in the late 1930s when authorities became concerned about the presence of unchaperoned children in the compounds, some of whom did household work for miners. If an African has "a small piccanin, . . . he is a domestic servant, and . . . any minimum wage would apply equally to persons of that sort."[51] The implication was that Africans would be unwilling to pay minimum wages. More fundamentally, though, the legislators' procrastination was influenced by their reluctance to change their own payment practices.

While other segments of the working class had, through official recognition of their unions, been allowed scope for advancement within the colonial hierarchy, domestic servants remained bound in personalistic terms to their employers for the entire span of the colonial period. Various amendments to the Natives in Employment Ordinance which were passed during the late 1940s and the 1950s gave workers the opportunity to take out cash allowances for housing and food rather than having them provided. Although technically applying to all workers, these amendments were made with skilled miners, teachers, and clerks in mind.[52] Those servants who could not tolerate the restrictive regime sought other options. In his 1957 market study in Lusaka, Nyirenda found several former servants among the marketeers. One of them told him: "I resigned because the dona used to blame me for the mistakes for which she was responsible." He had nearly struck her when she referred to him as *makaka* (monkey), "but because I

---

50. NAZ/SEC 2/76 1952. Annual Reports on African Affairs: Central Province, Broken Hill Urban District.

51. Northern Rhodesia. *Legislative Council Debates* 88 (1956), June 28–August 28, col. 296.

52. Ibid. 93 (1957), November 5–28, col. 368.

knew that if I did so I would be imprisoned, I made up my mind to leave her employment and become bwana-self in the market."[53]

Servants Aren't What They Used to Be

Resident whites were slow to acknowledge the implications of the economic and political changes that were transforming society around them. These processes also affected the domestic service institution, although many employers were unwilling to concede so. In their resistance to acknowledge the consequences of what was taking place, they turned to the one thing they had in common: their servants. The master-servant relationship was their chief contact with the "African." Alone among all African workers, men domestic servants were tolerated in white households. They were by definition considered socially and culturally distinct from their employers, inferior to them and capable of learning only by imitation. And old-time employers certainly believed they "knew" the African. "Look at Old Shadreck here": "Had him over forty years—ever since he was a piccanin in my kitchen. You ask old Shadreck what he thinks of all this political carry-on. Eh Shadreck? True enough, if old Shadreck were asked what he thought of 'all this political carry-on' he would undoubtedly have shaken his head sorrowfully and murmured 'Ah! Ah!' No good Bwana. Too much troubles. Very big troubles,—and cluckclucked sadly to himself as he emptied the ash tray, just as he had been doing for the past forty years. He would have told you this, not because he was old and tired . . . but because he would know . . . that this was what you wanted to hear."[54]

By "knowing" their servants, many whites considered that they knew "them all" and attributed political manifestations of African opposition to the work of agitators who lacked any real support, most certainly from their old Shadrecks. Yet the terms that governed employment and guided the behavior of servants and their employers at the locus of work produced such answers as old Shadreck's. And these terms were not impervious to outside influences.

Servant Problems

Not everything was in flux, of course. The stereotype of the faithful old Shadreck persisted, approximated no doubt in several real-life situations and lingering in the colonial mind as a prototype against which changes

53. A. A. Nyirenda, "African Market Vendors in Lusaka with a Note on the Recent Boycott," *Rhodes-Livingstone Journal* 22 (1957), p. 41.
54. Grace Keith, *The Fading Colour Bar* (London: Robert Hale, 1966), p. 16.

were negatively evaluated. Certainly there were men who faithfully had served and remained true to their employers' expectations. Some of them were experienced servants in long-time employment who on their master's death or retirement were rewarded for their good work. The retired employers of servants whom I interviewed in England in 1986 described several such cases and some of them tried against the odds of international currency regulations to send money to the trusted servants they had left behind. Evidence also persists of such practices in the colonial record. The 1943 will of Captain Hugh Abbot Green specified the payment of twenty-five pounds to his head servant and ten pounds each to six men who had worked as his messengers in various places throughout Northern Rhodesia. Most of these men were still alive then, some were still working, as was the headservant Mutuna Chifunda, who on the captain's death had been taken over by R. L. Moffat of Kasama. And sixty pounds were willed to the servants Muleyabai, alias Jack, and Silishebo, alias Office, in recognition of their long and faithful service to one Charles Tully. Awaiting their money at Livingstone, both men wished to take it in a lump sum to buy a span of oxen for plowing.[55]

Some employers who had left Northern Rhodesia for the neighboring countries requested authorities to allow their good and faithful Northern Rhodesian servants to join them abroad. Because of restrictions on recruiting Northern Rhodesian labor to work outside the country, special permission was needed. "I can't get on with the Southern Rhodesia boys," complained Mrs. W. Rodmore from Bulaway to the secretary for native affairs in Lusaka in 1943. She wrote "on behalf of my native who has been trying to come down to me. . . . This native Noah I have had in my employment for 10 years during my stay in Northern Rhodesia and I would like him back again as I understand him and he is an honest boy and being in sickly health myself he is good to my Kiddies during my illness."

It took five months to trace Noah, a Bemba man, who in the meantime had been employed as a servant in Luanshya. By mid-July he reached Bulawayo and, we hope, relieved Mrs. Rodmore of her troubles with the Southern Rhodesian servants, for as she put it: "having had him so long I cannot get used to my other boy."[56] From East London in South Africa, L. R. Whitaker similarly requested that her Lunda servant, Zumbo Karibyi, be allowed to travel to South Africa to work for her. Zumbo had been

---

55. NAZ/SEC 2/251. Native Legacies in European Wills, 1943–1947; Estate of Charles Tully. From Standard Bank of South Africa, Ltd., to the Provincial Commissioner at Livingstone, August 1947.

56. NAZ/SEC 1/1497. Domestic Servants Accompanying Europeans out of the Territory. Letter from Mrs. W. Rodmore, Hillside in Bulawayo to Secretary for Native Affairs, Lusaka, February 2, 1943.

employed in the Whitaker household at Ndola from 1939 to 1944.[57] Whether Zumbo joined the Whitakers, who were "keen to have him," is not clear from the record. No doubt many more servants than the few individuals referred to in the official record proved their worth on the employers' terms and were appreciated for it. It is equally certain that many servants were considered the bane of their employers' lives, and had it not been for the need for creature comforts, some employers would rather have been rid of them.

Such, at least, is the conclusion drawn from a protracted debate between 1943 and 1947 on the question of how many servants government employees were entitled to, whether they should be single or married, and how they should be housed. In the view of one high official, no domestic servants should be housed on the premises; to prohibit their residence would result in less noise and friction, more cleanliness, and less risk of infection. Such a course would all be very well, but only if the servants could be housed within half a mile of their place of work,—"but even then householders would find it most inconvenient to have no servant permanently on call on the premises. There would be difficulty about the morning tea being late and, in the wet weather, even the breakfast." The next-best alternative was to have one servant, but not his wife and family, on the premises. There would be no women and children to make noise and a servant always on call. The labor commissioner who wrote these remarks, noted that while it sounded attractive to have a single manservant always on the spot, it probably would not work. "A single native,could not be expected to live alone on a stand regularly. He would either go off to seek companionship or take a wife to keep him company."[58] He in turn suggested that domestic servants should be encouraged to have their wives with them and should be provided with married quarters.

The discussion floundered on the issue of standards for the servants' quarters. It was generally agreed that servant housing was deplorable and improvements were in order, but the question of how remained. Some proposals envisioned standards of a kind that were likely to have "repercussions if [African] civil servants found cooks and houseboys in so much better accommodation than them."[59] Then there was the question of whether or not the institution of domestic service would persist. Semipermanent servants' quarters would do adequately said the provincial commis-

57. Ibid. L. R. Whitaker, East London, South Africa to Chief Immigration Officer, Livingstone, April 4, 1945.

58. NAZ/SEC 1/1552. Local Government. Housing of Personal Servants of Government Employees, 1943–1947. Labour Commissioner, Lusaka, to Chief Secretary, November 18, 1943.

59. Ibid. Extract from Report of the African Housing Commission, Chief Secretary, African Housing on Employers' Stands, September 2, 1944.

sioner, "because conditions are changing rapidly and the system of employing male personal servants might be expected to change progressively year by year as indeed it was changing in the territories to the south. Long before the permanent quarters envisaged ceased to be serviceable it would probably be found that female servants had replaced male servants and they would be housed in an employer's house."[60] Eventually, the question was deferred. Housing for all races was in short supply, and wartime requirements took priority over servants' needs. When African civil servants in the late 1950s finally gained access to "superior" housing in an area bordering Chilenje township in Lusaka, their request for servants' quarters on their plots was declined by the city council.[61]

Experienced servants with good references who had worked for years in white households among the upper ranks of colonial officials saw their honorable occupation becoming less reputable during the postwar years. This decline was the result of three simultaneously ongoing processes: the continued urban influx of migrants fresh from the countryside, barely if at all educated and with no prior work experience; the coming, especially to the copperbelt, of large numbers of unskilled white workers and their families who had little prior experience with servants; and the gradual occupational differentiation within African society at large, through which better paid and more skilled jobs gradually came into the purview of more African men. These processes took place in a social and racial atmosphere that was becoming increasingly tense in economic and political spheres. The caricature of the faithful old Shadreck faded into the background as an almost unobtainable ideal from the good old days when servants, and with them all Africans, knew their place and kept to it. And servants, during the postwar years and the 1950s became increasingly viewed as subversive. No longer content with eavesdropping, servants had begun to ask questions.

For the domestic service institution to have continued to function "like in the good old days," both servants and their employers should have kept to their respective places. The records from the Labor Department, established in 1940, are filled with complaints from both sides. Labor officers, swamped with such complaints, ascribed their growing incidence chiefly to the domestic encounter of newcomers: young African boys fresh from the village and newly arrived working-class whites.[62] The white population doubled between 1936 and 1946, and by 1951 it had grown to 34,962.[63] Growing white immigration generated a boom in the employment market

60. Ibid. Provincial Commissioner.
61. *Central African Post*, May 28, 1958, p. 3; May 30, p. 1; May 30, E. M. Wilson, chairman of the African Affairs committee, referring to statements made by his African colleagues.
62. NAZ/SEC 1/1338.
63. Gray, *Two Nations*, pp. 200–201.

for servants, creating a great demand for well-skilled cooks who, for example, in Mufulira in 1943, were "in acute shortage." A labor officer in Mufulira noted that many old-time residents were still reluctant to pay decent wages and might prefer newcomers. "This of course," he added, "is also applicable to the old copperbelt houseboy who does his best to exploit the rookie from overseas."[64] Some of these old copperbelt houseboys found their way into better jobs in hotels and clubs, and in 1948 the labor officer in Kitwe suggested that "with the severe shortage of labor . . . only the poorer type of African is generally engaging in domestic service and that I think explains most of the trouble on both sides." Desertion was rife, and another labor officer suggested that employers had too much scope to cheat willing workers.[65] They each had a point: in a booming labor market servants shopped around for the best-paying jobs, and employers did not always pay their servants for completed work contracts.

Newcomers did not always know their obligations. To improve this situation, the obligations of employers of servants as stipulated by the Natives in Employment Ordinance were publicized in the papers in 1947.[66] In 1948 a pamphlet on the master-servant relationship was distributed widely among white mine workers on the copperbelt.[67] The lack of a shared means of communication made matters worse. Ewen Thomson recalled an incident from the copperbelt when a large, irate Afrikaans-speaking man came into his office with his African servant yelling, "I want this *munt* [derogatory abbreviation of *muntu*, the Bantu word for person] taken to court." It seems the man had hired this new servant and thrown his boots at the African for cleaning. The servant had taken the boots and put them on. Using two interpreters, Thomson found out that the servant had not understood what he was expected to do, and that the Afrikaaner had not explained how he was to go about polishing boots.[68] To facilitate some degree of communication between whites and Africans some of the mines began to offer courses in Kitchen Kaffir.[69]

Despite these attempts, complaints by servants about unpaid wages and unlawful retainment of *situpas*, and by employers about desertion, stealing, and insubordination continued throughout the ensuing years. Compared with earlier years, the postwar period through the 1950s regularly featured servant items in the newspapers in the form of news about burgla-

64. NAZ/SEC 1/1338. Mufulira, May 1948.
65. Ibid. Kitwe, 1947, 1948.
66. Printed government information pointed out the legal position according to the Annual Report of the Department of Labour (1947).
67. NAZ/NR 3/30. Labour Officers Conferences, 1947–1954. Minutes from Department of Labour and Mines, 1949.
68. Ewen Thomson, personal communication, July 15, 1986.
69. Annual Report of the Department of Labour (1951), p. 6.

ries under sensationalist headlines such as "7 years on 'Wine, Clothes and Women'" (about the sentence a twenty-three-year-old houseservant in Kitwe received in 1952 after cashing a check for his employer and spending the money on having a good time) or "African gang on the Copperbelt showed 'Great Cunning,'" (featuring a gang of three houseboys who had been responsible for 54 burglaries in Kitwe and gambled on the proceeds of the sale of stolen property).[70] The papers also contain many letters to the editor on two main themes: servants having "lost their pride," and stories about their stupidity. Immigrants from South Africa might have been used to a more summary form of justice and taken servant regulation into their own hands. In Kitwe in 1953, for example, one Girard Horn was fined five pounds for sjamboking his servant who "had been cheeky to him," and in 1954 in Mufulira, a white miner shot his neighbor's houseboy during a break-in attempt.[71] As late as 1958 the *Central African Post* found it necessary to spell out the employment regulations.[72] Not all incidents were equally dramatic. In 1961 an amusing case was brought to the Labour Office. The servant, using sickness as an excuse, had not reported to work. When the employer switched on his television, his servant appeared on a live jive program, apparently in excellent health. His absence was treated as a breach of contract for which a small fine was imposed.[73]

Servants and their employers probably each bore part of the blame for these problems. But so did the domestic service institution itself, for it did not change with quite the same pace as the surrounding society. The cost of living had risen rapidly during the war years and after, and servants' wages had not kept in tune with it. Officials dismissed suggestions for minimum wages, arguing that servants' wages were sufficient, especially when considering the perks: housing and castoffs from the employers' households.[74] Servants' wages were never controlled, and although informal standards to some degree were observed by various segments of the employing sector, and varied across urban and rural areas, the determination of a servant's pay was at his employer's discretion. Not only the rich had servants. The cost of a servant was pretty much what employers wanted it to be. Half of the white labor force on the mines in the early fifties were unskilled workers. The majority of these new immigrants had come with one primary aim:

70. *Central African Post*, August 28, 1952, p. 12; December 9, 1952, p. 1; December 12, 1952, p. 5.

71. *Central African Post*, August 7, 1953, p. 5, and February 17, 1954, p. 1.

72. "When You Engage an African: Mr. Richards Explains the Rules," *Central African Post*, January 10, 1958, p. 9.

73. NAZ/SEC 5/333 Northern Rhodesia Labour Department. Reports and Returns, 1961–1963.

74. "Control of Wages for Domestic Servants 'Not Possible' Says Secretary for Native Affairs," *The Livingstone Mail*, February 2, 1951, p. 13.

to make money.[75] Even casual white workers here earned incomes that surpassed what they could have earned almost anywhere else in the world. Many, and cheap, domestic servants enabled them to pursue what they believed to be the distinctive and superior values of the "European way of life."

Troubled Lives: The Employers

Many of these new employers took for granted the low-paid servants, always on call, and allowed their children to address them rudely and order them around. In their effort to emulate a lifestyle identified with high living and fast spending,[76] they also became more dependent on their servants' work. During the postwar period of labor scarcity, an increasing number of white women began to work away from home in offices and stores. "In something like 9 cases out of 10 women go out to work, usually leaving their children in care of servants," commented Mrs. M. G. Rabb, chair of the philanthropic Federation of Women's Institutes: "We insist not only on the motor cars, refrigerators and telephones of the West, but also on [a] plenitude of domestics and other servants. . . . In order to keep up with even the most average Jones, wives feel they must go out to work to meet the monthly bills, savings towards holidays, the sudden emergencies. Not to mention the inevitable entertaining at home, the parties at clubs. . . . Is it surprising that a child left in the care of a servant whose mental agility is lower than its own, should . . . develop a bullying, tyrannical sense of superiority?[77]

Women like Mrs. Rabb had less time to supervise their servants' work than had the generation of white women who came out to the colony between the wars. It is perhaps significant that the second edition of Emily Bradley's book on tropical household management was published in 1948, at a time when more women of working-class background and unfamiliar with household service joined the labor force than ever before. Uncertain about the expected place and role of servants and unfamiliar with the mores and manners of the class to whose lifestyle they aspired, they are likely to have needed advice and to have treated their servants with a mixture of familiarity and crudeness that was unusual in the occupation. It was a situation that caused trouble, as it did for Mrs. Hammergren from Ndola,

75. Holleman and Biesheuvel, *White Mine Workers*, p. 52.
76. Ibid., p. 12.
77. For indications on white women's employment, see Annual Report of the Department of Labour (1953), p. 18. Mrs. Rabb's speech, reprinted in lead article entitled, "Dangers to the Future of Our Children," *Central African Post*, March 30, 1955, p. 4.

who in 1952 was taken to the labor officer at the request of her coloured nurse girl, Dorothy Richards, on the matter of four pounds in outstanding wages:

> I am not prepared to pay her more than £2/8/0, the amount I first gave her. Five dresses the value of £10, 3 pairs of shoes has [sic] been ruined all of which she has been guilty whilst she was with me. Because she would not wash and clean the things, instead she through [sic] them in a box and pushed the box under the bed.
>
> She gets to work at eight or after, too late to take the children to the convent which costs me 3/6 every day for a taxi. She did not once get to work in the house to dress the children or give them their breakfast. In the evening she would not wait until the children come from the convent to feed and put them to bed instead she left the baby with the boy [the male servant] who expected 2/–every night for watching the baby until I got home. One afternoon the boy was not home so she just left the baby by herself on the cot and went off home.
>
> In view of all these facts and heaps more I am not prepared to pay her any more and feel that she does not even deserve the £2/8/0 as the damage done to my baby's clothes is more than she is even worth. Also I have had to give my job up [because of] her as I could not bear to see my things going to ruin and my baby being put to sleep in a cot with no sheet or pillowcase when there is plenty only she was too lazy to get them from the wardrobe. [78]

Mrs. Hammergren clearly depended on Dorothy Richards for relief from the burden of child care from early morning till the children went to bed. But the arrangement did not work out to her satisfaction, and Dorothy settled for the £2/8/0 she had been given of the monthly pay of £9 originally promised her. Many other white women depended as heavily on their servants.

Some "black peril" cases occurred during this period. Very few seem, as I noted in the previous chapter, to have taken place during the early, and interwar years. Incidents that took the form of violence against white women were likely to have been products of and reactions against the generally tense, and crude atmosphere that characterized the postwar servant-employer relationship. Among the seven examples I have identified of alleged or attempted rape and indecent assault between 1945 and 1960 in Northern Rhodesia, a sentence was imposed in only one; the rest were dismissed because of insufficient evidence. A young male servant who had fondled a four-year-old white girl received ten strokes by cane and was sent to a reformatory for five years. Two of the other cases involved "carnal knowledge of girls under 16." The remaining four concerned servants who were

78. NAZ/NR 3/348. Labour and Mines Department. Wages, Payments, and Individual Despatches, 195052. Mrs. Hammergren, Ndola, to Labour Officer, 1952.

alleged to have sexually assaulted their madams, some while arguing over outstanding wages.[79] More such incidents may have taken place than the few noted here, and not all of them are likely to have been brought to the court.

Sexual attacks of white woman by black men challenged the racial boundary and the hierarchy of domination that was its basis and they could not be tolerated. In the effort to restore order, minor offenses were sometimes punished with perhaps disproportionate severity, as in the case headlined in the press as the "Lusaka Phone Call Menace." It concerned an African houseboy, London Mukonka, who in 1957 was sentenced to eight strokes of a cane for having made three indecent telephone calls to two white women. His behavior was "unpleasant and degrading" and, in the judge's words, "in a multi-racial society it is essential to keep this type of offence down to a minimum."[80]

White women had problems in their relation not only with their servants but within the family as well. The postwar pursuit of high living and the superior "European way of life" was fueled by a general affluence that in the mining towns, according to a study from the late 1950s, was probably "unequaled in any other white community in Africa." Average earnings of white miners had risen more than 200 percent above the already generous wages they had earned in 1950. Even semiskilled white miners could earn as much as, if not more than, persons who were academically trained. In addition, furnished housing was provided almost free and compulsory savings schemes and pension funds provided for the future. The leisure-time lifestyle that developed centered on generous, if not hectic,[81] entertainment, clubs, and cars; many children were sent to boarding schools in Southern Rhodesia, South Africa, or overseas; and they and their parents took expensive holidays on the coast off South Africa or in Europe. While the copperbelt towns may have set the pace, in a scaled-down version it became the lifestyle in the rest of the towns, where the pursuit of wealth and comfort became an established element of "the European way of life."

The pursuit had its costs. A survey of white family life in the early 1950s showed a high level of instability: separations or divorce and problems especially with childrearing and young people. White women, and ser-

79. "African Attacks White Woman," *Livingstone Mail*, October 24 (1947), p. 5; "Indecent Assault," *Livingstone Mail*, November 24 (1949), p. 1; Criminal Case no. 67 of 1952, Ndola (juvenile of fifteen years charged with unlawful carnal knowledge of employer's daughter under eighteen years); Criminal Case no. 107 of 1952, Lusaka (charge of attempted rape of woman employer); Criminal Case no. 95 of 1954, Ndola (charge of defiling young European girl under age sixteen) *Law Reports of Northern Rhodesia* 5 (1949–1954), pp. 210–211; pp. 324–331; pp. 616–618; "African Stands over Girl's Bed," *Central African Post*, January 25, 1957, p. 1; and "Woman Tells of Bedroom Attack," *Central African Post*, May 14, 1958, p. 1.

80. *Central African Post*, June 19, 1957, p. 1.

81. Holleman and Biesheuvel, *White Mine Workers*, pp. vii, 12, 35–36.

vants, were blamed for these troubles. Commenting on a report from the social welfare department that showed the "perilous state of [white] family life in the territory," Governor Sir Gilbert Rennie in a speech at the Lusaka Business and Professional Women's Club in 1952 warned young wives of the dangers of their going out to work. "The family," he said, "is the basis of our social structure, and any undermining of that basis will imperil the future welfare and prosperity of the country." To safeguard the interests of the children and the home, white women, he suggested, should pay attention to social services and voluntary social work. This would give "the home—the right type of home—its proper place in our lives."[82] The governor, of course, was not alone in considering the home to be woman's place. A member of the legislative council had complained that the task of attending children was too easily pushed over on to African servants. He said: "we are a peculiar people, we hide away our small change and lock up our sugar and go out to the day's work, leaving those whom we regard as our chief possession and the greatest asset of the country in the charge of those who we are always assuring each other have no sense of responsibility. . . . I cannot think it is in the interest of the country for its children to spend such a large part of their time in the charge of servants. . . . I hope . . . that young married people may not feel obliged to deny themselves the greatest joy and privilege of home life for fear of the cost of bringing up a family."[83]

Judging from newspaper reports, the white colonial home was a far cry from joyous. In the mid-1950s, drinking and petting parties among white teenagers in Lusaka caught the headlines. Teenagers were accused of five-minute love competitions, in which "boy and girl are paired off for that time under the gaze of other teenagers. The pair who do it best are then acclaimed." There were also "petting parties," and the teenagers held drinking sessions in one another's homes "where beer, spirits and cocktails are the order of the day." According to the news report, parents said they could not control their children and that "their daughters won't cook, knit or sew." Instead they attended parties, often till the small hours. The lack of parental influence was blamed on the unsettled character of town life, with new immigrants coming and going, and on the lack of youth centers.[84] Yet one member of the legislative council squarely blamed career mothers for children's petting-party habits. They stemmed, he said, "from the fact that most married women work and see far less of their children than they should."[85]

82. *Central African Post*, May 29, 1952, p. 14.

83. Northern Rhodesia. *Legislative Council Debates* 67 (1950) January 4–13, cols. 140–142. Reverend E. G. Nightingale, nominated unofficial member representing African interests.

84. *Central African Post*, October 28, 1955, p. 1.

85. *Central African Post*, November 2, 1955, p. 1. E. W. Sargent, Member, Lusaka.

The influx of many new immigrants probably did contribute to "the perilous nature" of family life in Northern Rhodesia's towns in the 1950s, and some of these teenagers may well have been emulating the behavior of adults. Few women cooked for the family; their African men cooks did not train the madams' daughters. Some women had extramarital affairs and some single women more than one partner. In 1955 a "call girl racket" was revealed in Lusaka. Operating from one of the suburbs, a dozen white women and girls as well as some who worked independently took assignations by phone and met with both white and African men for commercial sex.[86] Interracial sex had always been a volatile issue and in the fifties became even more so in the tense political climate and exaggerated concern for maintaining the distinct standards of a multiracial society. The concerns both with "the proper home" and interracial sex must be viewed in that light.

Servant Lives

Many African men and a few women remained working in domestic service during the late 1940s and 1950s when new opportunities had opened up elsewhere. There was more differentiation in the occupational field, some extent of advancement in jobs previously restricted to whites, and collective bargaining. Representation in politics began, first in the form of African representative councils and urban advisory committees, and later membership in the legislative council. And party politics, developing from African welfare societies to the establishment of full-fledged political parties: the African National Congress (ANC) in 1949, and its rival, the Zambia African Congress (Zambia); when the Zambia party was banned in 1959, its successor, the United National Independence Party (UNIP) grew quickly. These processes also affected servants, involving both sexes, but differentially so.

New Lives for African Women?

In the field of political mobilization, women's branches operated as auxiliaries to the main parties that enlisted their services in voter registration drives, rallies, and demonstrations.[87] Few women had as dramatic a life history as Mama UNIP, Julia Mulenga Chikamoneka, who was one of the women protestors who demonstrated stripped naked to the waist at

86. *Central African Post*, October 14, 1955, p. 1; October 17, 1955, p. 1.
87. See Peter Harries-Jones' sensitive portrait of a woman political mobilizer on the copperbelt, Foster Mubanga, in his *Freedom and Labor*, pp. 23–43.

[180]

Lusaka's airport when Ian MacLeod arrived from London to discuss constitutional change. His proposal was unacceptable to African politicians. Women bared their breasts on this and many later occasions to publicly dramatize their lack of approval. Mama UNIP, who died in 1986, had worked as a nanny for several years in white households, including those of district commissioners, in big and small towns across the country: Serenje, Mumbwa, Ndola, Kabwe, and Lusaka. By 1951 she used her small savings to buy a tiny shop in Lusaka. Here the new political spokesmen would assemble for discussions, and Chikamoneka became actively involved in organizing.[88] When the nationalist leaders were arrested in the 1959 emergency, she organized a support movement to secure their release.

Like most other African women, Chikamoneka had not wanted to make domestic service a lifetime career. Colonial authorities had been unsuccessful in getting African women to enter domestic service, but they had better luck in turning out women teachers, nurses, and welfare assistants. Under programs for African advancement, more teachers' training schools were opened in the 1950s, and municipalities and mines expanded the variety of vocational and technical courses for the rapidly growing urban African population. Some women took part in these programs, but as Tables 5 and 6 show, they were not surprisingly far outnumbered by men. Special educational efforts directed at women were also launched. From the 1940s on, facilities for training African women as nurses' helpers had been available in the Lusaka hospital and before the end of the decade, the Salvation Army hospital at Chikankata offered nursing courses with government financial assistance.[89] By the early 1950s the mines offered training courses for women nursing assistants, and modified nurse training leading to a government certificate was established in the territory's hospitals in 1954.[90] Midwifery training was added in 1958.

During these same years both mines and municipalities increased their training of welfare workers, many of whom taught homecraft classes in cooking, home economics, dressmaking, and hygiene. In some of these courses government badges were issued to the women who had been successful, but which "could be withdrawn if the required standards [were] not maintained."[91] Such courses were designed to make urban wives, especially those married to "advanced Africans," improve their own household management.[92] The courses were not particularly well attended by urban African women, for many of whom the Western notion of housewifery was

88. "Chikamoneka: Shining Example to Women," *Zambia Daily Mail*, June 24, 1986, p. 4.
89. Northern Rhodesia. *Legislative Council Debates* 55 (1946), August 24–30, col. 11.
90. Annual Report of the Department of Labour (1952), p. 7; (1956), p. 7.
91. Ibid.
92. Ibid., 1957, p. 5.

[181]

not only alien but also irrelevant.[93] In this period of economic insecurity many women escaped being housebound and added to low household budgets by trading and vending. The colonial authorities blamed men for women's lack of enthusiasm for the welfare and training activites, thus avoiding the question of whether or not such courses were of any use to women.

These courses were not designed to increase women's active participation in the labor force. For aside from the short moment during the African womanpower campaign, the colonial government continued to view the home as the African woman's proper place. During discussion as late as 1961 in the legislative council concerning the government's lack of progress in educating African women and girls[94] this attitude was expressed: "We must remember that a speeding up in academic education only is not the answer. The most important teaching in life, I think, is at the mother's knee, and the African mother's love for her child is second to none, so she must be brought more and more into the field of domestic hygiene, child and home care and *house pride* [my emphasis]." The white member who made this point went on to suggest that: "the UNIP leaders . . . would do well to remember that their womenfolk's place is in the home, training their children and not parading at airports or around the Secretariat with miserable placards strung round their necks which they cannot read for a start"[95]

As the "winds of change" were sweeping also over this part of Africa, African women were, on the one hand, provided new vocational and training opportunities which placed a minority of them in teaching, nursing, and welfare work and, on the other, were being inculcated with Western-derived standards of housewifery and housepride.[96] These standards distorted the degree of interdependence that had existed between women's reproductive and productive work in rural households before the labor

93. Hortence Powdermaker describes a situation in which African women and men criticized the training program and the attitude of welfare workers in Luanshya, *Coppertown*, pp. 109–111.

94. A subcommittee of the advisory board on native education had prepared a report on female education in 1938 (prepared by Mabel Shaw), emphasizing that the aim of all female education should be to educate girls for wifehood and motherhood. Not till after the passing of the Colonial Development and Welfare Act were concerns about the academic nature of women's education raised, prompted by a report from the Colonial Office: Colonial Office, February 1943. African no. 1169. Advisory Committee on the Education in the Colonies. Report of a Sub-committee on the Education and Welfare of Women and Girls in Africa.

95. Northern Rhodesia. *Legislative Council Debates* 102 (1961), March 14–April 7, cols. 632–633. Comments by Mr. Malcomson.

96. Miss Freda Gwilliam and Dr. Margaret Read used this term when recommending the emphasis on girls' education (quotation marks in the original), in Report on the Education of Women and Girls in Northern Rhodesia (Lusaka, 1948), PRO CO 795/158, file no. 45469. Governor Rennie's comments on the report are enclosed in the file.

migration process began. They also contradicted the demands that urban life placed on low household incomes, prompting many women to pursue nonwaged income activities in the neighborhoods where they lived. The construction of gender roles in the labor force also changed qualitatively for men. With independence in view, African men clerks began to replace white women in bureaus and offices and to attend to customers in shops.[97] Taken together, these processes reaccentuated urban women's and men's different participation in the labor force.

Political Mobilization

Over these years, some servants did vacate their jobs and move on to better positions. We know little of who they are today, for it is unlikely that domestic service would be flaunted on a resume. Fines Bulawayo, in 1987 a member of the central committee, arose from the servants' ranks to become involved in politics on the copperbelt in the 1950s, initially putting to use as an interpreter his language skills acquired on the job. In 1959 he was the propaganda secretary of the ANC.[98] His may be a special case, yet many others may have moved up, for example, into jobs in the hotel and catering business, or out of the occupation altogether, establishing themselves, like Amon Chapusha, in small-scale business or marketing. Some of their children certainly moved up and are today to be found among the ranks of government employees. But some stayed put and continued their work even when the colonial flag went down.

How did servants react to the political mobilization of the 1950s and 1960s? Some high-ranking colonial officials made a point of not asking their servants political questions, wishing not to interfere because of their official position in the colonial administration. Others considered their servants not to have sufficient intelligence for engaging in politics and referred to their lack of education and union organization in explanations of why servants would not know how to mobilize. Yet a colonial official pointed out that some servants were shrewd. His and his wife's long-time servant Gideon, who lived in the compound, carried both a UNIP and an ANC card and could always show the right colors if stopped when walking to and from work or at home in the compound. This official suggested that if servants signed up as members, it was because the youth leagues of the two parties pressured them.[99]

Servants were snobs in their own way, some employers would say. They

97. *Annual Reports, Labour Department* (1959), p. 1; (1960), p. 1.

98. Robert I. Rotberg, *The Rise of Nationalism in Central Africa: The Making of Malawi and Zambia 1873–1964* (Cambridge, Mass.: Harvard University Press, 1965), p. 306.

99. Ishbel and Roy Stokes, personal communication, July 12, 1986.

derived their status from the employer's rank, and the servant of a high-standing official would be sure to act superior to those employed by lesser officials. In these households of higher rank, the larger, more specialized staffs persisted longer, and employers observed their servants carefully maintaining the hierarchy between indoor and outdoor work and distinct tasks. The servants' yardstick for a good job was based on this sense of status and specialization, and it was sometimes unsettled by the arrival of rookie employers. When Merran Fraenkel arrived in Lusaka in the early 1950s, she did not want a servant at first but relented in the end because of the poor amenities: with only a woodstove and cold water, cooking and personal hygiene became time-consuming tasks for a working woman. The missionary-trained Kaonde servant Thomas, who waited on her doorstep, offered himself as a cook and suggested that she employ several other servants. They both compromised: Thomas cooked *and* cleaned, and she agreed always to refer to him as cook, and she paid him a higher wage for doing double duty. She objected, though, to his request for a uniform. At her first dinner party, Thomas turned up dressed in old, ragged clothes, with unkempt hair, and smelly. His hint was taken. The next day she gave him money to buy a uniform.[100]

Thomas also refused to serve at table when she invited African dinner guests. He would cook, but she would do the serving. In the view of some servants, the young educated Africans were just "jumped-up nobodies." Mrs. Bush noticed their reactions when her husband, then the secretary for native affairs, in the late 1940s began to hold tea parties for the African Representative Council, which met once or twice a year. The members were largely young, educated men of whom the servants, according to Mrs. Bush, did not think highly. "It would not do," she recalled, "for our house-boys to wait on them and so I called our own children and their friends all aged 7 to 10 or so to hand round cakes and cups of tea." Afterward, she heard "much merry noise from the kitchen where our staff was holding a reception of their own."[101]

Several previous employers of domestic servants in Northern Rhodesia whom I interviewed or corresponded with in England related variations on these stories, depicting servants as conservative, uninterested and not actively involved in shaping the events that took place around them. Such statements reflect the view of the dominating class and factor out precisely the element of domination central to the servant-employer relationship. The observations inscribed in that discourse must be mapped out in relation to actual colonial practices within the domestic service institution and beyond it in society at large.

100. Merran Fraenkel (nee McCulloch), personal communication, July 9, 1986.
101. Mrs. Ronald Bush, personal communication, October 14, 1986.

It is true that some servants are likely to have had a hard time waiting at table for other Africans in white households for it contradicted everything most of them had previously learned from their madams. But snobbishness at work might be a screen. There was a changing world beyond the workplace, and employers knew very little about their servants' social involvements away from work. Faithful servants may have behaved like good old Shadreck while at work, but not away from it. The Fraenkels related the surprise of a high-standing colonial official in Lusaka when one day his trusted cook did not turn up. He was at a loss about what to think, for he had used to speak of how happy his servants were and how the cook spoke to him about everything.[102] "Everything" in this case did not include political activity. On that day in the early part of April 1953, the cook had been involved in organizing for the "Days of Prayer," the ANC's attempt at demonstrating opposition to the Federation, when few Africans reported to work in Lusaka.[103] Other servants were more vocal and would report to work after attending political rallies, telling their employers that after independence they would take over their homes and their employers' possessions.[104] Whites may have attributed such statements to subversive speeches made at political rallies only half understood by their simple-minded servants or to beerhall conversations that drunken servants had overheard, but in all likelihood they nevertheless took notice of them. During this period of heightened political activity, whites became more apprehensive about the servant population in their yards. More than other African workers, servants are likely to have borne the brunt of racial animosity because of their proximity and economic dependence on whites, some of whom saw independence as the end to their comfortable lives, fearing another Congo or Mau Mau that would set Africans against whites. On the other hand, some servants who had made white household work their professional career and whose welfare had been provided for in the process shared no antiwhite sentiments.

Servants' Lives and Work through Independence

The economic decline of the late 1950s reduced urban employment for both Africans and whites. It seems that the number of servants decreased over those years,[105] owing in all likelihood to the departure of whites. Those servants who stayed on in white households did so because of lack of

---

102. Merran and Peter Fraenkel, personal communication, July 9, 1986.
103. Rotberg, *Rise of Nationalism*, pp. 249–250.
104. Stokes; Herta Ficks, personal communication, July 10, 1986.
105. "Seems" because of the insufficiency of numerical data. There is a lapse in the time sequence provided in Tables 5 and 6.

other opportunities, and their persistence in this occupation of itself implies nothing about their political involvement or detachment. Also active participation became more difficult, for during the 1950s the colonial government increased the powers of the police, banned parties, made organized political meetings unlawful, and declared a state of emergency in 1956. The years from 1959 to the end of the Federation were fraught with protracted strife and emergencies.[106] Servants' political attitudes must have varied widely, according to what they saw as their alternatives in a rapidly changing society.

Zakeyo Muhango, a Ngoni servant in his mid-fifties,[107] had lived for eight months in Ndola on the copperbelt in 1956. He had had problems finding a job. It was the time the fighting for the country had begun, he related when I spoke with him. When calling on private houses to inquire about work, he sometimes met with the response: "Go away, let Kaunda find you a job." He in fact left the copperbelt, finding it "too tough" to live in that charged political atmosphere.

Zacchi, as he was known to his employers, was a quiet man and, like some of the other servants I interviewed,[108] had expected his welfare and security to be provided by his white colonial employers. His employers would not allow him to go to political rallies and they preferred that he did not visit the compounds. They used negative terms to describe the African participants in the struggle for political independence, calling them bad people who would corrupt his mind. Zacchi was scared: "those people [the African politicians] said we want you people to fight the Europeans to go and leave this country. But me, I was not wanting them to leave because we liked Europeans too much, because we had worked with them for a long time, you see."

The ANC had in 1953 encouraged a policy of noncooperation, the withdrawal of African labor from white farmers and contractors, and had organized campaigns against the color bar in hotels, restaurants, churches, post offices, cinemas, and shops.[109] Men such as Zacchi were concerned not to lose their jobs, and the nature and place of their work may have allowed them little time to picket shops and stores. Zacchi's reaction to the height-

---

106. Colin Leys, "The Growth of Police Powers and the 1959 Emergencies," in *A New Deal in Central Africa,* ed. Colin Leys and Cranford Pratt (London: Heinemann, 1960), pp. 126–137.

107. Personal interview at Handsworth Court, Lusaka, November 5 and 12, 1983, and January 21, 1984.

108. I collected life-history information from sixteen men and twelve women between 1983 and 1984 in Lusaka. Five of the men and four of the women were too young to remember much about preindependence politics. Of the others, slightly more than half had lived in southern Africa during those years. Those who had lived in Northern Rhodesia during the tense political atmosphere of the 1950s did not have much to relate.

109. Epstein, *Politics,* pp. 161–162.

ened political activity of the 1950s was one of three I noticed from the servants who had been working at that time. The second was participation, but with a sense of anxiety, for there was no way of knowing what the future would bring. In the recollection of some of these men, political rallies functioned much as boxing matches and tribal dances: they were something to be watched with vicarious pleasure. Vicarious, because these men assumed that they would always have to work as servants. And third, some quit service, trying to establish themselves in business. Judging from my interviews in 1984, their success had not been spectacular.

Some of these men had lived in Northern Rhodesia during the period of political mobilization before independence. Others had worked in domestic service across southern Africa and returned to Zambia around or shortly after independence, often accompanied by southern African wives. Some of the women with whom I discussed servant life and work were themselves from southern Africa and had come to Zambia at independence with men they had married in the south. They had worked as servants in South Africa and continued to work in service intermittently in Lusaka after their arrival. The Zambian women who had worked in domestic service in colonial Lusaka before independence had done so only in short stints, mainly as nannies or nursegirls. They had typically stopped work when they married. They had few observations to make about preindependence politics; their lives had for the most part revolved around their own households and interaction in the compounds.

The servants' experiences discussed here cover the range of those I sampled on a more systematic basis through a large survey in Lusaka, the details of which I turn to later. At this point, it is important to stress the two strands revealed in the experiences of the menservants: life-long domestic service within Northern Rhodesia, or a migratory experience in this job in the countries to the south.

Zacchi had been born in Broken Hill, probably the mid- to late 1920s. His Ngoni father had left Malawi before World War I, married a Nsenga woman from near Feira, and worked as a farmhand for an Afrikaans-speaking farmer near the railway line. He moved his household to Lusaka in 1951 and found employment with John Howard, one of Lusaka's oldest and largest contractors. His family lived in the contractor's compound and Zacchi got his first wage-paying job as a piccanin in the kitchen of an Afrikaans-speaking household. He held a number of jobs, all in Afrikaans-speaking households, gradually advancing from piccanin to houseboy, and learning to cook. He also worked a brief time with a contractor but left because he found the work too strenuous. In 1954 he married a Nsenga woman from Feira whom he had met in Lusaka. They lived in the servants' quarters and he worked as a houseboy. By 1955 his job also included cooking, but he left because there was too much work. The Afrikaans-speaking employer was unwilling to hire other servants and Zacchi had to clean, wash, and chop wood as well. His next job landed him as a cook to a farmer near Chilanga, some 25 kilometers south of Lusaka. When that employer left for South Africa in 1956, Zacchi went to Ndola where, as noted above, he did not remain long. Back in Lusaka he stayed a while with his parents and his wife in a compound, entering service again in the late 1950s, working in the household of a white South African woman until 1964, when that employer left for South Africa.

His first child, a girl, was born in 1959. She and the second-born daughter both died. The oldest surviving child, a son, was born in 1963, and in 1983 Zacchi and his wife had a total of five surviving children. He had continued to work as a servant, always to whites, but now no longer predominantly Afrikaans-speaking. In between jobs he took periods of rest in the compound or the village. When I met him, he had recently been hired as a general servant in an expatriate household after spending one year in the rural area. His future security had not been ensured by obliging colonial employers. He, like many other menservants who had worked in households of South African background during the years before independence, commented on their employers' hostility and unwillingness to remain in the country under a black government. But in 1980 a departing employer had given him a present of money with which he had secured land from the headman in his wife's area of origin and built a small house. His wife lived there with three of the children during the cultivation season and with him in town during the dry season. His oldest son, aged twenty, had failed school and was doing piecework in the employer's garden. Zacchi, this young man, and a girl of nine who was not in school, lived in the servant's quarters in Lusaka when I met him. On his monthly wage of K75, a weekly ration of K5 and a bag of mealie meal provided by the employer,[110] Zacchi had a difficult time making ends meet, sending money to his wife every month, buying school supplies for the only child who had not yet dropped out of school, and purchasing food and clothing. Although he complained about the harsh treatment he had received in some colonial households and said that people are nicer now, he was critically aware that today he does not have enough money to buy food, shoes, and clothing. Yet he keeps on working in the hope that the child who is still in school may become more successful.

I met BaBanda at his house in the compound in 1984. He was slightly better off than Zacchi. Born in 1925, he was fifty-nine years old and had been living permanently in Lusaka since returning from Johannesburg in 1971. BaBanda, a Chewa from Chipata, was one of the many men from the

---

110. In 1983 one U.S. dollar was worth approximately K1.60 (Kwacha) at the official bank exchange rate.

Eastern Province who had migrated directly to Southern Rhodesia and then on to the south. It was closer to walk to Southern Rhodesia on foot, he said, than to go to Lusaka or the copperbelt; it took just two weeks. Southern Rhodesia was traditionally recognized as the place for people from the Eastern Province and the Zambezi Valley to go for employment, and the development of the copperbelt in the late 1920s did little to offset this pattern.[111]

BaBanda first left Chipata in 1931.[112] It was easy to get a job, he said, and he worked for several years as a cleaner at a mine in Southern Rhodesia. He returned regularly to Chipata, where he was married, and he sent money home to buy cows. After a stint as a cleaner at another mine and a job in a Jewish bakery shop, he decided in the early 1940s to go to Johannesburg in South Africa. Wages were better there, and in addition he wanted to see what Goli was like. He began as a garden boy, then got a job as a houseboy, and within a year he was employed as a waiter in the King's Hotel. He worked there till 1953, when he went back to Chipata for three years. In 1956 he was once again at the King's Hotel, and only in 1971 did he return to Zambia.

Life was easy in South Africa, he said, and there were many pleasures one could enjoy in one's free time. But "home is home, and I was big then [had responsiblities] and I must see the relatives at home." Between 1971 and 1983, he had held four or five jobs as a cook, mostly in the households of expatriate Jews in Lusaka. When we met, he had been unemployed for almost a year. "They say I am too old," he explained. He had managed to build a house in the compound out of savings from his work in South Africa. The young wife he had married in 1971 was a market trader who earned enough to cover their daily food expenses. In addition, they were subletting two rooms in the house for a total of K30 per month. The three children of his late marriage were all in school, and although he did not face the same economic urgency as Zacchi, he would like to find a job again. For, as he said, "when a man doesn't work, his family gets into trouble."

BaNkuwa, a sixty-two-year-old Ngoni man, had an even more well-traveled history.[113] He left his grandparents at Chipata to go to Kitwe on the copperbelt in 1939 at the age of seventeen. His father was employed at the mine in Luanshya. Young Nkuwa first got a job as a garden boy in Kitwe and soon was moved into the kitchen as a piccanin. He left that job in 1940 and, wanting a change of scene, went to Ndola where he held a couple of jobs as kitchen boy in Afrikaans-speaking households. He lived in the yard

111. D. Niddrie, "The Road to Work: A Survey of the Influence of Transport on Migrant Labour in Central Africa," *Rhodes-Livingstone Journal* 15 (1954): 31–42; P. Scott, "Migrant Labor in Southern Rhodesia," *Geographical Review* 44 (1954), p. 33.

112. Personal interview in Mtendere township, Lusaka, June 9, 1984.

113. Personal interview in Mtendere township, Lusaka, May 22, 1984.

[the servants' word for their quarters in the garden], sharing a room with two other servants. He vividly recalled how they had had to use passes when leaving the European residential area to visit the compounds and how they enjoyed going to watch films in the welfare hall. When the employer left for South Africa in 1946, Nkuwa returned to Chipata. "They only gave me clothes as a present," he recalled. "No money. They were afraid that African people would get rich."

BaNkuwa remained a few months in Chipata, married, and then left the wife behind when in 1947 he headed for Bulawayo in Southern Rhodesia, where "everybody knew wages were better." He got work as a house- and tableboy in a British household and in 1948 sent money for his wife to come and join him. He worked for them till 1959, advancing to the position of cook. He and his wife liked living in Bulawayo. In his free time he watched football and went to the cinema. He also did ballroom dancing, foxtrot and jive. Suits for dancing were no problem, he said; they could be bought cheaply secondhand, and he earned enough to afford them. When the employers left for England, he went to Chipata for a short rest but returned to Salisbury, where he had been engaged as a cook in an Afrikaans-speaking household. He transferred with that household to Lusaka in 1963, working as a cook until the employers left in 1971 at the closure of the tobacco company in which the head of the household had worked. They were kind, he said. They built his house in the compound and helped his children become educated. He only had three, and they are all wage employed.

Between 1971 and 1982 he had had a series of jobs with expatriates of different nationalities; American, French, and German, sometimes with long periods of unemployment in between. He had been out of work for several months when I met him and complained that expatriate employers nowadays leave the country too soon and that there are too few jobs available for skilled cooks such as he. Because of her marital problems, a daughter and her two children were living with BaNkuwa and his wife in the house in the compound. His wife made some income from the sale of vegetables, and the adult children helped out economically. Not wanting to work in a Zambian household, BaNkuwa was taking his time looking for a job.

Unlike these men, fifty-two-year-old BaTembo had left domestic service at independence.[114] A Tumbuka, born at Lundazi in 1932, he had migrated together with his wife and his mother in 1953 to a farming area near Lusaka, Chisamba, where his father was a farmhand. His time as a servant began as a garden boy in a South African household in 1953. After two years in the garden, he advanced to houseboy and worked in that capacity for another five years. When the employers left in 1960, he became a general

---

114. Personal interview in Mtendere township, Lusaka, June 12, 1984.

servant in a British household for whom he worked till 1964. The Europeans did not treat servants well in those days, he said. There was too much work for too little money, and they would swear at servants, calling them "you bloody Kaffirs." BaTembo wanted to be his own boss, so with his small savings he bought a hawker's license to sell items of clothing.

He managed to build a house in a compound before his business folded in 1968. From that year through 1982, BaTembo was employed as a night guard in the ministry of education. He had been unemployed for a year when we met, but he did not want to work as a watchman again. Although the pay is slightly better than in domestic service, he found the job too dangerous. His desire for, and perhaps need of, a job as a servant was not particularly great either. "I am tired now," he said. He liked to sit around with his men friends and drink beer and had no thoughts of retiring to the village. At some point in his working life, he had learned to use a sewing machine. He owned one, and now and then he sold clothes to residents in the compound. BaTembo had married a second wife in 1978, with whom he had one child, who was attending school. The first wife lived in another compound, making a living as a market trader. Their four adult children had left home, all having completed Form 5. They no longer depended on the parents for support but could help them out instead.

These men's working lives in domestic service differ in many ways from women's. Mrs. Moyo, a Sotho woman from Lesotho, married a Tumbuka migrant in South Africa in the mid- or late 1950s.[115] Her experience in South Africa had much in common with that of the other southern African women I met, but when she came to Lusaka after independence she was more fortunate in the job field than most of them and the Zambian women. Before her marriage, she had worked as a cook for seven years. For people such as she who had little or no education, there were four wage-labor options in South Africa, she explained. If you lived in the rural area in the Transvaal, you could work as a farmhand, mainly at harvest time, and for this you were paid on a piecework basis. She had done so twice before being employed as a cook in an Afrikaans-speaking household. Cooking, sometimes combined with general housework, was the second option. The third was working as a nanny, which perhaps included some housework. Last, you could take in white people's laundry. This she did when she married. Her husband worked as a garden boy in an English-speaking household from the late 1950s till 1967. At that point he wanted to go home, and the employers helped repatriate his family. She had borne nine children of whom five died. In Lusaka, the husband found work as a cleaner at the university and they built a house in a compound. When he died in 1968, she was able to get a cleaning job there herself.

115. Personal interview in Mtendere township, Lusaka, March 17, 1984.

By custom, after her husband's death she was remarried to one of his brothers, and her youngest child was a product of that union. She felt she could not object to that custom, but never liked it. Her second husband already had two wives, one in the village and the other living in another section of the compound. When I met Mrs. Moyo, that husband had recently been retired from his job as a security guard and had gone to the village with the other town wife. She will not join him there. As she said, she had been used to managing economically on her own for he never gave her any household allowance. All her adult children had finished school, the daughters are married, and only the two youngest are still attending school. Given the nature of Lusaka's job market and her lack of education, Mrs. Moyo had a good job. She enjoyed her free time with church friends and neighbors, liked to have a beer once in a while, and joked about being too old to have boyfriends. Few of the Zambian women I spoke to had any long experience in domestic service during the colonial period, and since independence few women with little or no schooling have been able to find jobs like Mrs. Moyo's which would enable them to pursue a livelihood and not depend on economic support from husbands or men friends.

These servants had little or no schooling, and as opportunities in their society became wider and more diverse for educated Africans, many of them were left behind—that is to say, they continued to derive their living from being servants to others in more privileged positions. Their primary gain from a life of long-term domestic service was not an immediate one: it came from the houses and children's education that might provide security to them in old age in the form of shelter and economic support. But by no means all the elderly servants I met had achieved this gain. For this reason, some, like Zacchi, are still working today, and others who are worn out from a lifetime of manual labor live under dismal conditions in shelters or shacks in Lusaka's compounds, without relatives to support them and no money with which to return to their villages. The most striking example of this was an old couple, seated on the bare ground that functioned as the floor in the shell of a house an employer had helped them erect in the compound sometime in the late 1960s, which never had been finished.[116] The man, a Chewa from Malawi, had been born about 1910. As a youth he earned his first money as a tennis boy in Zomba. He worked over the years as a nurse-boy, houseboy, and finally cook, first in Southern Rhodesia, from where he subsequently moved on to Lusaka about the time of the World War II. There he married a Nsenga woman whom he had met in a compound and who occasionally worked as a nanny in white households. The two of them were keen ballroom dancers and they took part in competitions between the towns. They showed me a cup

116. Personal interviewed in Mtendere township, Lusaka, May 15, 1984.

they had won, and the old wife was agile enough to dance a few steps while she described her favorite ballroom dress. The gay atmosphere they described contrasted dramatically with the drab circumstances of their present lives. They had been among the audience at the preindependence political rallies, for as the old man said, "nobody could stop us." Yet he had nothing in particular to say about that period other than remarking that he knew then that he would be unable to get any other type of job. For such people as this couple, the political mobilization of the 1950s and the struggle for independence brought few tangible benefits.

PART II

Encountering Domestic Service

In Africa servants, like the poor, are always with us, and nobody seems to mind.
— Cullen Gouldsbury, *An African Year*

[4]

Research on and Life with Servants

Colonial anthropologists did not, as James Murray noted, study masters and servants. Because of tensions, there was little social interaction between anthropologists and white settlers and officials. Beyond highly ritualized encounters in colonial households by which the formalities of "calling" etiquette and the standards of white civilized society were observed, anthropologists may have had little opportunity to see how relationships between servants and employers were structured in everyday interaction. But this is not a sufficient explanation of why this particular occupational domain was left unexplored. And unexplored it was, for nowhere is it to be found in the established annals of Zambian labor history, colonial and present, even though, like most other whites, colonial investigators of anthropology and history kept servants. These workers seem, however, to have disappeared from social consciousness into oblivion.

Thus domestic service has been and, with a few exceptions, still is taken for granted, receiving a "no questions asked" approach from social scientists. Yet in postcolonial Zambia as in much of the rest of the world, servants are still with us. Part of the challenge of my research as it developed over the years has been to retrieve a sense of history—a changing one—of domestic service from among scattered archival records and between the lines of texts concerned with other issues. I also tried to establish a profile of domestic-service practices in postcolonial Zambia in the mid-1980s in order to explore the extent to which old habits had persisted. Finally, I sought to come to grips with what it meant to be a servant and an employer in the late colonial situation, and how these two places are experienced by the individuals who hold them today.

As a discussion of the methods of my research this chapter functions as a bridge between the colonial and the postcolonial periods in my examination of domestic service. I first reflect on the data-collecting procedures I used to give Part I its historical dimension. To provide a backdrop for Part III, I discuss my anthropological field research and attempts at participant observation, and comment on the intersubjective experience of the research process which has influenced my presentation and interpretation.

Making Servants Visible

Between 1981 and 1983 I sought to retrieve evidence about servants and their employers from the published literature on Northern Rhodesia and Zambia available in library collections in the United States, in particular, the Africana Collection at Northwestern University, my academic home since 1982. Simultaneously, I read whatever I could find of studies on domestic service in other places and other times in order to gain a comparative understanding of the processes that had shaped and changed this occupation over time in relation to demographic and economic shifts and different cultural and ideological influences. I spent the summer of 1982 in England, culling the official depository of colonial records from Northern Rhodesia at the Public Records Office in London in order to establish some sense of a historical trajectory of the legal measures and rules that had structured the place of servants in relation to employers and other workers over time.

This research provided a record of occupational roles rather than a sense of individuals with personal concerns of their own. In an attempt to infuse the record with that sense of personhood, I contacted people who had been employers of servants in Northern Rhodesia. Several British colleagues with research experience in southern Africa helped with advice and suggestions of contacts. In particular, J. C. Mitchell and Arnold Epstein, two of the prominent anthropologists associated with the urban research conducted at the Rhodes-Livingstone Institute during the 1950s, kindly tapped their memories about domestic-service practices at that time and made available special records for my use. I also placed an advertisement in the classified columns of the *London Times* in August 1982: "For a study of domestic servants in Lusaka, Zambia, during the colonial period and at present, I would appreciate hearing from anyone who has reminiscences, recollections or anecdotes. Of particular interest is information on terms of employment, level of wages and how it was calculated, accommodation, preference for servants from certain ethnic groups, and explanations of why so few women were employed as domestic servants. I am also interested in photographs of servants at work or at leisure." In March 1983 another advertisement went into the *Overseas Pensioner*, the newsletter of the Overseas Service Pensioners' Association in England. And in October

1983, a note about my study was featured in *News from Zambia*, a newsletter compiled from the Zambian press at the London office of Zambia Consolidated Copper Mines, one of the parastatal companies, whose editor, Dick Hobson, provided me with much information and many contacts. Its mailing list includes many members of the Zambia Society, an association comprised largely of former colonial officials interested in keeping up connections and sharing concerns and news about a country in which many of them lived for good parts of their lives. Among them, these notices yielded nine written responses, which prompted exchanges of questions and information. Some of the individuals who responded continued to offer their insights for the duration of my entire study, and their advice produced additional contacts over subsequent years.

Gradually I began to establish a profile of domestic service during the colonial period. There were still many gaps, and as yet I had little substantive information about the postcolonial situation. At that point, I proposed research in Zambia and applied for funding to investigate the dynamics of domestic employment on several levels: first, the changing structure of the labor force in domestic service, over time and in relation to national employment patterns; second, the changing content of the employer-employee relationship with special attention to the differences in work conditions of men and women; and third, the changing relationships among domestic workers and between them and other workers.

Having secured the necessary funding, I arrived in Lusaka at the beginning of October 1983. I spent nine months in Zambia during that field trip and returned for three months during the summer of 1985 to tie up loose ends and to pursue certain issues in more detail. Traveling between the United States and Zambia during those years, I made stops in England for additional archival work, including the collections at Rhodes House, and visited some of the people with whom I had corresponded. During summer 1986, I made several such calls in an effort to try to understand in particular what it was like to be a white employer of black servants during the political upheaval and rapidly changing times of the last decade of colonial rule. Because my attempts in Zambia to engage whites who had remained after the coming of independence in detailed discussion had been largely fruitless, in fall 1986, I sent some fifteen letters to people in Great Britain whose name had been given me by close contacts. Ten of them responded to my inquiries and helped me clarify the answers to a number of questions.

Research on Domestic Service

My research in Zambia led to the need for more archival work, the collection of employment and economic statistics, a survey of actual employment practices, biographical work, and some kind of participant observation. These various components of the research at times overlapped, but for the purpose of this discussion I present them as more discrete than in fact they were.

A Survey of Servants and Employers

Servants in Zambia today continue to be taken for granted. Everybody supposedly knows what having servants is like, what to expect and not to expect of them, and shares these insights with newcomers. But beyond anecdotes, little substantive information exists about servants and their employers in postcolonial Zambia. Domestic service has not been enumerated as a distinct employment category by the Central Statistical Office since 1968. Although the Zambia National Provident Fund (ZNPF) has operated a registration scheme of urban servants for pension purposes since 1973, not all employers register their servants. The ZNPF's figures for servants were not categorized by sex, and proved to be of little help as an indicator of the numerical size and composition of the occupation. To get at these and other factors, I had to construct a sample survey that would fairly encompass the kind of variations of domestic service practiced in Lusaka today. I wanted to explore whether or not, and if so, how, such factors as an employer's ethnic or national background, occupation, and the length of time of residence in Zambia or of keeping servants influenced employment practices. I also wanted to know whether or not a servant's ethnic background, education, employment experience, age, and sex shaped discernible differences in his or her experience in domestic service. And I wished to learn about about the kinds of lives servants and their employers lived beyond their interaction in the household setting.

The available statistics on Lusaka's population contained no information on the ethnic/national and occupational composition of residential areas. To construct a sample that would control for these factors, I drew on my own understanding of Lusaka's population composition and sought advice from local colleagues. I thus planned my sample as a survey of every tenth house in two of Lusaka's low-density areas, Woodlands and Kabulonga, which would allow an inclusion of servant-keeping householders who worked in government as well as in private business and who represented Zambians and several foreign nationalities. As the survey got under way, I quickly realized that the resident Asians and the Eurafrican population were being left out. To remedy this, I selected two areas that during the colonial period were designated specifically for them: an area with a heavy concentration of Asian traders and the former Eurafrican part of town. Appproximately every tenth house was surveyed there as well. This is to say that the sample survey was readjusted as it was undertaken to control

[200]

for those factors I was concerned to learn about. What at the outset I had hoped would become a random sample survey thus turned out to be in the nature of a quota sample.

I composed two questionnaires to use in the survey, one for the servant and one for his or her employer, which I had begun to work on before I arrived in Zambia. I had made a list of the of issues I wanted to explore and had given much thought to how and what kinds of questions to ask. When I arrived in Lusaka in October 1983, I discussed these issues with local colleagues, received their advice on what else to include in the survey and how to approach asking questions. I drafted a preliminary set of the two questionnaires, which I showed to my colleagues and pretested with the help of my chief assistant. Then I drafted the format of the questionnaires used in the actual survey.

To administer a survey of this kind required several participants. My chief assistant, Susan Antkiewicz, the wife of a North American history colleague at the University of Zambia, had been involved in a variety of research work in Lusaka and already in 1981 had indicated her interest in participating in my future research on domestic service. She and I each headed a team, the counterpart of which was a Zambian assistant. On the recommendations of colleagues, I engaged three Zambian students from the university for this work: Lameck Mwaba, who had just completed a B.A. in public administration and was unemployed; Stella Moyo, who held a B.A. in economics and was taking postgraduate courses in international law; and Ethel Chongo, who was studying for her B.A. in African development studies. We all met several times before beginning the actual survey, and I explained to them my interest in the domestic service occupation. They were puzzled at first, since they assumed—judging perhaps from syndicated American programs shown on local television—that everyone where I came from kept servants. They tested the questionnaire themselves, and in the end we eliminated a couple of questions that appeared intractable. Then we set out.

The survey required mobility. In my previous work in Lusaka I had used, first, a small motorcycle, then a bicycle, and finally public transportation in the form of the minibus to get to the compound. Clearly, this would not do. I was fortunate to be able to hire a Landrover and driver from the Institute of African Studies of the University of Zambia, where I was a research affiliate. The driver picked us up each workday at 1 P.M., dropped us in the residential areas at a spot I specified in advance, and collected us again at a specified place at 6 P.M. This was the time period during which, I thought, we would be most unlikely to upset servants' work in the household. The majority of the heavy tasks are done in the morning, and in some households servants have some time off after lunch, which in this part of former British Africa is between 1 and 2 P.M. We chose to continue till six

[201]

in the hope of reaching employers who worked away from home when they returned at five.

I had targeted the residential areas into subsets of house blocks, using aerial photographs and surveyers' plot maps. When the driver left us, Susan and her assistant would approach one subset and I and my assistant another. If no one was home at the house, or if the householder declined to be interviewed, we would go on to the next house. We would approach the gate, alert the guard or servant to the presence of visitors and ask him to inform the madam. If there was no gate, we walked directly to the front door. We would inform the householder about the nature of the survey and invite him or her to participate. If the invitation was accepted, we white women would accompany the householder, while our Zambian assistants interviewed the chief servant of the household. I insisted on conducting these interviews separately and encouraged the assistants to interview the servant in the servant quarters in order to get a glimpse of what the living conditions were like.

Studies of domestic service which involved interviews undertaken in South Africa and what then was Southern Rhodesia had led me to anticipate that my research team might encounter hostility from householders when we asked them questions about their servants,[1] but in fact we met very little. I attribute this to the more relaxed racial atmosphere in Zambia as compared with the countries in the south and to our approach: a white woman accompanied by a young Zambian perhaps did not give rise to the kind of suspicion that an all-Zambian research team might have in a city where everyone fears thieves and burglars. To be sure, some householders made excuses. But others who were busy invited us to return the next day. Without exception, the Zambian householders were the most approachable, which I attribute to traditional patterns of hospitality: we were often invited inside the house and seated before we had even got a chance to explain the reason for our coming. (There were amusing moments as a result, such as the time we already had been seated on the living room couch when the male Zambian householder told us he had just sacked his servant the day before—but wouldn't we like to talk to him about something else?) The hostility we did meet came from one clearly identifiable source: whites who had stayed put since the colonial period. From them we got more excuses—and closer to having the door slammed in our faces—than from anyone else.

One of the residential areas I had initially targeted for our work included a housing enclave for high-level government officials but once under way, I

1. Jacklyn Cock, *Maids and Madams: A Study in the Politics of Exploitation* (Johannesburg: Ravan Press, 1980), pp. 19–20, and A. K. H. Weinrich, *Mucheke: Race, Status, and Politics in a Rhodesian Community* (New York: Holmes and Meier, 1976), pp. 215–217.

decided we should not interview there, in order not to give the impression that we wanted to pry into the private affairs of public officials. For the same reason we also avoided the residences of ambassadors and consuls. We did, however, include lower level embassy personnel in the survey. Sometimes the pragmatics of pedestrian field research made such avoidance rules hard to observe. I recall one very hot afternoon when Ethel and I had been walking from door to door for what seemed like an eternity. Up came an ambassadors residence, and I said: "let's give it a try." The guard announced our presence, a servant was sent to collect us, and soon we were seated in a reception room and brought cold drinks. The ambassador's wife appeared and listened to our story. She was sorry, she said, but protocol prevented her from revealing household details. Yet she went on talking and talking. The embassy circles were a bit nervous then, for a long-time, trusted servant in the British High Commission had been involved in a check-forging scheme. This I knew, for it had been reported in the newspaper.[2] The rest of what she revealed remains confidential.

When we were allowed to interview, each member of the team went through his or her separate questionnaire. Susan and I rotated the Zambian assistants between us in order not to develop a procedural routine that became so fixed that it made us ignore the specifics of the given household. I did work more with Lameck, though. He and I would team up on several Saturdays, descending on private householders who otherwise worked away from home in the early morning. This had its embarrassing moments, for example, one Saturday morning when a male householder appeared in his dressing gown at the door. But he spoke Swedish, and I gave him a big Danish grin. We ended up having morning tea with him and his wife in their dressing gowns.

The questionnaires were designed to elicit information from both servant and employer about occupational background, the length and variety of their involvement with domestic service, the work regime, duties and responsibilities of both servant and employer, the composition of the households of the two parties, and leisure-time interaction and lifestyle of both. On the last issues we sought in particular to engage people in informal conversation, by conducting fairly structured small-talk on the completion of the formal questionnaire. If the assistants finished interviewing the servant before the interview with the employer was completed, they were instructed to come into the living room and seat themselves inconspicuously. On the other hand, we would extend our small talk if the assistants went on longer. All the assistants were multilingual and conducted their inteviews in Nyanja or one or other of the local languages. Susan and I interviewed most of the employers in English. Our linguistic

2. "Cook on Graft Charge," *Zambia Daily Mail*, October 17 (1983), p. 3.

problems occurred mainly in Asian households where in some cases the women we interviewed knew very little English. Yet our language skills were so limited in comparison to those of our Zambian assistants. (One afternoon I interviewed employers in a Norwegian-speaking household; I spoke Danish, and they spoke Norwegian. I remember my thrill when Lamack came back in: at least he could hear that I could speak something in addition to English.) The interviews lasted anywhere from half an hour to more than an hour. They were conducted during the three hottest months of the year, and I was offered more soft drinks during the duration of this work than I have ever consumed before. We were also sometimes offered alcohol, which whether we really would have liked it or not, we always declined.

On days when all the three Zambian research assistants were available, Ethel went off on a special assignment: interviewing servants and some employers in "the flats," the apartment buildings that a number of private firms, government, and parastatal companies have constructed to accommodate junior-level employees. When I decided it was necessary to extend this work, her younger brother, Kizito, a high-school student, received on-the-job training and helped her.

How reliable is the information we collected in these interviews? Some items such as wages, hours of work, holiday arrangements, length of employement, and ZNPF registration can be cross-checked, for both servant and employer were questioned about these matters. We as interviewers developed a sense of whether or not the person was honest in answering or merely telling a story. Some people were difficult to interview and consistently had to be prompted, whereas others were extremely easy to talk to and rapport developed quickly. To get at the question of how employers really viewed their servants, we asked them what advice they would give a newcomer who had never kept servants. Answers to this question revealed that regardless of whatever else they told us, employers do not trust their servants. While they would rather not bother about them, they feel they have to because they never know what they are up to. Most of these interviews contain litanies of complaints from both servants and employers; we found few households with relaxed interpersonal relations.

The members of the interviewing teams were instructed to write up, on the evening of the interview, a narrative of it, the characteristics of its setting, their reception, and whatever they learned outside the framework of the questions. These narratives tell, among other things, of the amusements and disappointments of the work, such as long walks in the hot sunshine knocking on too many gates, pursuit by ferocious dogs, the location of the tallest fences with the highest spikes in Lusaka, and hostile madams, British or southern African, posing in front of the main door with legs astride, arms on hips, saying, as only they can, "*Yiiis?*"—meaning, I suppose, "Who do you think you are to come here?" They also tell of the lives of a cosmopolitan crowd, friendly receptions, interesting conversations, and of invitations to come again. But first and foremost, they relate the spectacular difference between the life and circumstances of servants and those of the persons they work for.

Special Collections

During the interview period, I also spent time with the special collection of Zambiana and government documents in the university library, reading travel descriptions, biographies and autobiographies, novels—anything in which I could find information about servants and their employers. When the survey was completed, I spent some months perusing files in the National Archives of Zambia in Lusaka, and several days in the National Archives of Zimbabwe, looking at early records from the period when the two Rhodesias were administered from South Africa. In addition there were newspapers, magazines, and newsletters published during the colonial period, reports of colonial commissions, and law reports. Perhaps the driest of this reading, the reports of the Legislative Council, in fact gave me a better sense of the tensions among the colonial whites than any of the other documents. With it all, I was beginning to fill in the gaps in the record I had established before my arrival in Zambia.

My reading also raised new questions. Scattered remarks in labor reports, about servants' attempts to form unions in the postwar years, for example, made me eager for more information. I spoke to union officials of the Zambia Congress of Trade Unions at the Kitwe headquarters. While they found my observations interesting, they knew nothing about these attempts and could add little to what I already knew. But like everyone I spoke to during this research, they had their stories and anecdotes about servants and employers. And they were willing to talk about the prospects—which they considered to be negligible—for unionization among servants today. I also met mining officials and the mine archivist of Zambia Consolidated Copper Mines in Kitwe with the faint (but unfulfilled) hope that the records on miners' attempts to form a union in the late 1940s would contain information also about servants' union activities. I spent about a month in the ZNPF registration office for domestic servants in Lusaka going through records and discussing the servants' situation with its staff, as well as with the officials at the ZNPF headquarters. I spoke with statisticians in the Central Statistical Office about the problems of sampling domestic servants. I consulted officers at the labor exchange and looked at registration data, while Lameck interviewed some of the men lined up outside the office who hoped to find jobs as servants. Lameck inteviewed officers at the police station in one of the residential areas we had sampled

[205]

in order to get information about the types of cases employers and servants bring in. And Lameck and I interviewed personnel managers in a number of private firms and parastatal companies to learn about their policies in regard to paying for servants for certain ranks of employees.

Servants Everywhere

At this point in my work, servants had become anything but invisible. What I read about them in the records obviously still left them distant. But the reading was done against the backdrop of an urban setting, where every unemployed man is a potential servant. So I encountered them everywhere. During my cigarette breaks as I sat on the low wall surrounding the National Archives, men passing by would often approach me asking for work, telling me of their skills in domestic arts, whether or not they really had them, such as boiling eggs or peeling potatoes. Men, and sometimes women, would also call at the house where I happened to stay. This did not occur every day, but it happened often enough to dramatize the wretched employment situation in Lusaka. Some of these people would be men who had seen me when I visited my friends in the compound. From the point of view of the unemployed person, every white woman is a potential employer.

Living with Servants

In order to obtain the cooperation of both servants and their employers, I had to confront the question of how to gain access beyond the setting of formal interviews. Domestic service, perhaps because of its location within the private household, seems to invite nonconventional approaches for purposes of close-range research.[3] I considered two options: establishing my own servant-keeping household, using myself as a guinea pig to register the details of everyday interaction, or to move into already established households with persons who employed servants. I quickly negated the first option. Even if housing had been available in Lusaka's crowded housing market, I did not wish to live as a single housekeeper—in part because a household that was empty most of day was vulnerable to break-ins and thefts, in part because I anticipated that I would be an unsuccessful madam. Given my dislike of the domestic service institution, I would have paid what local residents term exorbitant wages, leave the organization of

3. See Evelyn Nakano Glenn, *Issei, Nissei, War Bride: Three Generations of Japanese American Women in Domestic Service* (Philadelphia: Temple University Press, 1986), pp. x–xvi, and Judith Rollins, *Between Women: Domestics and Their Employers* (Philadelphia: Temple University Press, 1985), pp. 8–11.

household tasks and their timing to the servant, and have trouble making authoritarian decisions about how, where, and when the servant's presence was required. I would have been too uncertain, too talkative, and too lacking the firmness that household manuals suggest madams exhibit. Keeping my own servant would have taught me nothing about other people's servant-keeping practices.

I chose the second option. From my experience of living as a paying guest in a private household while doing research in Lusaka in 1981, I knew that it would give me a strategic position from which both to observe and participate in the interactions around the daily routine of household activity. My plan was to stay in several households of varied national and occupational backgrounds which had engaged domestic servants for varying lengths of time. But in most servant-employing Zambian households there are pressures on space and resources with relatives living in and visitors coming and going, so I soon gave up the idea of staying in one. My desire to make a live-in arrangement with a household of British or southern African background who had remained in Zambia after independence was also soon quashed. Although I had introductions from former Northern Rhodesians in Britain and from long-time expatriates in Zambia and had discussed the matter at length with local whites who had many contacts with the kinds of households I was interested in, none of them wanted my presence. When meeting some of the old-timers, I was initially received with an overbearing curiosity that, when I persisted with my questions, turned into suspicion and in some cases outright hostility. "What's this study for, anyway?" was the response of one of these white madams when I inquired about contacts we both knew she had and which I knew would be helpful. Her assumption, in my interpretation of her remarks, is that since they live with them, matters about servants are supposed to be well known already, so what is there to know? The white women we interviewed in the survey who were old-timers were far from expansive in their comments. We had the impression they did not want to talk about their servants, at least not discursively.

The Englishwoman's home may well be her castle and her desire for privacy pronounced, yet there was something else at stake. I first blamed myself for their negative response. I do ask many questions and perhaps in a more straightforward manner than is considered polite by persons concerned with standards and etiquette. But so do many other people in Zambia today without being considered rude. Being a single woman might also have been a liability, a disturbing element in the private household. Yet, many householders in Lusaka accommodate nonmembers for varying lengths of time because of the acute housing shortage. Their reactions disturbed me. I finally concluded that their hostility, though directed toward me, arose because of the troublesome nature of my research topic. It is far easier to speak about servants as an investigator than to live with them as a householder. I had approached my research from a distance; I had not experienced the vexations that were part of the daily enactment of domestic service and the difficulties employers experience in their relationship with servants. Servants aren't what they used to be, such employers say, and there are more problems today in keeping them in their place and making them work satisfactorily. Servants and their problems are issues many of the old-time employers would rather not be reminded of, let alone be forced to explore by a probing researcher.

During 1983 and 1984 and again on my return in 1985, I lived for varying lengths of time in four households whose members were employed at the University of Zambia and had outlooks closer to my own. Two were from the United States, one from India, and one a Canadian-American household. With the exception of the last, they had all lived in other parts of Africa before coming to Zambia. The members of the Canadian-American household had previously lived in Zambia for some time. The servants were informed of my presence and told about my work. I paid a monthly fee for room and board and I asked my hosts to remunerate their servants out of it for the additional work my presence caused. I in turn tipped the servants when they had done special tasks for me and, following the practice of my hosts, brought presents to some of them on my return in 1985.

Although these households are not representative of the range of persons who employ servants, they exposed me to several variations of service arrangements and made me sensitive to both the joys and the problems of servant-employer relationships. Freed from housework, laundry, and cleaning, I had more time than I have ever had before or since for my own research activities. For out-of-the-ordinary events I might prepare a special dish (much in the manner of the Western husband who enjoys weekend gourmet cooking, leaving the dirty work and the dishes for the wife). Living in these different households, I was exposed to a wider circle of people in leisure-time interaction than I would have been had I established my own household. When learning about the nature of my research, most of the people I met offered comments from their own experience. Their anecdotes about life with servants and hints about tropical household management could fill another book. My understanding of the social lives of people who keep servants is influenced by this more extensive but less formal interaction and draws as well on information I collected in the sample survey.

Members of my households had lived in Lusaka for varying lengths of time, and although there were university teachers in each household, they managed their relationships with servants very differently. Crudely typecasting them, the Canadian-American couple who had lived in Lusaka for the shortest time, were "liberals" who tried to put as few demands as possible on their middle-aged woman servant. She lived in a nearby compound, commuted on a bicycle given to her by previous expatriate employers, arrived after breakfast and returned to her home before sunset. The household routine was accommodated to her health problems, and the employers sometimes helped her with her own economic household problems. The relationship within the household was caring, but in a distant way because of language problems. Of the households I lived in, the interpersonal atmosphere in this one seemed to me the most artificial.

The American single head of household, who had been in Lusaka a bit longer than the Canadian-American couple, had previously lived in Malawi, Kenya, and Nigeria. Because her working day of teaching and meetings was filled with personal contact, she insisted on privacy at home. She did not want her manservant to bother her, and their relationship was marked by distance. Beyond his daily routine of cleaning, washing, and a bit of garden work, she preferred to consider him irrelevant. She did not want to know what went on in the servants' quarters where several people lived; it was none of her business, she said. Because of this apparent noninterference, I thought for a long time that the relationship in this household was relaxed.

Members of the second American household had lived in Lusaka for about seven years, and the husband had spent time in Tanzania as well. They had employed one servant before the man who worked for them now. Their relationship to the servant could be labeled one of despair. As a newly arrived expatriate woman, the wife had initially wanted to be involved. Her trust and good will, however, had been misused; in one instance, there was a burglary, planned by her previous servant. Now after several years of employing them, she insisted that she couldn't "handle" servants. She disliked the idea of having them, although her husband was more positively inclined. They kept up jovial relations with their servant when he worked inside the house but she wanted nothing to do with his private life. She was as skilled at interpreting the servant's reactions as he was of hers. The atmosphere in the servant-employer relationship in this household was one of uncertainty: "you never know what he is up to." In my judgment, the routine in this household functioned smoothly.

I stayed the longest with my Indian hosts, who had lived in Lusaka since the early 1970s and spent several years in Ghana before that. They employed a full-time man servant whose wife did half-time work in the kitchen and, on her husband's day off, in the house. The servants had two children below school age. The relationship of employers with servants in this household could be typed as paternalistic. The employers assumed several caretaking functions for their servants' household, related lovingly to the servants' oldest child, and wished with the best of intentions to advise the servants on how to handle family life and household economy. Yet in a paternalistic relationship, one party is considered childlike. Although the employers were more well intentioned regarding their servants' welfare than any of the others with whom I lived, they experienced more trouble in the day-to-day running of household activity. More frustrations were expressed here, by the employers as well as by the servants, of the other not living up to expectations. The servants did not work properly, in the employers' view, and in the view of the servants, the employers did not help them enough. There were constant trials and tribulations in this household. As I experienced it, the atmosphere between servants and employers in this household was tense.

If these arrangements allowed me to enjoy the comforts of domestic service, they also confronted me with many of its problems. As a participating member of these households, it was impossible to keep up the anthropologist's stance as an objective observer. My observations were no longer those of academic distance but of daily encounters. I doubt that my presence to any large extent changed the manner in which these householders interacted with their servants, for they were reenacting practices that already had become routinized. There may have been fewer harsh words when I was around. But when I argued with my hosts or made suggestions about reforming practices, they would do things their way, not mine.

I tried not to argue with my hosts, hoping in that way to see household activity unfold as it perhaps would have done without my presence. But of course my presence did create a difference, for there was a new household member for the servant to contend with. Moreover, my position was ambiguous. I was not the person who brought in the bread, yet I seemed to have a lot of money. Sometimes I was out a lot, at other times I would spend a good deal of the daytime in the house. I had different visitors. Unlike most expatriates, I did not drive a car. I paid more attention to the servants than guests normally did. I engaged the servants in conversations and asked them questions. I tried to chat informally as I would do with persons in any household. My questions may at times have annoyed these servants, for who was I to snoop into their lives? They did talk to me without first being spoken to, however, and asked questions, about my assistants, what we were doing, and where I had been. They also asked for favors. And sometimes they appealed to me to raise particular issues with the employers. Yet my occasional role as intermediary between the two was limited. And although I was closer to the servants in terms of conversation, from their perspective my place was clear: I "belonged to" the employers and I had resources that were desirable.

In the second household described above, where the relationship with the servant was kept distant and noninterference was the order of the day, the servant stole what by Zambian standards was a large amount of cash and travelers' checks in foreign currency from the locked nightstand in my room. Even this servant who did not spend much time in the house knew every nook and cranny and what we kept there. This incident served to verify the employers' truism: a servant was not to be trusted. Only through this occurrence that directly involved me did I begin to understand, to know, some of the vexing meaning of life with servants in a city such as Lusaka.

It was through my intersubjective experience that I came to understand how distance between servants and their employers was systematically expressed and re-created in both space and social structure. I hope this extremely personalized experience in the field has enriched my analysis of contemporary servant-employer interaction without my losing sight of the class underpinnings of their relationship.

Lives: Servants and Their Employers

In order to qualify the generalizations I found expressed in the official records, I tried to capture the personal viewpoints and experiences of elderly servants and white former-employers who had lived through the last period of colonial rule. I did so by collecting biographies that focused on working lives from a number of individuals, in informal circumstances.

I met several persons, both servants and employers, who fitted these criteria when undertaking the sample survey. The occupational histories their life and work as servants or employers contained were complex and their observations interesting and informative. I could have called back on several of these households to engage the servant or the employer in longer-term discussion. I decided to not use this avenue because of the interference and intrusion into ongoing household activity such calls might impose on households I had selected as randomly as possible for sampling purposes. There was always in old-time white households that lingering curiosity of what I really was up to, and the suspicion, perhaps, of setting servants up for something. In some of these households in which servants spoke another Zambian language than Nyanja, which I know, I would have to bring along an assistant to interpret. This would add restrictive formality to an interviewing situation of, we hoped, free-flowing exchange, and perhaps make me more suspect in the view of white employers.

The life histories with focus on occupational experiences I did collect were obtained under more informal circumstances. I interviewed one lifetime servant in the neighborhood where I lived. His employers were friends of mine, and it was easier to gain rapport than through a stranger's household. The rest of the servants I spoke with, fifteen men and twelve women, lived in the compound where I had done my previous research in

Lusaka. My long-time assistant, who has lived there since its opening, identified these individuals for me. Several of them had now stopped work, some were still looking for jobs in domestic service, and some after a life of domestic toil had settled down to old-age poverty in urban retirement. Because of what I experienced as hostility from white old-time employers still living in Zambia, I interviewed former colonial employers who now live in England.

The information was obtained with difficulty and with much prompting on my part. Many of the servants I spoke to were not particularly articulate, perhaps as a result of their adjustment to a job in which they were expected always to be present without being seen and not talk unless they were spoken to. Most of them expressed surprise that anyone would be interested in such lives as theirs. Society devalues their work, and during the late colonial period servants who obediently and deferentially continued their work were considered to be politically suspect. Yet some of these old-time servants opened up, among them a couple of extremely good talkers who took pleasure in sharing their rich occupational histories with me. Some of them had enjoyed the perks of domestic service for whites and had in their own words led good and exciting lives that had taken them across the southern African continent. Others had experienced the domestic institution to be a particularly restricting one that had curtailed their own plans for living independent lives. Some had staged individual rebellions by quitting, yet many others stayed put. Most depressing to me, above all, was the sharp contrast between living conditions as these servants had known them and their life circumstances today: some of them had acquired nothing but a far-ranging and complex work history from their lifelong labor in domestic service.

I called on five households in England whose members had been long-time employers of domestic servants in Northern Rhodesia. Most of them had been members of the colonial administration and they had left the country at or soon after independence. They spanned two different cohorts of colonial employers: those who had come out in the days when the imperial order was taken for granted, that is, before the Great Depression, and those who had gone to Northern Rhodesia after World War II, when the colonial flags had begun to be taken down elsewhere. Generalizing from my limited data, it would not be incorrect to characterize the interwar generation as "paternal" in their relation to servants. The postwar group was more "liberal" in their attitude, yet also displayed a curious despair about servants who seemed to perform no longer according to old-time expectations.

Some of the members of these five households were among my original correspondents. That is to say that they are a somewhat biased sample. The persons who responded to my advertisements and who invited me into their homes had positive recollections of their life and work in Northern Rhodesia. People for whom life in the colony had been a troublesome experience did not respond to my call. My hosts were persons who were interested and concerned to exchange information about a country in which they had lived long and interesting periods of their lives and about individuals who often had been part of their lives for several years: their servants. They were also concerned to rectify the negative image of the colonizers to which they had been subjected in much of the scholarly literature of a previous generation.

My discussions with them did not take the form of structured interviews. They were extended informal conversations revolving around personal biography: reasons for coming to Northern Rhodesia, regional postings, marriage, the birth of children, rural versus urban locations, and social life and the nature of interaction among, between, and across the different racial groups. We discussed their changing experience of life with servants in relation to these settings and to the flow of events: the coming of the Federation, the rise of African political parties, and the general political mobilization before to independence.

In these conversations, I was particularly concerned to come to grips with the inherent paradox in such households as the colonial era was drawing to a close: the preparation in society at large of some Africans to take over the reins of the polity at independence, and the persistence within private households of a hierarchically structured labor process. These colonial employers did not find it necessary to revolutionize the domestic service institution from within. Postcolonial employers of servants, including Zambians, have not done so either. Gouldsbury's statement from the first decades of the century still pertains: "Servants, like the poor, are always with us, and nobody seems to care."

PART III

Colonial Legacies and Postcolonial Changes

Domestic servants lead miserable lives. In the past, they were smart. Today, cooks look like gardeners. If I had known this would become a woman's job, I would have sought work as a driver.

—BaNkuwa

[5]

Persistence and Change

From BaNkuwa's perspective, the position of servants in relation to other occupational groups has changed for the worse since Zambia became independent in 1964. A servant during the colonial period, dressed up in his Sunday best, was indistinguishable from a clerk. Today servants not only look miserable, they are also underpaid, most certainly when compared with those who employ them, no matter their color, and when compared with other unskilled workers.[1] Their occupation is alive, but not well.

In this chapter I explore the meaning of BaNkuwa's statement, beginning with a discussion of the growing inequalities in postcolonial Zambia and the widening gap between the tiny segment of well-situated urbanites and the rest of the population, most particularly between servants and other low-income workers. Next I present the findings of the large sample survey of servants and their employers I undertook in Lusaka in 1983 and 1984. With the survey as background and referring also to my subsequent research in 1985, I discuss the contemporary domestic service institution: who are the servants and the employers and how is the employment relationship characterized? The changes that my survey revealed, which taken together have transformed the occupation of domestic service, are the subject of Chapter 6. These changes stem largely from the nature of postcolonial economic developments, or lack thereof, in the new nation, and they affect the employers, the servants themselves, their work relationship, and the labor process in private domestic service. Throughout Part III, my discussion is focused on Lusaka, which after independence surpassed the copper-

1. See Table 7 in Chapter 7.

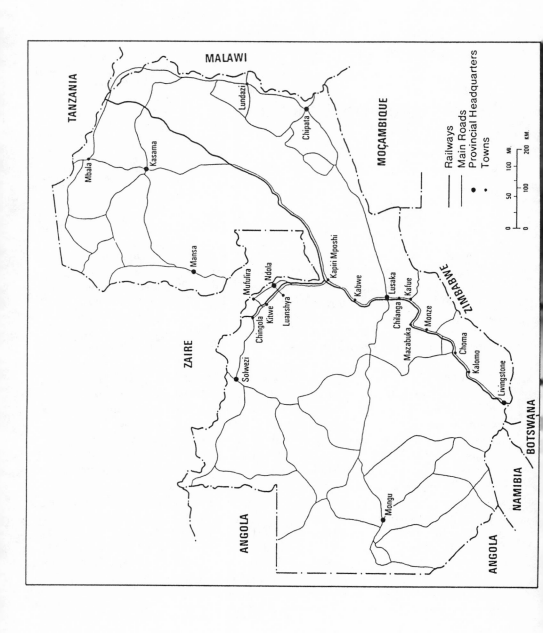

belt towns as the country's hub, the center for its elite, its politicians, and the international aid and development workers who are replacing the colonial era's predominantly British and South African expatriates.

Independent Zambia: Growing Inequities

A former colonial resident returning to Lusaka in the mid-1980s—twenty years or so after independence—would feel curiously at home in the social landscape. To be sure, many more black faces appear behind office desks, and tall office buildings break the horizons of a rapidly growing capital that for a long time looked like a ramshackle town. His remaining friends still employ servants, as does anyone of influence as well as persons of lesser means. While their discourse would seem familiar when they express their problems regarding servants, their complaints have become more pronounced. In spite of persistence of an entire occupational domain, there have been changes that are making the relationship between servant and employer more troublesome than it ever was before.

These processes must be examined against the background of overall changes in the postcolonial Zambian economy. At independence the rules and regulations that had structured the migrant labor system and given access to housing and work by race were scrapped. The educational system was greatly expanded. The government set about developing the economy by opening jobs for people with white-collar skills in its many new departments; import-substitution industries were built, offering work to some, and the construction business grew. Economic reforms in the late 1960s and early 1970s stimulated the indigenization of many commercial establishments. The government entered into a 51-percent partnership with a number of foreign firms and with the mining companies, placing them under the control of parastatal agencies. The multiparty government established at independence gave way at the end of 1972 to a one-party system and increased involvement by the state in the running of the economy.

A good deal has been written about these processes from economic and political perspectives,[2] and it suffices here to mention just those issues that directly affected the employment situation. The country inherited a lopsided economic structure, geared toward the export of mining products,

2. Among useful sources on postcolonial developments are the following: Cherry Gertzel et al., eds., *The Dynamics of the One-Party State in Zambia* (Manchester: Manchester University Press, 1984); William Tordoff, ed., *Politics in Zambia* (Manchester: Manchester University Press, 1974); William Tordoff, ed., *Administration in Zambia* (Manchester: Manchester University Press, 1980); Ben Turok, ed., *Development in Zambia* (London: Zed Press, 1979), and Klaas Woldring et al., eds., *Beyond Political Independence: Zambia's Development Predicament in the 1980s* (Berlin: Mouton, 1984).

and a tiny manufacturing base. After independence the structure of production continued to be grossly dominated by mining. Despite the rhetoric of successive development plans, agriculture was neglected. Rural livelihoods deteriorated because of the government's inability or unwillingness to improve the rural infrastructure and its reluctance to provide producer prices conducive to improving agricultural production. This situation was exacerbated in the 1980s by recurrent droughts. The rate of urbanization, already advanced by sub-Saharan African standards, accelerated from 20 percent of the total population in 1964 to 43 percent in 1980,[3] as more and more people, especially women, moved to the towns,[4] anticipating new developments and improved working opportunities.

Party officials made many statements emphasizing equality of opportunity for women and men in the new nation. Throughout the 1960s, when export earnings from mining were booming, some of the economic and gender inequalities that colonial policy had helped generate were temporarily covered up. Some women benefited during the initial employment boom, as the first and tiny cohort of better-educated women obtained jobs as typists, clerks, airline hostesses, secretaries, and lower-level administrative assistants in government and parastatal offices.[5] Their aspirations were beyond the reach of most urban Zambian women, and they became less attainable, even for women with some education, when export revenues from the sale of copper began to decline in the early 1970s. In 1974 the richest 2 percent of the households took home roughly 20 percent of the income, which was about the same as the share of the poorest 50 percent.[6] Public-sector employment has grown steadily since independence, prompted by the indigenization process. It continues to grow, so that when overall employment stagnated in the mid-1970s, increasing numbers of people came to look upon the government as their primary source of employment. Since the mid-seventies, the Zambian economy has more and more come to rely on infusions of foreign aid and loans, among them substantial amounts from the International Monetary Fund. Several devaluations, decontrol of prices, phasing-out of food subsidies, wage freezes, and runaway inflation have turned the making of a living into an uphill battle for most of the population.

3. Republic of Zambia, *Preliminary Report: 1980 Census of Population and Housing* (Lusaka: Central Statistical Office, 1981), p. 8.

4. M. E. Jackman, "Recent Population Movements in Zambia: Some Aspects of the 1969 Census," *Zambian Papers*, no. 8 (University of Zambia: Institute for African Studies, 1973), p. 17.

5. Ilsa M. G. Schuster, *New Women of Lusaka* (Palo Alto, Calif.: Mayfield Publishing Corporation, 1979).

6. Assefa Bequele and Rolf van der Hoeven, "Power and Inequality in Sub-Saharan Africa," *International Labour Review* 119 (1980): 383.

In spite of policy speeches that stress sexual equality, the new men in power retain several of the colonial government's biases. Gender is still not considered a critical factor, as evidenced in the first comprehensive census taken in the country on the eve of independence in 1963, which did not break down employment statistics by sex. The first postindependence census of 1969 did not exhibit any radical improvement. Gender statistics were given for the total labor force—men comprised 71.2 percent and women 28.9 percent[7]—but no further categorizations were provided. The compilers of the *Monthly Digest of Statistics* from the Central Statistical Office in Lusaka have of late begun to include a listing of female employees. The 1985 publication, using statistics from June 1980, lists a total of 26,310 Zambian women in wage employment across the country, slightly less than half of whom (11,080) were in community, social, and personal services. This figure can be compared with the total of 360,980 Zambian men, the majority of whom (101,030) are also clustered in the same occupations. The second-largest category of male wage employment, mining and quarrying, employed some 56,710 workers in June 1980.[8]

Paid domestic service has not been enumerated in the Zambian employment statistics since 1968, when a total of 36,491 men and 1,758 women were listed in the occupation.[9] Although their numbers were large, knowledge about or concern with the livelihood of domestic servants has remained at the level of folklore. The sample survey I undertook in Lusaka in 1983 to 1984 is the first research effort ever made to ascertain substantively the nature of this occupational domain in Zambia. According to my own conservative estimate, some 100,000 persons are employed as servants across the country, of whom slightly fewer than 25,000 are women. This figure excludes young persons who do household work for relatives in exchange for their care. The size of the domestic servants' work force is almost double that of miners, who numbered 53,740 in June 1983.[10] As in the past, three major economic sectors today dominate the Zambian labor market: mining, agriculture, and domestic service. The gradual emergence of secondary industry after independence has supplemented rather than restructured this pattern, and the main change has been a shift in the numerical proportion of the three sectors. Judging from my estimate, paid

7. Republic of Zambia, *Census of Population and Housing, 1969. First Report, August 1970* (Lusaka: Central Statistical Office, 1970), p. A19. I discuss the 1969 census, using preliminary census tapes on Lusaka's low-income urban population in my "When Sex Becomes a Critical Variable: Married Women and Extra-Domestic Work in Lusaka, Zambia," *African Social Research* 30 (1980): 831–849.

8. Republic of Zambia, *Monthly Digest of Statistics* (Lusaka: Central Statistical Office, 1985) 21, no. 2–3, supp., pp. 1, 7.

9. See Table 6, Chapter 2.

10. Republic of Zambia, *Monthly Digest*, supp., p. 8.

domestic service presently forms the largest single segment of the urban wage-laboring population in Zambia. While overall employment shrank in the economic decline that set in during the first half of the 1970s and still persists, domestic service, like government employment, has kept on growing.

Domestic service continues to be an important entry-level occupation for people with few marketable skills and for migrants newly arrived from the countryside. But for most of them this occupation remains a trap, and they would rather not work as servants if they had a choice. Their main inducement for seeking domestic work may be the prospect of getting housing with the job. The pressures on the economy have had their impact on the housing stock. Because of the scarcity of low-cost accommodation, more than half of Lusaka's population lives in squatter housing.

Domestic Service in Lusaka

Lusaka, the transportation center on the northbound railway, the garden city which S. D. Adshead planned along racially segregated lines as a the new site for the country's capital of 1935, had a population of 123,146 on the eve of independence in 1963. It has more than doubled in size every decade thereafter, from 262,425 in 1969, to 538,469 in 1980,[11] to an estimated 750,000 in the mid-eighties. As the locus of government activity, this city has been the center for announcement of laws and regulations designed to eliminate the inequities of the colonial era. Some of these new laws apply to domestic servants as well as to other workers and at least in theory should have improved their position in relation to other segments of the labor force. According to the new legislation, it continues to be the employer's responsibility to house low-paid employees, either directly in local authority housing or by paying a housing allowance. There are provisions relating to the protection of wages, annual leave, and paid public holidays. Servants were included under the provisions of the Employment Bill of 1965, although only after lengthy discussion in the National Assembly during which white former colonial residents continued to argue that matters between servants and their employers were better left to the two parties concerned.[12] To improve the servants' situation further, the Zambia National Provident Fund Bill of 1965 was amended in 1973, requiring among other things that employers of domestic servants in urban areas make a contribution toward their pensions.

11. Republic of Zambia, *Preliminary Report*, p. 8.
12. Republic of Zambia, *National Assembly Debates* 4 (1965), July 13–September 22, cols. 327, 357.

Many employers who were part of my sample survey were ignorant of, or chose to disregard, these regulations. According to Zambia National Provident Fund (ZNPF) figures, some 45,760 persons were employed in domestic service throughout the country's towns as of June 1983.[13] This figure includes house servants, cooks, nannies, and gardeners who are working for wages in private households in municipalities and townships. In my sample survey of 187 servant-keeping households in Lusaka, only one-third of the servants interviewed were registered with the ZNPF. If the ZNPF figure reflects an overall registration rate in one-third of all servant-keeping households, as I found to be the case in Lusaka, my previous estimate that a total of some 100,000 persons work as servants in urban Zambia is indeed conservative. Since Lusaka's population formed a quarter of the country's total urban population in 1980, I estimate that at least one-quarter of the total number of servants working presently are employed in the capital city.

The majority of these servants are in the employ of other Zambians. The remainder work in households that represent many nationalities and whose members for the most part reside in Zambia on a short-term contract basis. To cover a broad range of these categories, I constructed a sample survey in which the chief domestic servant and his or her employer were interviewed in low-density areas. In Zambia the low-density areas are where the white residences were in the colonial era, where houses were built on spacious plots. Distinctions in the housing market today follow not racial but class lines. While high-income Zambians have moved into the former white residential areas, the high-density areas have remained the locuses of the poor black urban Zambian population. My sample survey covered Woodlands, one of the white residential areas laid out behind the government buildings in Adsheads's plan for the capital. Most of it consists of low-density government housing, some of it run down, built in the 1950s or just before independence. It houses mainly government sector workers and is heterogeneous in race and nationality. Several Zambian government employees live there, as do many foreign nationals on contract to the government's plethora of departments. To include nongovernment employees, the survey was extended to cover parts of Kabulonga, a low-density residential area, in the main built privately on subdivisions of a large farm during the 1950s. The area has grown considerably since independence. Some residents here own their houses or rent them from private developers. Although some preindependence houses remain and their quality vary, Kabulonga is Lusaka's most posh residential area. It is inhabited disproportionately by people in private business, and white expatriates outnumber any other population group there. Interviews were also under-

13. Republic of Zambia, *Monthly Digest*, supp., p. 8.

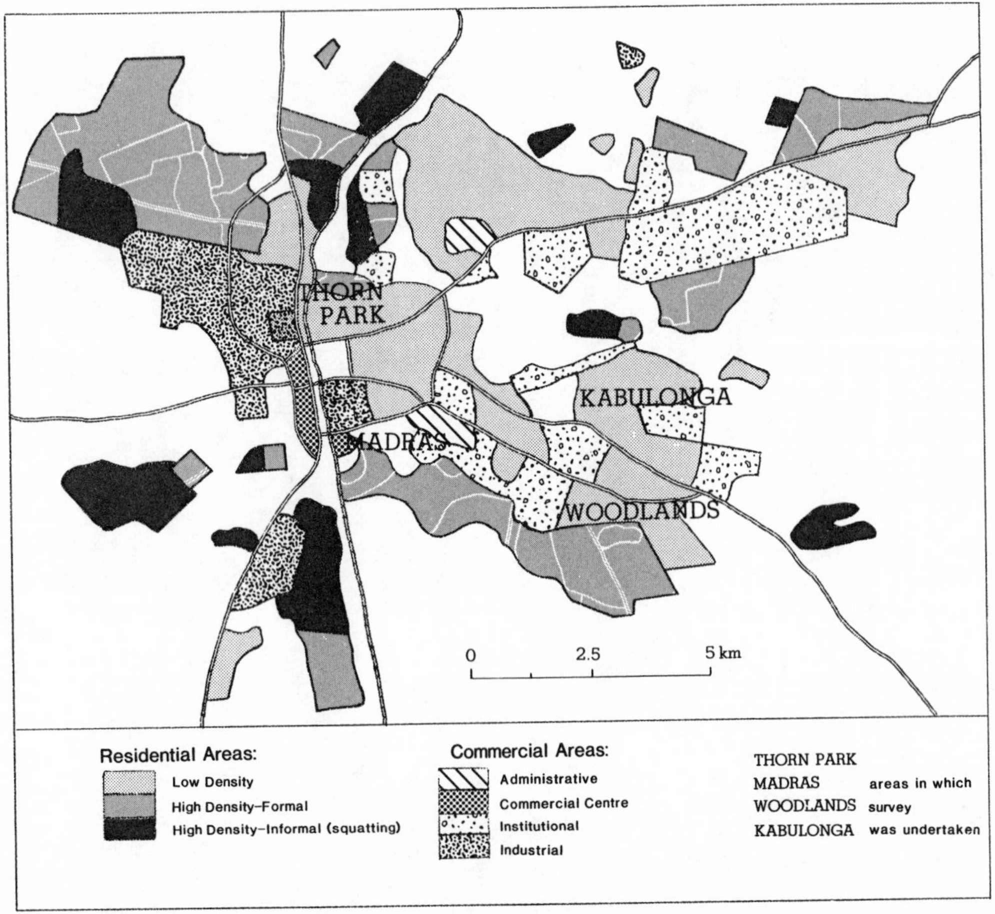

Residential Areas:

Low Density

High Density—Formal

High Density—Informal (squatting)

Commercial Areas:

Administrative

Commercial Centre

Institutional

Industrial

THORN PARK   areas in which
MADRAS   survey
WOODLANDS   was undertaken
KABULONGA

0   2.5   5 km

KABULONGA

WOODLANDS

THORN PARK

MADRAS

Map 4. Lusaka, residential and commerical areas, 1983

taken in the part of Lusaka which still houses an ethnically distinct population, namely resident Asians who engage mainly in trade and commerce.[14] A good number of their shops and houses still cluster in the locale assigned to them in the colonial period, then known as Madras. The colonial city also had, from the mid-1950s and on, a residential area allotted to the Eurafrican population, called Thorn Park. Interviews were undertaken there as well, although more black Zambians than Eurafricans live in the area today. The survey finally sampled some of the flats, operated by institutions such as the Bank of Zambia, Zambia State Insurance Company, Zambia Electricity Supply Corporation, and the University of Zambia. Construction of such flats was initially begun to alleviate the housing shortage in the postwar years and primarily to house single government employees at the lower echelons. Their chief purpose is still to accommodate junior employees, but because of the housing shortage in Lusaka, they also house entire households.

As discussed in the previous chapter, the purpose of the sample survey was to reveal patterns in employment practices possibly influenced by the employer's income, race/nationality, and length of time spent in Zambia, as well as patterns in the experiences of servants, shaped by such factors as age, sex, ethnicity, education, and length of employment. In its totality, the survey comprises a 5-percent sample of the areas investigated. Insofar as it covers the range of variation in terms of ethnic/racial and economic background characteristic of employers of servants throughout Lusaka, I consider the patterns revealed by the survey as typical for this occupational domain.

The Employers

In terms of broad ethnic/racial categories, the plurality of the households, 42 percent, who employed servants were black Zambians, followed by 33 percent whites and 25 percent Asians.[15] Most of these households were comprised of married couples; in only 1.8 percent were women single heads of households, mainly because of divorce or widowhood, and 1.2 percent were headed by men who lived without any permanent female companion. The majority of the men, 69 percent, worked in middle- to

14. I am using the term *resident Asians* to refer to persons from the Indian subcontinent who settled in this region during the colonial period, many of whom now are naturalized Zambian citizens. The term *expatriate Asians* refers to persons from that region who after Zambia's independence have taken contract jobs for shorter or longer durations with the intention of leaving the country when completing their contracts.

15. The category *white* includes three high-income coloured and three interracially married couples. Two couples of non-Zambian African background and four medium-income coloured couples are included in the *Zambian* category.

upper-level executive, managerial, technical, and consultant positions, most of them in government and parastatal companies, some in private firms. Some of these men pursued the professions of medicine, teaching, and law. Eleven percent were members of various diplomatic corps, mainly in advisory positions, and some were employed by foreign governments or international development agencies. Six percent, all resident Asians, engaged in local commerce. The sample also included two missionary households, one from Great Britain, the other from the United States.

More than half of the Zambian wives worked away from home, mainly in teaching, medical, and clerical positions. In contrast, only one-fifth of the expatriate Asian wives were in wage employment, and none among the resident Asian population. Most of the expatriate Asian wives were teachers, and slightly fewer than one-third of the white women were engaged in teaching, medical, or clerical work. The expatriate husband is often the chief contract employee when the couple arrives in Zambia, and women's low employment figures are likely to reflect the difficulty they experience in obtaining their own work permits. A total of 44 percent of the women surveyed did not earn any wage income. Close to 8 percent of these women did "hidden work": some of them painted, others did food catering, tailoring, hair care, and clerical work from their homes without a work permit. Some Zambian women conducted businesses, including fashion design, hair dressing, and cosmetology, from their homes, and a few had shops in nearby markets.

Employers of servants were not always willing to reveal what they earned. Fifty-one percent gave an estimate of their annual income before taxes; the remainder said either that they did not know or that they would not tell. The estimates they did volunteer for the chief wage earner ranged as follows: 24 percent earned between K5,000 and K15,000, 24 percent between K16,000 and K25,000 and 3 percent from K31,000 to more than K50,000 per year. The Zambians earned the least.[16] Most employers also enjoy many additional benefits, such as free or very inexpensive housing, free access to government hospitals and clinics, and, until the end of 1985, free education for their children in government schools. Many do not use the medical facilities and schools because standards have dropped. Expatriates on local contracts receive paid overseas leave at regular intervals as well as free transportation to and from Zambia and baggage allowances for themselves and members of their families at the beginning and conclusion of their contracts. In addition to their local wage in Zambian Kwacha, 21 percent of the employers, all expatriate, received "topping up" in their

---

16. The bank exchange rate for one U.S. dollar was approximately K1.60 in 1983. The rate had changed to K2.20 by mid-1985.

home country's currency—for example, the overseas supplementation allowance sometimes paid by the British government, and the "hardship allowance" the United States Agency for International Development gives to some employees in countries where the living conditions are considered difficult.

The white expatriates had lived in Zambia for periods of time ranging from a few months to most of their lives, with eight years the average length. Among them were 3 percent who had remained since the late colonial period. The expatriate Asians had spent an average period of seven years in Zambia, and the Zambians about five years in Lusaka, preceded and interrupted by transfers to other parts of the country and trips abroad.

The majority of all employers fell within the thirty-to-forty-year-old age bracket, although among whites there were as many in the forty-to-sixty age bracket as in the thirty-to-forty one. Half of the white households had no children, that is, the children were either grown up or away in boarding schools. The same was true for the expatriate Asian households. Household structures in the resident Asian community were more complex, however, because of the presence of extended-family members and their dependents. So, too, were Zambian households: they contained an average of seven persons, and three-quarters of them were comprised of extended families.

Regardless of background, these employers were a cosmopolitan crowd. More than half of the white employers, most of whom were from Western Europe, had spent several years elsewhere in Africa, the Middle East, the Far East, or Latin America. Most of them had employed servants when living in these countries, whereas fewer than 1 percent had ever done so in their country of origin. Slightly less than half of the expatriate Asian employers, who included members from many Indian-language groups as well as persons from Pakistan, Bangladesh, and Sri Lanka, had lived elsewhere in Africa before taking up contracts in Zambia; they were, from their countries of origin, also used to employing servants. More than half of the Zambian employers had spent time abroad, mainly for study purposes, most of them in Britain, others in North America, Scandinavia, or Eastern Europe. They represented many ethnic groups, with Bemba predominating, followed by Lozi and Ngoni. Taken together, various ethnic groups from Zambia's eastern province (for example, Nsenga, Chewa, and Tumbuka) comprised another large category of these householders. In the distant past, some of these groups such as the Bemba, Ngoni, and Lozi engaged in practices ranging from slavery to dependent labor. Most of the Zambians surveyed did not grow up in the rural areas where remnants of these practices might have persisted; they had their first encounter with paid domestic service in towns. Some, the sons and daughters of the tiny

African elite, had grown up in households that employed servants. But many more had had their first exposure to paid domestic service soon after they were married.

Most of these employers had seen several servants pass through their households. While 14 percent had only had one, the chief servant presently in their employ at the time of the survey, 45 percent had had between two and three, 26 percent between four and five, and 15 percent had had six or so many that they did not care particularly to be reminded of the turnover. The number of servants gone through did not necessarily reflect the length of time a householder had been a servant-employer in Zambia; some householders had dismissed several within their first year of employing servants, and others who had kept servants over the course of several years had only had a few.

The Servants

About two-thirds of the servants interviewed in the survey were men (N = 131), the rest women (N = 56). Given that we interviewed only the chief domestic servant, male or female, and that several of the households employed more than one servant, most of them men, and that in households where women were employed, any additional workers were always men, the overall male-to-female ratio in the sample is in reality even more skewed in favor of men. Since these 187 households employed among them a total of 311 full-time servants, 232 of whom were men and 79 women, women comprised about one-third of this occupational group. Of these households, 46 percent employed only one general servant; 41 percent had two servants: one inside the house and one in the garden or, alternatively, depending on the needs of the household, a nanny and a general servant; 10 percent kept three; and the remaining 3 percent of the households employed between three and four servants. In addition to servants, 34 percent of the households employed watchmen on the grounds.

Close to half of these servants (N = 94), regardless of sex, originated from the Eastern Province (Ngoni, Chewa, Tumbuka, Nsenga). The rest represented a variety of ethnic groups, with Tonga, Bemba, and Soli dominating. Some Shona from Zimbabwe, Chikunda from Zimbabwe and Mozambique, and Yao and Tonga from Malawi were among the menservants, and Ndebele and Shona from Zimbabwe, Chikunda from Mozambique, and Xhosa from South Africa were among the women servants.

About one-third of all the servants were in the twenty-to-thirty age bracket, yet 21 percent of the men ranged between the ages of forty-five and sixty-five, if not older. Twenty-one percent of the women servants were below twenty years of age, compared with 9 percent of the men. Twenty-seven percent of the women servants clustered toward the end of the childbearing years and older, ranging from the age of thirty-five to sixty or older. Twenty-two percent of the men were doing the job of a servant for the first time as compared with 24 percent of the women; 10 percent of the men, compared with 5 percent of the women, had worked as servants since before independence, many of them in long-time employment in white households, and most had worked exclusively for whites. The rest of the servants had held several servant jobs for varying lengths of time for employers of different nationality before entering their present position. Some of these servants had been in and out of service and other unskilled jobs. They explained these shifts as the result of the departure of employers, being fired, or their own decision to quit. Such decisions are prompted by a combination of factors including low wages, harsh treatment, and the servant's personal circumstances. In between jobs, several servants had returned to the rural area for a rest of shorter or longer duration. Some had intended that such periods of rural rest would not be succeeded by a return to the job as an urban domestic servant. Yet all these servants did return, including Zacchi in his mature years after realizing the difficulty of making a living in the rural area. Servants who for most of their time as able-bodied workers had been employed in towns found it difficult to adjust to village life and the work required in cultivation, which they had never done before. Half of the servants had gone to school for fewer than seven years. Twenty-two percent of the men compared with 30 percent of the women had less than a year's or no education at all, whereas 8 percent of both sexes had more than seven years of school.

Men and women servants had very different marital experiences, and I discuss the implications of this in Chapter 6. As many as 67 percent of the men were married and lived with their wives. Twenty percent of the men had not married, and 13 percent were divorced, widowed, or their wives lived in the rural areas. Thirty-five percent of the women servants were married and living together with their husbands, 13 percent had not married, and 52 percent were either divorced, widowed, living away from their spouses, or supporting children without the help of a husband.

Hiring

There are a variety of ways to go about hiring a servant. Judging from my survey, only 2 percent of the employers used the government's labor exchange office and newspaper advertisements. They were either newcomers to Zambia or, more commonly, persons who had had a large turnover of servants, were thoroughly frustrated and looking for a last resort. Before reaching that point, employers can call on several informal labor exchanges that exist in expatriate circles. From embassies and various development/aid organizations servants are often passed on together with the house once an employer leaves the country and a successor moves in, and these agencies often keep a listing of servants. Many prospective employers seek the advice of a trusted friend or another servant when hiring. The majority of Asians hired on personal recommendation. A total of 40 percent of the servants surveyed had been taken on after such personal recommendations. In contrast, Zambian employers are more likely to hire right "at the gate": servants on the lookout for work walk from door to door in the low-density areas, and 27 percent had been successful when inquiring about a job in this way.

The chief skill in short supply in this glutted market is cooking, especially among that small segment of the servant-keeping households who are entitled to several servants on company payroll.[17] These are primarily top-level government civil servants, managers in parastatal and private companies, and the like. Ten percent of the employers enjoyed such privileges, and an additional 12 percent had a portion of their servants' wages contributed. Good cooks, these employers claim, are few and far between, and embassies serve as the main recruiting platform. Such cooks charge higher than average wages. They are hard to get, and this difficulty is reflected in newspaper advertisements, which frequently feature requests for cooks.

Education was rarely considered a critical factor except by newly arrived white householders who preferred servants conversant in English. In 49 percent of the households, employers spoke to servants in English. Most of the one-quarter of Zambian employers who employed servants they had hired at their gate preferred young men newly arrived from the countryside with little education and no previous work experience. Such young boys, they say, can be better trained to perform the work in and around the house the way they want it done. Once thoroughly familiar with the running of the household, these young men are said to begin to take things for granted, become lazy, and are laid off and replaced by another newcomer. Thirty-four percent of the Zambian householders communicated with their servants in Nyanja, a language spoken in parts of the country's Eastern Province and the neighboring regions of Malawi and which comes close to functioning as a lingua franca in Lusaka; another 12 percent spoke a variety of Zambian languages with their servants. Five percent of the householders, mainly resident Asian and coloureds, spoke to their servants in Chilapalapa, and they also used Nyanja to some extent.

Special requirements such as cooking and education aside, servants are not hired so much for their skills as for their personality traits. Personality,

17. In order to gain information about the servant-keeping privileges granted to top-level employees, we interviewed personnel managers at the folowing headquarters : ZIMCO (Zambia Industrial Mining Corporation, Ltd.), ZCCM (Zambia Consolidated Copper Mines), Barclays Bank of Zambia Ltd., and Lonrho.

appearance, neatness, and cleanliness were the chief qualities employers, regardless of background, looked for when hiring a servant. These were followed, in order of importance, by traceable references and previous work experience. "We see how they look," one Zambian employer said. "If they don't look nice, we don't hire." Honesty was asked for as well. Other factors frequently considered were drinking habits, family status, church membership, and regional background. Depending on the household, employers looked for servants who were "good with children," "good with dogs," willing to do garden work, or any combination of the above. In one expatriate household without children, the treatment of the dog was the key to whether or not the employer, so he said, was satisfied with his servant.

The majority of the remaining employers of men servants preferred them to be married, on the assumption that a "family man" takes his job seriously since he has wife and dependents to support. An additional attribute desired by the minority of white employers with long-term residence in Zambia is membership in a fundamentalist church, such as the Watchtower Society. The employers assume that "church men" are more honest, hard working, and do not drink or play around with women. Of the 28 percent of the servants who claimed active church membership in the survey, a minority were Watchtower members, some of them working as lay preachers on their days off. A few employers who had been in the country for a long time said that Muslim men made good servants for they do not drink. Since Islam's presence in Zambia is minimal, Muslims were barely represented in my survey: only two servants claimed to be Muslim, one a Yao man from Malawi, where Islam is more widespread, and the other a long-term servant in a Muslim resident Asian trading household.

The colonial era's preference for servants from the Eastern Province and Malawi persisted in 33 percent of these employers. They said the servants from those parts of the country were hard workers, more reliable, and more used to domestic service work than others. The second-strongest preference, though expressed only by 6 percent of the employers, was for persons from the Southern Province, mainly Tonga speakers, who were said to be very industrious. Several other regional preferences probably reflected the experience of individual employers when living in different parts of the country. Some Zambian employers preferred servants from their own lingistic group, whom they claimed would more readily understand and execute the work in the household to the employer's satisfaction. But just as many took the opposite stance: servants from their own lingistic group would listen in too closely and get privileged information about the private affairs of the household. Since most servants and their Zambian employers know several African languages, these are not so much explanations as justifications for the employer's attitude to servants: they want a working relationship, and preferably one marked by distance. Fourteen percent of the employers considered ethnic or regional background irrelevant when hiring a servant; their decision "depended on the person." But 15 percent of the employers, mainly expatriate Asians and whites, had never bothered where their servants came from and had no idea of, or interest in, regional preferences. In their view, servants were all the same. Many of them did not believe much of what their servants said about their backgrounds anyway, for ethnicity can be assumed and reference letters and national registration cards fabricated.

Regardless of background, all the households in the survey employed men servants; Asian householders, except in a few cases, did not employ women.[18] The question of whether to employ a man or woman servant is influenced by the needs of the employing household, its willingness/ability to pay servant wages, and the personal idiosyncracies of the employers. Householders employing only one servant tended to prefer men. They claim that men servants are more flexible, able to do various tasks inside and outside the house, such as lifting and moving heavy furniture as well as the garden work. They are also "good to have around" for security reasons. Householders employing several menservants contended they did so out of what they called "Zambian habit": that it did not occur to them to employ women, that women rarely avail themselves for hire, and/or that the employment of women was fraught with problems. "Zambian habit" in this context appears to be a contemporary term for the employment convention that developed during the colonial period.

The women who did work as servants were employed largely in Zambian or white households. In cases where the wife of the household worked away from home for wages, these women had often been hired as nannies but in fact many did general housework. Between fifteen and twenty years old, relatively new to domestic service, often school dropouts after grade seven, and sometimes single mothers, these young women servants rarely stayed long in a job. Most of them were not accommodated on the premises, and their own domestic problems with children and struggles either to find or to get rid of a man interfered with their work performance. They were the category of servant about whom employers made the most insidious remarks. Perhaps reflecting employers' problems in finding and retaining them, requests for "reliable nannies" came second to skilled cooks in frequency in the newspapers' employment-offered columns.

Some women who were employed in white households were on staffs

18. The only explanation offered in the chief (and almost only) study of Asians within this region during the late colonial period is the following: "males must be hired as African nursemaids are virtually impossible to obtain, and the few who are available are expensive by local standards." In Floyd and Lillian Dotson, *The Indian Minority of Zambia, Rhodesia and Malawi* (New Haven: Yale University Press, 1968), p. 278.

with several other servants; they worked as maids together with male house servants, gardeners, and occasionally a cook. These women, whose ages ranged from thirty-five to sixty years, included all the non-Zambian women servants in the survey. Several of them had held many servant jobs before, some long term. Half of them had never been to school, and most were single heads of households. Some of them had settled down to a life as professional servants: they stipulated the terms and conditions of their employment when being interviewed and, according to some employers, were the kind of women who would take over the running of the household, making the madam feel she was being bossed around.

Aside from the servants who "came with the house" and those recommended by the employer's trusted friends, most servants were initially taken on for a probationary period, referred to by those involved as a "trial." First there would be an interview, in most cases by the wife in the employing household, who examined the servant about his or her prior work experience and stated the terms of the job. Most employers do not expect prospective servants to dicker over terms: if they do, their attempts are interpreted as signs that they are rude and may be likely to cause discipline problems. Only the newcomer, say the old hands, will allow herself to be duped this way. According to the servants, some employers are deliberately unclear during the interview about their intents concerning wage increases, vacation, and ZNPF registration, saying they first will have to see how the relationship works out before settling on terms.

The trial period ranged from one to three months in white and Zambian households to a couple of days to a week in Asian households. Some servants were not allowed to have their family living with them in the quarters during this time. In some Zambian households the trial period kept getting extended and many servants quit before their terms of employment were ever formalized. Many Zambian employers supervised the servant during this time, the wife sometimes taking time off from her own work to instruct the servant in the ways of her household. Such women spoke of "breaking in" their servants, a term that perhaps is shaped by their preference for hiring young adult workers, just arrived from the countryside. In some Asian households, during the first days of the trial period the householder would follow behind her servant to make sure that the work was done to her precise specifications. Most servants were promised higher pay on completion of the trial period, to be paid at monthly intervals, and many Asian employers gave their servants daily pay during this time. In addition to scrutinizing the prospective servant's personality and work habits, many employers also tested his or her honesty by leaving money, alcohol, items of clothing or food around. Most servants are aware of such testing practices and will work hard to make a good impression during the trial period.

Just as servants vary in the view of most of the people who hire them so do the employers in the opinion of servants. Although slightly more than half of all the servants interviewed were reluctant to indicate any preference for a particular type of employer, and 27 percent said that the quality of the job depended on the person regardless of color and background, the rest preferred, if given a choice, to work in white households. Their preferences were based on pay, treatment, and assistance. Whites do pay better, as I discuss shortly. The duties are more clearly defined in white households, servants say. And whites are more inclined to help a servant. But in Zambian households, especially where members of the extended family are present and others visit for short or long periods, servants are called on constantly without regard for them as people or consideration of their needs. Payment of wages is not always certain, because the Zambian householders themselves are often in an economic bind: their own children, relatives who are being supported while they go to school, and a continual stream of visiting relations place strains on the salaries of civil servants, teachers, nurses, and bank clerks, even in households where both spouses work. In these households, servants say, there are few handouts, for the employer's dependents will get them first, but at least there is no language barrier. In Asian households the work of servants is more closely supervised, their entry into and exit from the main house often tightly regulated, and some never get a day off. The wages may be better than in some Zambian households, but handouts are few. Servants understand, they say, why their Zambian employers may have a hard time economically, but Asians are stingy. According to servants, Asians always sell used clothes and worn-out things; if they give something to a servant, they think it is money wasted; they never trust you. Although they are stereotypes, these statements from the servant interviews capture some of the existing differences in employment practices. With regard to the Asian employers, my survey shows that expatriate Asians pay less than members of the long-term resident Asian population. According to the resident population, the new expatriate Asians are concerned to make as much money as possible while on contract in Zambia, for they come from countries where jobs even for highly skilled persons are limited. To reduce their local expenses, they pay their servants as little as they possibly can.

The Chores of Domestic Service

Once the trial period is completed and the employer is tolerably satisfied with the servant's work performance and does not dislike his or her personality, the servant settles in to the work routine and requirements of the new household. The tasks and duties vary with the job description, which was that of "general servant" for 41 percent of the servants interviewed. These servants were men who worked inside and outside the house. In white and Asian households they cleaned the house, did the laundry, ironed, set the table, washed the dishes, assisted in cleaning vegetables for cooking, and did the garden work. In an additional 7 percent of these households, all of them Zambian, the general servant did the cooking as well. In almost all Zambian households, bedrooms and their cleaning were off limits to servants, as was the washing of the madam's underwear. In some households, the servant's work followed a routine with distinct tasks such as laundry and ironing, assigned to specific days, whereas in other households the servant would be expected to do some of all these tasks every day. Most of the work was manual and labor intensive and done without the aid of labor-saving devices. In addition to having an inside staff of one or more servants, 38 percent of all households employed men for the sole purpose of gardening.

The second largest category of servants in the survey, 27 percent, did housework inside the house and some food preparation or cooking. Only 4 percent of the households surveyed employed servants exclusively for cooking and 31 percent had hired servants exclusively for housework. Ten percent of the servants did inside housework and childcare, and another ten percent engaged in these tasks as well as some cooking; this 10 percent were all women servants.

Given the diversity of chores most of these servants were expected to do, work never stopped and there was always some unfinished business for the

Patson Satepa, setting the table in Mazabuka, 1964. From the collection of Mary and Reginald Thompson. Reproduced with permission.

next day. The actual hours spent on the job were long—approximately ten hours a day—divided by a lunch break of one to three hours. Servants with long lunch breaks usually worked in the evenings until the dishes from the employers' dinner were washed and the kitchen closed up. Although most employers contended that their servants' jobs were easy, their work burden light, and that servants were slow and spent too much time doing the chores, they had difficulties separating hours required on the job from time off, especially when their servants lived on the premises. Servants' proximity to the workplace was often assumed to mean open availability, and demands were made on their time at the employers' convenience, particularly for purposes of watching the house. "They have got nothing to do and are here anyway," some employers would say. Increased workloads due to the presence of houseguests or the preparation for an entertainment function in the house were not generally considered extra work. The servant is employed anyway, supposed to be available, so why pay extra? Some, but not all, white employers with many social obligations stipulated at the initial interview that such work would be the servant's duty. In Zambian households servants were rarely given extra remuneration when the presence of extended family members and/or visitors necessitated that food be prepared and served at odd hours. In some households, guests were made to pay, or paid extra on their own initiative, and at times also left used clothes behind. In Asian households, some guests tipped the servants.

According to the statements of employers in the survey, most white employers gave their servants one and a half to two days off per week, typically the weekend from Saturday noontime onward plus a half day during the week. Most Zambian employers gave servants one and a half day off per week, as did the majority of Asian employers. Yet one-quarter of the servants in Asian households had only one day off per week, and one-fifth none whatsoever. When the servants themselves were interviewed, they reported getting less time off. Judging from their answers, as many as 44 percent never had any day off. This discrepancy in reporting likely reflects the fact that employers exploit the availability of servants domiciled on the premises on their days off, ignoring that the servant might have made his or her own plans.

Most white and Asian households usually give their servants an annual leave, ranging from two to four weeks. But in many Zambian households the turnover rate of servants is so fast that the majority rarely stay long enough for the question of leave to be considered. Some, but very few, servants in this survey were taken on vacation with their employers, as was the custom in the past. Some well-paid women servants had been on such trips to Zimbabwe, the Seychelles, and as far as Italy and England. One of the few cooks surveyed accompanied his employers on game-watching trips in Zambia's extensive game parks. Such "holidays with the family" do not provide time off for the servants, but simply shift the locus of work to a different place.

Remuneration

It is an oversimplification to state that whites pay better wages and provide better work conditions for their servants than do Zambians and Asians. Black Zambians also overwork their servants the most. Expatriate Asians pay the least of any householders and offer worse terms than do long-time resident Asians.[19] Within each of these categories in the survey there were variations, depending on whether or not the chief wage earner, usually the man in the house, was an upper-level government or company employee whose servants' salaries were paid as part of his contract. The actual wages varied from a monthly high of K180 to below K30, sometimes with no housing or housing allowance provided, but these figures are the extremes: the high of K180 was the wage of one embassy cook, and the low under K30 the amount paid to two young girls who worked as servants in flats. Between these extremes there appear to be three commonly accepted wage levels: a low-to-median range of K40–70 per month paid in 53 percent of all households, regardless of background; a middle range of K70–100 paid to 25 percent of the servants in white and some Asian households; a high range of K100–140 paid to 16 percent of the servants in white and some Zambian households on company payroll. Six percent of the servants received substandard wages, between K30 and K40. In terms of percentages, more women servants than men received low wages, whereas women slightly outnumbered men in the best-paying jobs. Thus 16 percent of menservants compared with 33 percent of women received wages below K50; 53 percent of men vs. 32 percent of women were paid below K80; 16 percent of both sexes received wages under K100; and 17 percent of men compared with 19 percent women were paid between K100 and K140 per month. In terms of specialization, men general servants and women nannies earned the least. Male inside house-servants and women working as nannies and doing some food preparation earned the middle range of wages, and servants of both sexes who cooked and did housework earned a little more. The few servants employed exclusively to cook were men, and they claimed the top wages.

About one-third of these households, primarily white and Asian, had registered their servants with the ZNPF and were paying the required monthly contributions to the servants' pension scheme. Employers commonly did not register servants until they had satisfactorily completed the

---

19. See Appendix 1 for my attempt to unravel the compounded effects of these factors by means of a regression analysis.

trial period. Since many servants in Zambian households never last beyond the trial period, Zambians rarely register them. "What is the point?" they would ask. "Servants come today and are gone tomorrow." They, as most of the other employers, also doubt that the ZNPF's pension scheme will work, and they question whether or not servants eventually will receive the money accumulated in their account on retirement. Because of their doubts, a tiny portion of the employers sought to make alternative arrangements to ensure their servants' future welfare. They established bank or post office savings accounts for their servants into which they placed a small sum of money, for example, K5, every month, admonishing the servant to do the same.

The level of servants' wages is not determined by any statutory minimum-wage legislation in Zambia, but the provisions of the General Employment Act of 1965 do apply to this occupation. These regulations stipulate lengths of annual vacation period based on how long a worker has been employed, sick leave, paid public holidays, and rules about dismissal— stipulations that most employers are unaware of or ignore. Rather, contemporary conventions, which parallel those of the colonial period with some innovations, guide payment practices. "The going rate" varies to some extent across neighborhoods, no doubt influenced in part by socioeconomic factors. It also varies according to national background and length of residence in the country. Many whites who have remained since the colonial period, complain that newcomers, especially those employed by international or foreign-based development agencies, are "spoiling" their servants by paying them "exorbitant" wages, thus upsetting long-held standards and disturbing the going-rate system. They cast their complaints in terms of the servants' future welfare: such overpaid servants will have trouble finding jobs once their present employers leave, as no one will be able to pay the wages they demand. Newcomers learn the conventions from residents in their neighborhoods. They also have access to the hints on household management and servant-keeping in Zambia which several development agencies include in their information packages and which some voluntary groups make available.[20] According to my survey, employers from Belgium and Holland pay the best wages, followed by North Americans and Scandinavians.

Going rates within neighboorhods, ethnic/national background of employers, the sex of the servant, and the employer's personal whims thus influence the wage paid to servants. Some servants on company payroll

20. For example, a pamphlet compiled by the American Women's Club in Lusaka, *Welcome to Lusaka: Information for Newcomers* (Lusaka: Teresianum Press, 1981), pp. 39–42, and in an information package that several international development organizations make available to their expatriate staff.

receive wages set by the firm, but in some cases, only a mini-mum/maximum range is set and employers have discretionary power to determine the exact wage.[21] In the final analysis, most servants' wages are decided by their individual employers and depend on the employer's will-ingness/ability to pay rather than on the servant's skills. Employers often take on new servants at a lower rate than they received previously, promis-ing an increase after the trial period. In Zambian households where ser-vants rarely complete the trial period, wages are seldom increased and servants are continually replaced at low wages. Most white and Asian householders give increases about once a year. The size of the increase is rarely adjusted to the rising cost of living but is determined by what the employer thinks the servant deserves. Like the beginning wage, increases are influenced not so much by the servant's skills and performance as by the employer's like or dislike of the person. "I just don't like this man," said one white woman. "He is not going to get a wage increase." This man was a cook in her employ for less than a year. She had no complaints about his job performance but could not stand him as a person.

Wages are also affected by what the employer assumes are the servant's needs, depending on marital status, age, and household size. Sometimes their reasoning is were spurious at best: "Servants don't eat like we do. They don't eat meat but like *nshima* and relish. They don't entertain." Some wages were deliberately kept low by employers who contended that their servants squander money and do not know how to budget.

Some servants receive benefits in addition to their cash wages. Those on company payroll usually receive free uniforms and work shoes, and some private employers provide their servants with a yearly issue of work cloth-ing, often at the servant's insistence. Most white and Asian households give Christmas bonuses, such as a small sum of money, food, and sometimes clothing. These same employers will also bring gifts to their servants when returning from holidays abroad. Now and then, all employers give some contribution in kind, such as irregularly issued rations of mealie meal, soap, meat, and other commodities that are in short supply. During the time of this survey, Lusaka was experiencing shortages of almost all house-hold basics: salt, sugar, cooking oil, flour, bread, and sometimes rice, soap, and detergent, and employers who had been able to stock up on these items would ration some of them out to their servants, in several cases deducting the cost from the servant's wages. Some servants also receive leftover food and castoff clothing, although many employers appear to have

21. Of the firms we interviewed, Barclays Bank had set terms guiding the servant wages of high-level officials; ZCCM had established a wage range within which such officials were free to decide on the exact level of servants' pay; and Lonrho allowed the official to determine the servants' wages.

taken to the practice of either selling such items to the servant or letting him sell them on commission in the low-income neighborhoods. Many servants get small advances from their wage or borrow outright from the employer, repaying the debts by installments from their wages.

Many employers claimed proudly that they extended medical care to their servants. Since medical care was free of charge in the university teaching hospital and government clinics spread across town, most of these employers only ensured that their servants went there when ill, either by giving them bus fare or by taking them by car. Some expatriate employers on company payroll had access to medical services in private clinics and health organizations. The privatization of health provision is a recent phenomenon in Zambia, a response to the deterioration of services and lack of drugs and supplies in the government hospitals. Some employers who are members of such clinics take their servants to the "private doctor" when illness strikes. Many employers considered such health problems as inconveniences, upsetting the household routine and interfering with the employers' jobs when servants had to be taken to and from hospitals and clinics.

The colonial practice of giving a weekly ration of foodstuffs to servants has since independence persisted in changed form in some households. In this survey, 45 percent of the servants received ration money, that is, a small sum given to the servant before the weekend. It ranged from K2 to K10, with 30 percent of all servants getting less than K5 on a weekly basis. A few employers, 4 percent, bought a bag of mealie meal, the main staple, every month for their chief servant instead of providing ration money. In Zambian households, most of the unmarried servants were fed, a practice that employers alleged would prevent servants' pilfering from kitchen stores. Some servants got tea and bread, if it was available, in the morning or at mid-morning. It is difficult to estimate the economic value of these contributions to the servants' budgets. Most of these handouts are given irregularly, at the employers' whim; they are rarely agreed upon or promised in advance, so that servants do not know what to expect and have difficulty reckoning with such contributions when deciding how to allocate their meager wages.

Housing

People who build houses in postcolonial Zambian cities continue to erect servants' quarters on the plot. If servants are not accommodated in them, such quarters may serve other purposes: sheltering members of the extended family, serving as the locus for the wife's unrecorded business, functioning as storage or being rented out by the inhabitants of the main house, a practice that is illegal. But most of the quarters continue to house servants, and 66 percent of the servants in this survey lived on the premises in tiny houses at the end of their employers' gardens. Four percent lived-in with members of the household; they were young girls working in flats. Nondomiciled servants lived in rented rooms or houses in Lusaka's low-income areas, the majority of them, 17 percent, in squatter settlements. A few servants were prohibited from living in the quarters because of the size of their families; their many children, the noise, the coming and going of so many people on the plot inconvenienced their employers. Some of the servants owned the houses they lived in. Only a small fraction of all servants, 4.3 percent, were given the statutory housing allowance to which low-income workers were entitled. [22]

Most servants who lived off-premises walked to work, spending between one-half and one hour to reach their work place. A few commuted on bicycle, often provided by a previous or the present employer. Most of those who lived so far away that they had to take the bus to work paid the fare out of their own pockets.

Of the servant-owned houses, the largest number, 6.4 percent, were in Mtendere, the first low-income settlement to be opened by the city council after independence, and the second-largest percentage, 5.9, were located in Misisi, one of the oldest squatter settlements in Lusaka. The rest of the houses were built or were under construction mainly in more recent squatter settlements. In many cases, the servants who owned these houses had provided long and faithful service to expatriates who on leaving the country had built or helped build a house for the servant. Most of these houses had been constructed from eleven to twenty years ago, a fact that indicates more recent employers have been less willing—or able—to help their servants in this way. Several of these servants did not live in their own houses. Slightly less than half of them housed relatives; the rest sheltered tenants who were charged monthly rents ranging from K15 to K35.

The majority of the servants who lived on the employers' premises were men. More women servants lived-out, and they spent more time walking between their residence and place of work than did men. Half of the servants in the resident Asian households did not live on the premises, whereas most of those employed by expatriate Asians did so.

The servants' quarters were dwellings of one to two rooms; they varied greatly in quality, some of them substandard at best. Where quarters comprised more than one room, employers sometimes used the additional space for storage. In most of these dwellings lived the servant's spouse, children and/or kin, and occasional dependents. The average household size in the quarters was five. "Furnished" quarters usually meant only the

22. In the mid-1980s, the lowest-paid government workers received K100–120 per month and a housing allowance of K30.

presence of a bed frame and a mattress, if that. Any additional furniture consisted of rickety chairs, tables, an occasional sideboard, cupboard, or shelf. All the quarters had piped cold water and lavatories, though not always inside the house. Hot water was available in very few quarters, but most had electricity. Most also had showers, but no modern cooking facilities. If hot water was available, the servant's household was usually requested to refrain from using it at certain times of the day. In some parts of Lusaka, employers also rationed their servants' use of cold water during the dry season when the general water supply was scarce.

These houses were not so much the servants' homes as extensions of the employers' space. For employers often restricted their servants' company and leisure-time activity. Only immediate relatives were allowed in many households, and no overnight visitors without permission. Some white and Asian households did not allow the servants' children inside the main house; servants' children were permitted to play with the employer's children only in the yard. The reason most typically given when explaining such arrangements was "hygiene" or "disease": servants' children supposedly carry intestinal worms and bugs, and for this reason also, employers often do not permit their own children to eat any food prepared in the servants' quarters. Some employers prohibit radio playing in the servants' quarters during the noon-hour rest and object to loud conversation from the quarters. During the time of this survey, an informal curfew was practiced in the most posh areas of Kabulonga; employers there required their servants to be inside the gate by sunset. Those servants who were fortunate enough to reside on premises that had separate servants' entrances could still come and go at night, but at their own risk. Burglaries were rampant throughout the city, and in these particular parts of Lusaka, residents took their own precautions against nightly intruders.

Given these restrictions on servants who live on premises, it is perhaps not surprising that 36 percent of servants would rather live away from their place of work. In their view, they would have more freedom and more friends to call on for assistance in situations of need if they lived in a compound. But more important, it is better to have one's own housing, they said, because the job of a servant is never secure. Employers come and go, and few servants are passed on with the house to the next employer. Yet 22 percent of the servants preferred to live on the premises, where housing is free and they do not have to walk far to their place of work. Life is quieter in the high-density areas, some said, and not as dangerous as in the compounds. Burglars who come to the low-density areas are not after the servants' few possessions but the valuables from the employer's house.

The premises on which servants live and work would not in 1985 impress the visitor to Lusaka with any semblance of the gardenlike atmosphere that Adshead had designed for the capital of 1935. The beautiful lawns and gardens have been hidden by ugly walls with cut glass or metal spikes, some of them so high that they conceal the house and its surroundings. Lusaka's change from a garden city to a city of fortresses began in the economic decline in the mid-1970s, when security-conscious residents, fearful of increasing burglaries, started erecting walls to protect their possessions. Metal burglar-bars on windows have also become widespread. In addition to security walls, many of the residents surveyed kept one or more guard dogs and had security guards on the grounds at night. Upper-level government employees and those in the managerial and supervisory ranks of parastatal, private, and international agencies were provided with around-the-clock guard services, paid by their employer. The most posh houses built most recently have high walls and a guard house where visitors report before being admitted to the premises. Today, a significant proportion of Lusaka's servant-keeping population is ensconcing itself behind protective barriers and looking with suspicion at anyone, including their servants, who do not belong in their carefully guarded interiors.

[6]

A Transformed Occupation

Although domestic service remains in Zambia today, the occupation has been slowly transformed from what it was in the colonial era. Its persistence masks changes at many levels: in the overall economy, within the servant-keeping population, among servants themselves, of the nature of work done in private households, and of the social relations in the labor process between servant and employer. In this chapter I discuss four specific aspects of this process: the degradation of work; the remaking of difference; the ongoing complaints; and the structuring of consent to the labor regime. Because most servants are men, the discussion refers almost exclusively to the work relationship between menservants and their employers. Much of what I have to say applies to women servants as well, but with a difference, and I take up the questions surrounding the changing gender dynamics in domestic service today in this chapter's last section.

The Degradation of Work

The work done by servants in private households in the mid-1980s has, according to my survey, been largely reorganized. Gone are the colonial era's task specializations, most certainly the distinct routines carried out by several different servants—the water boy, the bath boy, the wood boy. In many cases the majority of these tasks have been merged into the work of one general servant.

This reorganization shows some similarities to, as well as differences from, the process of deskilling which Henry Braverman identified as occurring during the development of the capitalist labor process in the United

States. His observations concern the destruction of old crafts which took place as scientific management was introduced and the unity that had characterized the craftperson's work became separated into conception and execution. The labor process thus was reorganized into deskilling and fragmentation, on the one hand, and the creation of an apparatus of conception on the other. Braverman's argument also concerned the expansion of capital into new areas, such as service industries, which transformed domestic work, for example, into an arena of capitalist relations. As capital conquered one sphere after another and as it itself became transformed within the spheres it had already conquered, so were old jobs destroyed and new ones created. [1]

Braverman's observations illuminate but also raise questions about the Zambian case. Its developing capitalism does not approach the stage he describes for the United States. Outside of a tiny sector, chiefly mining, most work continues to be labor- rather than capital-intensive. The availability of a reserve pool of labor has depressed wage levels to the point that it is cheaper to employ people than to use machines. Capital has barely moved into service industries and it has not commercialized private domestic service. Yet postcolonial capitalist developments in Zambia, such as they are, are nevertheless remodeling domestic service. The reorganization has had less to do with technological advances than with changes among the servant-keeping population and in the nature of work done in private households.

The deskilling that Braverman identified in the factory in the United States is taking place in reverse in domestic service in Zambia: once-separate tasks are being leveled out and merged into the work of one person, today's typical worker, the general servant. The chief householder still remains charged with the conception of the servant's work and its supervision. At the same time, among a tiny fraction of the servant-employing households some of the specialties of the colonial era persist, namely skilled cooks and dexterous houseservants who are men, and another specialty—the female nanny—is assuming unprecedented prominence. While I acknowledge its historical and economic background, the concept of the reorganization of work in domestic service in Zambia in the 1980s as a special process of deskilling is a useful one and I have applied it here to. the ongoing dequalification and degradation of the occupation.

Extrapolating from my survey, a composite description of a general servant in Lusaka would be a man in his late twenties, who arrived from the Eastern Province some seven years ago after dropping out of school; he lives on the premises and is now married and has a couple of children. His

1. Henry Braverman, *Labor and Monopoly Capital: The Degradation of Work in the Twentieth Century* (New York: Monthly Review Press, 1974).

wife does not do any wage labor. He has held about two places as a servant prior to his present job. As a general servant, he works both inside and outside the house; he does not cook. He works inside the house in the morning, and after his lunch break, in the garden. He sets the dinner table and returns to the kitchen to do the dishes and tidy up after his employers' dinner.

The reorganization of domestic service has been influenced to some extent by the availability in most servant-keeping households of basic amenities such as piped water, electricity, refrigeration, and flush toilets. But it is not the result of the application of labor-saving technology to household management. Even those employers surveyed who had labor-saving devices frequently did not allow servants to use them. Many employers consider servants to be clumsy and fear that they will break things. Many devices were broken down, or not used at all on the well-founded assumption that if they broke, spare parts would be unavailable. The servant's labor-intensive work is monotonous and routinized and offers him few opportunities for learning and expanding his abilities.

Working in this way, the servant develops no new skills and whatever special skills he might have acquired, say, in French cuisine, become inconsequential and are likely to be lost. In that sense, the contemporary servant's work is becoming deskilled. This process is partly a consequence of changes among employers—the entry into the servant-keeping population of more and more Zambians whose household management and cuisine require less elaborate standards than those of the colonial past, and of expatriate households, where the wives spend more of their time working in their own kitchens. The deskilling of domestic work is also influenced, at least at the time I did my research, by shortages of staple foods—flour, yeast, and cooking oil, not to mention spices and condiments—which makes it increasingly difficult for most employers "to keep house like in London." As a result, proportionately fewer skilled cooks than in the past graduate from on-the-job training in private domestic service in Zambia today.

The contemporary servant market is characterized by a paradox: on the one hand, it is glutted with potential servants; on the other, there are positions for cooks, for example, which are difficult to fill. The paradox reflects the coexistence of change and persistence in this occupational domain, epitomized by today's general worker and yesterday's skilled cook. And it is influenced by the mismatch of supply and demand factors in this particular segment of the labor market. There are indeed cooks available, but owing to the pressures of urban living, few of them can afford to wait for a well-paid job to open up in their specialty. Zacchi had to support a wife and dependents out of school and out of work. He told me with regret that he took the job as general servant in a white household, in which the madam herself carried out his specialty: cooking. His age mate, Nkuwa, was reluctant to follow Zacchi's example. Unlike Zacchi, he had support and therefore perhaps could afford to be choosy, defending his specialized skills as a cook against the devaluation of his labor. He was not optimistic about his job chances, for as he said with implicit reference to the new expatriates and their different standards of cooking: "the whites eat *nshima* now." (He was not implying that whites like Zambians eat nshima every day, but that white women do most of the cooking: nshima is supposed to be cooked by the wife in a Zambian household.) When asked whether he would work as a servant in a Zambian household, he smiled broadly, saying: "I can't cook Zambian food." We both laughed, knowing that of course he knew how to prepare Zambian food, but that he did not consider that task to be professional cooking. His point was not that he was unable to cook it but that he did not want to, for in a Zambian household he would be called on for many other duties. It would be below his dignity to be ordered around by another Zambian as a deskilled general servant. Nkuwa's comments implied, as did those of many others in the survey, that servants are critically aware of their failure to defend their specialized skills in domestic service today.

Remaking Difference

How the relationship between deskilled workers and those who control their labor is organized and structured in practice was not Braverman's interest. His was an abstract theory, not a concern with actual human interaction. In reality, both servants and employers bring intentionality to the workplace. They monitor their behavior in an uneasy relationship of cooperation and conflict that masks the essential ambiguity: its personalized nature. The personalized nature of the work relationship in postcolonial domestic service is not the product of a paternalistic ethos based on reciprocity of obligations between employers and servants. Rather, it is the result of the deteriorating economic situation and the general insecurity of living in society at large. These circumstances force persons with few means to make a living by working for those better situated, who in addition to getting housework done cheaply also get some one to be around the house in a role almost akin to a watchdog.

The colonial period's hierarchical relationship between servant and master was expressed mainly in racial terms, and the unequal relationship between the two interdependent parties accentuated, marked, and recreated a discourse that made the two even more unlike one another. The distinction between servant and employer is today no longer necessarily rationalized in racial terms, but more often in class terms. The antagonisms that such terms veil still revolve around the conception of the servant as other and one who is different, that is, less capable or worthy than the employer. This conception turns on the need to uphold the hierarchical distinctions within the private household—between servant and employer—so that work may go on. The conventions that today help recreate these distinctions have much in common with those of the colonial era. They are comprised of informal practices structured by tacit rules that in Giddens's terms institutionalize this domain of activity.[2]

These conventions are expressed in forms of address, in the structuring of everyday interaction, and in the way the two parties conceive of each other when away from work. The servants were in 68 percent of these households addressed by their first names. We noted 20 percent of employers referring to their menservants as houseboys, or boys, when describing the daily routine of the household. Six percent, all Zambians, addressed their married servants in a Bantuized idiom, for example, BaTembo for a man and MaBanda for a woman. Twelve percent of the employers addressed their servants by last name only, and a small fraction, 3 percent, mainly white expatriates, addressed their servants as, for example, Mr. or Mrs. Tembo. Servants were much more formal when addressing employers. Thirty-six percent addressed the heads in the employing household as Bwana and Madam; 28 percent used titles, for example, Sir, or Mr. and Mrs. Brown. Twenty-four percent of the servants in Zambian households addressed their employers in the terms from their respective languages for father and mother, or "father of," "mother of" followed by the name of a child. These are common African forms of address and serve, when used by servants, to acknowledge the status of the employer as a parent to whom respect and obedience is due. When talking of their experiences with different employers, many servants still referred to whites as *Wazungu* and Asians as *Mwenye*.[3] They would typically refer to their Zambian employers as "the owners."

As in any situation of inequality, the needs of the persons in authority determine to a large degree how their inferiors are treated. In the households where I observed daily interaction between servants and employers the servants were obsequious and almost inconspicuous. Most of them worked barefoot, knocked on the door when entering a room to clean it, and did not talk while being around you. Servants who took the initiative to engage you in conversation were considered intrusive. Employers felt imposed on by servants who asked questions about their work, their plans for

2. Anthony Giddens, *Central Problems in Social Theory* (Berkeley: University of California Press, 1979), pp. 65–73.

3. *Wazungu* (singular *muzungu*) is a Bantu term. Its basic meaning is "Europeans," or in general "white people." *Mwenye* is used for Asians.

vacation, and so forth. In most of these households, servants did not talk unless spoken to.

Employers' questions to servants are, of course, also intrusive. Because they know that employers do not want to become involved with their personal problems, many servants say nothing in answer, or simply make a downcast gesture. Some employers assume that their position of authority allows them to judge their servants' affairs, and admonish them, for example, to limit their families and to save money for a rainy day. Such patronizing advice is disliked by servants, who have their own plans, and for the most part, they make no comment. When they do speak to the employer, for example, if they need to attend a funeral, take a child to the clinic, need an advance from their wage or to borrow outright, they rarely address the employer directly. They may make their intention to speak known by a slight cough, or they go through the madam, asking her to tell the bwana about the matter at hand. Since most of these matters inconvenience the lives of the employers and the daily routine of the household, the employers are likely to nag before they, grudgingly, permit the servant to attend to them. In expatriate households where servants are not conversant in colloquial English, these encounters are often strained because of communication problems. Such employers generally assume that their servants are less capable of understanding English than in fact they are. To make their opinions clear, they speak slowly and in simplified language, conveying an attitude that infantilizes the servant.

Even in Zambian households where employers sometimes are addressed in the idiom of kinship, inequality is recreated every day in household interaction. Even if they treat you nice, say servants, you are still a servant. If you are out of place, they quickly put you back in your place. Zambians forget, servants say, that you are a fellow black—or, rather, that they are black themselves. Because of their inability or unwillingness to become involved with another black person's economic and social needs, Zambian employers resort to hierarchical practices of interaction with their servants. In their view, although they are of the same race, servants are still other, different from themselves: servants are members of poor families; they have been unfortunate in life; their needs and desires are different; they need less to make a living; in short, their world is inferior. Zambian employers make few efforts to improve their servants' world, for they pay their servants less than do most other employers and in this way help to maintain the class gap.

The social practices that structure conduct in these households help to ensure that servants never become members of them. Such practices are part of the ongoing interaction and they help to reproduce the structure of inequality that defines the relationship between servants and employer.

How do these practices become reproduced? Some newcomers to Zambia, and particularly people without prior experience of employing servants, are initially surprised by the practices that local residents recommend they follow. Some set out paying wages far beyond the going rates, having servants work fewer hours and insisting on doing some of the work themselves, listening to their servants' complaints and attending to their personal problems. Many of these employers insist on not locking up stores and personal things to avoid the feeling of being prisoners in their own homes. They will sit down with the servant and discuss the problems involved in making a living in Lusaka, ask questions about life in Zambia, about differences among the ethnic groups, and encourage servants to approach them freely and ask for help when necessary. Some women involve themselves with their servant's wife, encouraging her, for example, to take adult literacy classes if not trying to teach her and some of the children herself. They demonstrate handicrafts or supply the wife with materials so that she can work with skills she may already have, such as knitting and crocheting; a few of the women I encountered even taught the wife to use a sewing machine. These employers put themselves on a first-name basis with their servants and initially are lax in their household routine, saying "fine" when the servant asks for time off to attend to an unexpected matter. The routine breaks down in many cases, when the new employers realize that they have been taken advantage of. Some servants will exploit newcomers, hoping to get the most out of the situation while it lasts. Things may gradually begin to disappear from the house, and calls for assistance and money borrowing become too frequent. The result is dismissal, if the servant and his household have not already absconded.

Troublesome experieces of this nature typically take place during the first year or two of an expatriate household's residence in Lusaka. Because of the inequality that in the first place brings two persons together as servant and employer, their relationship revolves best around work, not personal friendship. And gradually, the woman householder begins to conform to the unwritten rules that structure interaction in domestic service in Zambia and becomes a madam. She locks up the valuables, communicates little with the servant if she happens to be around when he works, and she avoids involving herself in the personal affairs of the servant and his household. She never really trusts her servant and monitors his activities and changes of mood as he does hers. Then she sees other newcomers go through similar experiences and gradually begin to conform to the unwritten rules, and the cycle repeats itself. She smiles sadly when sharing these experiences with her neighbor, saying: "I told you so. They all learn," thus expanding rather than analyzing the folklore of domestic service.

What servants and their employers say about the other influences how they interact and helps to strengthen the relation of difference that distances them from each other.[4] Employers' views of servants can be observed not only in the workplace but in popular magazines, newspaper articles, and classified ads as well. One departing employer, for example, advertised the man who had worked for him in the following terms: "House servant, honest, good with dogs, references available"[5] And, on the other side, reckoning with employers' opinion of women servants, Grace Zulu sought to market herself as follow: "Good house girl available especially to foreigners. I speak good English, I am clean, I know how to wash and iron clothes, do all the work in the house, good to children; and I will be very honest with my job and to you."[6]

Such advertisements, which use the language of difference, in a way the language in which dogs are spoken of—servant as "pedigreed" with references—provoke no comment in Zambia.[7] There have been few shifts in the attitudes of the servant-keeping population. Employers buttress their sense of privilege and power by not, in the servants' practical language, treating them as human beings. By accounting for the relationship in terms of difference, employers also free themselves of any responsibility for creating that difference. The servant, for his part, says that he belongs to the common man and so therefore he must work for those who are different and better stationed, the *Apamwamba* or the Wazungu,[8] though he does so grudgingly. Nor has the succession from white to black among the servant-employing population altered the language and closed the distance of difference. Although some Zambian employers will say that, *after all*, servants are also human beings, the discourse of their daily interaction with servants remains the same. Seeing the other as different, servants and employers rationalize their unequal relationship in terms of such difference.

4. Johannes Fabian, *Time and the Other: How Anthropology Makes Its Object* (New York: Columbia University Press, 1983), pp. 25–35.

5. *Times of Zambia*, January 1, 1985.

6. *Times of Zambia*, March 9, 1985.

7. One advertisement did cause uproar, but for other reasons. A Mufulira woman calling herself Elizabeth placed the following ad for two days in succession: "A clean, non smoker middle aged coloured nanny needed to look after one year old baby; a well furnished little cottage and good salary offered." *Times of Zambia*, January 24 and 25, 1984. She was immediately taken to task in letters to the editor, one of them signed "colourless coloured" who asked: "Who is a coloured? What has colour to do with employment? Are we in Babylon or are we in Northern Rhodesia, or South Africa where colour is the passport? . . . I would like to advise this lady to stop behaving like she is in a South African zoo." "Racist Lizzie Caned," *Times of Zambia*, February 4, 1984, p. 4; and "Employer is Racist," *Times of Zambia*, April 10, 1984.

8. *Apamwamba*, a Nyanja term meaning literally "those on the top." They are the persons who live in *mumayaadi* (i.e., in the low-density areas), and have assimilated the style of life of the colonial wazungu whom they are replacing. In status terms, *wazungu* could just be another way of saying apamwamba. Professor Mubanga Kashoki helped clarify these terms for me.

Everyday Trials and Tribulations

The labor process in domestic service turns on the shared need for security: in the form of household comfort and protection of material property for the employer, of economic survival for the servant. A new kind of personalized dependency has been forged between these two unlike partners. Employers describe servants as "a blessing in disguise" and the servants in their turn say " you can never rely on them." In their everyday discourse, servants and employers talk about each other in a language of trouble and tribulations that conveys the contradictory concepts each uses about the other. Following Giddens, I suggest we must reckon with the concepts these actors themselves apply in the course of their ongoing conduct.[9] For each of them knows, in a practical sense, a great deal about the workings of the institution because they participate in it. What they say about each other does not constitute a description of their relationship; their statements are *part* of that relationship. As such, their statements about each other affect their ongoing interaction.

Contemporary employers will quite readily join the chorus of old-hands, lamenting that servants are not what they used to be and, to be sure, a good servant is hard to get. They are said to be inefficient, lazy, lacking any sense of foresight; they are not to be relied upon, they never tell the truth; they are irresponsible, they squander their money and disappear without notice. They just never learn and do things their own happy way. "Their way" includes eating different foods and not entertaining as the employers do; they have strange cultural ideas. Their relations to wives, dependents, in-laws, their work habits and notions of time and duty differ. Employers speak almost as if servants were a different species. Expatriate and Zambian employers make these statements, couching the difference between them and the other in terms of lifestyle attributes if not different culture. Employers pass these bits of knowledge on to one another, recreating the notion of servants as distant, and different from themselves.

In the counterdiscourse of servants, the employers are said to talk too much, to be rude, and they walk behind you. Zambian employers are too proud, they don't respect servants, and don't treat them like human beings. Expatriate employers are too odd, they make unreasonable demands; one day they love you, the next they hate you, you just never know. You work hard all day, five days, if not more per week, month after month, on a slave wage, and still they complain that you lack action and initiative. Their ideas about work are inconsistent: they want the beds turned down just so, or else. Their demands change: when they go on leave, they pay

9. Giddens, *Central Problems*, pp. 245–248.

you the same wage, though you only have to work in the garden, watch the house, and tidy up before they return. They have weird pantry and storage rules. You know what they have and where it is, yet they hide their valuables and tempt your honesty. The owners, as many servants refer to their Zambian employers, do not share or help out. They are stingy.

Most employers complain about their servants for many reasons and view them as a mixed blessing. A quarter of the employers surveyed said they could do without servants and would rather not have them. "Servants," they say, "are trouble. More trouble than they are worth." Yet they keep hiring them, considering them "a necessary evil." They have a hard time defining what it is they want in a servant beyond vague intangibles such as a good personality, or their being good with children. Because servants are hired not so much for their skills as for their personality, employers have difficulty ensuring their full cooperation, since servants do not know what to expect. Some take on servants because both spouses work, and because they have children. Others because of the weather: the tropical climate and the red dust that creeps in everywhere, the frequent need to change clothes, and the corollary of piled-up laundry and constant ironing to get rid of putsi flies—in short, they say there is too much housework. Others again have been used to servants for so long that although they do not really like them, they still find them useful to have around. Many rationalize their need for creature comfort by saying that at least they create jobs for persons who otherwise would not be employed. Paradoxically, most employers agree that they never really trust their servants, yet they employ them because of their need for security.

Most servants complain about bullying and mistreatment, lack of consideration, and, not least, low wages. They would like to have different jobs, and 75 percent of the servants surveyed said they hoped their children would not end up in domestic service. Yet they go on working in a job for which they say they are paid substandard wages because of lack of choice in the employment market. They need their employers in order to survive.

Post-colonial employers and servants in Zambia thus need one another in a very special sense that makes both sides vulnerable. The frictions that troubled domestic service during the colonial period continue to characterize it, but the concerns of the two parties have become accentuated because of the runaway economy. Security-conscious private householders, who live in a city where petty theft, break-ins, and armed robberies serve as regular means of material redistribution, need servants on the premises to guard their material possessions. This creates a dilemma. Since employers never really trust their servants, they need to watch them as well. The atmosphere in the household is openly characterized by distrust: employers lock up their valuables; more than one-third surveyed said they retained their servants' National Registration Cards (which is illegal) in the belief that it would deter a servant from absconding or help in tracing one who had done so. You never know, they claim, what kind of company the servant keeps; he or she may be in cahoots with thieves. There is no end to the stories, most of which are true, of long-trusted servants who suddenly stole from their employers. Thus no matter how many complaints you have about the servants' work efficiency, you maintain a modicum of good relations to prevent them from turning against you.

Servants on the other hand, although most receive substandard wages, continue to work in a manner that does not upset the employer too much. They depend on intermittent handouts to supplement their meager pay. Those who work for expatriate employers cherish hopes of receiving a gratuity when the employer leaves the country. Those who work in Zambian households today try to improve their conditions by looking for better-paying jobs. All servants hope that their present employers will help them find better situations in food service, for example, or as janitors at the employer's place of work. Meanwhile, they set their own limits as to what is tolerable in terms of workload and supervision. Because the market is shrinking, unless the work is plainly intolerable, many servants stay put, and the problems between them and their employers continue.

Structuring Consent

Unlike during the colonial period, when coercive rules and regulations governed employment according to a hierarchical regime, today consent to the labor process in domestic service is based on shared need for security. The conduct of servant and employer continues to be framed by an unequal interdependence fraught with ambiguities. These arise from the fact that the interpersonal nature of the relationship masks its fundamental class basis. Social practices, spoken of in a vocabulary centered on problems and trouble, help to maintain and reproduce this class relationship. In some of the existing work on servants such behavior has been analyzed as examples of submission to a personalized regime, in others as rituals of deference.[10] But although their relationship to their employers differs from that of other workers because of the personalized nature of the labor process in domestic service, servants are wage laborers and part of the working class, at least in objective terms. I suggest that studies of the relation between workers and employers in other occupational domains may throw light also on domestic service.

To make the class aspect of the worker-employer relation central to a

10. Judith Rollins, *Between Women: Domestics and Their Employers* (Philadelphia: Temple University Press, 1985), pp. 155–173.

discussion of domestic service requires a refocusing of the questions. Rather than asking why servants defer to the hierarchical interpersonal regime in domestic service, why their work performance is poor, and why they are untrustworthy, we might ask why at all they work as hard as they do under a labor regime that compensates them so poorly.

Their employers attribute problems with servants to extraneous factors such as servants' lack of education, their family ties and complications, cultural conventions, and so forth, which servants bring with them into the workplace. In his work concerning a Chicago machine shop, Michael Burawoy demonstrated how the organization of work relations on the shop floor was dominated by "making out"—a sort of game workers played with the rules that governed the tasks assigned by the management.[11] Such games are not frivolous play, but practices designed to do battle with the conditions of work. Through them workers sought to manipulate the tasks within the context of the established rules. Workers, in other words, do not confront their imposed conditions as passive objects; they actively seek to affect them. But by manipulating the rules, workers also lessen the potential for class conflicts to arise between themselves and management, for both parties must cooperate to some extent with one another so that both can continue with their different job tasks. The games workers play generate consent to the rules and allow the system to go on without challenge.[12]

Why do domestic servants in Zambia consent to work in a hierarchically structured employment situation in return for low wages? To answer this question I follow Burawoy, suggesting an explanation that uses factors characteristic of this particular work locus, rather than features that employers allege are peculiar to the servants' personal lives. Among these factors are low pay, poor work conditions, and short-term employment prospects.

In terms of the purchasing power of their wages, servants are worse off today than during the colonial era. Other segments of the working class have also been affected by runaway inflation, but the wage gap between servants and these other groups has widened increasingly. While servants during the colonial period got rations as part of their employment package, few do so today; in fact, the ration system was legally abolished at independence. Although some employers hand out food and used clothing occasionally, such handouts rarely form a regular contribution which the servant can count on in his or her own budget. Domestic servants are not organized and their conditions of work not regulated by any union agreements. The regulations of the 1965 Employment Act are unknown or ig-

11. Michael Burawoy, *Manufacturing Consent: Changes in the Labour Process under Capitalism* (Chicago: University of Chicago Press, 1979).
12. Ibid., pp. 66–93.

nored, and the ZNPF servant registration scheme ensuring them pensions is not widely complied with. These omissions facilitate a despotic organization of work within the household and take us to the next factor: poor work conditions.

The majority of today's servants are general servants who work both inside and outside the house. In such a generalized work regime, a servant's previous skills, as I suggested earlier for example in cooking, become redundant when the new expatriate madam insists she likes to cook and asks her manservant to scrub the toilet bowl, wash her undies and cut the lawn. Some servants, like Zacchi, openly regretted not being allowed to cook for his white employers. But not all general servants who had cooking skills divulged it to their new employers. Keeping such knowledge to themselves they resisted any additional claims employers might place on their already overtaxed labor time. The working hours are generally long, although there may be a lunch break and the employer says there is not much work to do in and around the house, and the servant spends too much time doing it. But if they weren't doing it, there would be something else, for "work never stops," and although the servant lives in quarters on the premises, time is rarely at his own disposition; he simply is available, or made to be so at the employer's discretion.

The work conditions and the daily routine have to be agreeable first and foremost to the employer, who sets the rules and dislikes being inconvenienced by a servant's wish to change his weekly day off from Saturday to Sunday so that he can attend church. The servant is subject to arbitrary and personalized domination—despotic, benevolent, or otherwise. If the servant's ways confront the employer's, he is said to be cheeky, insolent, rude, or irresponsible: "they never learn." What servants do learn is to consent to this regime. To carry out orders and do whatever meaningless work they are asked to do. They know that if they cannot tolerate the regime, there are many others to replace them. But they do not consent as passive automatons to orders handed down from above. They work at their own ease, and one of the games of "making out" in domestic service is to keep up the appearance of always working so that one is not pressed with new demands. By saying that servants are slow and lazy, the employers themselves expect a low work input and use it as a standard for evaluating their servants' work and to structure the future allocation of tasks within the household. While the servant fears losing his job if he does not consent, the employer never really trusts him and accommodates to some extent to the slow routine so as not to upset him unduly and antagonize him. Working alongside each other in this process of mutual monitoring, the inequality inherent in the situation is never confronted, and the relationship between the two parties, mediated by a precarious and skewed interpersonal dependence, is continually reproduced.

[256]

Servants know that their tenure is likely to be short, for today's expatriate employers come and go, and middle- and upper-income Zambians are transferred across the country frequently. In addition, if the job does not work out, prospective employers can hire from a market glutted with potential replacements. Because they are so easily replaceable, some servants are reluctant to take their annual leave even if it is offered to them. They fear the employer might hire a temporary replacement to whom he takes a better liking. To prevent this, sometimes a servant leaves his wife, or a young adult son or relative, behind to do the work in the house when he himself goes elsewhere for a break. In fact, some employers insisted on the servant's wife being left behind in order not to be inconvenienced when the manservant took his vacation time. "They never go anywhere together, anyway," some employers say. Some servants accommodated within limits they set to the employers' whims and tried to make the best out of it while it lasted, hoping to receive help and assistance in return for proper consent and that a new job might materialize once the employer leaves. In new jobs, the work routine with similar expectations on either part is reproduced again.

Those servants who work in the lowest paid jobs with the worst work regimes contest it by shopping around for better jobs. They are the ones who have come today and are gone tomorrow, and who leave without giving notice. Given their low wages, they work no longer or no more than they consider fits their remuneration, and some also help themselves to what they view as their due from the employers' household.

What servants and their employers grapple with in their troubled interaction is fundamentally an economic issue: the creation of survival and security in which they each have a different stake. Some extent of cooperation is necessary for it to be achieved, which requires consent and accommodation on both their parts. To explain the reasons for their different roles in the process, employers call up rural-urban, cultural, and ethnic differences. But what employers consider to be inherent characteristics of servants themselves, features they bring with them into the workplace "because they are different," arise at the locus of work itself and independently of the particular individuals who happen to fill the positions as servants. What employers and servants say about each other therefore reflects the practical knowledge they apply in the course of their conduct at the locus of work and helps reproduce that conduct. So, servants work slowly because, as explained above, work never stops. Knowing that his or her servant does no more than asked, and slowly at that, the employer repeats orders and says servants are lazy, for they never take any initiative. In the servant's language, the repetition of orders amounts to talking too much or too loudly; and checking up on his work by walking behind him amounts to supervising. The servant does not take any initiative for if he did, he would not get any better pay, and if he speeded up his work, he would be assigned another task. And if he argues about ways of doing things, he is said to be rude and cheeky. So he says nothing and is called insolent.

Yet the employer tries not to go too far. For with servants, you just never know; you cannot really trust them. Therefore, you should not upset them too much for there could be repercussions, such as a burglary by the servant you just fired. So, some extent of pilfering is tolerated, for after all you do not trust your servant. And if, after you have asked him five times to deal with some plants in the garden in a certain way and he still does not do so, you stop; you do not want to nag too much. After all, this servant has not to your knowledge been involved in anything against you, he has been with you for some time, knows your whims, and you dread the thought of getting used to a new servant who you may not like or may trust even less than this one. On they go, the servant intentionally being slow and, as expected by his employer, in need of constant supervision; the employer purposefully checking up and, as expected by the servant, never really trusting.

In this way the participants in domestic service bring their practical understanding of the wider surroundings and the circumstances of their interaction to bear on their conduct in a process of mutual monitoring that creates consent to, and reproduces, their unequal relationship. Intentionality, as shown in these examples, is a routine feature of the conduct of servants and employers. Their efforts to anticipate each other's moods so as not to upset the precarious balance required in their employment relationship mutes the potential for conflict between them and the work goes on. The tacit rules they set for themselves in their mutual conduct stem from their knowledge of how to go about doing things, given the circumstances of domestic service and the nature of the broader economic surroundings. Conceptualized as structuring properties, such social practices are not barriers to action but rather are involved in its production. This is Giddens's notion of the duality of structure,[13] according to which actors draw on the knowledge they have of one another's conduct in the production of their interaction in domestic service. In the process, their conduct also reconstitutes the institution they interact in without changing the fundamental inequality that underpins it.

The Woman Question in Postcolonial Domestic Service

The typical domestic worker today is the male general servant and for this reason my discussion about the problems between servants and their

13. Giddens, *Central Problems*, p. 71.

employers in the daily performance of domestic work centered on men. In households employing women servants, the same process is played out but with an added dimension of sexual tension. Women are now entering domestic service in larger numbers than ever before, and the causes and consequences of their entry need to be explored.

What did BaNkuwa have in mind when he said: "If I had known this would become a woman's job, I would have sought work as a driver?" His reference, as I understood him, was to the general deskilling of postcolonial domestic service, rather than to the replacement of men by women in the occupation. It is the fact of having to cook for Zambian employers that makes domestic service a woman's job in the view of long-time menservants. In traditional Zambian households, the wife cooked for her husband. Some contemporary Zambian wives continue to do so, while their servant is allotted the job of cooking for the children—yet many more of them assign the task to their menservants. BaNkuwa, who was a skilled cook and proud of it, did not want to work in a Zambian household; he did not want to do "woman's work.

Women in Zambia today are not replacing men domestic servants for they work primarily as nannies. Boserup's often quoted thesis about the link between economic development and the gender division in domestic service needs to be reevaluated, at least for this case. With economic development, Boserup suggested, the domestic service sector would grow and in the process tend to become more feminine.[14] Two observations certainly warrant attention in the Zambian case.

First, the kind of economic development envisioned by Boserup was predicated on a theory of modernization which has not held up too well when applied to the economic experiences of many developing countries. Zambia's economic growth has not been accompanied by an expansion in urban employment commensurate with the increase of the labor force. After the unsuccessful campaign for African womanpower in the postwar years, men did not leave domestic service for there was little work for them in other occupations. This pattern has persisted after independence, and as we have seen, employment statistics show dramatically that Zambian women continue to have difficulties in finding waged work.

The second factor concerns the construction of gender, the diverse ways it enters into economic and social relations in different societies and the way it changes, or persists, over time. These processes need to be examined in studies of economic change and their different effects on women and men. In Boserup's scheme, broad contrasts were noted: in most of Latin America servants are female and in much of Africa they are male.[15]

14. Ester Boserup, *Woman's Role in Economic Development* (New York: St. Martin's Press, 1970), p. 104.
15. Ibid.

But her reference to the important role African women played in cultivation hardly explains the persistence of men in domestic service. While women's work in cultivation certainly is important, its significance has varied in different countries over time owing to colonial and postcolonial changes in agricultural policy and markets, as well as to natural disasters. Indeed, the entire question of whether or not, when, and where men dominated in this particular occupational sector in Africa, is difficult to answer at the present time because of the anecdotal nature of our knowledge. In the Zambian case, the economic development process has followed a different pattern from that anticipated by Boserup. This process and local cultural practices have helped facilitate the construction of the gender division of labor in domestic service in such a way that women are considered less suitable for such work than men.

Domestic service in Zambia is thus not at the present time undergoing a gender transition from male to female. Men remain in service, and women's entry is simply extending an already established occupational domain. Most of the women who enter service are not taking over men's jobs, but do tasks associated with child care. We might speak rather of an unfolding recomposition of the gender division of labor in domestic service in Zambia.[16]

This process of gender recomposition is influenced by several interrelated factors, of which I briefly discuss three: the ongoing change in demographics of the servant-keeping population to Zambian background and its corollary, the decline in the expatriate population; the general deterioration and stagnation in the urban economy, which is expanding the labor supply to include women as potential servants; and the persistence of a variant of colonial gender ideology which construes the gender of women servants in terms of sexuality and continues to restrict their employment prospects.

As a result of the indigenization of the economy in the wake of independence, black Zambians today numerically dominate the servant-keeping population. There has been a substantial drop in the number of expatriates employed, from 32,100 (12 percent of the workforce) in 1964 to 11,900 (less than 1 percent) in 1985. One expatriate category, whites, comprised almost

---

16. I prefer this to the theory of labor market segmentation which Evelyn Nakano Glenn uses in her study of Japanese American women servants in the United States: *Issei, Nisei, War Bride: Three Generations of Japanese American Women in Domestic Service* (Philadelphia: Temple University Press, 1986), pp. 12–14. Factors such as race and sex are here held to direct women into the secondary labor market characterized by precarious security and low rewards. A "ghetto effect" results, for segmentation is reproduced by patterns of institutionalized discrimination. Such an explanation is not satisfactory in the Zambian case. It does not account for the inequality between men's and women's positions within this particular sector, and it fails to examine the way in which overall gender stratification feeds into this particular sector of the labor market without displacing men.

10 percent of the urban population during the late colonial period, and their numbers have fallen considerably since independence. By 1969 they accounted for only about 4 percent in Lusaka, Kitwe, and Ndola, and in 1980 under 2 percent.[17] Because of the differences in childbearing and childrearing patterns between Zambian women today and the white women of the colonial era, a special niche has opened up within domestic service for women to work as paid nannies for their wealthier countrywomen. This is not to say that African women never worked as nannies during the colonial period, but they were the exception, not the rule. Colonial white women had fewer children than do today's Zambian mothers. Because many children were sent to schools in Southern Rhodesia, South Africa, or Great Britain, their mothers had fewer worries about their day-to-day supervision than have postcolonial Zambian women. Zambian women householders thus need nannies to attend to their children while they themselves go out to work. And many Zambian women who do not work away from home want relief from child care if they can afford it. Creches and nursery schools do not have the facilities to accommodate the growing number of preschool children, and even if places in such institutions were available, they would be too expensive for most Zambian mothers. Nannies are cheaper.

A small proportion of Britons and white South Africans have remained in Zambia since independence, but the majority of today's expatriates originate from other countries throughout the world. Few have ever lived in racially structured colonial settings. They rarely accept the received wisdom passed down by the previous colonial generation about the problems involved in employing African women as servants. Expatriates who accept contracts in Zambia are usually older householders with teenage children who often are attending boarding schools in their home countries; thus their needs for domestic help are different from those of most Zambian householders. Those expatriates who do have small children sometimes employ nannies, and some let women servants do the general work inside the house, occasionally including the cooking. Those who employ nannies have the same turnover problems as those experienced by Zambian women householders. Asian householders continue to employ African women as servants rarely if ever.

Zambian women seek jobs in domestic service as a last resort, particularly in situations of family crisis, and because they have few alternatives. If they can avoid it, domestic service is not a lifetime choice. The hours are long, the remuneration poor, and further, service conflicts with the demands of married life. Although those demands place limits on women in

17. The Economist Intelligence Unit, *Country Profile: Zambia, 1987–1988* (London, October 1987), p. 14; Anthony O'Connor, *The African City* (London: Hutchinson, 1983), pp. 103–104.

ways that vary by class, by rural versus urban residence, and by age, most women are, within those limits, fairly autonomous in the everyday management of their own domestic work. That autonomy is lost, however, in paid domestic service.

My survey shows that the women who worked in domestic service fell into two broad categories. They were young school dropouts from rural areas who had come to town, sometimes leaving a child behind with relatives, and worked in very low-paid jobs, primarily as nannies, sometimes live-in, in Zambian households. Or they were middle-aged, close to or beyond the end of their childbearing years, long-term urban residents, often single heads of households because of divorce or death of a spouse. They worked in better-paid jobs as indoor household servants, especially in expatriate households, and lived-out with children and dependents.

Women's work in domestic service thus differs from men's in many respects. Women's chief activity focuses on child care and tasks associated with it, their jobs have the highest turnover rates, and they earn, with a few exceptions, by far the lowest wages (since it is assumed that they "last" a shorter time than men owing to their personal problems). Proportionately fewer women than menservants live in, and women's employers frequently do not pay the statutory housing allowance to low-income workers on the assumption that their women servants are wives or dependent members of households and therefore have shelter elsewhere.

The "nanny problems" of Zambian women begin with the birth of their first child. At this point in their household's development cycle they typically fetch, or are brought, a distant female relative from the countryside, often a teenage girl who has dropped out of school or whose parents are unable to pay for her education. She is fed and clothed and shares sleeping space with other members of the household, yet is at their beck and call. She rarely lasts from the birth of one baby to the next, which is to say at most two to three years. Problems of discipline quickly arise, for the young girls dislike being ordered around and want freedom to explore the city as well. If they stay for three years, they are generally returned at the end of that time or collected by their parents, the rationale being that to "detain" them longer might reduce their marriage chances. The longer they stay in town, the more likely they are to be "spoiled," that is, made pregnant, which reduces the size of the bridewealth their fathers or guardians may claim. Because of the ties of distant kinship, Zambian women householders can neither command the complete obedience nor control the full labor of these young girls. After their trials with usually several young country relatives, they turn next to paid women servants, who cause even greater problems. Many householders prefer rural women who are new to town for they are assumed to be less venturesome in matters of sex. Their period of service is deliberately kept short, to avoid the possibility of familiarity developing and the likelihood of intimate encounters with the male house-holder.

Once their last-born child has entered school or the older children are considered responsible enough to watch their younger siblings, Zambian women hire men servants. They recount their experiences of employing women in a troubled voice: women servants are insolent and cheeky; they only do the work they feel like doing; in addition, they steal; they go through your underwear and toiletries. But worst of all, before you know it they move into the bedroom and take over the house. As part of the collective consciousness of Zambian women who employ their country-women, stories of women servants usurping the place of the wife abound and are featured in popular newspaper columns and women's magazines.[18] The sexuality issue thus continues to shape the gender construction of women servants in postcolonial Zambia; the race of those who frame it has changed, but for women who must work in the occupation, the effect re-mains the same.

The Postcolonial Sexuality Argument

In the view of Zambian women householders, the "woman problem" in domestic service arises from the loose morals of their female domestics, who are always on the lookout for a man either to marry or to "keep them nicely." Being kept nicely in Zambia means receiving shelter, food, and clothing. This oversexed image Zambian women householders attribute to their female domestics is not a product of the tasks these women do in service or of their biology. Rather, as Michelle Rosaldo has observed, such a construction results from the meanings that women's activities acquire through actual social interaction.[19] Poor women's attempts to secure their own and their dependents' livelihood through support from a spouse or a consort clash with middle- and upper-income Zambian women's needs for child care. For the woman who takes a job as nanny seeks to quit as soon as she has some economic means in her own household.

To account for this tension, we must explore the power dynamics of gender within the household, the *structuration*, in Giddens's term, of relations between the sexes[20] within it and the way these dynamics enter into, and affect, women's and men's places in the wider social context. Paid domestic work does not in the Zambian view constitute proper women's

18. For example, "Georgette, My Wife," *Woman's Exclusive* 5 (Lusaka; 1983): 7, 9, and 17, and popular Zambian columnist Kapelwa Musonda, "House Servant Outwits Owner," *Times of Zambia*, January 8, 1985, p. 4.

19. Michelle Z. Rosaldo, "The Use and Abuse of Anthropology: Reflections on Feminism and Cross-Cultural Understanding," *Signs* 5 (1980): 399–400.

20. Giddens, *Central Problems*, p. 115.

work, for it is considered not "natural" for a woman with small children to leave her own household to attend to someone else's. While on the one hand they seek economic support from men, they wish to be able to act independently of them on the other. Most urban studies in Zambia have shown that male/female relations are filled with anxiety and that relationships are very unstable.[21] Regardless of the different ethnic backgrounds of the towns' populations, the gender dynamics within households turn on an age- and male-based hierarchy of authority. Across class, male-female relations are largely asymmetric, and although of course there are exceptions this observation is widespread enough to establish that, generally, husbands assume domestic authority. Marital relations are often fraught with tensions, in part due to the persistence of customary marriage practices permitting polygyny, and, perhaps influenced by this, to the existence of a double standard that condones extramarital sex for men. Women will go to great expense to buy love medicines to attract a man's love and assure his financial support.[22] Yet they also know that they cannot rely on men. Unlike in many West African countries, cultural norms in Zambia do not oblige men to distribute part of their income to wives for household purposes. The money allocation system between husband and wife depends entirely on his goodwill. Even if Zambian men have ample economic means, only a portion of their disposable income reaches their own households.

While women seek to get and maintain support from men, they also are concerned to ensure the day-to-day survival of their children and to make economic gains in their own right. As they grow older, and their children leave the household, Zambian women become less concerned with the pursuit of men's attentions and concentrate their efforts on making an income they control themselves. This shift helps account for women's dual participation pattern in domestic service, which I identified earlier: the young women who come and go in the low paid jobs are struggling to establish their own domestic menages, whereas the middle-aged and older women in longer-term employment and at better wages often are single heads of their own households after divorce or death of their husbands. Men may come and go in their lives, for they do not mind being kept nicely, yet they do not want men around on a permanent basis. Extrapolating from their own and their adult daughters' experience, they say that

21. Bonnie B. Keller, "Marriage and Medicine: Women's Search for Love and Luck," *African Social Research* 26 (1978): 489–505, and "Marriage by Elopement," *African Social Research* 27 (1979): 565–585; and Ilsa M. G. Schuster, *New Women of Lusaka* (Palo Alto, Calif.: Mayfield Publishing Company, 1979).

22. Keller, "Marriage and Medicine"; Benetta Jules-Rosette, *Symbols of Change: Urban Transition in a Zambian Community* (Norwood, N.J.: Ablex Publishing Corporation, 1981), pp. 129–163.

men cannot be relied on: "as soon as they see someone they like, men drop their wives, or they take another one on the side."

These tensions exist also in Zambian servant-employing households. Husbands may feel freer to pursue sex and change partners than women because under matriliny offspring are considered women's children who in case of divorce would belong to her group. Zambian women householders seek to identify themselves sexually as their husband's women at the same time as they are aware that husbands have other choices. They will make statements to that effect, if not about their own husbands, then about a neighbor's. To prevent extramarital relations from happening within their own household, they prefer to employ menservants. Although a couple of cases were brought to my attention in which a manservant was alleged to have molested the employer's young adult daughter, male sexuality has not entered popular folklore to affect the way the male servant's role was constructed in gender terms. The class gap between him and the employer is generally held to account for the difference between them, the manservant being merely seen as a poor, unskilled worker, unfortunate perhaps because of lack of education or family circumstances, leading a different life and having needs and problems quite unlike those of his employer.

If menservants were spoken of in a language of difference, women servants were even more so. As I noted in the preceding section, Zambian women who employ their countrywomen as servants speak of them in invidious terms. Their distrust of their women domestics expresses itself in a discourse of sexuality which accentuates and dramatizes their women servants' struggle for a livelihood. It also distances female employers from their less fortunate countrywomen who may have neither husbands nor homes of their own. These expressions veil a difference of lifestyle, a class gap, which they make sure not to bridge. Yet they do have one thing in common, although for different reasons: their interest in men. The servant wants a person to support her and her children so that she no longer needs to do someone else's domestic work, and her female employer wants a husband, certainly to support her children and to legitimate her economic and social pursuits as a mature social person, properly married. Their shared interest creates sexual hostility which further distances them from each other.[23]

The oversexed gender image Zambian women householders attribute to their women servants is a product of the way they interpret their women servants' activities and interaction and brings about a special body politic within their own households. Since they believe that their women servants

23. Laurel Bossen describes a Latin American variation on this theme involving different cultural factors from those prevalent in the Zambian case: "Wives and Servants: Women of Middle-Class Households, Guatemala City," in *Urban Life: Readings in Urban Anthropology*, ed. G. Gmelch and W. Zenner (New York: St. Martin's Press, 1980), pp. 190–200.

may indulge in sexual affairs with their husbands, they restrict them by rules that reduce their opportunity for contact with the male household head. The chief rules revealed in my survey concerned bedrooms and the preparation of food. Both domains are sexually charged: in the rural societies described in the ethnographic literature of this region these domains were surrounded by special precautions: spatial segregation by age of sleeping quarters, restrictions on women's cooking for men during menstruation, and abstinence from intercourse before important celebrations and events.[24] Neither men nor women servants were allowed to enter bedrooms in most of the Zambian households in the survey, and in several of them women servants were asked not to cook for the male head of household. In these cases the Zambian women householders feared that their female servants would mix love potions into the husband's food in order to attract his sexual attentions. For the most part, those servants who did cook were men, and even in some of these cases the wife took personal charge of preparing her husband's main meals. As a result of their own effort to encourage their husbands' attentions, many of these women bear children at regular intervals. And because of their need for child care, they tolerate the presence of their Zambian nannies. As these nannies come and go, their employer's problems with them are reenacted and the structured inequality between the two main protagonists recreated anew.

Although the coming of independence broke the hegemonic fusion of gender ideology and employment practice which helped keep African women out of domestic service during the late colonial period, women's sexuality in the view of some Zambians today continues to exercise a constraint on their employability. The parties who advocate this view have changed, for colonial white women's fear of African women's sexuality is today expressed by Zambian women who employ their countrywomen as servants. The concerns of both these categories of women centered on their husbands' opportunity for extramarital involvement with, in the colonial case, a woman of the other race, and in the postcolonial case, one of the other class. The gender ideologies that built on these fears reflect the prevailing socioeconomic orders of their time in both their patriarchal and class dimensions. The pronounced accent on women's sexuality in the postcolonial gender ideology is linked in complex ways to the hierarchical gender dynamics within households and the growing class gap that the economic downslide since the early 1970s has been fostering in Zambia.

24. For examples of some of these practices, see Audrey A. Richards, *Chisungu: A Girl's Initiation Ceremony among the Bemba of Zambia* (London: Faber and Faber, 1951), Victor W. Turner, *The Drums of Affliction: A Study of Religious Processes among the Ndembu of Zambia* (Oxford: Clarendon, 1968), and C. M. N. White, "Elements in Luvale Beliefs and Rituals," *Rhodes-Livingstone Papers*, no. 32 (1961).

[7]

Lives beyond the Workplace

How do servants, members of their households, and people with whom they interact when not at work experience lives in a depressed economy beset by recurrent scarcities of basic consumer goods and runaway inflation? How do they manage economically, and what are their alternatives to domestic service? What kind of social life and leisure time do they have? And what of their employers—how are these questions answered for them? In this chapter I explore these questions, and discuss the action that servants have taken to improve their position vis-à-vis other members of the working class and in society at large. I also examine some of the implications that the persistence of domestic service has for the debate about development in Zambia today. My discussion centers on today's most typical domestic worker, the male general servant, but whenever it is relevant I highlight the different experiences of women servants.

Domestic Service: A Way of Life?

Given their substandard wages, how indeed do servants manage to make a living? A general servant receives an average monthly wage that is gone before he has purchased his own household's basic staples. A minimum monthly budget, featuring meat or fish twice a week as a complement to nshima, the maize porridge, plus very basic essentials, would in 1983 require K119 to feed a household of two adults and two children. Few servants come close to earning that, and many have more than two children and sometimes other dependents as well. The wages most servants receive barely cover the purchase of a minimum of basic necessities such as mealie meal, charcoal, cooking oil, salt, sugar, soap, and detergent. If these necessities are bought, little if nothing remains for meat, relish, eggs, milk, bread, and tea not to mention clothes, school fees and uniforms or the expenses occasioned by the inevitable arrival of relatives.

To find the answer to the question, I asked two general servants I knew well to record their daily expenses, one for a two-month period, the other for three months. Their budgets are detailed in Appendix 2, as is the minimum monthly budget described above. There are several differences between the two servants. Edson, who kept his records for two months, was at the time a twenty-four-year-old general servant who had worked in the household of an expatriate Asian couple for five years. His wife, Gertrude, had recently been taken on part time; the madam suffered a back problem and was teaching Gertrude to cook Indian food to relieve herself from strenuous activity. Gertrude was also expected to do the general housework on Edson's day off. Theirs was the only Asian household in which I found an African woman cooking, and one in less than a handful of Asian households that employed African women in any capacity. Edson earned K75 and Gertrude K44 a month; Edson's wage was raised to K85 after the first month of his budget record. They had two children below school age, and Gertrude was pregnant with their third child. Euclid, who kept his records for three months, was a general servant in the household of a North American couple for whom he had worked for three years. He was thirty-five years old and recently remarried after a divorce; he and and his new wife had one small child. He earned K82 a month. Both these men had gone to school for about seven years. Their wives were barely literate.

Although they received different wages and the composition of their households varied, they had one thing in common with most of the servant households in my survey. Their income was insufficient to afford their households a minimum of necessities. In Edson's household, meat or fish was eaten approximately once a week, in Euclid's fish only. Their children hardly if ever got milk; most of the time they had to suffice with a diet of nshima and relish. The children beyond nursing age were undernourished. Judging from their budget records, Edson's household ate better than Euclid's. The difference was to some extent made up from Euclid's garden. He, like some other servants, had access to a garden plot in or behind the employer's garden on which he grew vegetables and maize. It provided a limited supplement but not one sufficient to cover the household needs. Under these circumstances, the weekly ration money that some servants are given is used for food and to some extent tides them over to month's end; Euclid received a weekly ration of two Kwacha.

Did income-generating activities on the part of servants' wives help relieve the shortfall in wages? Even though Gertrude, and she was an exception, worked half time, her small wage did not make a large difference in a low budget. Some, but very few, wives surveyed were occasionally asked to lend a hand with household chores for which they were paid on a piecework basis. In a few of the expatriate households, the work inside and outside the house was done by a servant couple who were paid separately. A few wives earned their own incomes, some as servants employed elsewhere and others engaging in small-scale vegetable trading in nearby markets or sewing dresses for sale from home. But the vast majority of servants' wives earned no money of their own. They cooked the meals in their own households, swept the quarters, took care of children, and otherwise "just sat" (Zambian-English term for the activity of persons who are not wage employed).

The male breadwinner is supposed to provide for everything his household needs. Although adult relatives from the extended family were accommodated in some of the servant households, most of them were on the lookout for work and they rarely contributed to the household's support. Their presence taxed the already meager resources of their hosts. A few menservants pursued income-generating activities on the side. A couple of them did tailoring work and one did tin-smithing. Their hope was to save money, to build a house in a compound or to set themselves up in business so that they could leave their servant jobs behind.

For most general servants, the employer's charity is the final recourse. Handouts of household necessities, leftover food, and new and used clothing are welcomed and come to be expected. In the mornings Edson and Gertrude got leftover tea, a slice of bread, and their oldest girl got milk and bread. Edson's employers regularly purchased the children's shoes. Both Edson's and Euclid's households received gifts at Christmas and presents when their employers returned from overseas leaves. But when assistance is not forthcoming, some servants help themselves and the problem of pilfering, if not outright theft, arises.

Alternatively or in addition, servants ask for advances from their pay to cover unanticipated expenses. Many servants, including Edson and Euclid, asked for pay advances regularly or borrowed from their employers and then paid back in installments. As debts accumulate, servants become more dependent on their employer's good will and hope that the debts will be written off. Sometimes they are, and for a while no further advances are given. Some employers establish a limit, often the amount of the servant's monthly wage, beyond which they do not permit borrowing. Once it is reached, a schedule of monthly payments is begun, during which time the servant is unable to borrow.

While many employers function as their servants' loan bank, some servants allocate some of their funds to a rotating credit system known as *chilimba*. Two (or more) persons who trust one another alternate in handing over an agreed-upon portion of their wage, for example, K20, to the

Edson Banda with Faides and Joe, Lusaka 1984. Author's photograph.

Gertrude Banda with Faides and Joe, Lusakla 1984. Author's photograph.

Euclid Nkumbula at work in the kitchen, Lusaka 1984. Author's photograph.

Euclid Nkumbula, daughter Nellie, and wife Betty, Lusaka 1984. From the collection of Henry Antkiewicz. Reproduced with permission.

other every month. A servant involved in chilimba who receives a monthly wage of K70 keeps K50 from his own wage during the month it is his turn to hand over money to his partner. But every second month he has K20 in addition to his own wage. This extra enables him to some degree to meet the financing of larger purchases, clothes, for example, often in installments. In this way, chilimba may help to stretch the budget. Twenty-six percent of the servants in the survey practiced chilimba at the time of the interview. Many more had done so previously but had given it up for a variety of reasons, including the move of their partner or because they had been cheated. The servants who engaged in chilimba were not young people new to town but mainly older people, and proportionately more older women than menservants. Young servants in their first job would say that they did not know anyone they could trust enough to start chilimba.

Servants may also resort to a lending practice known as *kaloba* to meet such unexpected expenses as the funeral of a father for which the employer has refused an advance because he has helped cover expenses for the funerals of several relatives. According to kaloba practices, borrowed money has to be repaid within a month at 50 percent interest. To repay it, access to chilimba funds is convenient, as is the prospect of a pay advance in next month, although the latter alternative makes the servant more dependent on the employer than the former. A couple of servants in my survey had turned kaloba into a profit-making venture. They used their access to wage advances to develop a loan-shark business. Borrowing from their employer in the middle of the month, they lent the money to someone else at kaloba rates. When they received the repayment with interest at the next mid-month, they returned the amount owed to the employer and pocketed the profit.

The chilimba system is not unique to servants. There is anecdotal evidence that it spread with migration during the colonial period. From Broken Hill in the late 1930s, Wilson reported that "nearly every African man . . . , married or single, has a partner with whom he pools his wages, alternatively, each month,"[1] and Epstein gives examples from the African township in Ndola on the copperbelt in mid-1950s.[2] The practice persists in today's low- to middle-income townships among various occupational groups such as orderlies, clerks, and secretaries. Chilimba, other rotating credit systems,[3] and various borrowing arrangements in Zambia have not

---

1. Godfrey Wilson, "An Essay on the Economics of Detribalisation in Northern Rhodesia, Part 2," *Rhodes-Livingstone Papers*, no. 6 (1942), p. 77.

2. A. L. Epstein, *Urbanization and Kinship: The Domestic Domain on the Copperbelt of Zambia 1950–1956* (New York: Academic Press, 1981), pp. 52–54.

3. Peter Hayward, personal communication, has noted two rotating credit systems among fishermen in Zambia: *muyambiro* and *kamukole*.

been the subject of any inquiry in their own right.[4] If they spread with the system of migratory labor, they may have arisen in response to the expansion of the cash nexus and have offered a practical financial arrangement understood by all in the multiethnic context of the growing colonial cities.

Chilimba and servants' use of a variety of borrowing systems provide evidence of the careful short- and long-term planning they apply in their attempt to make a living on scarce resources. "Stretching the money," as servants explain the function of chilimba, shows no lack of foresight. Such practices make available to servants the kind of credit they are unlikely to obtain in downtown banks because of lack of collateral. They also spare them from spending money on bus fares and wasting time in bank lines, for most banks are far away from the low-density residential areas in which most servants live and work. Euclid used his employer as a bank and loan association. He pursued a two-fold strategy: he asked his employer to retain part of his current wage as well as give him an advance on the next month's pay. These two transactions were carefully recorded in a book the employer kept for that purpose, and Euclid would often write notes when he wanted some of "his" money. Euclid knew the exact disposition of his money and corrected any errors in his employer's calculations. His accounts were intricate, for he earmarked funds from the two transactions for different purposes. Euclid used the "savings" from the regular wage on an intermittent basis throughout the month to pay for food, thus ensuring his urban household a bare minimum. He occasionally used advances from the next month's pay for installments on the purchase of a cow that he kept in his mother's village. He was a matrilineal Tonga from the Southern Province and was presumably seeking to accumulate a nest egg to offer him some security when he no longer worked in town. By contrast, Edson's household spent all of its income on living expenses every month. He was a matrilineal Nsenga from the Eastern Province who had neither land nor cattle; his mother had divorced his father and remarried in the city; there were no uncles left in the village, and Edson would have a hard time making customary claims on land.

Most servants struggle to make ends meet. To ease their struggle, some servants "farm out" children to country relatives. Some servants who up-

---

4. In an article that summarizes information on this topic from across Africa, the authors mention chilimba in Zambia and Zimbabwe but provide no substantive information on the arrangement. See Marvin P. Miracle, Diane S. Miracle, and Laurie Cohen, "Informal Savings Mobilization in Africa," *Economic Development and Cultural Change* 28 (1980): 701–724. Most of our African examples of rotating credit associations come from West Africa. For an excellent and detailed study of this subject in another part of the world, see Carlos G. Velez-Ibanez, *Bonds of Mutual Trust: The Cultural Systems of Rotating Credit Associations among Urban Mexicans and Chicanos* (New Brunswick, N.J.: Rutgers University Press, 1983).

hold use rights to land in the villages let their wives alternate between town and countryside, tending fields during the rainy season and keeping house during the dry season. But most servants have neither land nor cattle. And some do not have relatives who are able to keep their children. Many of them ended up in service jobs in the first place because of family circumstances that prevented them from progressing in school. And few of the servants I met had been able to save anything from their meager wages.

Occupational Alternatives

In their own view and that of fellow Zambians, servants lead miserable lives, doing a job from which there is nothing to gain and which has no future. When asked if she would consider taking a job as a servant, a woman resident in a high-density township answered emphatically, "Over my dead body!" She was of South African background, and had had her first wage-labor experience as a domestic servant in the south: there was "no way" she would do it again. Women, as I discussed earlier, enter domestic service as a last resort. For most, the preferred alternative is to be a wife and mother in one's own household. Yet economic pressures and strained marital relations provoke many women to seek some means of making money. When they do, they usually do not turn to domestic service but to trade and vending. Such activity allows them to continue to supervise their households, while in most cases they earn more than they would from domestic service. My previous work in Lusaka has shown how, over the course of their adult lives, many women intermittently conduct small-scale trades from their homes, in the streets and at markets.[5] No matter how small-scale their activity is, however, they need startup capital and the lack of it may force some women to seek work as servants: but this is a temporary measure.

Domestic service is an occupation without a future. Servants often feel trapped, with no options. They do not make enough money to set themselves up in a craft or trade, and in addition, their working hours do not leave them time to engage in any other money-earning activity. Only few can expect to move up in the ranks of the servant hierarchy, to become cooks in managerial households on company payroll. Once there, the pay compares unfavorably to that of the lowest-paid unionized worker on the payroll in the same company. Thus most servants depend for their future on their employers. Some well-intentioned households assist servants in

5. I have discussed women's trading and household activities in several articles, among them "The Urban Informal Sector as a Development Issue: Poor Women and Work in Lusaka, Zambia," *Urban Anthropology* 9 (1980): 199–225, and "Negotiating Sex and Gender in Urban Zambia," *Journal of Southern African Studies* 10 (1984): 219–238.

getting a driver's license; others secure them jobs in their company as janitors, messengers, orderlies, hospital attendants, or as cooks or waiters in hotels, bars, and private clubs. Such jobs are much preferred over domestic service because of their regulated hours, higher wages, and stipulated benefits. These jobs comprised the main avenue for upward mobility among the former servants I interviewed in Mtendere township.

The general consensus among former servants as well as nonservants was that they would rather have their children return to the rural areas to farm than see them employed as servants. When they make such statements, members of the older generation are envisioning a nonexistent ideal; they forget that they themselves left their villages to seek better economic opportunities in towns. Living conditions and economic prospects in the rural areas have so deteriorated in many regions[6] that returning to them is at present a worse option than the urban job as a servant. Though some servants have rights to land in their villages and some even have rights to cattle, resettling in a rural area requires resources—to purchase seed and fertilizer, perhaps to build a house—that most servants do not have. The growing disparity in the cities between the few who are well situated and the many who have nothing to sell but their labor power is increasingly becoming characteristic of the rural areas as well.[7] The few resources a returned townsman would bring to his village are likely to disappear quickly, given customary claims on his generosity. If he keeps his resources to himself and appears to be stingy, he may cause envy among his relatives. In some cases, these tensions have resulted in accusations of witchcraft. If the migrant goes back to the city (as many, like Zacchi, eventually do), he is likely to return there in poorer health than when he left and, without savings; he will have few other options but to reenter the domestic service market. It is a typical scenario and helps to explain why 45 percent of the servants I surveyed did not keep up connections with their villages of birth or their parents' home villages. One-third of these servants had been born in towns, and the rest had not been back to the village since their first departure. The lack of economic means and poor education that precipitated their departure also prevent them from returning to the villages.

Some young menservants who are recent entrants into the paid labor force study for their school-leaving certificates when off duty, still hoping that school credentials will open up new doors. Others have hopes of becoming drivers, as few formal credentials are necessary for the job. But positions as drivers are not easy to find—this occupation claimed the third

6. Peter Stromgaard, "A Subsistence Society under Pressure: The Bemba of Northern Zambia," *Africa* 55 (1985): 39–59.

7. Thayer Scudder and Elizabeth Colson, *Secondary Education and the Formation of an Elite: The Impact of Education on Gwembe District* (New York: Academic Press, 1980).

largest number of registrants at the labor exchange in September 1983. The largest number of job seekers looked for work in domestic service, and about half of them did find places.

Domestic service remains the only wage-paying alternative to which the young aspiring job-seekers return once their attempts to escape it have failed. Many of the young men I surveyed had left the job after an initial stint of less than a year. Some went back to their villages, only to return to the city. Some held various jobs as general workers, all of them temporary (it is well known that a number of Lusaka firms and companies take on temporary workers to cut costs). Some young men took jobs as security guards but left this higher paying occupation (at least when compared with domestic service) because of its awkward hours and the dangers associated with it. Within a couple of years, these young men had returned to the servant ranks. And there many of them are likely to remain. In the words of a twenty-four-year-old general servant with a wife and two children who was in his second job: "This is the only job for people like us who are not educated. Once a servant, always a servant!"

Accommodation and handouts of food and clothing in addition to wages are probably sufficient factors to continue to attract workers to domestic service, especially newcomers fresh from the countryside who are unable to find housing in Lusaka's crowded townships. Compared with rural poverty, and with the irregularity of other available jobs and the uncertainties of self-employment, domestic service offers at the present time at least a regular income and a subsistence level of survival for many families. Most of these servants, rarely themselves the sons and daughters of servants, hoped to ensure with their limited means that their children would go to school and never have to enter the occupation. But such hopes were more realistic during the late colonial period, for education was the chief means of upward mobility for the first generation of young adults immediately after independence. Since then, the educational system has not expanded at a rate sufficient to accommodate all children of school age. Because of their substandard wages, servants will have a hard time sending their children through school even if they are lucky enough to get places for them. With the high dropout rate on the one hand and the increased requirements of job applicants for degrees and certificates on the other, parents have little certainty that their struggle for their children's education eventually will pay off.

Fenced-in Lives

Today's economic structure in Zambia enables a tiny segment of the population—but one of diverse ethnic composition—to enjoy what in the past would have been considered racial privileges: large houses and gardens, servants to attend to their needs, poolside parties, sundowners on the porch, and private clubs. Today's servant-keeping population does not form a socially united community. They have in common only that they all employ servants whom they rarely trust but require nonetheless for security reasons, and they all are inconvenienced by the inflationary economy and recurrent scarcities.

Life for the financially privileged is fraught with fear and lived in an atmosphere of paranoia: valuables are hidden away, property is locked up. To prevent their servants from stealing as well as from seeing how many things they own, many employers lock up closets, cupboards, and chests of drawers, and some lock up bedrooms and studies as soon as the servant has finished cleaning them. Some householders remove their best pots and pans, cutlery and plates from the kitchen every evening, locking them up in store-rooms or bedroom closets. Kitchen staples—cooking oil, rice, sugar, salt, tea—are regularly locked up away from the kitchen. Refrigerators and deep freezers are sometimes placed in back rooms rather than the kitchen and locked. Many householders do not display their valuables in the living room so that they are not within view from the outside. Television sets, videos, radios, stereos are put in the master bedroom at night, and some people lock their bedroom doors from the inside. Employers try not to have much cash in the house, while at the same time making sure that they do have some bank notes at hand just in case "the burglars" should come—on the assumption that it is wiser to hand over money than be beaten or shot. They devise "advance warning systems," for example, putting empty bottles on window sills which burglars might shatter as they try to break in. Some households sleep in relays, so that at least one person is awake and alert at all hours. If a burglary occurs, often people stay behind locked bedroom doors and let the thieves take the few things left in the living room and kitchen rather than confronting possibly armed men. Nightwatchmen and servants have little power to deter thieves, who may beat them up or simply offer them a cut of the take. Dogs kept outside may be killed or poisoned. Not all employers have telephones; even if there is a phone, it may not work; and if the phone works, a call to the police station would make little difference. The police have too few cars, or gasoline might be unavailable, and so they would be unlikely to arrive at the scene before the burglars had gone. The police are notoriously ineffective in tracking down burglars after the fact. If they are caught, burglars are likely to be beaten, but when they recover from their bruises, they may simply go back to it again. While this is the worst scenario, all employers have experienced some aspect of it. Most urban residents go to bed fearing the night and worrying about what the morning will reveal.

Fear is not restricted to the house. Cars are burgled during the daytime;

people are robbed while waiting for the red light to change at one of Lusaka's few light-controlled intersections. (Stories abound of people being robbed from their cars at gunpoint and left to walk home at night in little or no clothing.)

Because of the general insecurity of living, a good deal of leisure time is spent at home, where now more entertainment takes place than during the colonial period. Expatriates and Zambians who can afford them have VCRs. Guests from across town tend to be invited for daytime gatherings during weekends. Informal visits and unannounced calls occur mostly before sunset. Dinner parties may feature guests predominantly from the immediate neighborhood, and those who come from a distance leave home fearing the drive and what they may encounter on their return. Many dislike this sense of being prisoners in their own homes and insist on going out from time to time to retain a wider sphere of interaction.

Lusaka offers a variety of entertainments appealing to expatriates, although many complain about the city's dearth of "culture." The amateur theater tradition that was started during the colonial period persists together with its club and bar. It regularly stages productions of both African and non-African pieces. The city has several movie houses that specialize in films glorifying the martial arts. The culture-promoting societies sponsored by national governments are present, too: the Alliance Française and the British Council. They, some of the foreign embassies that include representation from Eastern European and Asian countries, and the United States Information Service promote special events and some have libraries. There are also special-interest groups such as a Horticultural Society which sponsors yearly exhibits and competitions, a Wildlife Conservation Society, an Ornithological Society, and a variety of others. Attendance at most such events is predominantly non-Zambian.

Beyond their problems with servants, burglaries, and the country's economic ills, Lusaka's residents have little in common. Expatriates are likely to interact with Zambians at work, during work-related functions, and in civic and philanthropic groups such as Rotary International, the Jaycees, Round Table, and Lions, and when going to restaurants and bars. Those who are members of private sports clubs play tennis, squash, and golf, and drink beer in the club's bar with their Zambian fellow players. There is also a riding club, polo club, fencing club, and flying club whose memberships are predominantly expatriate. Dinner parties may feature a few Zambian colleagues, perhaps accompanied by wives. But many expatriates complain that it is difficult to establish close personal friendships with Zambians. Social invitations are rarely reciprocated; interests are said to differ. Those expatriates who have made efforts often leave the country with a sad feeling of never really having gotten to know the local population. Their knowledge of ordinary Zambians' way of life is limited to occasional car trips through a high-density area where they may have stopped briefly to bring, fetch, or search for a servant or buy beer during a shortage. And for some, the low-income areas function as "sights," which they point out to visitors new to the country.

Some expatriates' desire to "know the African" changes to "knowing Africa"—meaning the game parks, Victoria Falls, and exotic birds with which Zambia is richly endowed. Camping trips and visits to these places are the highlights of many expatriates' African experience in Zambia and they help create an image of an Africa that probably never was. In some of the game parks, visitors may rough it on walking safaris, sleeping for a few nights in huts or tents. Providing a break from the prisonlike existence in Lusaka, such trips feature specialized servants reminiscent of the colonial past: skilled cooks and inside servants in the lodges and tea boys among the inventory of walking safaris.

Not all expatriates who take jobs in Zambia are interested in getting to know the local population and exploring the region. Some (specifically the Asian expatriates) accept contracts in Zambia for the sole purpose of getting a job because of the glut of people with their skills and qualifications in their home countries. The response of one Asian woman in my survey reflects the attitude: "What is there to know?"

Asians, like the other regional or racial groups represented in my survey, socialized primarily with persons of their own group. These broad groups are comprised of a number of subgroups. The Asian population, for example, had several divisions of which the most marked were those between long-time residents in Zambia and expatriates on temporary contracts, and between Hindus and Muslims. Further splits exist between various country, home region, and language backgrounds—people from India versus those from Pakistan, people who speak Gujarati, and those who speak Bengali, or Hindi, and so forth. Within each of these groups, people met for specific religious and cultural events. The white expatriates also sort themselves out into broader regional groups, for example, North Americans, Scandinavians, and then distinct national groups: the British, the Germans, the French, those from the Netherlands, and so on.

The mingling across subgroups that happens at times results largely from shared professional interests. It produces a number of informal circles or cliques, such as the embassy crowd, the development people, university teachers, corporate managers and directors, and missionary circles. In households where both spouses work away from home and in different areas, socializing involves a broader realm of people than in households where only one spouse is wage employed.

While husbands attend meetings of their sex-segregated service clubs, women also have their auxiliary circles and service organizations, such as the American Women's Club, various church groups, the Business and

Professional Women's Club, the Women's Institute, and the YWCA. Many of these groups have social work as well as recreational functions, and some are places where expatriate women meet elite Zambian women. Groups of women from different residential areas meet informally for recreation and exercise. White expatriate husbands and wives spend more leisure time together than do Asians and Zambians. Yet several white women expressed the view that life in Zambia was hard on marriages and gave examples of couples who had divorced while living there. Support groups of friends and relatives are lacking in Zambia and it takes time to develop new ones. The general fear and insecurity is stressful and takes its toll. One is thrown back on oneself, but there are today, more than during the colonial period, possibilities for interaction across nationality, race, and sex lines which may provide opportunities not before explored.

Patterns of leisure-time activity among the members of Zambian servant-employing households are shaped to a great extent by the household's economic means and are in general more sex-segregated than they are among expatriates. Except for the fraction of Zambian households where the chief wage-earner is in a high-level position, incomes are smaller than those of most expatriate households. Also, there are more strains placed on their incomes, because Zambians have larger families and regardless of economic position they are likely to be additionally burdened by relatives from the extended family in need of support or education. Few Zambians renounce such responsibilities although some high-ranking officials I surveyed did place a limit on relatives they would be willing to support.

Membership in clubs is beyond the means of many Zambian households, so it is those Zambian men who are managers, directors, in the professions, and in upper-level government jobs whom expatriates will meet for games of tennis or golf, for a drink, or occasionally invite for dinner. Except for occasional visits to watch them play and to share a drink with them, the Zambian wives rarely accompany their husbands to the clubs. Husband, wife, and children may attend church together, but for the most part their social networks do not overlap. Women's social life includes women co-workers, neighbors and church friends, and relatives. Some women are members of such groups as the Business and Professional Women's Association and the YWCA, and some are active with expatriate women in fundraising activities for a variety of purposes, including the welfare of children and the plight of poor women in the townships. In the mid-1980s the Zambia Association for Research and Development established itself in preparation for the 1985 meeting in Nairobi that concluded the United Nations Decade for Women. This group has begun to raise critical questions about sex discrimination in the economic and political domain. These efforts involve a small number of professional women who can afford to spend time concerning themselves with social issues. The interactional sphere of most Zambian women is more limited. They get together with other women for events that symbolically celebrate their female sexuality—"kitchen parties" before weddings, when the prospective bride's women friends and relations give presents for the new home and and join in ribald song, commentary, and dance to prepare her for her new role as a wife, and baby showers. These parties offer a contemporary parallel to the initiation rites that took place in several of the region's rural societies not so long ago. They are accompanied by much beer drinking and conviviality.

Such events are welcome interruptions of the dreary routine of attending to household needs, often in isolated circumstances. In many Zambian households, husband and wife share little beyond the bedroom. Women are expected to cope with the pressures of maintaining the household, searching out scarce foods, queuing for necessities, without the help or emotional support of husbands. Men still eat separately in many Zambian households, and spend time where and with whom they like, unquestioned by their wives. Women friends offer each other much needed support systems.

Servant Interaction: Households, Neighborhood, and City

"They don't entertain like we do," say employers about their servants' leisure activities. Obviously not; servants cannot afford to. How they have a good time reflects their low salaries, not some essentially different outlook on life from that of their employers.

Servants' leisure-time interaction takes place in several social arenas which I discuss in turn: in and around the quarters with members of their households; with other servants from the neighborhood and visitors who call on them; in low-income areas across town; and in the city's downtown.

Social interaction within the servant's household is shaped by the age- and sex-based hierarchical division of authority common to most Zambian households. Some servants treat their wives in a very authoritarian manner, prohibiting them from doing tasks that take them far from the quarters. Euclid's new wife, for example, was not allowed to go shopping in a small grocery store some fifteen minutes' walk from their house. Edson was more liberal, or perhaps Gertrude was more independently minded, for she went downtown by bus to do errands and walked to the nearest compound to purchase vegetables at the market. Visitors are entertained with Zambian food prepared by the wife if their hosts can afford it. Otherwise they are given only something to drink. When leaving, visitors are usually escorted to the nearest bus stop, where the host will wait until the bus has arrived, for it is considered impolite to let visitors depart without company.

[281]

A lot of socializing takes place outside of the quarters. Men seat themselves on chairs, women and children sit on the ground. Some servants
have transistor radios and listen to music or the football games that are
transmitted every weekend. Radios and record players are coveted possessions. Listening circles may include visitors and servants from neighbors'
houses. When the householders are away at work during the daytime, a
good deal of interaction and conversation take place between servants in
the neighborhood across garden fences and within yards. They exchange
news about the comings and goings of their employers, the imminent
departures of some, and the possibilities of getting jobs elsewhere. On
weekends in one of the neighborhoods in which I lived, one of the menservants played a homemade guitar, drawing a crowd of children and adult
servants of both sexes around him. Euclid was a fine drummer, but it took
the arrival of a young relative of the employers, who was himself a music
student, for his employers to discover that he had such skills.

Some servants took pride in decorating their interior living space. Although the majority of the servants' quarters described by my assistants as
part of the survey looked drab, some servants tried their hands at interior
decoration. Walls would feature current or outdated calendars, family photographs, pictures cut out of magazines, and occasionally Zambian curios.
Shelves and tables would sometimes support a vase with plastic flowers.
One servant in one of the neighborhoods where I lived enjoyed making
arrangements of natural flowers and would decorate the employer's and his
own living room. A variety of bric-a-brac from the employer's house might
be on display as well: cosmetics bottles, discarded plates, and trays.

Radios are coveted possessions, as are record players. When Edson
wanted to borrow money to buy a secondhand record player, his employer
refused, warning him of the recurrent expenditures he would have for a
long time because of the need to purchase records. The employer's refusal
reflects a paternalistic concern and an implicit judgment that he knew
better than Edson how to handle Edson's money. And his attitude circum-
vents the central issue: Edson's desire to be able to listen to music, an
activity in which he took pleasure, and his freedom to pursue it. Euclid had
a different desire: he wanted to buy a secondhand sofa and chairs for his
living room and he needed an advance from his wage to do so. His employer advised him against it, primarily because he suspected the furniture was
stolen, but also because he considered it an unnecessary item for Euclid to
spend money on. Euclid went ahead and bought furniture, although not
from the suspect source. Rather than being deliberate attempts at emulating the lifestyle of their employers, these examples show the servants'
affective pursuits as well as their desire to have pleasant living surroundings.

Servants who live in the compounds do most of their socializing with people in their neighborhoods. Because of their long working days, they socialize mainly on weekends and their half days off. Servants who live in backyard accommodation in the low-density areas have relatives and friends in the compounds and go there to visit. Those who are fond of beer go to the bars and taverns in the compounds on weekends (some employers are familiar with the effects of such visits, as the housework on Mondays may proceed rather slowly). Since the low-density areas rarely feature shops and markets, servants make some of their purchases in the compounds as well. When needing special advice, they also consult experts in the compounds. When Gertrude's smallest child fell ill after a rural visit, she insisted on taking her to the compound for treatment because she feared the child had been bewitched in the village. When the *nganga's* (African doctor's) treatment did not help and the child got worse, the employer demanded that Gertrude take the child to the hospital where she was treated for a serious case of anemia.

Some servants attend churches in the compounds, and others go to the churches in the town's low-density areas. Euclid was a lay preacher in a suburban Lutheran church; his budget shows how seriously he took the church's challenge to help your poorer fellow men, for from his low wage he managed to give tiny donations at church services. He studied the Bible at home and would call on the madam for clarification of old-fashioned English words. Once, when reading the Old Testament, he asked where Egypt was and what kind of place it might be. When hearing about the Nile river and its delta, he commented that Egypt had to be a wonderful place to keep cattle. Euclid went to church alone, leaving the wife and child behind. Edson would have liked to go to church but was prevented from doing so by the madam, who felt she would be inconvenienced if she did not have a full-time servant at work on Sundays.

There are few shops in the low-density areas, and servants have to purchase many necessities downtown or at markets in the compounds. Because of the scarcities of basic consumer goods and the limited diversification of the local manufacturing sector, servants and their employers shop in many of the same stores when buying necessary household items such as cooking oil and bath soap, shoes and clothes, and pots and blankets. Because of their low wages, servants have little purchasing power in that market and, knowing the prices, they are forcefully reminded of their poverty when unloading their employers' cars. A week's supply of goods in many cases costs more that the amount a servant receives for a month's work.

Lusaka's hospital, most clinics, banks, and institutions of the state are spread across the downtown area at a distance from most residential areas. Visits to them place servants in contact with a broad range of people and prompt them to develop interactional skills and exercise civic duties that have little to do with their work as servants in private households. Edson appeared in court to testify on behalf of a relative. Unless they coincide with the servant's full or half day off, visits to such institutions directly interfere with the work routine and they inevitably annoy the employers. So do the unanticipated claims servants sometimes make for time off to attend funerals or call on a sick relative, especially when an out-of-town visit is involved. Funerals are elaborate affairs in Zambia, requiring a person's attention for more than just a couple of hours and an outlay of money as well. From the servant's perspective, a funeral is an occasion for showing respect for the deceased on the one hand and for strengthening ties to the surviving kin on the other. Because of classificatory kinship, a servant may have several persons in the same relationship to him as father, or as mother, or mother's brother, and so on. In the view of many employers, servants use funerals to get time off, and some employers limit the number of funerals for which they will be willing to release their servants.

Unlike their employers, servants have no discretionary budget to use on entertainment such as movies and football games, but their interests bring them together on rare occasions. The sportsground in the residential area off the University of Zambia campus in Lusaka was in 1983 the stage for a football game between the area's servants and their employers. Sports, like the hunting trips that colonial officials would take accompanied by their servants when on up-country tours, make men equal competitors and temporarily conceal the structure of inequality in society at large. To improve their position in that wider setting, servants struggle not only against their employers but on other fronts as well.

Servants, Class, and Development Questions

The place of domestic servants, qua wage workers, has remained problematic after independence although the class divisions within Zambia have grown more conspicuous. Whether or not servants today constitute a class and, if they do, how class consciousness is formed is an open-ended question. Attempts to answer it must take into consideration postcolonial economic developments that have adversely affected rural livelihoods and severely depressed the wage-labor market. These developments significantly influence servants' circumstances and future prospects. Servants' struggle to improve their situation takes place on three fronts: at work, in their own households and in social interaction, and in public in their relation with agents and institutions of the state. This threefold struggle, rather than any previous identification of servants as a class in terms of their relation to the means of production, is relevant to the explanation of the process of class formation and how class consciousness is made or unmade.

For how long will servants remain content with "half a loaf," saying, as many did when interviewed, that it is better than none? Today in Zambia the class division between worker and employer is no longer masked by race. Servants consent to an exploitative work regime out of fear of losing their jobs. Yet while consenting, they also actively contest the hierarchical rules of the game, and class distinctions enter into the relationship between servant and employer and help to politicize personal relations. Through their work, servants become excellent judges of character and skilled at sizing-up their employers. They use this skill politically, working no more and no longer than they themselves consider appropriate to their low wages. They bend the rules established by the employer to suit their own interests. "Go slow" routines, deliberate misunderstandings, apparent forgetfulness, not answering intrusive questions are all ways servants actively contest their labor regime while consenting to it so as not to lose their "half loaf." Work-related behavior that appears to be part of a personal survival strategy is thus directed against the employers and indirectly against the state, which for so long has taken little interest in what to its representatives appears to be merely personal squabbles in private households.

Servants' political outlook is shaped not only at the workplace but also by interactional activities in their own households and at leisure. Their attempts to keep wives at home and out of work reinforce the conventional hierarchical gender division and make the man servant an autonomous actor at least within his private household domain. It relieves him from the double burden of performing paid domestic labor as well as private household work, and enables him during his limited time off to interact with people who earn their living in different ways.

The servants in the survey spoke about the people they associated with. They were servants in the neighborhood, relatives and friends in the compounds, and churchmates. Their emphasis that they did not choose their friends because of shared ethnicity but "because of the person" may reflect the combined impact of two factors: the official political ideology of "One Zambia, One Nation," and the multiethnic character of Zambia's towns, where residential areas show little ethnic clustering. Spending leisure time in different neighborhoods, with residents in the compounds, attending church, and visiting shops and government offices gives servants a view of what lives outside of domestic service are like, and they use this knowledge for critical comparisons. They know what the gap is between their wages and those of many other workers. They are concerned with how to improve the livelihoods of their children when their own circumstances are so poor. Those who are literate read the newspaper while the employer is at work and are aware of labor unrest and strikes in other fields. Many servants vote in elections; they know who the candidates and what their platforms are (these platforms have never included issues specific to servants).

What are the prospects for class action among this category of workers in

Zambia today? Servants are one of the few remaining segments of the Zambian labor force which are not unionized. But as noted earlier, there are several factors that may militate against collective mobilization among servants. In this monopsonistic market employers have tremendous power. Because of the ready availability of replacements of what has become de-skilled labor, servants fear losing what little they do have. They refrain from complaining when hiring and firing is heavily influenced by personal factors.

Regarding the question of labor unions, 36 percent of the servants in my survey argued that servants definitely should have a union, that it would help improve their work conditions. But 48 percent said they doubted a union would be effective. Another 13 percent were even more negative, saying that unions would never work; relationships in domestic service would always be determined by the employers. And 3 percent simply said they would not be able to join a union because they could not afford to pay a union membership fee. Nevertheless, the union issue has engaged some servants' minds in the past and continues to do so at present. Some servants have tried to organize in the hope of improving wages and work conditions and to force employers to pay their ZNPF contributions. For in practice, matters between employers and servants continue to be handled at the individual level without regard to the legislation embodied in the Employment and the ZNPF bills. One such effort was the formation in 1973 of the National Domestic Houseservants Association of Zambia, the result of activities among servants in Lusaka (although it seems at one time to also have involved a group on the copperbelt, the Copperbelt Domestic Servants' Association). The Lusaka group, claiming four hundred members in 1974, aimed to protect, improve, and legitimate the professional interests of domestic servants. It argued for stricter compliance with the ZNPF registration scheme, higher pay, better living quarters, and the provision of uniforms. The group also called for the formation of UNIP party branches in the low-density residential areas so that servants could obtain party cards (which are needed in order for a person to rent a house in a low-income township). The association's officials felt that without party membership cards, servants would be discriminated against in the housing market. According to Fanwell Mukatulwa, chief spokesman for the association, "without forming branches in these places of so-called *Apamwamba* townships or yards, the party and government cannot know the enemies of the party."[8]

8. This account is pieced together from handwritten letters filed in the Lusaka offices of the *Times of Zambia* and published write-ups on July 19, 1973; August 17, 1973; April 1, 1974; November 25, 1974; January 17, 1975; March 18, 1978; June 10, 1978; September 20, 1978; and December 23, 1978. It is unclear from these communications whether or not the association ever registered with the Registrar of Societies, although an intent is indicated several times.

By 1979, however, the Houseservants Association withered away as its predecessors had in the past. Fanwell Mukatulwa appears to have obtained a better job in Livingstone with the Fiat motor assembly plant,[9] and in 1983 no one—neither union oficials nor servants interviewed—remembered the association. There may have been other attempts by servants to organize. As far as I know, the most recent effort at union formation took place in Kitwe on the copperbelt in October 1983. Reacting to it, Newstead Zimba, the general secretary of the Zambia Congress of Trade Unions, offered the comment heard many times during the colonial period, that a servants' union would be "unmanageable." He remarked (erroneously) that servants were "under" the National Union of Hotels and Catering Workers. His condescending answer to a servant who suggested the formation of a union was that "if he was looking for a job he should go to the Hotel and Catering Workers rather than mislead houseservants."[10]

The record of other countries suggests that unions for servants can be "managed." In several Latin American countries servants have formed associations or unions. In Zimbabwe a union was established for domestic workers immediately after independence in 1980 at the same time that the minimum wage was raised. South Africa (until recently) had a number of local domestic servants' associations which in December 1986 were combined as a registered labor union under the Congress of South African Trade Unions. Trade unions for servants can certainly be established and registered, as these examples show, but whether they can appreciably improve the working conditions of servants and upgrade their position in relation to other unionized groups remains to be seen. Given the postcolonial history of trade unionism in Zambia and the attitudes of officials, it is doubtful that a trade union for servants would be effective. Furthermore, statutory instruments barring strikes and free collective bargaining have diminished the influence of trade unions.

Servants' failure to form unions does not necessarily mean they lack class consciousness. They did try to fight when they could both before and after independence, indicating that they considered their work position problematic and wanted to change it. Their class consciousness during the colonial period may perhaps be best described by Gluckman's term *situational*,[11] and it did produce some features of an urban servants' work culture and status system that influenced their activities in some contexts. Servants were snobs, as one retired employer recalled. They took their status from their employers and they had a hard time accepting the job of

9. According to the registration files of the Zambia National Provident Fund.
10. "Kitwe Domestic Servants Form Union," *Zambia Daily Mail*, October 18, 1983, p. 3.
11. Max Gluckman, "Anthropological Problems Arising from the Industrial Revolution," in *Social Change in Modern Africa*, ed. Aidan Southall (London: Oxford University Press, 1961), pp. 68–70.

Table 7. Increases in annual average earnings in Zambia, by occupational sector, 1954–1965

| Sector | Annual percentage increase in average earnings | | | | | | Average annual earnings in 1965 (Pounds) | |
| | African | | | Non-African | | | African | Non-African |
	1954–1963	1964	1965	1954–1963	1964	1965		
Agriculture, forestry, fishing	5.4	33.3	(−2.3)	5.0	5.7	(−15.6)	86	1,182
Health services	5.7	26.7	*	4.2	−2.6	*	*	*
Electricity and water	7.7	26.0	21.3	4.6	15.1	0.8	194	2,137
Commerce	8.0	23.6	19.6	3.4	6.1	11.6	232	1,239
Mining and quarrying	8.5	22.8	12.8	2.1	0.4	4.4	413	2,689
Education	7.3	22.2	*	4.0	−7.0	*	*	*
Central and local government (exc. health and education)	8.7	17.4	16.8*	4.2	−3.2	16.0*	229	1,450
Manufacturing	9.6	17.3	19.7	2.5	9.6	5.7	243	1,564
Transport and communications	9.5	13.1	0.8	3.5	3.7	2.6	243	1,539
Construction	7.1	10.9	5.2	3.2	5.4	13.2	161	1,755
Domestic services	5.2	5.3	10.2	—	—	*	108	—
Other private services	7.3	0.8	16.8*	3.1	−0.3	16.0*	229	1,450
Total	8.3	19.4	20.4	2.8	3.9	6.2	230	1,749

N.B. Figures in parentheses indicate a change of base in the 1965 statistics.
*No separate data is yet available on government and private earnings in the service sector in 1965.
Source: Republic of Zambia. Manpower Report. A Report and Statistical Handbook on Manpower, Education, Training and Zambianization 1965–1966, issued by the Cabinet Office (Lusaka: Government Printer, 1966), p. 68.

serving for African guests in white households when the political climate began rapidly to change in the 1950s. Several long-time servants enjoyed peaceful retirements on the support of good employers, and most of their children had gone to school and helped support them as well. But when engaging in class action, consciousness had a different focus. For there was a vast generalized urban working class beyond domestic work with whom servants could and did at various times develop relationships. The circumstances that made such shifts possible have changed to a great extent today where servants derive little material benefit from sharing their Zambian employers' status. In objective terms, servant wages are at the bottom level of wage scales in Zambia (see Table 7). They compare in many ways with the level of incomes made by informal sector workers. The "slave job" aspect about which servants speak may refer to more than just their low wages; it may imply a notion about an unremovable job status they are particularly concerned not to pass on to their children. Very few of the servants interviewed in my research were themselves the sons and daughters of servants. Most of them objected strongly to the idea of their own children working as servants, and within their limited abilities they tried to do what they could to prevent this. Their concern about exiting from domestic service, in their own lifetime or through their children, suggests that a consciousness focused on this particular occupation is yielding to a renewed realization of the shared problems that confront working-class lives in urban Zambia.

In the view of most of the servants interviewed, domestic service is "just another job", although a disliked one that at the present time puts men and women to work on different terms and in unlike ways. The growing number of women and young people who are entering service since independence has the potential to create factions within the ranks along lines of generation and gender. Because of its economic vulnerability each faction may continue simply to try to preserve its "half loaf." If the economy continues its downward turn, domestic servants may hold on more tenaciously to their disliked jobs as ever fewer options become possible. If as a result, sons and daughters of servants increasingly follow in their parents' footsteps and a servant class develops, it may perhaps devise new and radical means to protect its interests.

Development Questions

The kind of development that might solve Zambia's problems, including those of servants, would entail an overall "change process characterized by increased productivity, equalization of the distribution of the social product, the emergence of indigenous institutions whose relations with the

[289]

outside world and particularly with the developed centres of the international economy are characterized by equality rather than dependence or subordination."[12] In this ideal world, everyone would be productively engaged and earn a living wage without having power wielded over them by those richer than they, and women would not be dominated by men. The availability of alternative labor opportunities would make the servant market a sellers' market, and householders would have to pay living wages for whatever services they contracted.

These utopian conditions have not been achieved anywhere. They were approximated in the United States during a period of economic growth when native-born American women left service. They were replaced by immigrant labor. This continues to be the case today, as it is in much of northwestern Europe. So it was in Nigeria, to give an African example, during the oil boom, when indigenous Nigerians left domestic service for better jobs, and alien Africans succeeded them as household workers.[13]

Given the poor economic performance of the Zambian economy, no utopian scenario is likely to be realized. The process currently ongoing in the West, the movement of capital into service industries, including private domestic service, transforming them into arenas of capitalist relations where contractually employed workers are freed from the ambiguous personalized regime characteristic of domestic service, also belongs to a distant and perhaps unforseeable future. One is forced, then, to confront the question of how to reform this occupational domain within the wider context that presently structures it. Barring an overnight restructuring of the Zambian economy and its dependent relationship with outside markets, and perhaps the outright disappearance of domestic service, what can be done to ensure servants a living above bare subsistence level? Should the employment situation improve somewhat, men are more likely to be the beneficiaries than women, given women's secondary status in the labor market historically. In all likelihood an improved situation would simply mean that more women would move into the male stronghold of general household work as men moved out and up. Such a shift would likely be accompanied by a deemphasis on sexuality in the cultural construction of women servants' gender role. But in my own view, domestic service will continue to grow, with its current division of labor by gender. The processes ongoing in Zambia today will sustain the growth of the population segment who now employs servants. These processes will widen the gap

12. E. A. Brett, *Colonialism and Underdevelopment in East Africa: The Politics of Economic Change, 1919–1939* (London: Heinemann, 1973), p. 18.
13. During the oil boom, Nigerian servants priced themselves out of the market, leaving it to alien Africans who were willing to work for much reduced wages. According to one source, after the expulsion of aliens in 1983, Nigerian servants changed the rate to what it had been before the aliens undercut it. "Of Aliens and Foreigners," *African Business*, June 1985, p. 23.

between those who are economically well situated and those who have nothing but their potential to labor.

Employers, Zambians and expatriates alike, are quick to assure you that they at least provide poor people with a job. Their implicit rationalization, that it is better to work than not to work, may be correct, but for the wrong reasons. To be sure, a large number of people are employed. But their work represents far more than a way of passing time. It contributes appreciably to the social welfare of the employing classes and makes available to them at extremely low cost child care and household maintenance facilities that neither the state nor private business have been able or willing to furnish. Some observers have referred to domestic service as a form of "misemployment," meaning the underutilization if not wasteful use of labor that is unproductive.[14] But except for the very few households in postcolonial Zambia who employ large domestic staffs in part for public display, the work of most servants does not so much represent underutilization and waste as naked exploitation of labor power. In return for substandard pay, servants perform tasks that wealthier households cannot do without.

Servants' lives could be improved appreciably, if employers would observe the few rules and regulations that in postcolonial Zambia are supposed to guide the employment of servants, and which in theory should improve their conditions compared with the colonial period. Could labor union activity by servants help them to force their employers to observe these requirements? There is no reason to believe that unionizing would be the only or best way in the future to seek changes in domestic service. But just because attempts to wrest improvements from the system have failed in the past does not mean they always will. The political climate has changed and new links have been forged between the existing unions and the state in ways that do not always benefit the common worker. Economic conditions have also worsened. Servants are realizing that their opportunities to leave domestic service have declined and that the broad mass of unskilled workers are not doing much better than themselves. Under these conditions, servants may become increasingly impatient with their "half loaf" and begin to frame their claims for improvements in unconventional ways such as demonstrations and riots. In my opinion, plans for improvement must address the connection between women's deteriorating wage labor conditions in service as compared with men's and their roles as unpaid household workers, as mothers and wives.

Whatever else development might mean for domestic service in Zambia, it means choice and autonomy. Both can prove subversive to people in

14. Alan Gilbert and Josef Gugler, *Cities, Poverty, and Development: Urbanization in the Third World* (London: Oxford University Press, 1982), pp. 68–69.

power—men who are heads of state and men who are heads of households. Those in power—heads of households, those who employ servants—and men and women servants play different and often contradictory roles in shaping the domestic service domain in the way it is presently structured. But this structure is not preordained or unchangeable. Everyone will have a part to play in reforming domestic service. At least in the short term, men and women servants and their male and female employers will have to participate in removing from this occupation the aspects of personal subordination and exploitation which deprive servants of their sense of personhood.

[8]

Servants Everywhere: Conclusions

The troubles women householders and their servants encounter in their unequal relationship in private households in Zambia are by no means unique to that country, although to be sure they are influenced by cultural and ideological notions particular to their society. Yet in spite of its problems, the institution of domestic service endures, in Zambia as elsewhere. How has it changed over time in other societies? What can be learned from the differences between the Zambian experience and that of other countries? The reasons that domestic service has survived in the industrial West are not difficult to understand. Much has been written concerning women's entry into the labor force and the conflicts that have arisen as a result in the domestic domain concerning their responsibilities as housewives and mothers. The working woman's need for relief from housework and child care is well documented.

Paid household work has not disappeared as an important occupation in contemporary Western society and it persists, if not grows, in many developing countries as well. As the Zambian case demonstrates, the occupation has not everywhere been feminized, and it is incorrect to assume that generally "when women enter a job, men leave it."[1] It has, however, been restructured. The late twentieth-century domestic servant has many faces, among them the live-in servant, the day worker, and the employee of franchised cleaning companies. This restructuring is influenced by economic transformations and resulting shifts in the makeup of the labor force in the West. Recent estimates indicate that some 43 percent of women

---

1. Rae Andre, *Homemakers: The Forgotten Workers* (Chicago: University of Chicago Press, 1981), p. 245.

employed outside the home in the United States hire household help.[2] In addition, increased longevity and the lack of institutional care has increased the need of retired persons for paid household workers. This growing demand is being supplied by a new generation of hired hands, among whom are both women and men.

Paid household work thus has a history, and one that is ongoing. Studies from across the disciplines, but particularly in economic and social history, published in growing numbers since the early 1980s, have delineated parts of the domestic-service story from the end of the feudal period in France, when women began to outnumber men servants, to the late twentieth century in North America, when live-in women servants are being replaced by day workers.[3] But recent transformations of paid domestic work have barely received scholarly attention. In this last chapter, I explore briefly the comparative dynamics of paid household work in order to spell out specifically what the lesson of the Zambian case is in this wider context.

The Unfolding Story of Domestic Service

Modernization and industrialization have not brought about the demise of domestic service in the Western world. Its persistence is not to be seen as an anachronistic survival of feudal or premodern features into the late twentieth century. This sort of analogy is misleading, for personalism, asymmetry, and dependence do not belong to a specific mode of production but can develop under a variety of socioeconomic conditions. Preindustrial and feudal analogies retard the study of the new guises in which domestic service is appearing and of the processes that are bringing them about. They obscure the fact that domestic service appears to be growing as an occupation in the advanced capitalist systems of the West.

The variety of forms which domestic service is assuming in the late twentieth century must be explored against the background of economic processes that are shaping our contemporary world as well as of gender dynamics that characterize relations between women and men within households. The new international division of labor in the global economy draws its momentum from a combination of processes: partial deindustrial-

---

2. Carol Kleiman, "Maid Services Clean Up as Demand Escalates," *Chicago Tribune*, August 17, 1986, sec. 8, p. 1.

3. Faye E. Dudden, *Serving Women: Household Service in Nineteenth-Century America* (Middletown, Conn.: Wesleyan University Press, 1983); Cissie Fairchilds, *Domestic Enemies: Servants and Their Masters in Old Regime France* (Baltimore, Md.: Johns Hopkins University Press, 1984); Sarah C. Maza, *Servants and Masters in Eighteenth-Century France: The Uses of Loyalty* (Princeton, N.J.: Princeton University Press, 1983).

ization in the West, relocated manufacturing in some parts of the Third World, and general economic decline in other parts, including Zambia.[4] The worldwide economic pattern so far has been one of decline and growth, coupled with spatial relocation in which once important economic activities have retrenched while others, mostly very different ones, have grown.[5] Stagnation and unemployment have been evident everywhere. Large trade deficits, huge debt burdens, and regional disparities are as characteristic of the United States today as they used to be, and still are, in many developing countries.[6] In the process, the gender division of labor in household work is becoming accentuated.

The Reorganization of Paid Domestic Service in the United States

Against this background of overall economic decline over the last decade, high technology and service-oriented work have experienced growth in some regions. In the course of this process, the composition of wage labor forces is changing, not only by sector, but also by sex. Several studies in the United States indicate that men hold the top jobs in these fields and that women dominate at their low-paid end. Today, because of economic pressures, many more women with preschool children are working away from home than ever before. They include women who are single heads of households and wives of unemployed husbands.

Regardless of class, women are still vulnerable to American society's stereotype of what a housewife should be. They judge their housework by standards that date back to a time when most married women were full-time homemakers and many had servants.[7] The studies on this subject show the same distressing result: that women remain principally in charge of child care and housekeeping; that although men may help out now and then, women put in many more hours; and that although new household technology has relieved women of the heavier tasks, it has not reduced the

4. Folker Fröbel, Jürgen Heinricks, and Otto Kreye, *The New International Division of Labour* (Cambridge: Cambridge University Press, 1980).

5. Saskia Sassen-Koob, "The New Labor Demand in Global Cities," in *Cities in Transformation: Class, Capital, and the State,* ed. Michael P. Smith (Beverly Hills, Calif.: Sage, 1984), pp. 139–172.

6. June Nash, "The Impact of the Changing International Division of Labor on Different Sectors of the Labor Force," in *Women, Men, and the International Division of Labor,* ed. June Nash and Maria Patricia Fernandez Kelly (Albany: State University of New York Press, 1983), pp. 3–38.

7. Annegret S. Ogden, *The Great American Housewife: From Helpmate to Wage Earner, 1776–1986* (Westport, Conn.: Greenwood Press, 1986), p. xii.

actual work load.[8] Both the single wage-earning mother in a low-paid service job and the junior executive in a dual-earner household need relief from housework and child care.

Who are the new domestic helpers and what makes them turn to an occupation that a previous generation of workers were only too willing to leave? Some are the wives of unemployed husbands. Others are workers who themselves are laid off after closures of manufacturing plants and who have been unable, or are unprepared, to find new jobs in high technology or service-oriented occupations. Because of economic retrenchment such as factory closings, some have been forced to make mid-life switches.[9] Some are unskilled women trying to earn an income for their households or supplement a social security check; others are minority women who face discrimination in the labor market because of race, sex, and sometimes lack of education.[10]

Finally, there are the recent immigrants, some without legal documents, who find in paid household work a hard-earned solution to the problem of making a living in the metropolises of the United States. Some of them are trained as teachers or nurses but because of their illegal status they cannot seek work in these fields. A few studies indicate and scattered observations suggest that the ethnic composition of a region's domestic workers may reflect to a certain degree the port of entry and the existing ethnic mix of the city. Among Chicago's recent household workers are many Polish and Mexican women; in New York and Boston, Irish women have been taking jobs as nannies, especially since their home island's economic decline in the early 1980s; many West Indian women work as servants in East coast cities; the West coast cities have women servants from Mexico and from Southeast Asia. Central American women toil at household labor in all these areas. These immigrant domestics are overwhelmingly women, for men, even when they speak little English, more readily find low-paid jobs as casual laborers.

Economic slowdown, industry layoffs, sectoral shifts from manufactur-

8. Sarah F. Berk, ed., *Women and Household Labor* (Beverly Hills, Calif.: Sage, 1980); Susan Strasser, *Never Done: A History of American Housework* (New York: Pantheon Books,1982); Ruth S. Cowan, *More Work for Mother: The Ironies of Household Technology from the Open Hearth to the Microwave* (New York: Basic Books, 1983); and Sarah F. Berk, *The Gender Factory: The Apportionment of Work in American Households* (New York: Plenum Press, 1985).

9. David M. Katzman, *Seven Days a Week: Women and Domestic Service in Industrializing America* (New York: Oxford University Press, 1978), p. 46; Daniel E. Sutherland, *Americans and Their Servants: Domestic Service in the United States from 1800 to 1920* (Baton Rouge: Louisiana State University Press, 1981), pp. 58–59.

10. Evelyn Nakano Glenn, *Issei, Nisei, War Bride: Three Generations of Japanese American Women in Domestic Service* (Philadelphia: Temple University Press, 1986); Judith Rollins, *Between Women: Domestics and Their Employers* (Philadelphia: Temple University Press, 1985).

ing to service industries, and new immigration are thus producing a vast pool of both skilled and unskilled workers who are willing to take low-paid jobs as domestics. Many receive no pension and medical benefits, and employers do not always pay their social security taxes. Some of these new hired hands live in, but many more do day work. Even with this vast supply of workers, there are employers who complain that, just as in Zambia, good help is hard to find.

Employment agencies have arisen in response to the household needs of Americans who can afford and are willing to pay for help. They place the butlers, cooks, housekeepers, and nannies requested by affluent householders who set stringent standards for their full-time servants. In addition, like employers in Zambia, they have age and ethnic preferences. According to one newspaper story, some are so security conscious that they ask placement agencies to undertake police checks and administer lie-detector tests before hiring a prospective servant.[11] These employers do pay social security taxes and offer a variety of fringe benefits.

Another area of domestic service is also enduring in changed form. The occupation of nanny has been undergoing a process of upgrading through the establishment of nanny schools, which have proliferated quite recently, sometimes associated with universities. The American Council of Nanny Schools in 1985 listed twelve, and in 1986 thirty, teaching and placement centers across the country. At its Delta College Nanny Program in Michigan, prospective nannies can register for a six-week certificate program that includes courses in American family structure, child development, infant and toddler care, family communication, health care, nutrition, etiquette, and dress. Placement is available for the graduate, who is considered an "in-home childcare professional."[12] The services of these nannies are expensive, yet demand seems far to outpace supply.[13] For those who can afford them, nannies who can provide the individual care that a working mother cannot may be preferable to private or institutional day care.

Other aspects of domestic service are being commercialized. Failing to find a satisfactory servant through classified advertisements or placement services, the person in need of household help can call on a professional cleaning company. The number of such franchises has increased so rapidly that professional housecleaning/maid service was described as the fastest-growing business in the United States in 1986, outpacing fast-food franchises, which used to hold the lead.[14] They are solving the problem of keeping the house clean for working people as well as for those two-career

---

11. "The Hired Help," *Chicago Tribune*, August 7, 1983, sec. 14, p. 1.
12. Delta College Nanny Program brochure.
13. "Nannies, American Style," *Chicago Tribune*, April 23, 1986, sec. 7, p. 15.
14. Kleiman, "Maid Services."

couples Lisa Belkin describes, "who work all day and barely have time to change clothes and meet clients for dinner at night."[15]

Some of these cleaning companies stress professionalism and scientific management in the labor process. Merry Maids, one of the fastest-growing franchises, with 325 offices in forty states in 1986, uses a training film to teach workers exactly how to execute cleaning tasks. It supplies them with a computer printout of their tasks before sending them to a client. The company employs more than 2,500 workers and cleans approximately 30,000 homes a week. Such companies employ both women and men, many on a part-time basis. Dirtbusters, a New York City firm, is staffed by many aspiring actors who do not regard such labor as work but rather consider it to be a job that enables them to do their "real" work, acting.[16]

The story of domestic service is thus still unfolding in the United States. Within this occupational domain coexist several labor processes, none of which is dominant in shaping it at the present time. There is live-in or day work, characterized by a personalized arrangement, most likely determined by the employer's whims and without contractual obligations. Then there is the situation of the professional servant, that is, the butler, house-keeper, cook, or certified nanny, in which contract and a more specialized division of labor are observed, giving the worker more autonomy in the relationship with the employer. Finally, there is the service of the cleaning company, whose workers are paid by the hour and the division of labor is defined by the management.

Domestic service in the United States today is thus a complex occupation, difficult to conceptualize categorically in Braverman's terms. Paid household work is being reorganized, certainly. On the one hand, domestic service appears in labor forms that to varying degrees have become structured contractually by capitalist relations prevalent in the wider economy while retaining many personalized features. At the same time, specialization *and* degradation are taking place. The training of skilled nannies, butlers, and cooks exemplifies the specialization process,[17] and the use of scientific management principles by such firms as Merry Maids illustrates the degradation process and the gradual transformation of private household service into a capitalist labor arena. For anthropologists concerned with the study of work and its changes, these phenomena are opening up a dynamic field of research in which to raise questions about the making and changing of gender roles, the construction of relations between worker and

15. Lisa Belkin, "Modern Households Wave White Rag, Ending the Age-old War against Dirt," *Chicago Tribune*, April 18 (1985), Section 5, p. 5.

16. Kleiman, "Maid Services."

17. William Hall, "You Rang? Butlers Are an Endangered Species, but a School in Palm Springs Is Determined to Carry On," *Chicago Tribune*, January 6, 1988, section 7, pp. 21–22.

employer, and the relationship of these processes to the broad economic changes that are taking place around us.

The Zambian Case

To look at the history of domestic service in the United States can illuminate the Zambian case but also forces us to ask questions about the differences between the two countries. Although private domestic work in Zambia has not yet undergone a gender transition from male to female and been affected by commercialization as it has in the United States, the lack of economic expansion is having an impact on the occupation. Urban labor supplies, including potential servants of both sexes, are booming while wage labor jobs are getting fewer and farther between. Because of the lack of overall economic growth in Zambia, culturally constructed gender conventions in domestic service have persisted relatively unchanged. Men remain the preferred servants, and the contemporary expansion in the servants' ranks is due in large degree to the employment of women as nannies.

Employers of servants in Zambia in the past sometimes drew on comparative insights concerning economic trends when discussing the gender question in domestic service. To rationalize their dismissal of African women's potential in domestic service, colonial officials made spurious analogies to situations elsewhere. Lord Gladstone, the high commissioner in South Africa, for example, remarked in 1910 that African fathers in the Rhodesias were as unlikely to send their daughters into domestic service in white colonial homes as were Essex farmers to allow their daughters to go to London to become coachmen or chauffeurs. Yet many British women did just this sort of work when men were away fighting during World War I, and through subsequent decades in Britain and elsewhere women have increasingly taken on work that once was gender-typed as male.

Lord Gladstone's comparison is misleading, not so much for its insistence on what Rhodesian and Essex farmers wanted or did not want for their daughters, but for its failure to take the different economic conditions of Rhodesia and Britain into account. In the campaign for African womanpower in Northern Rhodesia during the post–World War II years, J. P. Law made a similar mistake when he suggested that African women in Northern Rhodesia might be expected to follow the experience of their sisters in Southern Rhodesia, who, he said, were going into secondary industry and skipping the stage of working in private homes. In fact, although some, but not many, Southern Rhodesian women were employed in the new industries, they did not skip the stage of working in private homes, for they began gradually to replace men in private domestic service during the postwar economic expansion in that country.[18] But in Northern Rhodesia such secondary industry hardly developed. Contrary to Law's suggestion, white Northern Rhodesians did not go through the butler/footman stage to doing it themselves and in the process skipping the stage of the female domestic servant. They never had to do the housework themselves and barely even reached the beginnings of a stage of employing African women as servants. They continued to employ menservants, for except during a brief moment of the postwar years, there was an ample male labor force to work in industry as well as private homes. Thus the economic trajectory that Law suggested for domestic service was not particularly applicable to Northern Rhodesia.

The continued dominance of African men in domestic service in Northern Rhodesia is a result partly of different economic developments as compared with those occurring in the neighboring countries to the south, in Europe, and in the United States. These economic factors combined with cultural and ideological factors to influence employers' choice of men over women as servants. Because they viewed African women in sexual terms, white women householders were reluctant to employ them as servants. Since there was a large supply of African menservants, white women employers were able to exert their preferences. But it was not only white colonial society that shaped domestic service. There was an African response as well. For most certainly, African fathers, husbands, and guardians did not want their female dependents to go to work as domestic servants in white colonial households. In most African societies as elsewhere, a woman's place was in the household under male supervision. More important, African women themselves preferred work in and around their own households to underpaid domestic service under another woman's supervision. Their own households provided them with a setting in and from which they could act autonomously from men in a variety of nonwaged economic activities that served to maintain not only the needs of their children but also their own designs on leading independent lives.

18. According to census figures, 37,896 African men as compared with 1,887 African women were employed in domestic service in Southern Rhodesia in 1941. In 1946 the employment of women servants had almost doubled to 3,638, while men's employment as servants grew by only one-quarter to 47,705. *Southern Rhodesia, Report on the Census of Population of Southern Rhodesia Held on 7th May, 1946* (Salisbury: Central Statistical Office, 1946), pp. 326–327. Between 1946 and 1956 women's employment in service doubled again, to 7,994, while men's employment increased by about one-third, to 63,584. *Federation of Rhodesia and Nyasaland, Census of Population 1956* (Salisbury: Central Statistical Office, 1960), pp. 69–70. The 1962 census did not categorize employment by sex, and the 1969 census's categorizations by sex into employment groupings are too broad to distinguish domestic service as a separate occupation. The employment tables in the *Monthly Digest of Quarterly Digest of Statistics* (Salisbury: Central Statistical Office) and the postcolonial *Quarterly Digest of Statistics* (Harare: Central Statistical Office) are not categorized by sex.

They could, I suggest, better subvert men's authority by working in and around their own households than by holding jobs as domestic servants.

The gender division in domestic service continues to be shaped by these cultural and ideological factors, framed by patterns of male authority and women's desire for autonomy, in postcolonial Zambia, where economic developments have not led to a decline in the occupation. Regardless of their ethnic or national background, employers continue to prefer menservants. Zambian women householders employ Zambian women primarily as nannies, not as domestic servants, and as soon as they no longer need help with child care, they hire menservants. Thus there has not been the kind of transition in the occupation from male to female which took place in industrializing Europe and North America and which may be occurring in some other developing countries. What is taking place in Zambia might more correctly be described as a recomposition within the division of labor in domestic service: more women are working as nannies than ever before, while men persist as the chief household workers. This recomposition, and other shifts in the status and nature of domestic work, are the results of the complex interplay of economic and local cultural factors. Only when we have grasped the nature of this interplay can we understand why in private domestic service in Zambia it is, "naturally," men who complain that housework never stops.

Household work in all its various forms—live in, day work, or commercialized contract cleaning—hinges on a labor process whose nature and gender division have throughout time been influenced by demographic factors, socioeconomic and political conditions, and local cultural practices. Regardless of time and place, these types of work have depended for their continuance on a relationship that distances the workers from the employers.

Employers of servants in Northern Rhodesia and Zambia were not alone in relating to their domestic workers as distant companions. Household workers everywhere were in their employers' households but never of them. Servants everywhere were different from their employers. In each case, the way difference was explained had to do with cultural assumptions that took various and changing forms. This difference was never a "natural" difference: the dominant position of the employers in this relationship should not be taken for granted. It should be problematized in each context and questions raised about it. It is best seen as an emerging property, the product of an unequally structured labor process enabling those with greater access to resources to play the role of masters.

The comparative study of domestic service shows that this process has been generally problematic and has given rise to "trouble." The only way that two participants meeting in the same space and time within the private household could be turned into worker and employer was through creating a distancing relationship between them. Servants and employers everywhere became each other's other. In my view, part of the uniqueness of the Zambian case arises from the colonial experience and local cultural practices. During the colonial period in Northern Rhodesia, white masters considered their servants inferior to themselves because of race and tribal culture. Economic developments in Zambia since independence have not dented the might of employers but widened the opportunity gap between them and their servants. Their relationship is uneasy, especially in black Zambian households. The antagonisms inherent in the relationship are fueled by the servants' failed expectations of a new and better life, and by the knowledge that the boss has not changed at all, he just looks different. The present thus has been fashioned by the past in many ways even though the occupation itself has been transformed because of overall changes in the economy. In their discourse with and about servants postcolonial employers use terms rooted in class-based assumptions but which produce the same effects on social relationships in domestic service: distance and difference.

The content of such distinctions are, however, not given. They are, as this study demonstrates, made—they are the products of social interaction. The social practices that structure relationships of difference within domestic service are both enabling and constraining, and therefore they contain within them the seeds of change. Servants, their employers, and members of society at large all play parts in shaping domestic service in its present form. This form is not preordained, but is a product of their mutual interaction; thus they face the challenge of changing it. On occasion, perhaps they will produce radical shifts in the kinds of social relationships I have been concerned with here. The story of the relationship between servants and their employers in Zambia thus has no single or final conclusion. I can only hope that by revealing this part of it, my work will prompt others to fill in its gaps and to keep track of its future.

Appendix 1   Servants' Wages

I carried out a regression analysis in order to explore the impact of several factors on the monthly wages paid to servants.[1] These factors were: ethnic/national background of the employer; the employer's work, or rather the employment sector he/she was occupationally engaged in; the length of time he/she had lived in Zambia; the servant's sex; and his or her age. I first ran separate regressions for each of these factors, that is, for each of the independent variables, using dummy variables in the first two regressions (to code for the qualitative ethnicity and type of the employer's work). Dummy variables are simply 1, 0 type variables that code for the presence/absence of the qualitative factor of interest. If a qualitative variable has, say, 5 categories, as in the employer's ethnicity variable discussed below, then the variable is coded using four 1, 0 variables, leaving out one category to serve as the "reference" category for that variable, against which the other dummy variables can be compared. The coefficient for the dummy variables indicate the size of the difference between each category and the category to which each is compared, that is, the omitted "reference" category. I then ran a multiple regression to show the impact of all the variables considered together.

The ethnicity/national background variable was coded using dummy variables for each of the following categories: Zambians; Asians; Coloureds; others (Afro-Americans). The omitted "reference" category was the white employers category. The employer's occupation variable was coded using the following set of categories after first omitting the category of persons

1. I am grateful to Malcom Dow for his advice in setting up this regression analysis and for his help in interpreting the results.

[303]

who were employed in international organizations, foreign government offices, and foreign development agencies: GRZ (employees of the Government of the Republic of Zambia); PRIV (employees in private companies); SELF (self-employed); and MISC (other and non-specified). NOY is a continuous level variable referring to the length of time the employer had lived in Zambia, and AGE a continuous level variable referring to the servant's age. All of the variables considered simultaneously yielded the following regression equation (sample size N = 168):[2]

Monthly salary = 8.59 + [−2.73 ASIAN − 1.91 ZAMBIAN − 1.94 COLOURED − 1.38 OTHER]
      (.000)   (.002)   (.02)   (.15)

+ [.276PRIV − 1.63 MISC − .67 GRZ]
   (.59)   (.053)   (.12)

+ .10 AGE − .67 SEX − .11NOY
   (.015)   (.08)   (.11)

R² = .397

The square brackets placed around the sets of ethnicity and employer's work dummies signify that these variables should be seen together as coding for these two qualitative variables. The numbers in parenthesis beneath each regression coefficient refer to the corresponding statistical significance level associated with each coefficient.

The adjusted R square (R² = .397) for this multiple regression equation indicates that close to 40 percent variance in monthly salary is explained by this set of independent variables. The analysis shows the employer's ethnic/national background to be the variable that most significantly influences the servant's monthly wage level. That is, the magnitude of this set of coefficients is considerably greater than for the other variables in the equation. Compared with the omitted category of white employers, Asians pay lower wages (significance level .000); the rest of the employers pay slightly more than Asians, although still less than whites. The type of work the employer has (occupation) does not influence the wage paid to the servant in any statistically significant way. The servant's age is statistically significant (.015), and the positive sign of the regression coefficient shows, perhaps not surprisingly, that the older the servant is, the higher is his/her wage. Comparing men with women servants, that is, looking at the coefficient of the sex variable, reveals that women tend to be paid less; and although the significance level (.08) is not significant at conventional levels (that is, .05), it indicates a nontrivial trend. The analysis also shows that even when the ethnicity/nationality variable is held constant, age and sex still have significant effects on wage levels.

2. The total sample size of the survey discussed in Chapter 6 is 187. In the regression analysis I excluded 21 interviews undertaken in servant-employing households living in flats. The sample size used in the regression is thus 168.

Appendix 2   Servants' Budgets

To get an indication of how servants managed on their low wages, I sought to establish a minimum monthly budget. Two semi-skilled Zambian workers and their wives advised me concerning the bare essentials a monthly income had to cover.

A Minimum Budget

A minimum monthly budget for a household consisting of two adults and two children, excluding expenditures on clothing and support given to relatives, would feature the following items (prices given reflect approximate costs in 1984):

1 bag (50kg) mealie meal	K 23
1 gallon cooking oil	K 10
2 bags charcoal (cooking fuel)	K 10
5 kg sugar	K 4
1 kg salt	K 1
Relish (vegetables and meat) @ K15/week	K 60
Soap (5 bars)	K 5
Washing powder (3 packets)	K 6
Total	K 119

This budget, for a minimum of necessities, allows no discretionary expenses. Although it is a bare minimum, it requires a wage higher than that received by the majority of servants interviewed in my survey. They man-

age only with difficulty, as the two budgets I describe below illustrate. I
asked two menservants whom I knew well to record their incomes and
daily expenditures in notebooks I provided. I explained why I was interested in this aspect of their personal housekeeping, instructed them in how
to record their transactions, and paid each of them K10 per completed
month for the duration of the exercise. I asked occasionally, but I hoped
not intrusively, if they remembered to keep their books during this period.
It is likely that some expenditures were not recorded. Nevertheless, their
budgets show clearly that their available incomes were hardly sufficient to
cover any but the most basic expenditures, if even those, in 1984.

Edson's Household Budget

Edson and his wife, Gertrude, worked in an expatriate Asian household,
Edson as a full-time general servant working inside the house and on the
grounds and Gertrude half-time in the kitchen to help out with the cooking
and to replace Edson when he was not on duty. They lived on the premises
and had two children, Faides and Joe, below school age; Gertrude was
pregnant with their third child. The following budget lists Edson's report of
income and expenditure over a two-month period, beginning at the time
that Edson was paid his monthly wage.

Date	Income	Kwacha	Date	Expenses	Kwacha
April 29	Wage (Edson)	75.00	April 30	1 bag (25 kg) mealie meal	11.20
April 29	Wage (Gertrude)	45.00	April 30	Cooking oil	7.50
			April 30	Margarine	0.74
			April 30	Meat	3.00
			April 30	To Gertrude's father	20.00
May 1	Advance of wage	50.00	May 1	Fish (fresh)	2.00
			May 1	Kapenta (dried fish)	1.00
			May 1	Bread	0.60
			May 2	Sweater (Faides)	18.50
			May 2	Sweater (Joe)	14.50
			May 2	Dress (Faides)	16.95
			May 3	Rape	0.60
			May 3	Cabbage	0.60
			May 3	Oranges	0.80
			May 4	Tomatoes	0.50
			May 4	Bread	0.75
			May 5	Paraffin	5.20
			May 5	Ice cream	0.70
			May 8	Bread	0.75
			May 8	Brown sugar (2 bags)	1.36
			May 8	Transport	0.60

Date	Income	Kwacha	Date	Expenses	Kwacha
			May 8	Soap (powder)	2.50
			May 8	Soap (bar)	0.60
			May 10	Fish (fresh)	2.50
			May 10	Kapenta	1.00
			May 10	Beans	0.90
			May 10	Matches	0.30
			May 10	Sugar cane	0.30
			May 12	Vaseline	1.85
			May 12	Eggs	1.15
			May 13	Rape	0.80
			May 13	Oranges	0.40
			May 14	Bread	0.53
			May 14	Meat	4.00
			May 14	Margarine	0.74
			May 14	Transport	0.60
			May 14	Tomatoes	0.40
			May 15	Tomatoes	0.20
			May 15	Salt	0.50
			May 15	Fish (fresh)	2.00
			May 15	Bread	0.60
			May 15	Transport	1.60
			May 15	Kapenta	1.00
			May 17	Pork meat	3.75
			May 17	Rape	0.60
			May 17	Bread	0.53
			May 17	Milk	0.60
			May 17	Soap (bar)	0.60
			May 18	Oranges	0.40
			May 18	Bread	0.53
			May 20	Bread	0.55
			May 20	Milk	0.30
			May 20	Tomatoes	0.40
			May 20	Kapenta	1.75
			May 21	Transport	0.70
			May 21	Peanuts (ground)	0.60
			May 22	Pork meat	3.75
			May 22	Transport	0.50
			May 22	Eggs	0.80
			May 23	Okra	0.70
			May 23	Kapenta	1.00
			May 23	Beans	0.90
			May 23	Tomatoes	0.50
			May 23	Fish (fresh)	4.00
			May 23	Sugar cane	0.55
			May 28	Transport	1.10
			May 28	1 bag (25 kg) mealie meal	11.20
			May 29	Meat	3.00
			May 29	Eggs	0.60
	Total income	170.00		Total expenses	172.63

Appendix 2

Date	Income	Kwacha	Date	Expenses	Kwacha
May 30	Wage (Edson)	85.00	May 30	Shirt and shorts (Joe)	13.35
May 30	Wage (Gertrude)	44.00	May 30	Underwear (Edson)	5.50
May 30	From Karen	10.00	May 30	Underwear (Faides)	2.50
			May 30	Sweater (Gertrude)	8.00
			May 30	Meat	4.00
			May 30	Transport	0.60
			June 1	Okra	0.80
			June 1	Peanuts	0.20
			June 2	Rape	0.80
			June 2	Beans	1.20
			June 2	Cooking oil	1.00
			June 3	Ice cream	0.70
			June 4	Stamps	0.60
			June 4	Rice	1.65
			June 4	Chitenje (Gertrude)	10.00
			June 4	Juice	1.60
			June 4	Buns	0.80
			June 4	Transport	0.80
			June 4	Milk	0.30
			June 5	Pork meat	5.63
			June 5	Oranges	0.45
			June 5	1 bag (25 kg) mealie meal	11.20
			June 6	Transport	0.65
			June 6	Blanket	27.95
			June 7	Cooking oil	7.36
			June 7	Soap (powder)	1.70
			June 7	Sugar (2 kg)	1.66
			June 7	Transport	1.30
			June 9	Rape	0.60
			June 9	Paraffin	3.70
			June 11	Transport	0.45
			June 11	Bread	1.06
			June 11	Okra	0.80
			June 11	Rape	0.60
			June 11	Milk	0.30
			June 12	Oranges	0.50
			June 12	Meat	2.50
			June 12	Bread	0.53
			June 12	Soap (powder)	2.50
			June 12	Transport	0.60
			June 13	Soap (2 bars)	1.20
			June 16	Meat	3.75
			June 17	Kapenta	1.75
			June 17	Eggs	0.60
			June 18	Transport	1.40
			June 18	Rape	0.60
			June 18	Tomatoes	0.60
			June 18	Soap (bar)	0.70
			June 18	Peanuts (ground)	0.85

Date	Income	Kwacha	Date	Expenses	Kwacha
			June 18	Buns	0.40
			June 20	Pork meat	3.75
			June 20	Biscuits	0.95
			June 20	Bread	1.10
			June 21	Rape	0.60
			June 21	Eggs	1.95
			June 22	Okra	0.60
			June 23	1 bag (25 kg) mealie meal	11.20
			June 24	Meat	4.00
			June 24	Bread	0.53
			June 25	Fish (fresh)	2.00
			June 25	Beans	0.90
			June 25	Kapenta	1.00
			June 25	Bread	0.53
			June 27	Okra	0.50
			June 27	Meat	4.50
			June 27	Fish	1.50
			June 27	Soap (bar)	0.70
			June 27	Tomatoes	0.50
			June 27	Transport	0.30
			June 28	Oranges	1.00
			June 29	Bread	1.00
			June 29	Bread	0.53
			June 29	Transport	0.33
	Total income	139.00		Total expenses	178.26

Edson and Gertrude spent all their available money on daily household necessities and a few items of clothing. Their expenditures from late April through late May 1984 almost equaled their income, including an advance of Edson's wage for the next month. Their household ate a daily diet of maize porridge, nshima, and featured meat or fish approximately once a week. One pound of meat in 1984 cost between K3 and K5, depending on the cut, so they were by no means overindulging. Their diet features milk and eggs intermittently, and once in a while Edson bought biscuits or ice cream from a bicycle vendor for the children. Edson's wage was increased by K10 after the first month of his record keeping. Expenditures on clothing for the children (May 2) and themselves (May 30) strained their tight budget. These expenses could not have been afforded unless Edson used his access to advances of money from his employer. Gertrude bought a sweater at the end of May. May and June are the coldest months in Lusaka, where temperatures sometimes fall below 0 degrees Celsius. Because of the cold, they also bought a blanket (June 6). In June, Gertrude bought a *chitenje*, a piece of brightly colored cloth that Zambian women wrap around the body like a skirt. Their expenditures for June exceeded their means. I suspect Edson during that month had gotten an advance of some

50 Kwacha from his employer; it would just about have balanced the budget for the late May to late June period.

Euclid's Household Budget

Euclid worked as a general servant for a North American couple. His wife, Betty, and their small daughter, Nellie, lived with him in the servants' quarters on the premises. The wife did not earn any income in her own right. Euclid's reported income and expenditures for a three-month period are featured below.

Date	Income	Kwacha	Date	Expenses	Kwacha
March 24	Ration	2.00	March 24	Bread	0.53
March 26	Wage	82.30	March 25	Bread	0.53
March 26	Advance from	40.00	March 25	Transport to church	0.50
	April's wage		March 25	Offering in church	0.20
			March 26	Installment on furniture	120.00
			March 26	Sugar	1.56
			March 26	Biscuits	0.50
			March 27	Tomatoes	0.20
			March 28	Okra	0.20
March 30	Ration	2.00	March 30	1 bag (25 kg) of mealie meal	17.60
			March 30	Soap (bar)	0.95
			March 31	Soap (bar)	0.65
			April 1	Meat	3.00
			April 2	Fish	2.50
April 7	Ration	2.00	April 7	Cooking oil	6.60
			April 7	Eggs	1.20
			April 8	Biscuits	0.18
			April 11	Okra	0.20
			April 11	Bus	0.20
			April 12	Kapenta	1.00
April 15	Ration	2.50	April 15	Kapenta	0.50
			April 16	Fish	1.00
			April 16	Sugar	0.60
			April 16	Bus	0.20
			April 16	Offering in church	0.40
			April 18	Soap	0.95
			April 21	Bus	0.20
April 21	Ration	1.50	April 21	Sweet	0.03
	Total income	132.30		Total expenses	162.18

Date	Income	Kwacha	Date	Expenses	Kwacha
April 23	Wage (remaining half)	42.30			
April 24	From Karen	10.00	April 24	Guava	0.03
			April 24	Bus	0.20
			April 24	Eggs	1.95
			April 24	Vaseline	1.95
			April 24	Mealie meal	8.80
			April 25	Six batteries	6.00
			April 25	Fish	2.50
			April 25	Transport money	1.70
			April 26	Soap	1.70
			April 26	Bread (two loaves)	1.06
			April 27	Okra	0.20
			April 27	Gave my sister	2.20
April 28	Ration	2.00	April 28	Sugar	0.85
			April 29	Tomatoes	0.20
			April 29	Sweets	0.20
			April 29	Bread (two loaves)	1.06
			April 30	Biscuits	0.18
			April 30	Gave to blind man	0.20
			April 30	Chitenje (for Betty)	9.00
			April 30	Fish	2.00
			April 30	Sweet	0.03
			April 30	Vegetables	0.20
			May 1	Milk	0.38
			May 1	Sugar	2.00
			May 1	Bread	0.53
May 5	Ration	2.00	May 5	Buns	0.50
			May 5	Matches	0.20
			May 6	Buns	0.60
May 12	Ration	2.00	May 13	Fish	1.00
			May 16	Offering in church	0.05
			May 17	Sweet	0.05
			May 18	Buns	0.35
May 19	Ration	2.00	May 20	Fish	1.00
			May 20	Sweet	0.03
			May 20	Sugar	0.59
			May 21	Okra	0.30
			May 22	Buns	0.30
	Total income	60.30		Total expenses	50.09

Date	Income	Kwacha	Date	Expenses	Kwacha
May 23	Wage	82.30	May 26	Mealie meal	8.80
May 26	Ration	2.00	May 27	Milk	0.78
May 27	From Karen	10.00	May 27	Chicken	6.50
			May 28	Bread	0.53
			May 29	Fish	2.00
			May 30	Greens	0.60

Date	Income	Kwacha	Date	Expenses	Kwacha
			May 31	Sugar	1.00
			June 1	Cotton thread	1.00
			June 1	Dress (Nellie)	5.00
			June 1	Shoes	12.00
			June 1	Soap (powder)	3.60
June 2	Advance of June's wage	29.00	June 2	Bag	27.95
June 3	Ration	2.00	June 3	Soap (powder)	5.50
			June 4	Rice	2.00
			June 6	Belt	2.50
			June 8	Transport (to village)	16.00
			June 8	Transport from Kanzoka to Mazabuka	7.00
			June 11	Transport (coming back)	16.00
			June 11	Fish (fresh)	6.00
			June 12	Battery	4.60
			June 13	Biscuits	0.80
			June 14	Sweets	0.30
June 15	Ration	2.00	June 15	Rice	2.00
			June 20	Meat	3.00
			June 21	Bread	0.53
			June 21	Soap	1.00
			June 22	Fish	2.00
June 23	Ration	2.00	June 23	Soap	1.75
			June 24	Mealie meal	11.20
	Total income	129.30		Total expenses	151.94

Euclid tried to manage his household budget more frugally, or tightly, than Edson did. Euclid's household ate meat or fish less often than Edson's. Over the period of three months that he recorded his expenditures, Euclid once bought a chicken (May 27), a two and a half to three pounds of fowl worth K6.50, an item Edson did not allow his household. Otherwise, Euclid was a very thrifty man. His budget for the month from late March through late April is thrown off balance because of installment payments on furniture (March 26), which Euclid could only pay by obtaining an advance from the next month's pay. Even then, Euclid's budget from late March through late April is unbalanced. He may have used some of the "special savings" that the employer kept track of (see Chapter 7). Like Edson, Euclid also had expenditures on clothing for the family (April 30, June 1). He controlled expenditures from late April through late May extremely carefully, having his household eat a daily diet of nshima, fish once a week, and greens from his garden. His late May through late June budget is off balance, in part because of transportation costs incurred during a visit to his village in the Southern Province (June 8–11); he also bought a travel bag.

His employer may have helped pay his travel expenses, which would just about have balanced his budget for that month. Euclid's possible economic transactions in the rural area, for example, with relatives, and perhaps occasional support to his former wife and her children are not reflected in this budget; neither are the earnings he sometimes made from playing drums in the village. Euclid spent part of the weekend time away from his residence with a woman friend and he is likely to have spent money on her. Euclid also, like Edson, once in a while bought small packages of biscuits and sweets to please his young daughter. Despite his tight budget, Euclid gave small sums of money at church as well as to a blind beggar on the main street in Lusaka's downtown.

Index

Index

Library of Congress Cataloging-in-Publication Data

Hansen, Karen Tranberg.
  Distant companions.

  Includes index.
    1. Domestics—Zambia—History—20th century.
2. Sexual division of labor—Zambia—History—20th
century.   3. Master and servant—Zambia—History—
20th century.   4. Zambia—Social conditions.
5. Zambia—Colonial influence.—I. Title.
HD6072.2.Z33H36   1989   88-47771
                        331.7′6164046′096894
    ISBN 0-8014-2217-5 (alk. paper)